Roland 1910

THE GREAT EVENTS
BY
FAMOUS HISTORIANS

A COMPREHENSIVE AND READABLE ACCOUNT OF THE WORLD'S HISTORY, EMPHASIZING THE MORE IMPORTANT EVENTS, AND PRESENTING THESE AS COMPLETE NARRATIVES IN THE MASTER-WORDS OF THE MOST EMINENT HISTORIANS

NON-SECTARIAN NON-PARTISAN NON-SECTIONAL

ON THE PLAN EVOLVED FROM A CONSENSUS OF OPINIONS GATHERED FROM THE MOST DISTINGUISHED SCHOLARS OF AMERICA AND EUROPE, INCLUDING BRIEF INTRODUCTIONS BY SPECIALISTS TO CONNECT AND EXPLAIN THE CELEBRATED NARRATIVES, ARRANGED CHRONOLOGICALLY, WITH THOROUGH INDICES, BIBLIOGRAPHIES, CHRONOLOGIES, AND COURSES OF READING

EDITOR-IN-CHIEF

ROSSITER JOHNSON, LL.D.

ASSOCIATE EDITORS

CHARLES F. HORNE, Ph.D.
JOHN RUDD, LL.D.

With a staff of specialists

VOLUME XVIII

The National Alumni

CONTENTS

VOLUME XVIII

LIST OF ILLUSTRATIONS

VOLUME XVIII

AN OUTLINE NARRATIVE

TRACING BRIEFLY THE CAUSES, CONNECTIONS, AND CONSEQUENCES OF

THE GREAT EVENTS

(THE GREAT WARS OF READJUSTMENT)

CHARLES F. HORNE

IN speaking of 1861 and the years that followed, we deal with the still smouldering ashes of recent fires. There are yet leaders of thought and action in the United States who fought in the great campaigns of 1861–1865. More than half the reigning sovereigns of Europe could give us interesting anecdotes of what they thought of the American war when it broke out. Catholic Italians are still refusing to take part in the government that seized the States of the Church in 1860 and 1870. Elderly Frenchmen still hate with a personal hatred the Germans against whom they strove in vain in 1870–1871.

These events have not yet faded into that academic past where wholly unprejudiced judgment becomes possible. Whatever opinion on them one may express, he finds other persons, honest men and able scholars, in warmest protest against him. "I see now how history is manufactured," said a naval officer who had been through the recent Spanish-American war, "and I will never trust another word of it. Probably the only real fault of Nero lay in being too honest and simple-minded for the game in Rome; and Seneca wrote about the Cæsars for a political campaign." Despite this pessimistic view, there are a few broad outlines and world-wide consequences of events too self-evident to be misunderstood. Let us in the ensuing outline look only to those.

Following on the colossal upheavals and revolutions of 1848–1849, the decade previous to 1860 had seen at least two gigantic wars, one in the Crimea, one in Italy. The next decade encountered three even more colossal. Then for more than thirty years the general peace of the world met little interruption except from minor conflicts. This warlike period seems therefore to have been volcanic and temporary, a period of readjustment to new conditions. The contest everywhere was connected more or less with the advances of democracy, the coming of the common people into power, and the establishment of strong, clearly marked nationalities. Thus the war of 1859 had been an expression of Italy's yearning for both independence and union. So, too, the Civil War in the United States was fought partly in defence of "State sovereignty," that is, independence; partly to preserve the Union, that is, nationality; wholly because of slavery, that is, the denial of man's equality, of democracy.[1]

CIVIL WAR IN THE UNITED STATES

President Lincoln was elected by the Republicans of the North in the autumn of 1860. Without waiting for his inauguration, several Southern States withdrew from the Union, some of them unwillingly and with sad words of adieu. Virginia, whose ancient leaders had done so much to create the central Government, could hardly bring herself to abandon it. When her citizens chose a special convention to consider the question of secession, a majority of the delegates elected received instructions to cling to the Government at Washington. Congress hastened to offer every sort of concession to the seceding States. But every concession was rejected by the States farthest south. The die was cast; and when President Lincoln in his inaugural address asserted that his oath of office bound him to preserve the Union at any cost, civil war became inevitable. The American flag was fired on at Fort Sumter, and the President called for volunteers to defend it.

Since they must fight, the slave States of the middle tier decided to strike with their Southern comrades rather than

[1] See *Secession of the Southern States*, page 1.

against them. The same Virginia convention that had before opposed secession now approved it, though with a proviso that the ordinance be submitted to the people. Richmond was made the capital of the Southern Confederacy, and the Potomac River became the border-line between two hostile sections.

The troops from either side gathered on the frontier, and the forces of the North were defeated in the first serious battle, at Bull Run.[1] The South thought the war was over, and began to celebrate its triumph. But President Lincoln called for five hundred thousand more volunteers, and they came forward readily, eagerly, to "fight for the flag." The war did not fairly begin until 1862, when a series of gigantic conflicts ensued between such well-matched foes, contested with such courage and devotion, and resulting in such terrific slaughter as the world had not known since the "Battle of the Nations" at Leipsic and the downfall of Napoleon.

In February, 1862, General Grant captured Fort Donelson. This action was especially noteworthy for the short and sharp negotiations in which Grant demanded an immediate and unconditional surrender. Happily the irritation caused by certain expressions therein long since passed away. Admiral Farragut captured New Orleans in April.[2] But General McClellan, attempting to strike a decisive blow against the capital of the Confederacy, was obliged to retreat.[3] Then General Lee invaded the North in his turn, but was defeated by McClellan at Antietam. The President, watching anxiously for a favorable moment, took advantage of this victory to proclaim the emancipation of all the slaves in the rebellious States.[4]

In December, 1862, and May, 1863, unsuccessful attempts were made to drive Lee back on Richmond; and then he once more took the initiative and invaded the North. The gigantic three-days' battle at Gettysburg was the military turning-point of the war. Again and again were the Confederates beaten back in their desperate charges against the Union lines. When at last Lee acknowledged the uselessness of the assault and with-

[1] See *The Battle of Bull Run*, page 26.
[2] See *The Capture of New Orleans*, page 46.
[3] See *McClellan's Peninsula Campaign*, page 53.
[4] See *Emancipation in the United States*, page 70.

drew his exhausted forces, the star of the Confederacy had set.[1] At the same time Grant was following up Farragut's work by capturing Vicksburg, the last Southern stronghold on the Mississippi. The great river, the "backbone of the Confederacy," was wholly in Northern hands, and the railway line by which the Confederates drew supplies from beyond that river was severed.[2]

To follow further the military operations of the war is only to trace the desperate resistance of a defeated but still defiant people. The Union fleet closed one Confederate port after another, extending its remarkably effective work of blockade along the entire coast. Grant, summoned from his victories in the West to take command in Virginia, began his famous "hammering" campaign, using the superior numbers of his forces to destroy Lee's army, the chief reliance of the Confederacy. The war became a holocaust in the thousands of its victims. Sherman, Grant's lieutenant, having crushed the Confederates in the West, cut loose from his line of communication and supply and marched his army across the richest State of the South, destroying the source of its supplies.[3] He reduced the area of resistance to a comparatively small circle around Richmond, where at last Lee surrendered in April, 1865. The war was over.[4]

In addition to Farragut's celebrated victories at New Orleans and Mobile, the struggle had produced at least two naval combats of peculiar and world-wide interest. Up to 1862, for as many thousands of years as history can trace, the navies of the world had been built of wood. A ship's walls offered small resistance to cannon-shot. But now American inventors both North and South determined to sheathe their vessels in iron armor. The result was the production of the first two "ironclads," the Merrimac and the Monitor, which by their amazing battle transformed the navies of the world. Every Power in Europe began with all possible haste to build iron ships.[5]

Equally important perhaps in its result was the action of England in permitting Confederate cruisers to be built in British

[1] See *The Battle of Gettysburg*, page 77.
[2] See *The Fall of Vicksburg*, page 110.
[3] See *Sherman's March to the Sea*, page 135.
[4] See *The Surrender of Lee*, page 153.
[5] See *The Monitor and the Merrimac*, page 38.

shipyards. From the point of view of business rivalry this was a most successful step. The merchant-vessels of the United States were practically driven from the ocean, and the carrying trade of the world fell more than ever into British hands. The most noted of these privateers was the Alabama, from whose name the whole subject is usually referred to as the "Alabama question." This swift and daring cruiser captured sixty-five vessels in all, and destroyed four million dollars' worth of property. A Union sloop-of-war finally discovered her in the harbor of Cherbourg, France, and waited for her to come out. In the sea-duel that followed the Alabama was sunk. But she had done her work.[1]

EFFECTS OF THE AMERICAN WAR

As to the manner in which this American war was regarded abroad, the European governments can take but little pleasure in looking back upon their attitudes. Their sympathies (with the exception of Russia's) were with the South, not because of any question of right or wrong involved, but because Southern victory meant a rebuff to the common people, a strengthening of aristocratic government, and above all a division of the great Republic between two hostile powers whose antagonisms would leave Europe free to seize Southern America, as she was seizing Africa and Asia.

Even during the war operations were begun that would never have been attempted but for the division of the Union. Napoleon III, with some dream of forming a vast world-wide union of the Latin races, quarrelled with Mexico. His French armies overthrew the republican government there and established a precarious empire, to whose throne he invited the Austrian Prince Maximilian. The British Government also seemed more than once on the point of quarrelling with President Lincoln and lending active aid to the South. Parliament was held in check first by the resolute attitude of Queen Victoria, inspired by Prince Albert, then by the slowly awaking sympathies of the English common people for the struggle against slavery, and finally by realizing what American privateers might do to British commerce.

[1] See *Destruction of the Alabama*, page 124.

The downfall of the Confederacy changed the face of affairs. The strong have many friends. England virtually adopted the United States as an ally. Napoleon III was notified that the presence of his French troops in Mexico was a violation of the Monroe Doctrine. He apologized, and withdrew them; and his brave but helpless puppet Maximilian, who had shot hundreds of Mexicans for "rebellion," was captured and shot in his turn. It was amazing to see what a different matter this was, and how deeply the sympathies of the civilized world were roused by the victim's unhappy fate.[1]

A far greater man than he had already perished and left unfinished a far greater work. President Lincoln, as all the world knows, had fallen, assassinated in the hour of victory. His death made almost impossible the difficult work of reconstruction, of restoring some sort of real harmony to the shattered American Union. The man whose wisdom and moderation had dominated the land in war would doubtless have guided it in peace with the same far-sighted calm. His death left confusion and divided counsels. It was impossible that the South should be kept permanently under military rule as a conquered country. Yet where her white citizens were permitted to resume control, they began passing laws that practically reduced the blacks to slavery again. Naturally the Republican Congress interposed; the voting power was taken away from all "rebels" and given to the blacks, and for a time the former slaves governed their former masters.

Those were sad days for the South, days that few men look back to with approval. Whatever may be the ultimate solution of the negro question, it has not yet been discovered. For a dozen years a Republican Congress persisted in retaining control of the South by negro votes, and not until the centennial year of 1876 was this policy wholly abandoned. Then the close presidential election between Hayes and Tilden led to a compromise, and the South was left to settle her negro problem by herself.

Meanwhile the nation as a whole was rising like a phœnix from the desolating ruin of the war. In 1866 the first successful Atlantic cable connected her business centres with those of Europe

[1] See *The Fall of Maximilian*, page 186.

and crowned with triumph a resolute and protracted struggle whose details read like the extravagance of romance.[1] In 1867 Alaska was purchased from Russia. The career of expansion which had led the United States southward to the Gulf of Mexico and westward to the Pacific now drew her northward beyond the Arctic Circle. Each despised purchase has proved a treasure in its turn.[2]

Two years later the Pacific railroad was completed, connecting one ocean with the other, another link in the girdle that nineteenth-century enterprise carried round the earth.[3] Nor was Europe behind in industrial advances. The same year (1869) that saw the completion of the Pacific railroad saw also the opening of the Suez Canal.[4] The new railway saved the globe-circler from the long voyage round South America; the new canal cut Africa from his route. Vasco da Gama and Magellan, the triumphant explorers of four centuries before, had been superseded by these modern engineering works.

CHANGES IN THE BRITISH EMPIRE

Canada also shared in the general prosperity. The world-movement toward closer union, emphasized in Italy and the United States, led to a Canadian movement for federation, and in 1867 all the provinces except Newfoundland followed the example already set by Upper and Lower Canada and joined in establishing the Dominion of Canada.[5]

Two years later the great Hudson Bay Company, which for two hundred years had ruled like a sovereign power over all the vast wilderness of the bleak Canadian Northwest, yielded to the march of progress and surrendered to the people its antiquated autocratic authority.[6] A few years previously the famous East India Company had also abandoned its effort to govern a foreign land, and surrendered its charter to the British crown. Soon afterward Queen Victoria was declared Empress of India. The

[1] See *The Laying of the Atlantic Cable*, page 175.
[2] See *Purchase of Alaska*, page 206.
[3] See *The Completion of the Pacific Railroad*, page 287.
[4] See *The Opening of the Suez Canal*, page 275.
[5] See *Canadian Confederation*, page 196.
[6] See *The Abolition of the Fur Companies*, page 258.

decade of the 'sixties was thus noteworthy in changing the conditions of English dominion. The empire became more imperial and at the same time more democratic.

Africa, last of the continents to be developed, received also a vast stimulus in the discovery in 1867 of the wonderful diamond-mines in the Orange Free State.[1] This led to rapid colonization in Southern Africa. Gold also was discovered in the Transvaal Republic, and soon England was once more crowding the Boers northward, claiming a protectorate over British subjects in the Transvaal region.

In Continental Europe democracy was still engaged in struggle. In Italy men looked yearningly toward Rome and Venice, the two districts left outside the pale; and in 1862 Garibaldi tried to duplicate his celebrated Sicilian victories by a sudden dash on Rome. The city was protected by French troops; so rather than hazard war with Napoleon, the Italian King ordered out his own soldiers, and they checked Garibaldi in the Battle of Aspromonte and made him prisoner. A convention, however, was arranged with Napoleon, by which the French were gradually to withdraw from Rome and leave it unprotected. Meanwhile the condition of Austrian affairs opened for the Italians an unexpected road to Venice.

THE SEVEN WEEKS' WAR

A genius had arisen among the Prussians, the great statesman, Von Bismarck. He saw a way to turn to his own country's advantage the tendencies of the age, and to establish anew a German Empire as united as that of the ancient days. Of course to a Prussian this meant an empire with Prussia at its head and Austria crowded out altogether. Bismarck announced grimly that German unity could be cemented only by "blood and iron," and in anticipation of what would follow he prepared Prussia thoroughly for war.

In 1863–1864 the flimsy German confederation of States quarrelled with Denmark over the possession of the German duchies on the Danish border; and Prussia and Austria, as representatives of the confederation, marched their armies forward and seized the disputed duchies. The German States wrangled

[1] See *The Discovery of Diamonds in Africa*, page 225.

among themselves as to the disposition to be made of the spoils, and Prussia grasped the lion's share. Then the lesser States, encouraged by Austria, began strengthening their military resources in threatening fashion. War broke out in June, 1866. A Prussian army, fully prepared for the event, marched at once into the little States that had upheld Austria. Their feeble armies were defeated and their territories occupied almost before they realized that war had begun. Meanwhile Bismarck had formed a secret alliance with Italy, by which Venice was to be restored to the arms of its ancient motherland. Italy also declared war against Austria.

This "Seven Weeks' War," as it has been called, brought about such results as perhaps only Bismarck had foreseen. By Europe in general, Austria was still regarded as the strongest German State. Her lesser German allies were supposed to balance Italy, and so a long conflict was anticipated by which Austria and possibly Italy would be the eventual gainers.

Prussia, however, was supplied with a new tool of war, a very rapid firing "needle-gun," or rifle, and she had a great general in the person of Count Von Moltke. Her troops converged with splendid military precision on the Austrians and defeated them in a great battle at Sadowa or Koeniggraetz. The result was decisive. Vienna lay open to the invaders; and the Austrian Emperor hastened to sue for peace.[1]

In Italy the Austrians had been victorious, overcoming their opponents by land, and also by sea in a noted naval battle at Lissa. Nevertheless, through the success of her ally, Italy won her stipulated reward in the recovery of Venice. Prussia herself received substantial territorial additions appropriated from the little German States she had overrun; and, more important still, she broke up the old confederation and established another of which she herself was the leader. Austria agreed to withdraw entirely from the German world, of which under one name or another she had been for so many centuries the strength and the leader. The term "Germany" in mediæval days had meant the Austrian court and its satellites; hereafter it was to mean Prussia and the German people.

[1] See *The Austro-Prussian War*, page 163.

Even in Austria itself democracy gained by the war. During the earlier Italian war of 1859 the Bohemians had said openly, "If we win, we shall get nothing; if we lose, we shall get a constitution." And in fact the Austrian Emperor granted a constitution to his people in 1860, but soon withdrew it, declaring that it had proved an evil. Thus the war of 1866 had found the Austrian Government still autocratic, and it was only the grim necessities of this further defeat that wrung from the Emperor another, and this time irrevocable, constitution. Austria was the last of the European States except Russia to abandon absolutism. Even Hungary, the despised and trampled on, was allowed to become self-governing. The very name of the Austrian Empire was changed, and it became Austria-Hungary, a dual State in which the ancient Asiatic Huns have equal voice with their Teutonic neighbors.

THE FRANCO-PRUSSIAN WAR

How had these tremendous changes among neighboring States affected Napoleon III, the self-constituted "dictator of Europe"? He had been allowed no voice in them. When Frenchmen saw Prussia suddenly grown so strong upon the Rhine border, Italy strengthened also, and France by comparison gone back in the scale of power, they felt that they had been played with, that Napoleon's leadership of Europe was but a pretence. He saw that his position grew doubtful. He was but a shadow after all; and the same public opinion which had made him could unmake him. He demanded of Bismarck that France also be permitted to increase her territory among the little Rhine States. But Bismarck, with a victorious army in readiness at his call, stood out as the protector of Germany and peremptorily refused to let one foot of German soil be alienated to France. Napoleon, his armies being unready, perforce submitted. After that a Franco-Prussian war was only a question of time and preparation.

Its direct cause arose out of the troubles in Spain. The Spaniards, after long endurance of the rule of their depraved and abandoned Queen Isabella, finally in 1868 rose in rebellion and declared the land a republic. Napoleon thought to have a hand in that game also, but soon abandoned the idea, and left the various Spanish factions to quarrel among themselves.[1] In 1870 they concluded to restore a monarchical form of government, and offered their throne to a German prince, a distant relative of King William of Prussia. France at once protested against this additional Prussian "aggrandizement." Bismarck, knowing his country fully prepared for the struggle, purposely aggravated his opponents' rage, and the Franco-Prussian War began.

It was one series of disasters for the French. Their armies proved unready and badly supplied. The South German States, with Bavaria in the lead, joined readily with Prussia in what they considered a struggle for the defence of German territory. The French forces, driven back at every point, were defeated in the great Battle of Gravelotte; and finally an army of two hundred thousand men, headed by Napoleon himself, was compelled to surrender at Sedan.[2]

Napoleon's popularity, already at lowest ebb, perished completely with the disaster at Sedan. As the scandalous lack of preparation for the war had become more and more apparent, Frenchmen everywhere had begun to cry out for the deposition of the Emperor and the restoration of the republic. At the news of Sedan, Paris took the lead, and its citizens under the guidance of M. Jules Favre formed the Republic that is still existent today.[3]

The new Government had to take up the war amid the confusion and defeat into which the incompetency of the Empire had plunged it. The Germans, pressing steadily forward, began their celebrated siege of Paris. French armies of militia, raised from the provinces by desperate efforts, attacked the German besiegers again and again, but without success. Paris surrendered early in 1871, and the war was at an end.[4]

By the terms of peace France paid an enormous money indemnity, and she also yielded up the provinces of Alsace and Lorraine. Oddly enough, she made these sacrifices to a power that had not been in existence at the beginning of the war.

[1] See *Revolution in Spain*, page 243.
[2] See *The Battle of Sedan*, page 302.
[3] See *The Third French Republic*, page 321.
[4] See *The Siege of Paris*, page 333.

This was the German Empire. Bismarck's proudest hopes had been crowned with complete success. Moved by the excitement and patriotic enthusiasm of successful war, the South German States had united with those of the North in forming a close union, with Prussia as its head. The German Confederation had become the German Empire as we know it to-day, and William, King of Prussia, was proclaimed Emperor of Germany.[1]

Another land to profit by the war was Italy. When the French troops were perforce removed from Rome to fight at home, the Italian armies advanced to occupy the ancient capital. The soldiers of the Pope made, by his orders, only a formal resistance, so as to show to the world that they were compelled to yield to force. Then they surrendered, and the Pope, the same Pius IX who had seen such vicissitudes of fortune in 1848, refusing all accommodation with the Italian Government, shut himself up as a prisoner in his palace of the Vatican. Rome was made the capital of the completed kingdom. Italy was a unit at last.[2]

France, thus foiled and defeated on every side, had not even yet drained her bitter cup. Many Frenchmen had protested against making peace with Germany on the hard terms offered them. The Parisians were especially enraged that the German troops had been permitted to parade through the capital. The new republican Government under President Thiers had a difficult task to reconcile all parties. They temporarily transferred the seat of government from Paris to Versailles; and almost immediately afterward the Parisian mob broke into revolt, drove the regular officials from the city, and set up an independent government of their own, the "Commune." So Paris underwent a second siege, this time from French troops. As the Communists found their cause grow desperate, they resolved to destroy the city which they could not defend, and set it on fire in several places. The Government soldiers, enraged at this vandalism, shot down the Communists by hundreds even after they had surrendered.[3]

Tranquillity was soon restored, and France with marvel-

[1] See *The Unification of Germany*, page 340.
[2] See *Completion of Italian Unity*, page 316.
[3] See *The Rising of the Commune*, page 351.

lous recuperative powers reasserted her ancient strength. The world entered on a period of peace and prosperity. In 1872 the "Alabama question" between England and the United States, a dispute which in earlier days would have led to war, was settled by the first famous appeal to "international arbitration." A court was formed of members appointed by five different Governments. To this court the contending parties submitted their claims, and by its decision they pledged themselves to abide. The result was in favor of the United States, and the British Government paid the award. Arbitration began to assert itself as a substitute for war.[1]

Yet that sudden Parisian outbreak of 1871 suggests solemn thoughts. Democracy has often shown within itself that same black gulf of anarchism, of ruthless crime and savage destruction. For the present, the middle classes with their thoughtful sober sense appear to be everywhere safely in control of the world of civilization; but anarchy still seethes below.

[1] See *The Geneva Arbitration*, page 367.

[FOR THE NEXT SECTION OF THIS GENERAL SURVEY SEE VOLUME XIX.]

SECESSION OF THE SOUTHERN STATES

A.D. 1861

JEFFERSON DAVIS   ABRAHAM LINCOLN

The doctrine that the several States of the American Union were sovereign, and that in entering the Union they did not resign their sovereignty, but were at liberty to withdraw at will, was intimated or implied in various acts and resolutions, and debated tentatively through many years, until it was plainly formulated by John C. Calhoun, of South Carolina. It was strenuously disputed at that time by President Andrew Jackson and other statesmen, but, as an abstract doctrine, was accepted probably by the greater part of the Southern people. It came to the supreme test when, in 1861, ten States attempted to enforce it, and the great Civil War followed. As President of the Confederacy, Jefferson Davis was officially the head and front of that attempt, and there can be no better or more authoritative presentation of the argument in its favor than his, which is given herewith. On the other hand, there is no clearer statement of the argument against it than that contained partly in President Lincoln's inaugural address, and partly in his first message to Congress, which also follows.

JEFFERSON DAVIS[1]

WHEN, at the close of the War of the Revolution, each of the thirteen colonies that had been engaged in that contest was severally acknowledged by the mother-country, Great Britain, to be a free and independent State, the confederation of those States embraced an area so extensive, with climate and products so various, that rivalries and conflicts of interest soon began to be manifested. It required all the power of wisdom and patriotism, animated by the affection and engendered by common sufferings and dangers, to keep these rivalries under restraint, and to effect those compromises which it was fondly hoped would insure the harmony and mutual good offices of each for the benefit of all. It was in this spirit of patriotism and confidence in the continuance of such abiding good-will as would for all time preclude hostile aggression, that Virginia ceded, for the use of the confeder-

[1] From Jefferson Davis's *Rise and Fall of the Confederate Government* (New York, 1881: D. Appleton and Company), by permission.

ated States, all that vast extent of territory lying north of the Ohio River, out of which have since been formed five States and part of a sixth. The addition of these States has accrued entirely to the preponderance of the Northern section over that from which the donation proceeded, and to the disturbance of that equilibrium which existed at the close of the War of the Revolution.

It may not be out of place here to refer to the fact that the grievances which led to that war were directly inflicted upon the Northern colonies. Those of the South had no material cause of complaint; but, actuated by sympathy for their Northern brethren, and a devotion to the principles of civil liberty and community independence, which they had inherited from their Anglo-Saxon ancestry, and which were set forth in the Declaration of Independence, they made common cause with their neighbors, and may, at least, claim to have done their full share in the war that ensued.

By the exclusion of the South, in 1820, from all that part of the Louisiana Purchase lying north of the parallel of 36° 30′, and not included in the State of Missouri; by the extension of that line of exclusion to embrace the territory acquired from Texas; and by the appropriation of all the territory obtained from Mexico under the Treaty of Guadalupe-Hidalgo, both north and south of that line, it may be stated with approximate accuracy that the North had monopolized to herself more than three-fourths of all that had been added to the domain of the United States since the Declaration of Independence. This inequality, which began, as has been shown, in the more generous than wise confidence of the South, was employed to obtain for the North the lion's share of what was afterward added at the cost of the public treasure and the blood of patriots. I do not care to estimate the relative proportion contributed by each of the two sections.

Nor was this the only cause that operated to disappoint the reasonable hopes and to blight the fair prospects under which the original compact was formed. Discriminating duties upon imports favored the manufacturing region, which was the North; burdening the export region, which was the South, and so imposing upon the latter a double tax: one by the increased price of articles of consumption, which, so far as they were of home production, went into the pockets of the manufacturer; the other by the diminished value of articles of export, which was so much withheld from the pockets of the agriculturist. In like manner the power of the majority section was employed to appropriate to itself an unequal share of the public disbursements. These combined causes—the possession of more territory, more money, and a wider field for the employment of special labor—all served to attract immigration; and, with increasing population, the greed grew by what it fed on.

This became distinctly manifest when the so-called "Republican" Convention assembled in Chicago, on May 16, 1860, to nominate a candidate for the Presidency. It was a purely sectional body. There were a few delegates present representing an insignificant minority in the "Border States," Delaware, Maryland, Virginia, Kentucky, and Missouri; but not one from any State south of the celebrated political line of 36° 30′. It had been the invariable usage with nominating conventions of all parties to select candidates for the Presidency and Vice-Presidency, one from the North and the other from the South; but this assemblage nominated Abraham Lincoln, of Illinois, for the first office, and for the second, Hannibal Hamlin, of Maine, both Northerners.

Lincoln, its nominee for the Presidency, had publicly announced that the Union "could not permanently endure, half slave and half free." The resolutions adopted contained some carefully worded declarations, well adapted to deceive the credulous who were opposed to hostile aggressions upon the rights of the States. In order to accomplish this purpose, they were compelled to create a fictitious issue, in denouncing what they described as "the new dogma that the Constitution, of its own force, carries slavery into any or all of the territories of the United States"—a "dogma" which had never been held or declared by anybody, and which had no existence outside of their own assertion. There was enough in connection with the nomination to assure the most fanatical foes of the Constitution that their ideas would be the rule and guide of the party.

Meantime the Democratic party had held a convention, composed as usual of delegates from all the States. They met in Charleston, South Carolina, on April 23d, but an unfortunate disagreement with regard to the declaration of principles to be set forth rendered a nomination impracticable. Both divisions of the convention adjourned, and met again in Baltimore in June. Then, having finally failed to come to an agreement, they separated and made their respective nominations apart. Stephen A. Douglas, of Illinois, was nominated by the friends of the doctrine of "popular sovereignty," with Mr. Fitzpatrick, of Alabama, for the Vice-Presidency. Both these gentlemen at that time were Senators from their respective States. Mr. Fitzpatrick declined the nomination, and his place was filled with the name of Herschel V. Johnson, a distinguished citizen of Georgia.

The convention representing the conservative, or State rights, wing of the Democratic party (the President of which was the Honorable Caleb Cushing, of Massachusetts), on the first ballot, unanimously made choice of John C. Breckenridge, of Kentucky, then Vice-President of the United States, for the first office, and with like unanimity selected General Joseph Lane, then a Senator from Oregon, for the second. The resolutions of each of these two conventions denounced the action and policy of the Abolition party as subversive of the Constitution and revolutionary in their tendency.

Another convention was held in Baltimore about the same period by those who still adhered to the old Whig party, reënforced by the remains of the "American" organization, and perhaps some others. This convention also consisted of delegates from all of the States, and, repudiating all geographical and sectional issues, and declaring it to be "both the part of patriotism and of duty to recognize no political principle other than the Constitution of the country, the Union of the States, and the enforcement of the laws," pledged itself and its supporters "to maintain, protect, and defend, separately and unitedly, those great principles of public liberty and national safety against all enemies at home and abroad." Its nominees were John Bell, of Tennessee, and Edward Everett, of Massachusetts, both of whom had long been distinguished members of the Whig party.

The people of the United States now had four rival tickets presented to them by as many contending parties, whose respective positions and principles on the great and absorbing question at issue may be briefly recapitulated as follows:

1. The "Constitution-Union" party, as it was now termed,

led by Bell and Everett, which ignored the Territorial controversy altogether, and contented itself, as above stated, with a simple declaration of adherence to "the Constitution, the Union, and the enforcement of the laws."

2. The party of "Popular Sovereignty," headed by Douglas and Johnson, who affirmed the right of the people of the Territories, in their Territorial condition, to determine their own organic institutions, independently of the control of Congress; denying the power or duty of Congress to protect the persons or property of individuals or minorities in such Territories against the action of majorities.

3. The "State Rights" party, supporting Breckenridge and Lane, who held that the Territories were open to citizens of all the States, with their property, without any inequality or discrimination, and that it was the duty of the General Government to protect both persons and property from aggression in the Territories subject to its control. At the same time they admitted and asserted the right of the people of a Territory, on emerging from their Territorial condition to that of a State, to determine what should then be their domestic institutions, as well as all other questions of personal or proprietary right, without interference by Congress, and subject only to the limitations and restrictions prescribed by the Constitution of the United States.

4. The so-called "Republicans," presenting the names of Lincoln and Hamlin, who held, in the language of one of their leaders, that "slavery can exist only by virtue of municipal law"; that there was "no law for it in the Territories, and no power to enact one"; and that Congress was "bound to prohibit it or exclude it from any and every Federal Territory." In other words, they asserted the right and duty of Congress to exclude the citizens of half the States of the Union from the territory belonging in common to all, unless on condition of the sacrifice or abandonment of their property recognized by the Constitution—indeed, of the only species of their property distinctly and specifically recognized as such by that instrument.

On the vital question underlying the whole controversy—that is, whether the Federal Government should be a government of the whole for the benefit of all its equal members, or (if it should continue to exist at all) a sectional government for the benefit of a part—the first three of the parties above described were in substantial accord as against the fourth. If they could or would have acted unitedly, they could certainly have carried the election, and averted the catastrophe which followed. Nor were efforts wanting to effect such a union.

John Bell, the Whig candidate, was a highly respectable and experienced statesman, who had filled many important offices, both State and Federal. He was not ambitious to the extent of coveting the Presidency, and he was profoundly impressed by the danger which threatened the country. Mr. Breckenridge had not anticipated, and it may safely be said did not eagerly desire, the nomination. He was young enough to wait, and patriotic enough to be willing to do so, if the weal of the country required it. Thus much I may confidently assert of both those gentlemen; for each of them authorized me to say that he was willing to withdraw, if an arrangement could be effected by which the divided forces of the friends of the Constitution could be concentrated upon some one more generally acceptable than either of the three who had been presented to the country. When I made this announcement to Stephen A. Douglas—with whom my relations had always been such as to justify the assurance that he could not consider it as made in an unfriendly spirit—he replied that the scheme proposed was impracticable, because his friends, mainly Northern Democrats, if he were withdrawn, would join in the support of Lincoln, rather than of anyone who should supplant him (Douglas); that he was in the hands of his friends, and was sure they would not accept the proposition.

It needed but little knowledge of the *status* of parties in the several States to foresee a probable defeat if the conservatives were to continue divided into three parts, and the aggressives were to be held in solid column. But angry passions, which are always bad counsellors, had been aroused, and hopes were still cherished, which proved to be illusory. The result was the election, by a minority, of a President whose avowed principles were necessarily fatal to the harmony of the Union.

Of 303 electoral votes, Lincoln received 180; but of the popular suffrage of 4,676,853 votes, which the electors represented, he obtained only 1,866,352, something over a third of the votes. This discrepancy was owing to the system of voting by "general ticket"—that is, casting the State votes as a unit, whether unanimous or nearly equally divided. Thus, in New York, the total popular vote was 675,156, of which 362,646 were cast for the so-called Republican (or Lincoln) electors, and 312,510 against them. New York was entitled to 35 electoral votes. Divided on the basis of the popular vote, 19 of these would have been cast for Lincoln, and 16 against him. But under the "general ticket" system the entire 35 votes were cast for the Republican candidates, thus giving them not only the full strength of the majority in their favor, but that of the great minority against them superadded. So of other Northern States, in which the small majorities on one side operated with the weight of entire unanimity, while the virtual unanimity of the Southern States counted nothing more than a mere majority would have done.

The manifestations which followed this result, in the Southern States, did not proceed, as has been unjustly charged, from chagrin at their defeat in the election, or from any personal hostility to the President-elect, but from the fact that they recognized in him the representative of a party professing principles destructive to "their peace, their prosperity, and their domestic tranquillity." The long-suppressed fire burst into frequent flame, but it was still controlled by that love of the Union which the South had illustrated on every battlefield from Boston to New Orleans. Still it was hoped, against hope, that some adjustment might be made to avert the calamities of a practical application of the theory of an "irrepressible conflict."

Few, if any, then doubted the right of a State to withdraw its grants delegated to the Federal Government, or, in other words, to secede from the Union; but in the South this was generally regarded as the remedy of last resort, to be applied only when ruin or dishonor was the alternative. No rash or revolutionary action was taken by the Southern States, but the measures adopted were considerate, and executed advisedly and deliberately. The Presidential election occurred (as far as the popular vote, which determined the result, was concerned) in November, 1860. Most of the State Legislatures convened soon afterward in regular session. In some cases special sessions were convoked for the purpose of calling State conventions—the recognized representatives of the sovereign will of the people—to be elected expressly for the purpose of taking such action as should be considered needful and proper under the existing circumstances.

These conventions, as it was always held and understood, possessed all the power of the people assembled in mass; and therefore it was conceded that they, and they only, could take action for the withdrawal of a State from the Union. The consent of the respective States to the formation of the Union had been given through such conventions, and it was only by the same authority that it could properly be revoked. The time required for this deliberate and formal process precludes the idea of hasty or passionate action, and none who admit the primary power of the people to govern themselves can consistently deny its validity and binding obligation upon every citizen of the several States. Not only was there ample time for calm consideration among the people of the South, but for due reflection by the General Government and the people of the Northern States.

President Buchanan was in the last year of his Administration. His freedom from sectional asperity, his long life in the public service, and his peace-loving and conciliatory character were all guarantees against his precipitating a conflict between the Federal Government and any of the States; but the feeble power that he possessed in the closing months of his term to mould the policy of the future was painfully evident. Like all who had intelligently and impartially studied the history of the formation of the Constitution, he held that the Federal Government had no rightful power to coerce a State. Like the sages and patriots who had preceded him in the high office that he filled, he believed that "Our Union rests upon public opinion, and can never be cemented by the blood of its citizens shed in civil war. If it cannot live in the affections of the people, it must one day perish. Congress may possess many means of preserving it by conciliation, but the sword was not placed in its hand to preserve it by force." (Message of December 3, 1860.)

Ten years before, John C. Calhoun, addressing the Senate with all the earnestness of his nature, and with that sincere desire to avert the danger of disunion which those who knew him best never doubted, had asked the emphatic question, "How can the Union be saved?" He answered his question thus: "There is but one way by which it can be [saved] with any certainty; and that is by a full and final settlement, on the principles of justice, of all the questions at issue between the sections. The South asks for justice, simple justice, and less she ought not to take. She has no compromise to offer but the Constitution, and no concession or surrender to make. Can this be done? Yes, easily! Not by the weaker party; for it can of itself do nothing—not even protect itself—but by the stronger. But will the North agree to do this? It is for her to answer this question. But, I will say, she cannot refuse if she has half the love of the Union which she professes to have, nor without exposing herself to the charge that her love of power and aggrandizement is far greater than her love of the Union."

During the ten years that intervened between the date of this speech and the message of Buchanan cited above, the progress of sectional discord and the tendency of the stronger section to unconstitutional aggression had been fearfully rapid. With very rare exceptions, there were none in 1850 who claimed the right of the Federal Government to apply coercion to a State. In 1860 men had grown to be familiar with threats of driving the South into submission to any act that the Government, in the hands of a Northern majority, might see fit to perform. During the canvass of that year, demonstrations had been made by quasi-military organizations in various parts of the North, which looked unmistakably to purposes widely different from those enunciated in the preamble of the Constitution, and to the employment of means not authorized by the powers which the States had delegated to the Federal Government.

Well-informed men still remembered that, in the convention which framed the Constitution, a proposition was made to authorize the employment of force against a delinquent State, on which Madison said: "The use of force against a State would look more like a declaration of war than an infliction of punishment, and would probably be considered by the party attacked as a dissolution of all previous compacts by which it might have been bound." The convention expressly refused to confer the power proposed, and the clause was lost. While therefore in 1860 many violent men, appealing to passion and the lust of power, were inciting the multitude, and preparing Northern opinion to support a war waged against the Southern States in the event of their secession, there were others who took a different view of the case. Notable among such was the New York *Tribune*, which had been the organ of the abolitionists, and which now declared that, "If the cotton States wished to withdraw from the Union, they should be allowed to do so"; that "any attempt to compel them to remain, by force, would be contrary to the principles of the Declaration of Independence and to the fundamental ideas upon which human liberty is based"; and that "if the Declaration of Independence justified the secession from the British Empire of three millions of subjects in 1776, it was not seen why it would not justify the secession of five millions of Southerners from the Union in 1861." Again, it was said by the same journal that, "Sooner than compromise with the South and abandon the Chicago platform," they would "let the Union slide." Taunting expressions were freely used, as, for example: "If the Southern people wish to leave the Union, we will do our best to forward their views."

All this, it must be admitted, was quite consistent with the oft-repeated declaration that the Constitution was a "covenant with hell," which stood as the caption of a leading abolitionist paper of Boston. That signs of coming danger so visible, evidences of hostility so unmistakable, disregard of constitutional obligations so wanton, taunts and jeers so bitter and insulting, should serve to increase excitement in the South, were consequences flowing as much from reason and patriotism as from sentiment. He must have been ignorant of human nature who did not expect such a tree to bear fruits of discord and division.

In November, 1860, after the result of the Presidential election was known, the Governor of Mississippi, having issued his proclamation convoking a special session of the Legislature to consider the propriety of calling a convention, invited the Senators and Representatives of the State in Congress to meet him for consultation as to the character of the message he should send to the Legislature when assembled.

While holding, in common with my political associates, that the right of a State to secede was unquestionable, I differed from most of them as to the probability of our being permitted peaceably to exercise the right. The knowledge acquired by the administration of the War Department for four years, and by the chairmanship of the Military Committee of the Senate at two different periods, still longer in combined duration, had shown me the entire lack of preparation for war in the South. The foundries and armories were in the Northern States, and there were stored all the new and improved weapons of war. In the arsenals of the Southern States were to be found only arms of the old and rejected models. The South had no manufactories of powder, and no navy to protect our harbors, no merchant-ships for foreign commerce. It was evident to me, therefore, that, if we should be involved in war, the odds against us would be far greater than what was due merely to our inferiority in population. Believing that secession would be the precursor of war between the States, I was consequently slower and more reluctant than others, who entertained a different opinion, to resort to that remedy.

While engaged in the consultation with the Governor, just referred to, a telegraphic message was handed to me from two members of President Buchanan's Cabinet, urging me to proceed "immediately" to Washington. This despatch was laid before the Governor and the members of Congress from the State who were in conference with him, and it was decided that I should comply with the summons. I was afterward informed that my associates considered me "too slow," and they were probably correct in the belief that I was behind the general opinion of the people of the State as to the propriety of prompt secession.

On arrival at Washington I found, as had been anticipated, that my presence there was desired on account of the influence which it was supposed I might exercise with the President in relation to his forthcoming message to Congress. On paying my respects to the President, he told me that he had finished the rough draft of his message, but that it was still open to revision and amendment, and that he would like to read it to me. He did so, and very kindly accepted all the modifications which I suggested. The message was afterward somewhat changed, and, with great deference to the wisdom and statesmanship of its author, I must say that, in my judgment, the last alterations were unfortunate—so much so, that when it was read in the Senate I was reluctantly constrained to criticise it. Compared, however, with documents of the same class which have since been addressed to the Congress of the United States, the reader of Presidential messages must regret that it was not accepted by President Buchanan's successors as a model, and that his views of the Constitution had not been adopted as a guide in the subsequent action of the Federal Government.

The popular movement in the South was tending steadily and rapidly toward the secession of those known as "planting States"; yet, when Congress assembled on December 3, 1860, the representatives of the people of all those States took their seats in the House, and they were all represented in the Senate, except South Carolina, whose Senators had tendered their resignation to the Governor immediately on the announcement of the result of the Presidential election. Hopes were still cherished that the Northern leaders would appreciate the impending peril; would cease to treat the warnings, so often given, as idle threats; would refrain from the bravado, so often and so unwisely indulged, of ability "to whip the South" in thirty, sixty, or ninety days; and would address themselves to the more manly purpose of devising means to allay the indignation and quiet the apprehensions, whether well founded or not, of their Southern brethren. But the debates of that session manifest, on the contrary, the arrogance of a triumphant party, and the determination to reap to the uttermost the full harvest of a party victory.

ABRAHAM LINCOLN

Inaugural Address

Fellow-Citizens of the United States:

In compliance with a custom as old as the Government itself, I appear before you to address you briefly, and to take in your presence the oath prescribed by the Constitution of the United States to be taken by the President "before he enters on the execution of his office."

I do not consider it necessary at present for me to discuss those matters of administration about which there is no special anxiety or excitement. Apprehension seems to exist, among the people of the Southern States, that by the accession of a Republican Administration their property and their peace and personal security are to be endangered. There has never been any reasonable cause for such apprehension. Indeed, the most ample evidence to the contrary has all the while existed and been open to their inspection. It is found in nearly all the published speeches of him who now addresses you. I do but quote from one of those speeches when I declare that "I have no purpose, directly or indirectly, to interfere with the institution of slavery in the States where it exists. I believe I have no lawful right to do so, and I have no inclination to do so." Those who nominated and elected me did so with full knowledge that I had made this and many similar declarations, and had never recanted them. And more than this, they placed in the platform for my acceptance, and as a law to themselves and to me, the clear and emphatic resolution which I now read:

"*Resolved*, That the maintenance inviolate of the rights of the States, and especially the right of each State to order and control its own domestic institutions according to its own judgment exclusively, is essential to the balance of power on which the perfection and endurance of our political fabric depend, and we denounce the lawless invasion by armed force of the soil of any State or Territory, no matter under what pretext, as among the gravest of crimes."

I now reiterate these sentiments; and, in doing so, I only press upon the public attention the most conclusive evidence of which the case is susceptible, that the property, peace, and security of no section are to be in any wise endangered by the now incoming Administration. I add, too, that all the protection which, consistently with the Constitution and the laws, can be given, will be cheerfully given to all the States, when lawfully demanded, for whatever cause—as cheerfully to one section as to another. There is much controversy about the delivering up of fugitives from service or labor. The clause I now read is as plainly written in the Constitution as any other of its provisions:

"No person held to service or labor in one State, under the laws thereof, escaping into another, shall, in consequence of any law or regulation therein, be discharged from such service or labor, but shall be delivered up on claim of the party to whom such service or labor may be due."

It is scarcely questioned that this provision was intended, by those who made it, for the reclaiming of what we call fugitive slaves; and the intention of the lawgiver is the law. All members of Congress swear their support to the whole Constitution—

to this provision as much as any other. To the proposition, then, that slaves, whose cases come within the terms of this clause, "shall be delivered up," their oaths are unanimous. Now, if they would make the effort in good temper, could they not, with nearly equal unanimity, frame and pass a law by means of which to keep good that unanimous oath?

There is some difference of opinion whether this clause should be enforced by National or by State authority; but surely that difference is not a very material one. If the slave is to be surrendered, it can be of but little consequence to him, or to others, by which authority it is done. And should anyone, in any case, be content that his oath should go unkept, on a mere unsubstantial controversy as to how it shall be kept?

Again, in any law upon this subject, ought not all the safeguards of liberty known in civilized and humane jurisprudence to be introduced, so that a free man be not, in any case, surrendered as a slave? And might it not be well, at the same time, to provide by law for the enforcement of that clause in the Constitution which guarantees that "the citizens of each State shall be entitled to all privileges and immunities of citizens of the several States"? I take the official oath to-day with no mental reservation, and with no purpose to construe the Constitution or laws by any hypercritical rules. And while I do not choose now to specify particular acts of Congress as proper to be enforced, I do suggest that it will be much safer for all, both in official and private stations, to conform to and abide by all those acts which stand unrepealed, than to violate any of them, trusting to find impunity in having them held to be unconstitutional.

It is seventy-two years since the first inauguration of a President under our National Constitution. During that period fifteen different and greatly distinguished citizens have, in succession, administered the executive branch of the Government. They have conducted it through many perils, and generally with great success. Yet, with all this scope for precedent, I now enter upon the same task for the brief constitutional term of four years, under great and peculiar difficulty. A disruption of the Federal Union, heretofore only menaced, is now formidably attempted. I hold that, in contemplation of universal law, and of the Constitution, the Union of these States is perpetual. Perpetuity is implied, if not expressed, in the fundamental law of all national governments. It is safe to assert that no government proper ever had a provision in its organic law for its own termination. Continue to execute all the express provisions of our National Government, and the Union will endure forever—it being impossible to destroy it, except by some action not provided for in the instrument itself.

Again, if the United States be not a government proper, but an association of states in the nature of contract merely, can it, as a contract, be peaceably unmade by less than all the parties who made it? One party to a contract may violate it—break it, so to speak; but does it not require all lawfully to rescind it? Descending from these general principles, we find the proposition that, in legal contemplation, the Union is perpetual, confirmed by the history of the Union itself. The Union is much older than the Constitution. It was formed, in fact, by the Articles of Association in 1774. It was matured and continued by the Declaration of Independence in 1776. It was further matured, and the faith of all the then Thirteen States expressly plighted and engaged that it should be perpetual, by the Articles of Confederation in 1778. And finally in 1787 one of the declared objects for ordaining and establishing the Constitution was "to form a more perfect union."

But if destruction of the Union, by one, or by a part only, of the States, be lawfully possible, the Union is less perfect than before, the Constitution having lost the vital element of perpetuity. It follows, from these views, that no State, upon its own mere motion, can lawfully get out of the Union; that resolves and ordinances to that effect are legally void; and that acts of violence within any State or States, against the authority of the United States, are insurrectionary or revolutionary, according to circumstances.

I therefore consider that, in view of the Constitution and the laws, the Union is unbroken, and to the extent of my ability I shall take care, as the Constitution itself expressly enjoins upon me, that the laws of the Union be faithfully executed in all the States. Doing this I deem to be only a simple duty on my part; and I shall perform it, so far as practicable, unless my rightful masters, the American people, shall withhold the requisite means, or, in some authoritative manner, direct the contrary. I trust this will not be regarded as a menace, but only as the declared purpose of the Union that it will constitutionally defend and maintain itself.

In doing this there need be no bloodshed or violence; and there shall be none, unless it be forced upon the national authority. The power confided to me will be used to hold, occupy, and possess the property and places belonging to the Government, and to collect the duties and imposts; but beyond what may be but necessary for these objects, there will be no invasion, no using of force against or among the people anywhere. Where hostility to the United States, in any interior locality, shall be so great and universal as to prevent competent resident citizens from holding the Federal offices, there will be no attempt to force obnoxious strangers among the people for that object. While the strict legal right may exist in the Government to enforce the exercise of these offices, the attempt to do so would be so irritating, and so nearly impracticable withal, I deem it better to forego, for the time, the uses of such offices.

The mails, unless repelled, will continue to be furnished in all parts of the Union. So far as possible, the people everywhere shall have that sense of perfect security which is most favorable to calm thought and reflection. The course here indicated will be followed, unless current events and experience shall show a modification or change to be proper, and in every case and exigency my best discretion will be exercised, according to circumstances actually existing, and with a view and a hope of peaceful solution of the national troubles, and the restoration of fraternal sympathies and affections.

That there are persons in one section or another who seek to destroy the Union at all events, and are glad of any pretext to do it, I will neither affirm nor deny; but if there be such, I need address no word to them. To those, however, who really love the Union, may I not speak? Before entering upon so grave a matter as the destruction of our national fabric, with all its benefits, its memories, and its hopes, would it not be wise to ascertain precisely why we do it? Will you hazard so desperate a step while there is any possibility that any portion of the ills you fly from have no real existence? Will you, while the certain ills you fly to are greater than all the real ones you fly from—will you risk the commission of so fearful a mistake?

All profess to be content in the Union if all constitutional rights can be maintained. Is it true, then, that any right, plainly written in the Constitution, has been denied? I think not. Happily the human mind is so constituted that no party can reach to the audacity of doing this. Think, if you can, of a single instance in which a plainly written provision of the Constitution has ever been denied. If, by the mere force of numbers, a majority should deprive a minority of any clearly written constitutional right, it might, in a moral point of view, justify revolution—certainly would if such right were a vital one. But such is not our case. All the vital rights of minorities and of individuals are so plainly assured to them by affirmations and negations, guarantees and prohibitions, in the Constitution, that controversies never arise concerning them. But no organic law can ever be framed with a provision specifically applicable to every question which may occur in practical administration. No foresight can anticipate, nor any document of reasonable length contain, express provisions for all possible questions. Shall fugitives from labor be surrendered by National or by State authority? The Constitution does not expressly say. May Congress prohibit slavery in the Territories? The Constitution does not expressly say. Must Congress protect slavery in the Territories? The Constitution does not expressly say.

From questions of this class spring all our constitutional controversies, and we divide upon them into majorities and minorities. If the minority will not acquiesce, the majority must, or the Government must cease. There is no other alternative; for continuing the Government is acquiescence on one side or the other. If a minority in such case will secede rather than acquiesce, they make a precedent which, in turn, will divide and ruin them; for a minority of their own will secede from them whenever a majority refuses to be controlled by such minority. For instance, why may not any portion of a new confederacy, a year or two hence, arbitrarily secede again, precisely as portions of the present Union now claim to secede from it? All who cherish disunion sentiments are now being educated to the exact temper of doing this.

Is there such perfect identity of interests among the States to compose a new Union, as to produce harmony only, and prevent renewed secession? Plainly, the central idea of secession is the essence of anarchy. A majority held in restraint by constitutional checks and limitations, and always changing easily with deliberate changes of popular opinions and sentiments, is the only true sovereign of a free people. Whoever rejects it, does, of necessity, fly to anarchy or despotism. Unanimity is impossible; the rule of a minority, as a permanent arrangement, is wholly inadmissible; so that, rejecting the majority principle, anarchy or despotism, in some form, is all that is left.

I do not forget the position assumed by some, that constitutional questions are to be decided by the Supreme Court; nor do I deny that such decisions must be binding, in any case, upon the parties to a suit, as to the object of that suit, while they are also entitled to very high respect and consideration in all parallel cases, by all other departments of the Government. And while it is obviously possible that such decisions may be erroneous in any given case, still, the evil effect following it being limited to that particular case, with the chance that it may be overruled, and never become a precedent for other cases, can better be borne than could the evils of a different practice. At the same time the candid citizen must confess that if the policy of the Government upon vital questions affecting the whole people is to be irrevocably fixed by decisions of the Supreme Court, the instant they are made in ordinary litigation between parties in personal actions the people will have ceased to be their own rulers, having to that extent practically resigned their Government into the hands of that eminent tribunal.

Nor is there in this view any assault upon the court or the judges. It is a duty from which they may not shrink to decide cases properly brought before them, and it is no fault of theirs if others seek to turn their decisions to political purposes. One section of our country believes slavery is right and ought to be extended, while the other believes it is wrong and ought not to be extended. This is the only substantial dispute. The fugitive-slave clause of the Constitution, and the law for the suppression of the foreign slave-trade, are each as well enforced, perhaps, as any law can ever be in a community where the moral sense of the people imperfectly supports the law itself. The great body of the people abide by the dry legal obligation in both cases, and a few break over in each. This, I think, cannot be perfectly cured; and it would be worse, in both cases, after the separation of the sections than before. The foreign slave-trade, now imperfectly suppressed, would be ultimately revived, without restriction, in one section; while fugitive slaves, now only partially surrendered, would not be surrendered at all by the other.

Physically speaking, we cannot separate. We cannot remove our respective sections from each other, nor build an impassable wall between them. A husband and wife may be divorced, and go out of the presence and beyond the reach of each other; but the different parts of our country cannot do this. They cannot but remain face to face; and intercourse, either amicable or hostile, must continue between them. It is impossible, then, to make that intercourse more advantageous or more satisfactory after separation than before. Can aliens make treaties easier than friends can make laws? Can treaties be more faithfully enforced between aliens than laws can among friends? Suppose you go to war, you cannot fight always; and when, after much loss on both sides, and no gain on either, you cease fighting, the identical old questions, as to terms of intercourse, are again upon you.

This country, with its institutions, belongs to the people who inhabit it. Whenever they shall grow weary of the existing Government, they can exercise their constitutional right of amending it, or their revolutionary right to dismember or overthrow it. I cannot be ignorant of the fact that many worthy and patriotic citizens are desirous of having the National Constitution amended. While I make no recommendation of amendments, I fully recognize the rightful authority of the people over the whole subject, to be exercised in either of the modes prescribed in the instrument itself; and I should, under existing circumstances, favor, rather than oppose, a fair opportunity being afforded the people to act upon it. I will venture to add that to me the convention mode seems preferable, in that it allows amendments to originate with the people themselves, instead of only permitting them to take or reject propositions originated by others, not especially chosen for the purpose, and which might not be precisely such as they would wish to either accept or refuse. I understand a proposed amendment to the Constitution—which amendment, however, I have not seen—has passed Congress, to the effect that the Federal Government shall never interfere with the domestic institutions of the States, including that of persons held to service. To avoid misconstruction of what I have said, I depart from my purpose not to speak of particular amendments so far as to say that, holding such a provision now to be implied constitutional law, I have no objections to its being made express and irrevocable.

The Chief Magistrate derives all his authority from the people, and they have conferred none upon him to fix terms for the separation of the States. The people themselves can do this also if they choose; but the Executive, as such, has nothing to do with it. His duty is to administer the present Government as it came to his hands, and to transmit it, unimpaired by him, to his successor. Why should there not be a patient confidence in the ultimate justice of the people? Is there any better or equal hope in the world? In our present differences, is either party without faith of being in the right? If the Almighty Ruler of Nations, with his eternal truth and justice, be on your side of the North, or on yours of the South, that truth and that justice will surely prevail, by the judgment of this great tribunal of the American people.

By the frame of the government under which we live, the same people have wisely given their public servants but little power for mischief; and have, with equal wisdom, provided for the return of that little to their own hands at very short intervals. While the people retain their virtue and vigilance, no administration, by any extreme of wickedness or folly, can very seriously injure the Government in the short space of four years.

My countrymen, one and all, think calmly and well upon this whole subject. Nothing valuable can be lost by taking time. If there be an object to hurry any of you in hot haste to a step which you would never take deliberately, that object will be frustrated by taking time; but no good object can be frustrated by it. Such of you as are now dissatisfied, still have the old Constitution unimpaired, and, on the sensitive point, the laws of your own framing under it; while the new Administration will have no immediate power, if it would, to change either. If it were admitted that you who are dissatisfied hold the right side in the dispute, there still is no single good reason for precipitate action. Intelligence, patriotism, Christianity, and a firm reliance on Him who has never yet forsaken this favored land are still competent to adjust, in the best way, all our present difficulty.

In your hands, my dissatisfied fellow-countrymen, and not in mine, is the momentous issue of civil war. The Government will not assail you. You can have no conflict without being yourselves the aggressors. You have no oath registered in heaven to destroy the Government; while I shall have the most solemn one to "preserve, protect, and defend" it.

I am loth to close. We are not enemies, but friends. We must not be enemies. Though passion may have strained, it must not break, our bonds of affection. The mystic cords of memory, stretching from every battlefield and patriot grave to every living heart and hearthstone all over this broad land, will yet swell the chorus of the Union, when again touched, as surely they will be, by the better angels of our nature.

First Message to Congress

It might seem, at first thought, to be of little difference whether the present movement at the South be called "secession" or "rebellion." The movers, however, will understand the difference. At the beginning, they knew they could never raise their treason to any respectable magnitude by any name which implies violation of law. They knew their people possessed as much of moral sense, as much of devotion to law and order, and as much pride in and reverence for the history and the government of their common country as any other civilized and patriotic people. They knew they could make no advancement directly in the teeth of these strong and noble sentiments. Accordingly they commenced by an insidious debauching of the public mind. They invented an ingenious sophism, which, if conceded, was followed by perfectly logical steps, through all the incidents, to the complete destruction of the Union. The sophism itself is that any State of the Union may, consistently with the National Constitution, and therefore lawfully and peacefully, withdraw from the Union without the consent of the Union or of any other State. The little disguise that the supposed right is to be exercised only for just cause, themselves to be the sole judges of its justice, is too thin to merit any notice.

With rebellion thus sugar-coated they have been drugging the public mind of their section for more than thirty years, and until at length they have brought many good men to a willingness to take up arms against the Government the day after some assemblage of men have enacted the farcical pretence of taking their State out of the Union, who could have been brought to no such thing the day before.

This sophism derives much, perhaps the whole, of its currency from the assumption that there is some omnipotent and sacred supremacy pertaining to a State—to each State of our Federal Union. Our States have neither more nor less power than that reserved to them in the Union by the Constitution—no one of them ever having been a State out of the Union. The original ones passed into the Union even before they cast off their British colonial dependence; and the new ones each came into the Union directly from a condition of dependence, excepting Texas.

And even Texas, in its temporary independence, was never designated a State. The new ones only took the designation of States on coming into the Union, while that name was first adopted by the old ones in and by the Declaration of Independence. Therein the "United Colonies" were declared to be "free and independent States"; but, even then, the object plainly was not to declare their independence of one another or of the Union, but directly the contrary, as their mutual pledge and their mutual action before, at the time, and afterward abundantly show. The express plighting of faith by each and all of the original thirteen in the Articles of Confederation, two years later, that the Union shall be perpetual, is most conclusive. Having never been States, either in substance or in name, outside of the Union, whence this magical omnipotence of "State Rights," asserting a claim of power lawfully to destroy the Union itself?

Much is said about the "sovereignty" of the States; but the word even is not in the National Constitution, nor, as is believed, in any of the State constitutions. What is "sovereignty" in the political sense of the term? Would it be far wrong to define it "a political community without a political superior"? Tested by this, no one of our States, except Texas, ever was a sovereignty. And even Texas gave up the character on coming into the Union; by which act she acknowledged the Constitution of the United States, and the laws and treaties of the United States made in pursuance of the Constitution, to be for her the supreme law of the land. The States have their *status* in the Union, and they have no other legal *status*. If they break from this, they can only do so against law and by revolution. The Union, and not themselves separately, procured their independence and their liberty. By conquest or purchase the Union gave each of them whatever of independence or liberty it has. The Union is older than any of the States, and, in fact, it created them as States. Originally some dependent colonies made the Union, and in turn the Union threw off their old dependence for them, and made them States, such as they are. Not one of them ever had a State constitution independent of the Union. Of course, it is not forgotten that all the new States framed their constitutions before they entered the Union; nevertheless dependent upon, and preparatory to, coming into the Union.

Unquestionably the States have the powers and rights reserved to them in and by the National Constitution; but among these, surely, are not included all conceivable powers, however mischievous or destructive; but, at most, such only as were known in the world, at the time, as governmental powers; and, certainly, a power to destroy the Government itself had never been known as a governmental—as a merely administrative power. This relative matter of national power and State rights as a principle, is no other than the principle of generality and locality. Whatever concerns the whole should be confided to the whole—to the General Government; while whatever concerns only the State should be left exclusively to the State. This is all there is of original principle about it. Whether the National Constitution, in defining boundaries between the two, has applied the principle with exact accuracy is not to be questioned. We are all bound by that defining, without question.

What is now combated is the position that secession is consistent with the Constitution—is lawful and peaceful. It is not contended that there is any express law for it; and nothing should ever be implied as law which leads to unjust or absurd consequences. The nation purchased with money the countries out of which several of these States were formed; is it just that they shall go off without leave and without refunding? The nation paid very large sums (in the aggregate, I believe, nearly a hundred millions) to relieve Florida of the aboriginal tribes; is it just that she shall now be off without consent or without making any return? The nation is now in debt for money applied to the benefit of these so-called seceding States in common with the rest; is it just either that creditors shall go unpaid or the remaining States pay the whole? A part of the present national debt was contracted to pay the old debts of Texas; is it just that she shall leave and pay no part of this herself?

Again, if one State may secede, so may another; and when all shall have seceded, none is left to pay the debts. Is this quite just to creditors? Did we notify them of this sage view of ours when we borrowed their money? If we now recognize this doctrine by allowing the seceders to go in peace, it is difficult to see what we can do if others choose to go, or to extort terms upon which they will promise to remain. The seceders insist that our Constitution admits of secession. They have assumed to make a national constitution of their own, in which, of necessity, they have either discarded or retained the right of secession, as they insist it exists in ours. If they have discarded it, they thereby admit that, on principle, it ought not to be in ours. If they have retained it, by their own construction of ours, they show that to be consistent they must secede from one another whenever they shall find it the easiest way of settling their debts or effecting any other selfish or unjust object. The principle itself is one of disintegration, upon which no government can possibly endure.

If all the States save one should assert the power to drive that one out of the Union, it is presumed the whole class of seceder politicians would at once deny the power and denounce the act as the greatest outrage upon State rights. But suppose that precisely the same act, instead of being called "driving the one out," should be called "the seceding of the others from that one," it would be exactly what the seceders claim to do; unless, indeed, they make the point that the one, because it is a minority, may rightfully do what the others, because they are a majority, may not rightfully do. These politicians are subtile and profound on the rights of minorities. They are not partial to that power which made the Constitution and speaks from the preamble, calling itself "We, the People."

It may well be questioned whether there is to-day a majority of the legally qualified voters of any State, except perhaps South Carolina, in favor of disunion. There is much reason to believe that the Union men are the majority in many, if not in every other one, of the so-called seceded States. The contrary has not been demonstrated in any one of them. It is ventured to affirm this even of Virginia and Tennessee; for the result of an election held in military camps, where the bayonets are all on one side of the question voted upon, can scarcely be considered as demonstrating popular sentiment. At such an election, all that large class who are at once for the Union and against coercion would be coerced to vote against the Union.

THE BATTLE OF BULL RUN

A.D. 1861

HORACE GREELEY

When Fort Sumter, in Charleston Harbor, was bombarded and compelled to surrender (April 12-13, 1861), it could no longer be doubted that war was inevitable, and President Lincoln called for seventy-five thousand volunteers to suppress the insurrection. These were forthcoming without delay—in fact, more were offered than could be accepted. Most of those from the Western States were concentrated at Cairo, Illinois, while those from the Eastern States were forwarded to Washington. As soon as these were uniformed and armed, there was an impatient popular demand that they be marched against the enemy without delay, regardless of the fact that they needed thorough organization and discipline in order to become an effective army. The most noticeable form of this demand was the cry "On to Richmond!" which appeared first in the New York *Tribune*, edited by Horace Greeley, whose narrative of the consequent battle we give herewith. The important effect of that battle was not purely military; for as soon as the people of the North had recovered from their surprise at the defeat, they set to work to make stronger and better preparations for continuing the conflict. The correspondents of European papers wrote it up in such a way as to convince their readers that there could be no doubt as to the speedy triumph of the Confederacy, and this enabled the Confederate Government to sell bonds in Europe and thus raise funds for carrying on the war. At the same time the victory confirmed the Southern people in their belief that the South was invincible. Thus this battle—the greatest, up to that time, that had ever been fought on this continent—had an important influence in prolonging the contest.

THE movement of the Union Grand Army, commanded in the field by General Irvin McDowell, but directed from Washington by Lieutenant-General Winfield Scott, began on Tuesday, July 16th. General Royal O. Tyler's column, in the advance, bivouacked that night at Vienna, four and a half miles from Fairfax Court House. It rested next night at Germantown, two miles beyond Fairfax; and, on Thursday, at 9 A.M., pushed on, to and through Centerville, the Confederates retiring quietly before it. Three miles beyond that village, however, they were found strongly posted at Blackburn's Ford, on Bull Run, and, on being pressed, showed fight. This was at 1.30 P.M. A spirited conflict, mainly with artillery, resulted, the Confederates being in heavy force, under the immediate command of General James Longstreet. The Unionists, more exposed, as well as outnumbered, finally drew back. The losses were nearly equal: eighty-three on our side; sixty-eight on the other. Sherman's battery, Captain Romeyn B. Ayres, did most of the actual fighting, supported by Colonel Israel B. Richardson's brigade, consisting of the First Massachusetts, Twelfth New York, and Second and Third Michigan. Regarded as a reconnoissance in force the attack might be termed a success, since the result demonstrated that the main Confederate army was in position along the wooded valley of Bull Run, half-way between Centerville and Manassas Junction, and purposed to remain.

General McDowell's army was moved up to and concentrated around the ridge on which Centerville is situated during the 18th and 19th, with intent to advance and attack the enemy, posted along Bull Run and between that stream and Manassas Junction, on Saturday, the 20th. But delay was encountered in the reception of adequate subsistence, which did not arrive till Friday night. On Saturday three days' rations were distributed and issued, and every preparation was made for moving punctually at two o'clock next morning. Meantime General P. T. Beauregard, maintaining an absolute quiet and inoffensiveness on his front, and fully informed by spies and others of every movement between him and Washington, had hastily gathered from every side all the available forces of the Confederacy, including fifteen thousand, or nearly the full strength, of General Joseph E. Johnston's Army of the Shenandoah, and had decided to assume the offensive and attack our forces before General Robert Patterson could come up to join them. Had the advance been made on Saturday, as originally intended, it would have encountered but two-thirds of the force it combated; had it been delayed a few hours longer, the Federal troops would have stood on the defensive, with the immense advantages of knowing the ground and of choosing the positions whereon to fight. Such are the casualties and fatalities of war.

Bull Run is a decent mill-stream, fordable in summer at

intervals of half a mile to a mile. Its immediate valley is generally narrow and wooded, enclosed by bluffs, neither high nor very steep, but affording good positions for planting batteries to command the roads on the opposite side, so screened by woods and brush as to be neither seen nor suspected until the advancing or attacking party is close upon them. This fact explains and justifies General McDowell's (or Scott's) order of battle. This was, briefly: to menace the enemy's right by the advance of our First division on the direct road from Centerville to Manassas Junction, while making a more serious demonstration on the road running due west from Centerville to Groveton and Warrenton, and crossing Bull Run by the Stone Bridge; while the real or main attack was to be made by a column fifteen thousand strong, composed of the Second (David Hunter's) and Third (Samuel P. Heintzelman's) divisions, which, starting from their camps a mile or two east and southeast of Centerville, were to make a considerable détour to the right, crossing Cub Run, and then Bull Run, at a ford known as Sudley Spring, three miles above the Stone Bridge, thus turning the enemy's left, and rolling it up on the centre, where it was to be taken in flank by our First division (Tyler's) crossing the Stone Bridge at the right moment, and completing the rout of the enemy. The Fifth division (D. J. Miles's) was held in reserve at Centerville, not only to support the attacking columns, but to guard against the obvious peril of a formidable Confederate advance across Blackburn's Ford to Centerville, flanking our flank movement, capturing munitions and supplies, and cutting off the line of retreat. The Fourth division (Runyon's) guarded communications with Alexandria and Arlington; its foremost regiment being about seven miles from Centerville.

The movement of the Federal army was appointed for 2.30 A.M., and the battle should have been opened at 6 A.M.; but the raw troops never had been brigaded before this advance, and most of their officers were without experience; so that there was a delay of two or three hours in the flanking divisions reaching the point at which the battle was to begin. General Tyler, in front of Stone Bridge, opened with his artillery at 6.30 A.M., eliciting no reply; and it was three hours later when Hunter's advance, under Colonel Ambrose E. Burnside, crossed at

Sudley Spring; his men, thirsty with their early march that hot July morning, stopping as they crossed to drink and to fill their canteens.

Every movement of the Federal forces was revealed by Beauregard, watching them from the slope two or three miles west, by the clouds of dust that rose over their line of march; and regiment after regiment was hurried northward by him to meet the imminent shock. No strength was wasted by him upon, and scarcely any notice taken of, the feint on his right; but when Burnside's brigade, after crossing at Sudley, had marched a mile through woods down the road on the right of Bull Run, and come out into a clear and cultivated country, stretching thence over a mile of rolling fields down to the Warrenton turnpike, he was vigorously opened upon by artillery from the woods in his front, and, as he pressed on, by infantry also. Continuing to advance, fighting, followed and supported by Hunter's entire division, which was soon joined on its left by Heintzelman's, which had crossed the stream a little later and farther down, the attacking column reached and crossed the Warrenton road from Centerville by the Stone Bridge, giving a hand to William T. Sherman's brigade of Tyler's division, and all but clearing this road of the enemy's batteries and regiments, which here resisted our efforts, under the immediate command of General Joseph E. Johnston.

Here Simon G. Griffin's battery, which, with James B. Ricketts's, had done the most effective fighting throughout, was charged with effect by a Confederate regiment, which was enabled to approach it by a mistake of the Federal officers, who supposed it one of their own. Three different attacks were repulsed with slaughter, and the battery remained in our hands, though all its horses were killed. At 3 P.M. the enemy had been driven a mile and a half, and were nearly out of sight, abandoning the Warrenton road entirely to the victorious troops.

General Tyler, on hearing the guns of Hunter on the right, had pushed Sherman's and soon afterward Keyes's brigade over the Run to assail the enemy in his front, driving them back after a severe struggle, and steadily advancing until checked by a heavy fire of artillery from batteries on the heights above the road, supported by a brigade of infantry strongly posted behind breastworks. A gallant charge by the Second Maine and Third Connecticut temporarily carried the buildings behind which the enemy's guns were sheltered; but the breastworks were too strong, and our men, recoiling from their fire, deflected to the left, moving down the Run under the shelter of the bluff, covering the efforts of Captain Alexander's pioneers to remove the heavy abatis whereby the enemy had obstructed the road up from the Stone Bridge. This at length had been effected; and Schenck's brigade and Ayres's battery, of Tyler's division, were on the point of crossing the Run to aid in completing the Federal triumph.

But the Confederates, at first outnumbered at the point of actual collision, had been receiving reënforcements nearly all day; and at this critical moment General Kirby Smith, who that morning had left Piedmont, fifteen miles distant, with the remaining brigade of General Johnston's army, appeared on the field. Cheer after cheer burst from the Confederate hosts, but now so downcast, as this timely reënforcement rushed to the front of the battle. Smith almost instantly fell from his horse, wounded; but the command of his brigade was promptly assumed by Colonel Arnold Elzey, who pressed forward, backed by the whole reassured and exultant Confederate host, who felt the day was won.

A correspondent of the Richmond *Dispatch* wrote: "Between two and three o'clock large numbers of men were leaving the field, some of them wounded, others exhausted by the long struggle, who gave us gloomy reports; but, as the firing on both sides continued steadily, we felt sure that our brave Southerners had not been conquered by the overwhelming hordes of the North. It is however due to truth to say that the result at this hour hung trembling in the balance. We had lost numbers of our most distinguished officers. Generals Bartow and Bee had been stricken down; Lieutenant-Colonel Johnson, of the Hampton Legion, had been killed; Colonel Hampton had been wounded. But there was at hand the fearless General whose reputation as a commander was staked on this battle: General Beauregard promptly offered to lead the Hampton Legion into action, which he executed in a style unsurpassed and unsurpassable. General Beauregard rode up and down our lines, between the enemy and his own men, regardless of the heavy fire, cheering and encouraging our troops. About this time a shell struck his horse, taking his head off, and killing the horses of his aides Messrs. Ferguson and Hayward. General Johnston also threw himself into the thickest of the fight, seizing the colors of a Georgia regiment and rallying them to the charge. His staff signalized themselves by their intrepidity, Colonel Thomas being killed and Major Mason wounded. Your correspondent heard General Johnston exclaim to General Cocke just at the critical moment, 'Oh for four regiments!' His wish was answered; for in the distance our reënforcements appeared. The tide of battle was turned in our favor by the arrival of General Kirby Smith from Winchester, with four thousand men of General Johnston's division. General Smith heard, while on the Manassas railroad cars, the roar of battle. He stopped the train and hurried his troops across the fields to the point just where he was most needed."

The Federal soldiers, who had been fighting thirteen hours, weary, hungry, thirsty, continually encountering fresh regiments, and never seeing even a company hurrying to their own support, became suddenly dismayed and panic-stricken. Elzey's and Jubal A. Early's fresh battalions filled the woods on their right, extending rapidly toward its rear, firing on them from under cover, and seeming, by their shots and cries, to be innumerable. Two or three of the regiments recoiled, and then broke, rushing down to the Run. Jefferson Davis, who had left Richmond at 6 A.M., reached the Junction at four, and galloped to the battle-field just in time, it was said, to witness the advance of his cavalry, fifteen thousand strong, under Lieutenant-Colonel J. E. B. Stuart, on the heels of the flying troops. He telegraphed that night to his Congress as follows: "Night has closed upon a hard-fought field. Our forces were victorious. The enemy was routed, and fled precipitately, abandoning a large amount of arms, ammunition, knapsacks, and baggage. The ground was strewed for miles with those killed, and the farmhouses and the ground around were filled with wounded. Pursuit was continued along several routes, toward Leesburg and Centerville, until darkness covered the fugitives. We have captured several field-batteries, stands of arms, and Union and State flags. Many prisoners have been taken."

Before 3 P.M. there had been fitful cannonading and skirmishing, but no serious engagement, on the left. But, when a defeat on the right became manifest, General Johnston again ordered General Richard S. Ewell to advance and attack, which he did, but was received by the Second brigade, Colonel T. A. Davis, with so rapid and spirited a fire of canister that he precipitately retreated. There were still more than three hours of good daylight when the Confederates saw the routed right rushing from the field, like frightened sheep, yet their pursuit amounted to nothing. They came across Bull Run, preceded by their cavalry, and seem to have taken a deliberate, though rather distant, survey of the Fifth division, drawn up in good order along the slope west of Centerville and eagerly expecting their advance. But they appear to have been aware that their victory was a lucky accident, and they did not choose to submit its prestige to the chances of another fray. Having gratified their thirst for knowledge, considerably out of musket-shot, they returned to their previous hiding-places in the woods skirting Bull Run.

During the fore part of the night some Union men, who had not been stampeded, went down toward the battle-field and brought away one or two guns, which had been abandoned in the flight, but not captured by the enemy. The Fifth division, constituting the reserve, now become the rearguard of the army, remained in position until after midnight; when, under orders from General McDowell, it began its deliberate retreat.[1]

[1] Between the panic-stricken fugitives and the victors were not merely the reserve (Fifth) division, which remained in position, and had not fired a shot, but the First (Tyler's) division forming our left, which had suffered little loss, but had signally repulsed the demonstration made upon it at the close of the fight; while the better portion of our beaten right and centre, including the regular infantry and cavalry, still stood its ground and sternly faced the foe. Major Barry, our chief of artillery in the battle, in his official report, after noticing the loss of ten of his guns at the close, through the flight of their supporting infantry, says: "The army having retired upon Centerville, I was ordered by General McDowell in person to post the artillery in position to cover the retreat. The batteries of Hunt, Ayres, Tidball, Edwards, Green, and the New York Eighth Regiment (the latter served by volunteers from Wilcox's brigade), twenty pieces in all, were at once placed in position; and thus remained until 12 P.M., when, orders having been received to retire upon the Potomac, the batteries were put in march, and, covered by Richardson's brigade, retired in good order and without haste, and early next morning reoccupied their former camps on the Potomac."

General McDowell reported our losses in this engagement at 481 killed and 1011 wounded, but says nothing of how many wounded or others were taken prisoners.[1] General Beauregard reports his loss at 269 killed and 1533 wounded; in all, 1852; saying nothing of any loss in prisoners, of whom two or three hundred were taken by our soldiers in the early part of the battle and forwarded to Washington. He says he had sent 1460 wounded and other prisoners to Richmond. He adds: "The ordnance and supplies captured include 28 field-pieces of the best character of arms, with over 100 rounds of ammunition for each gun, 37 caissons, 6 forges, 4 battery-wagons, 64 artillery horses completely equipped, 500,000 rounds of small-arms ammunition, 4500 sets of accoutrements, over 500 muskets, and 9 regimental and garrison flags, with a large number of pistols, knapsacks, swords, canteens, blankets, a large store of axes and intrenching-tools, wagons, ambulances, horses, camp and garrison equipage, hospital stores, and some subsistence."[2]

At 7 A.M., Monday, the 22d, the last Union stragglers and wounded left Centerville, which a Confederate cavalry force was about to enter. But there was no pursuit, and no loss on our part after the battle, but of what our men threw away. Beauregard explains his failure to pursue, after the Union discomfiture: "An army which had fought like ours on that day against uncommon odds, under a July sun, most of the time without water

[1] Among our killed were Colonel James Cameron, brother of the Secretary of War—of the Seventy-ninth New York (Highlanders); Colonel Slocum, and Major Ballou, of the Second Rhode Island; and Lieutenant-Colonel Haggerty of the Sixty-ninth New York. Among our wounded were General David Hunter and General S. P. Heintzelman, commanding divisions; Colonel Oliver B. Wilcox, of Michigan; Colonel Gilman Marston, of the First New Hampshire; Colonel A. M. Wood, of the Fourteenth New York; Colonel H. W. Slocum, of the Twenty-seventh New York; and Colonel N. L. Farnham, of the Eleventh New York (Fire Zouaves). Colonel Wilcox was also taken prisoner, as well as Colonel Michael Corcoran, of the Sixty-ninth New York (Irish), and Major James D. Potter, of the Thirty-eighth New York.

[2] His statement of the number of muskets taken at "over five hundred," including all those dropped by our dead and wounded, proves that the stories told by excited correspondents and other fugitives, of our men throwing away everything that could impede their flight, were gross exaggerations.

and without food, except a hastily snatched meal at dawn, was not in condition for the toil of an eager, effective pursuit of an enemy immediately after the battle. On the following day, an unusually heavy and unintermitting fall of rain intervened to obstruct our advance with reasonable prospect of fruitful results. Added to this, the want of a cavalry force of sufficient numbers made an efficient pursuit a military impossibility."

The forces actually engaged in this celebrated battle, so decisive in its results and so important in its consequences, were probably not far from twenty-five thousand on either side;[1] while the combatants actually on the battle-field, or so near it as to be practically at the disposal of the respective commanders, were, on either side, not far from thirty-five thousand. But the Confederates, who were somewhat the fewer at daybreak, fought under the encouraging stimulus of a knowledge that every hour, as it passed, added to their strength; that each railroad train arriving at the Junction brought fresh brigade after brigade to their support; and these, as they arrived, were hastened to that part of the field whereon their services could be most effective: while the Union men, who had been called to arms at two in the morning, and had generally thrown aside their knapsacks and haversacks to facilitate their movements, had been fourteen hours marching—some of them on the double-quick for miles—or fighting, and were utterly exhausted and faint with hunger and thirst; while not a single company had been added to their numbers. Some regiments fought badly, and had been demoralized and dispersed before the general catastrophe; but the great majority evinced a courage and devotion which, under favoring auspices, would have commanded victory. They gave way only when hope seemed dead—when the ever-increasing hosts of their foes not only outnumbered them in their front, but filled the woods on their right flank, exposing them to an enfilading fire, which they could not return with effect; and, their defeat once confessed, the

[1] Pollard says, "Our effective force of all arms ready for action on the field, on the eventful morning, was less than thirty thousand men." This was before the arrival of that portion of Johnston's army led to the field by Kirby Smith, or the brigade of Early—to say nothing of the reënforcements that were received during the day from the direction of Richmond.

confusion and panic of their flight are explained, not excused, by the fact that, owing to the long détour they had necessarily made in advancing to the attack, pursuant to the plan of battle, their line of retreat lay in part along the front of the foe, much of whose strength was actually nearer to Centerville than they were when the fortunes of the day turned against them.

The causes of this disaster, so shamefully misstated and perverted at the time, are now generally understood. No one could, at this day, repeat the misrepresentations that for the moment prevailed, without conscious, palpable guilt and ignominy. The true, controlling reasons of the Federal defeat were, briefly, these:

1. The fundamental, fatal error on that side was that spirit of hesitation, of indecision, of calculated delay, of stolid obstruction, which guided all military councils, scattering their forces and paralyzing their efforts. Had any real purpose of suppressing the rebellion been cherished by General Scott, he never would have scattered the eastern forces along the line of the Potomac and Chesapeake, from Cumberland to Fort Monroe, divided into three or four distinct armies, under the command of militia officers who had never smelled burning powder unless in a squirrel-hunt. His advance across the Potomac, after being put off as long as possible, was made, as we have seen, on May 24th.

2. The flagrant disobedience and defection of General Patterson, unaccountable on any hypothesis consistent with the possession, on his part, of courage, common-sense, and loyalty.

3. The failure of General Scott to send forward with General McDowell a force adequate to provide against all contingencies. The fact that twenty thousand volunteers remained idle and useless, throughout that eventful Sunday, in and immediately around Washington—Scott having obstinately resisted entreaties that they should be despatched to the front; insisting that McDowell had "men enough"; that he needed no cavalry, etc.—of itself attests strongly the imbecility and lack of purpose that then presided over our military councils.

4. The Confederates were kept thoroughly acquainted by their friends, left in the Union service, with all that took place or was meditated on that side, and so were able to anticipate and baffle every movement of those armies. Thus, a military map or plan of the region directly west of Washington had been com-

pleted for the War Department barely two days before the Union advance reached Centerville; but, the movement being rapid, the Confederates left here many articles in their hasty flight, and, among them, a copy of this map, which was supposed to be unknown to all but a few of our highest officers.

5. The fall, very early in the action, of General David Hunter commanding the Second or leading division, was most untimely and unfortunate. He was so seriously wounded that he was necessarily borne from the field. General Heintzelman, commanding the Third division, was also wounded, not as severely, but so as to disable him. General McDowell either had control of Runyon's division, guarding his line of communication, or he had not. If he had, he should have ordered the bulk of it to advance that morning on Centerville, so as to have it well in hand to precipitate on the foe at the decisive moment; or, if he was so hampered by Scott that he was not at liberty to do this, he should have refused to attack, and resigned the command of the army, rather than fight a battle so fettered.

6. The original call of President Lincoln on the States, for seventy-five thousand militia to serve three months, was a deplorable error. It resulted naturally from that obstinate infatuation which *would* believe, in defiance of all history and probability, that a revolt of nearly ten millions of people was to be put down in sixty or ninety days by some process equivalent to reading the Riot Act to an excited mob and sending a squad of police to disperse it. Hence, the many prisoners of war taken with arms in their hands, in West Virginia and Missouri, had up to this time been quite commonly permitted to go at large on taking an oath of fidelity to the Constitution—a process which, in their view, was about as significant and imposing as taking a glass of cider. The Government had only to call for any number of men it required, to serve during the pleasure of Congress, or till the overthrow of the rebellion, and they could have been had at once. Regiments were pressed upon it from all sides; and the hotels of Washington were crowded by keen competitors for the coveted privilege of raising more batteries and fresh battalions.

7. It is impossible not to see that the Confederate troops were better handled during the conflict than the Union men. General McDowell, who had not participated in any former bat-

tle but that of Buena Vista, where he served as aid to General Wool, appears to have had very little control over the movements of his forces after the beginning of the conflict.

8. Although the Federal army, before that disastrous fight, was largely composed of the bravest and truest patriots in the Union, it contained also much indifferent material. Many, in the general stagnation and dearth of employment, had volunteered under a firm conviction that there would be no serious fighting; that the Confederates were not in earnest; that there would be a promenade, a frolic, and ultimately a compromise, which would send everyone home, unharmed and exultant, to receive from admiring, cheering thousands the guerdon of his valor. Hence some regiments were very badly officered, and others gave way and scattered or fled just when they were most needed.

THE MONITOR AND THE MERRIMAC

A.D. 1862

JOHN DENISON CHAMPLIN[1]

Early in the Civil War the United States Government had iron-clad gunboats built for service on the Mississippi River and its great tributaries. Some of these, all of which were named for Western cities, were launched within a hundred days from the laying of the keel, and they performed efficient service, notably in the capture of Fort Henry, on the Tennessee, in February, 1862, and in assisting the land forces at the Battle of Pittsburg Landing a month later. The Confederates also constructed ironclads, some large ones being produced by putting a sloping roof of railroad iron on a wooden vessel. Such were the Louisiana at New Orleans, the Virginia (popularly known as the Merrimac) at Norfolk, Virginia, and the ram Tennessee in Mobile Bay. But the crowning achievement in this line, which revolutionized naval warfare, was the Monitor, built at the Brooklyn Navy-Yard, by John Ericsson, which arrived in Hampton Roads just in time to be of the highest service to the United States forces there. Great as this service was, it was somewhat exaggerated, for the Merrimac was not seaworthy and could not have gone to New York or Philadelphia. Captain Ericsson deserved all the fame that his achievement gave him. But he was not the inventor of the revolving turret for war-ships. That idea was originated by Theodore R. Timby, then a resident of Poughkeepsie, New York, and patented by him in 1842.

THE Merrimac, one of the finest steam-frigates in the United States Navy, had been set on fire and scuttled when the Gosport Navy-Yard was abandoned in April, 1861. The noble vessel sank to the bottom before the flames had injured her much, and the Confederates soon raised her, cut down her upper deck, and built upon her a very strong timber covering, with sloping sides, like the roof of a house. The outside of this was plated with iron thick enough to be proof against shot from the most powerful guns then in use. Her bow and stern were both under water, and her bow was made sharp and fitted with a cast-iron beak, to be used as a ram. This novel war-vessel, which was

[1] From John D. Champlin's *Young Folks' History of the War for the Union* (New York: Henry Holt and Company), by permission.

finished early in March, 1862, and renamed the Virginia (though her new name did not stick to her), was armed with ten heavy guns, four on each side, one in the bow, and one in the stern, and was put under the command of Captain Franklin Buchanan, formerly of the United States Navy.

The Confederates hoped that this vessel would enable them to open Hampton Roads, which the ships of the Union had kept closely blockaded since the beginning of the war, and which had been the starting-place of the naval expeditions that had done so much damage to their coasts. Vague rumors of this new engine of war had found their way North, and created no little fear, for it was suggested that she might easily ascend the Potomac and destroy Washington, or steam into the harbor of New York and fire the city with her shells, or force the inhabitants to buy safety with a vast sum of money. These rumors probably had the effect of hastening the Government in building ironclads, several of which had already been planned.

At last, without any warning, the dreaded sea-monster made her appearance in Hampton Roads. About noon of Saturday, March 8, 1862, a large black steamer, accompanied by two smaller vessels, was seen coming down Elizabeth River. It was at once thought to be the long-expected Merrimac, and her approach was signalled to the fleet. The Union vessels then in the Roads were the sailing-vessels Cumberland, 24 guns; Congress, 50 guns; and St. Lawrence, 50 guns; the steamers Roanoke and Minnesota, each of 40 guns; and several small steamers. The Cumberland and the Congress lay off Newport News; the others were off Fort Monroe, about six miles distant. Captain Marston, of the Roanoke, who commanded the fleet, at once started with his steamer and the St. Lawrence for Newport News.

The drums of the Cumberland and the Congress beat to quarters, and the ships were prepared for action. Their crews watched curiously every movement of the Confederate battery, of which they had heard such terrible reports. On she came, steaming slowly toward them, her chimneys belching black smoke, and her flag fluttering defiantly in the breeze, while the two little steamers followed close behind. When she was about a mile distant the Cumberland opened fire upon her, but the "house afloat," as some of the sailors called her, came on without replying. As she passed the Congress, that vessel poured a broadside into her, but the balls bounded from her mailed sides as if they were made of india-rubber. The Merrimac, conscious of her strength, steamed grimly on through the iron storm which would have sunk any common vessel, and steered directly for the Cumberland, which lay with her side toward her so as to bring her broadside to bear.

The Cumberland opened a heavy fire on the monster which she could not escape, and the Merrimac, amid the flash and roar of her guns and enveloped in a pall of smoke that nearly hid her from view, went with a crash through the side of the doomed ship. The Cumberland shivered from end to end, and when the Merrimac drew slowly back it was found that her iron beak had passed through her, making a ragged hole into which the water rushed rapidly. The Merrimac then fired broadside after broadside into her sinking foe; but the gallant men of the Cumberland, never dreaming of surrender, stood by their guns to the last. In three-quarters of an hour after she was struck the noble ship went down in fifty-four feet of water, with her flag flying at the peak. The dead and the wounded sank with her; of the rest of the crew, some swam to the shore and some were picked up by small boats; but of three hundred seventy-six men, one hundred twenty-one were lost.

Meanwhile the two little vessels, the Beaufort and the Raleigh, had been firing into the Congress, and three other small gunboats —the Patrick Henry, the Jamestown, and the Teazer—joined them in the attack. The Congress replied bravely to their fire until the fate of the Cumberland showed her commander what he had to expect, and he ordered her to be run ashore, so that the enemy could not ram her. The Merrimac then fired shells into her with great effect, dismounting her guns, and killing many of her men. At last her commander, Lieutenant Joseph B. Smith, and a large part of her crew, having fallen, and the ship being on fire in several places, her colors were hauled down. Some of her men were taken prisoners by one of the Confederate steamers, and some escaped to the shore; but many were killed or wounded, and only about half of her crew of four hundred thirty-four answered the roll-call next morning.

The three frigates that had left Fort Monroe to go to the

aid of these unfortunate ships had grounded in shallow water, and had watched the unequal struggle more than a mile away, powerless to help. After the destruction of the Cumberland and the Congress, the Merrimac and the gunboats bore down to attack the others. The Roanoke by this time had got off, with the aid of tugs, but her machinery being damaged she returned to Fort Monroe. The Merrimac drew so much water that she could not get within a mile of the stranded vessels, so she fired shells at them from a distance, the gunboats helping her with their fire. The Minnesota was struck several times, and many of her men were killed or wounded. At last the St. Lawrence was pulled off by tugs and taken back to Fort Monroe, but the Minnesota remained fast in the mud. She kept up a fire on the enemy, but without any effect on the armor of the Merrimac, and it seemed as if she must soon suffer the fate of the Congress. But the day was fast waning, and about seven o'clock the Confederates left their prey and steamed slowly back toward Norfolk.

Saturday night was a dismal one at Fort Monroe, and few eyes closed in sleep. The return of the Merrimac on the morrow was a certainty, and there appeared to be little chance of saving the Minnesota. What the monster would do next, was a question that no one could decide. General John E. Wool, the commander of the Fort, telegraphed to Washington that probably both the Minnesota and the St. Lawrence would be captured, and that it was thought the enemy's vessels would pass the Fort.

About nine o'clock in the evening a queer-looking vessel came into Hampton Roads, and anchored near the Fort. It was a novel steam-battery—the now famous Monitor—which had been building near New York under the eye of her inventor, John Ericsson, a Swede by birth, but long a resident of the United States. Much had been heard of this vessel, and a great deal had been promised for her by her builder, but when she came into the Roads everybody was disappointed. What could this puny thing do against the great Merrimac, more than five times her tonnage! Her sides were but little above the water, and nothing was to be seen on her deck but a kind of round iron box in the middle, a pilot-house forward, and a small smokestack aft.

At a mile's distance she might be taken for a raft—indeed, the

Confederates well described her when they called her a "Yankee cheese-box on a plank." But when one went on board, her great strength was seen: her deck was plated with shell-proof iron, and her round box, called a turret, was made of iron plates eight to nine inches thick. Inside this turret, which was made to turn round, were two eleven-inch Dahlgren guns, placed side by side, so that both could be fired together at the same object. Ordinary ships have to be turned so as to bring their guns to bear on an enemy, but by revolving the turret of the Monitor her guns could be fired forward, backward, or sidewise, without changing the position of the ship. Her bow, too, was made strong and sharp, so that she could ram in the side of an enemy's vessel. This odd-shaped craft had been named by her inventor the Monitor, because, he said, he expected that she would be a monitor to the great nations of Europe, and teach them that the days of old-fashioned ships had passed away forever.

The authorities at Washington, frightened at the prospect of a visit from the Merrimac, had telegraphed to have the Monitor sent there as soon as she should arrive at Fort Monroe; but Captain Marston, thinking it important to do what he could to save the rest of the fleet, ordered Lieutenant John L. Worden, her commander, to go to the aid of the Minnesota. The little vessel therefore went up in the night and took a position alongside the Minnesota, between her and the Fort, where she could not be seen by the Confederates, but could be ready to slip out in case the Merrimac and her gunboats came to finish their work.

The whole bay and the shores were lighted up by the flames of the Congress, which had been burning many hours. Her guns went off one by one as the fire reached them, and at last, a little after midnight, her magazine, which contained five tons of gunpowder, went off with a grand explosion, which threw the blazing fragments of the ship over the waters to a great distance around.

The Monitor did not have to wait long, for early on Sunday morning the monster was seen coming down again, followed by two gunboats crowded with troops. The Confederates evidently hoped to board the Minnesota and capture both her and her crew, and this is probably the reason they did not destroy her the night before.

As the Merrimac approached, the Monitor slipped out from behind the Minnesota and steamed straight at her. She looked like a pygmy beside the great mailed battery, whose black sides rose higher than the top of her turret. The crew of the Merrimac did not know what to make of the odd little craft, that had appeared as suddenly as if it had risen from the depths of the sea, but they soon found out that it had teeth, for when the Monitor had come within a hundred yards of her foe, she opened fire with her great guns. The Merrimac, astonished at her reception, threw open her ports and poured into her several broadsides such as had sunk the wooden ships; but the steel shot glanced as harmlessly from her turret as had the balls of the Cumberland and the Congress from her own armor the day before, and her crew cried out in wonder, "The cheese-box is made of iron!" From eight o'clock until noon the battle raged. The Monitor, more easily managed than her antagonist, sailed round and round the Merrimac, firing and receiving her broadsides in return, the two being often so near to each other that their sides touched. Once the Merrimac got aground, but getting afloat again she turned savagely upon the Monitor and ran directly at her, hoping to run her down. But though she struck her so hard that the Monitor's crew were nearly thrown off their feet, she did not damage the vessel in the least.

The Merrimac, finding that she was only wasting her ammunition on the Monitor, fired a shell into the Minnesota, setting her on fire. Another shell struck the boiler of a tugboat near the Minnesota and blew her up. But the Monitor was not to be cheated in this way. She steamed up between the Minnesota and the Merrimac and renewed the battle. The Merrimac now trained her guns on the Monitor's pilot-house, which was built of wrought-iron beams a foot thick. A solid shot broke one of these beams, and drove it inward an inch and a half. Lieutenant Worden, who at the time had his eyes close to a slit between the bars, watching the Merrimac, was severely wounded in the face so as to lose his eyesight for a long time. He was therefore obliged to give up the command to Lieutenant Greene, who continued the fight. But after a few more broadsides, the Merrimac, finding that she could do nothing with her enemy, gave up the battle and steamed back to Norfolk, followed by her gunboats.

The breaking of the beam in the pilot-house was the only damage the Monitor received, although she was struck twenty-two times. The Merrimac's iron beak was twisted, some of her armor plates damaged, her smoke- and steam-pipes riddled, and her anchor and flagstaffs shot away. Two of her guns also had their muzzles shot off. The Monitor returned to Fort Monroe and remained there on the watch for her rival, but the Merrimac did not see fit to try her mettle again. The Minnesota was lightened and put afloat again in the following night, to the delight of her captain and crew, who had fought her so nobly and under such trying circumstances.

Honors were showered on Ericsson, the inventor, and on Worden, the commander, of the Monitor, for all felt that to them was due the deliverance from great peril. Chief Engineer Stimers, who was on the Monitor during the battle, wrote to Captain Ericsson as follows: "I congratulate you on your great success. Thousands have this day blessed you. I have heard whole crews cheer you. Every man feels that you have saved this place to the nation by furnishing us with the means to whip an iron-clad frigate that was, until our arrival, having it all her own way with our most powerful vessels." But the Monitor did far more than save a few ships and a fort—it settled the question of naval power in favor of the Union, and taught the nations of the Old World who wished to see our country divided that it would be dangerous for them to interfere in the quarrel. The Government, which had built the Monitor on trial, recognized her great value and at once began to construct other vessels of the same model, and by the next year the United States had a fleet of iron ships afloat able to defend their coasts against the navies of all the rest of the world.

Lieutenant Worden was so shocked by the concussion of the shot which had so nearly blinded him that he was insensible for some time. When he came to himself his first question was, "Have I saved the Minnesota?"

"Yes," was the reply, "and whipped the Merrimac."

"Then I don't care what becomes of me," he answered.

McKean Buchanan, brother of the commander of the Merrimac, was a paymaster on the Congress at the time of the battle; but, desiring to do active duty, he asked the commander to give him a place on the upper decks. He served gallantly through the action, and in his report to the Navy Department he said, "Thank God, I did some service to my beloved country."

Lieutenant Joseph B. Smith, the commander of the Congress, who was noted for his bravery, fell before the ship surrendered. When his father, the veteran Commodore Joseph Smith, who was on duty at Washington, saw by the first despatch from Fort Monroe that the Congress had raised the white flag, he only remarked quietly, "Then Joe's dead." The feeling that his son would never surrender his trust while alive was well founded. The ship's flag was not lowered until his son had fallen.

THE CAPTURE OF NEW ORLEANS

A.D. 1862

LOYALL FARRAGUT[1]

One of the chief Federal successes of the year 1862 was that won by the naval expedition of Captain David Glasgow Farragut at New Orleans. He compelled the surrender of the city after a warlike exploit which at once made him a conspicuous figure among naval heroes. The defences of New Orleans, the largest city in the South, were very strong, as it was of the utmost importance to the Confederate Government to hold the place and command the mouths of the Mississippi. Seventy-five miles below New Orleans were two formidable forts, and a little farther down a chain was stretched across the river. At each end of the chain were earthworks. In the river between the chain and the forts were five rafts loaded with inflammable materials. Here also were thirteen gunboats, an iron ram, and an iron-clad floating battery.

Farragut was to be assisted by Commander David D. Porter with a mortar-fleet of twenty-one schooners. Sailing for the Gulf of Mexico, in the sloop-of-war Hartford, Farragut reached Ship Island, February 20th. The two forts—St. Philip, on the north bank of the Mississippi, and Jackson, on the south bank—mounted about forty and seventy-five guns, respectively. To force his way through the obstructions and past the forts, overcome the hostile fleet, ascend to New Orleans, and demand its surrender—this was Farragut's task. His fleet, including Porter's, consisted of six sloops-of-war, sixteen gunboats, twenty-one schooners each carrying a thirteen-inch mortar, and five other vessels. On April 18th they were all in position. For six days and nights a ceaseless fire was kept up by the mortars—mainly on Fort Jackson—but beyond a few casualties to the garrisons, no serious damage was done. As Farragut impatiently observed, the bombardment served chiefly to warn the enemy of the intended attack by his ships. Farragut, who had never put much faith in the use of the mortars, determined to run by the forts. The following account of this feat and the success that followed it is by the son of the intrepid officer who performed this great service for his country.

FARRAGUT had made up his mind to run by the forts at the close of the fifth day's bombardment; but the necessity of repairing damages to two of his vessels delayed him twenty-four hours longer. He had intended to lead the column in his flag-

[1] From Loyall Farragut's *Life of Admiral Farragut* (New York: D. Appleton and Company), by permission.

ship Hartford; but in the final disposition he gave that post to Captain Theodorus Bailey, at his own earnest request, who hoisted his red flag on the gunboat Cayuga.

As early as April 6th Farragut had reconnoitred the forts in broad daylight, going up within cannon-shot of Fort Jackson in the Kennebec, where he sat in the cross-trees, glass in hand, till the Confederate gunners began to get the range of his ship. The attempt to pass was to be made in the night of April 23d; and, as the moon would rise about half-past three o'clock in the morning, the fleet was warned to expect the signal for sailing at about two o'clock. In this, as in the case of nearly all important operations early in the war, the enemy were mysteriously apprised of what was to be done. On the 23d the forts hardly fired a shot all day, though Porter kept up a terrific bombardment.

In answer to a despatch from General Mansfield Lovell in New Orleans that day, General John K. Duncan, commanding Fort Jackson, wrote: "Heavy and continued bombardment all night and still progressing. No further casualties, except two men slightly wounded. God is certainly protecting us. We are still cheerful, and have an abiding faith in our ultimate success. We are making repairs as best we can. Our barbette guns are still in working order. Most of them have been disabled at times. The health of the troops continues good. Twenty-five thousand [in reality about five thousand] thirteen-inch shells have been fired by the enemy, one thousand of which fell in the fort. They must soon exhaust themselves; if not, we can stand it as long as they can."

At sunset the wind had died away, except a slight breeze from the south, and there was a haze upon the water. Lieutenant Commanding C. H. B. Caldwell was sent up in the Itasca to examine the obstructions and find whether the passage was still open. At eleven o'clock he gave the signal that it was, and about the same time the enemy opened fire on him, sent down burning rafts, and lighted the immense piles of wood which they had prepared on the shore near the ends of the chain.

Soon after midnight the hammocks were stowed, and the work of quietly clearing the ships for action began. At five minutes before two o'clock the signal to weigh anchor—two ordinary red lights at the peak of the flagship—was displayed; but it was half past three, the hour of moonrise, before all was ready. In the light of the blazing rafts and bonfires, moon or no moon made little difference now.

Porter with his gunboats, and Swartwout in the Portsmouth, had been directed to move up-stream to Fort Jackson and engage its water battery while the ships were going by, which they promptly did.

Captain Bailey led off with his division of eight vessels, whose objective was Fort St. Philip, and all of them passed through the opening in the cable. Both forts opened fire upon his flagship, the Cayuga, soon after she had passed the hulks. Five minutes later she was pouring grape and canister into St. Philip, and in ten minutes more she had passed beyond range of that work, to find herself surrounded by eleven Confederate gunboats. Three of them attempted to board her at once. An eleven-inch shot was sent through one of them at the close range of thirty yards, and she immediately ran aground and burned up. The Parrott gun on the forecastle drove off another; and Bailey was preparing to close with the third, when the Oneida and the Varuna, which had run in close to St. Philip, thus avoiding the elevated guns of the fort while they swept its bastions with grape and shrapnel, came up to the assistance of the Cayuga. The Oneida ran under full steam into one of the Confederate ships, cut her nearly in two, and left her to float down-stream a helpless wreck. She fired right and left into the others, and then went to the assistance of the Varuna, which was ashore on the left bank, hard pressed by the Governor Moore and another, said to be the Manassas. The Varuna was rammed by them both, and sank at the end of fifteen minutes; but in that time it is said that she put three eight-inch shells into the Governor Moore, and so crippled her with solid shot that she surrendered to the Oneida; and she drove five eight-inch shells into another, which sent her ashore. Still another of her shells exploded the boiler of a Confederate steamer.

The Pensacola steamed steadily but slowly by, firing with great deliberation and regularity, doing special execution with her eleven-inch pivot gun and rifled eighty-pounder. But this was not done without receiving a heavy fire in return, and her losses (thirty-seven men) were the greatest of any in the fleet. She promptly sent her boats to the assistance of the sinking Varuna.

The Mississippi was fought regularly in line, like the Pensacola, but escaped with light losses. She encountered the ram Manassas, which gave her a severe cut on the port quarter below the water-line and disabled her machinery. But she riddled the ram with shot, boarded her, and set her on fire, so that she drifted below the forts and blew up.

The Katahdin ran close to the forts, steamed by rapidly, and got near the end of the line, where she put a few shots into the ironclad Louisiana. The Kineo ran by close under St. Philip, and then assisted the Mississippi in handling the ram Manassas; but she was afterward attacked by three gunboats at once, and, her pivot-gun carriage becoming injured, she withdrew and continued on up-stream. The Wissahickon ran ashore before she reached the forts, got off, passed them, and above ran ashore again. Most of these operations were carried on in darkness occasioned by the thick smoke, lighted, however, by the lurid flashes of more than two hundred guns.

The Hartford, bearing Flag Officer Farragut, led the second division of the fleet. She was under way at 3.30 A.M., and twenty-five minutes later opened with her bow guns on Fort Jackson, receiving a heavy fire from both forts. Twenty minutes thereafter, in attempting to avoid a fire-raft, she grounded on a shoal near Fort St. Philip. At the same time the ram Manassas pushed a raft upon her port quarter, and in an instant she was on fire. A part of the crew went to fire quarters and soon subdued the flames, while the working of her guns was steadily continued and she was then backed off into deep water. This movement turned the ship's head down-stream, and it was with some difficulty that she was turned around against the current; but this was finally accomplished, and she continued to steam up the river, firing into several of the enemy's vessels as she passed. Among these was a steamer full of men, apparently a boarding-party. She was making straight for the Hartford when Captain Broome's gun, manned by marines, planted a shell in her, which exploded, and she disappeared.

Watson remarks that the Admiral stood during the critical period coolly giving his orders and watching the ship slowly turn, referring occasionally to a little compass which was attached to his watch-chain, though most of the time during the engagement he was forward observing the conflict.

The Brooklyn got out of her course, ran over one of the hulks, and became entangled in the raft, where she suffered a raking fire from Fort Jackson and a pretty severe one from St. Philip. Scarcely was she disentangled and on her way up-stream when she was butted by the Manassas, which, however, had not headway enough to damage her much, and slid off in the darkness. Then she was attacked by a large steamer, but gave her the port broadside at fifty yards and set her on fire. Groping along through a black cloud of smoke from a fire-raft, she came close abreast of Fort St. Philip, into which she poured such tremendous broadsides that by the flashes the gunners were sent running to shelter, and for the time the fort was silenced. The Brooklyn then passed on, and engaged several of the enemy's gunboats at short range. One of these, the Warrior, came under the port broadside, when eleven five-second shells were instantly planted in her, all of which exploded, setting her on fire, and she was run ashore. The Brooklyn was under fire an hour and a half, and her losses were almost as severe as those of the Pensacola. The Richmond, a slow ship, brought up the rear of the second division, steaming steadily and working her guns with great regularity. Her commander attributed her small losses mainly to the complete provision of splinter-nettings.

The Sciota, carrying Fleet Captain Bell, led the third division. She steamed by the forts, firing as she passed, and above them burned two steamboats. She sent a boat's crew to receive the surrender of an armed steamer, but it was found to be fast aground. The Iroquois passed within fifty yards of Fort Jackson without injury, but was subjected to a terrible raking crossfire from Fort St. Philip, and was also raked by the McCrea with grape-shot and langrage. She drove off the McCrea with an eleven-inch shell and a stand of canister, and afterward passed through a group of rebel gunboats, giving each a broadside of shell as she went by. Her losses were heavy. The Pinola passed up in line, firing her eleven-inch pivot-gun and Parrott rifles at the flashes of Fort Jackson's guns, which at first were all that could be seen; then she emerged from the cloud of smoke, stood over toward Fort St. Philip, and in the light of the blazing rafts received the discharges of its forty guns. She was the last vessel that passed the forts, and got up in time to put one or two shells into the gunboats of the enemy.

The Kennebec got out of her course, became entangled in the rafts, and did not get free till it was broad daylight and too late to attempt a passage. The Itasca, arriving in front of Fort Jackson, received a shot in her boiler, which made it impossible for her to proceed, and she was turned down-stream. The Winona got astray among the hulks and lost so much time that when she came within range of Fort Jackson it was daylight and the fleet had passed on. The first three or four shots from the fort swept away the entire crew of her rifled gun, save one man. Still she kept on, until the lower battery of Fort St. Philip opened on her at less than point-blank range; this was too much for her, and she prudently headed down-stream and ran out of the fire.

Thus was accomplished a feat in naval warfare which had no precedent, and which is still without a parallel except the one furnished by Farragut himself, two years later, at Mobile. Starting with seventeen wooden vessels, he had passed with all but three of them against the swift current of a river but half a mile wide, between two powerful earthworks which had long been prepared for him, his course impeded by blazing rafts, and immediately thereafter had met the enemy's fleet of fifteen vessels, two of them ironclad, and either captured or destroyed every one of them. And all this with a loss of but one ship from his own squadron. Probably few naval men would have believed that this work could have been done so effectually, even with ironclads.

The magnitude of this novel enterprise was scarcely realized at the North when the first news was received. It was heralded that Farragut had simply "run by the forts," and there was an evident desire on the part of some to belittle the importance of the circumstance, although it was afterward acknowledged, by both Federal and Confederate reports, that he had passed under a terrific fire.

Captain Bailey, in the Cayuga, preceding the flagship up the river to the Quarantine Station, captured the Chalmette regiment encamped on the river-bank.

On the morning of the 25th, the Cayuga still leading in the progress up-stream, the Chalmette batteries, three miles below New Orleans, were encountered. The Hartford and the Brooklyn, followed by several others coming up rapidly, soon silenced them—and now the city was fairly under Union guns. This result had cost the fleet thirty-seven men killed and one hundred forty-seven wounded.

Farragut appointed eleven o'clock of the morning of the 26th as the hour "for all the officers and crews of the fleet to return thanks to Almighty God for his great goodness and mercy in permitting us to pass through the events of the last two days with so little loss of life and blood."

McCLELLAN'S PENINSULA CAMPAIGN

A.D. 1862

ROSSITER JOHNSON[1]

When the dismal news of the defeat and retreat at Bull Run spread through the North, after the first shock of surprise and mortification the general sentiment was tersely expressed by a Methodist minister, the Reverend Henry Cox, who was conducting a camp-meeting in Illinois. The news of the battle came while he was preaching, and he closed his sermon with the words, "Brethren, we'd better adjourn this camp-meeting, and go home and drill." Everybody recognized that nothing was lacking for the National troops in the way of courage and patriotism, but much was wanting in the way of organization and discipline. For the acquisition of these, probably the best man was chosen in General George B. McClellan; and while he organized and drilled the great Army of the Potomac to the entire satisfaction of Government and people, they, on the other hand, gave him their boundless confidence and showed remarkable patience in waiting for him to use the instrument he had prepared. How he did it is told in this chapter. When his army returned fruitless from its promising march up the Peninsula, and this was closely followed by a second defeat on the battle-ground of Bull Run, the war spirit at the North reached its lowest ebb, and one result was seen in the autumn elections, which went heavily against the Administration. It was relieved somewhat by McClellan's victories at South Mountain and Antietam, and, more than many expected, by President Lincoln's proclamation of emancipation.

WITHIN twenty-four hours after the defeat of McDowell's army at Bull Run (July 21, 1861) the Administration called to Washington the only man that had thus far accomplished much or made any considerable reputation in the field. This was General George B. McClellan. He had been graduated at West Point in 1846, standing second in his class, and had gone at once into the Mexican War, in which he acquitted himself with distinction. After that war the young captain was employed in engineering work till 1855, when the Government sent him to Europe to study the movements of the Crimean War. He

[1] From Rossiter Johnson's *History of the War of Secession* (New York: Bryan, Taylor and Company, 1895), by permission.

wrote a report of his observations, which was published under the title of *The Armies of Europe*, and in 1857 resigned his commission and became chief engineer of the Illinois Central Railroad, and afterward president of the St. Louis and Cincinnati. He had done good work in northwestern Virginia in the early summer, and now at the age of thirty-five was commissioned Major-General in the regular army of the United States, and made commander of all the troops about Washington.

For the work immediately in hand this was probably the best selection that could have been made. Washington needed to be fortified, and McClellan was a master of engineering; both the army that had just been defeated and the new recruits that were pouring in needed organization, and he proved preëminent as an organizer. Three months after he took command of fifty thousand uniformed men at the capital he had an army of more than one hundred thousand, well organized in regiments, brigades, and divisions, with the proper proportion of artillery, with quartermaster and commissary departments going like clockwork, and the whole fairly drilled and disciplined. Everybody looked on with admiration, and the public impatience that had precipitated the disastrous "On to Richmond" movement was now replaced by a marvellous patience. The summer and autumn months went by, and no movement was made; but McClellan, in taking command, had promised that the war should be "short, sharp, and decisive," and the people thought, if they only allowed him time enough to make thorough preparation, his great army would at length swoop down upon the Confederate capital and finish everything at one blow.

At length, however, they began to grow weary of the daily telegram, "All quiet along the Potomac," and the monotonously repeated information that "General McClellan rode out to Fairfax Court House and back this morning." The Confederacy was daily growing stronger, the Potomac was being closed to navigation by the erection of hostile batteries on its southern bank, the enemy's flag was flying within sight from the capital, and the question of foreign interference was becoming exceedingly grave. On November 1st General Scott, then seventy-five years of age, retired, and McClellan succeeded him as General-in-Chief of all the armies.

Soon after this his plans appear, from subsequent revelations, to have undergone important modification. He had undoubtedly intended to attack by moving straight out toward Manassas, where the army that had won the battle of Bull Run was still encamped, and was still commanded by General Joseph E. Johnston. He now began to think of moving against Richmond by some more easterly route, discussing among others the extreme easterly one that he finally took. But, whatever were his thoughts and purposes, his army appeared to be taking root. The people began to murmur, Congress began to question, and the President began to argue and urge. All this did not signify; nothing could move McClellan. He wished to wait till he could leave an enormous garrison in the defences of Washington, place a strong corps of observation along the Potomac, and then move out with a column of one hundred fifty thousand men against an army that he believed to be as numerous as that, though in truth it was then less than half as large. It is now known that, from the beginning to the end of his career in that war, General McClellan constantly overestimated the force opposed to him.

On January 10, 1862, the President held a long consultation with Generals Irvin McDowell and William B. Franklin and some members of his Cabinet. General McClellan was then confined to his bed by an illness of a month's duration. At this consultation Mr. Lincoln said, according to General McDowell's memorandum, "If something was not soon done, the bottom would be out of the whole affair; and if General McClellan did not want to use the army, he would like to borrow it, provided he could see how it could be made to do something."

Immediately upon McClellan's recovery, the President called him to a similar council and asked him to disclose his plan for a campaign, which he declined to do. Finally the President asked him if he had fixed upon any particular time for setting out; and when he said he had, Mr. Lincoln questioned him no further. A few days later, in a letter to the President, he set forth his plan, which was to move his army down the Potomac on transports, land it at or near Fort Monroe, march up the peninsula between York and James rivers, and attack the defences of Richmond on the northern and eastern sides. The President at first disapproved of this plan, largely for the reason that it would require so much time in preparation; but when he found that the highest officers in the army favored it, and considered the probability that any general was likely to fail if sent to execute a plan he did not originate or believe in, he finally gave it his sanction, and once more set himself to the difficult task of inducing McClellan to move at all. And yet the President himself still further retarded the opening of the campaign by delaying the order to collect the means of transportation. Meanwhile General Johnston quietly removed his stores, and on March 8th evacuated Centerville and Manassas, and placed his army before Richmond. This reconciled the President to McClellan's plan of campaign, which he never had liked.

The order for the transportation of McClellan's army was issued on February 27th, and four hundred vessels were required; for there were actually transported one hundred twenty-one thousand men, fourteen thousand animals, forty-four batteries, and all the necessary ambulances and baggage-wagons, pontoons, and telegraph material. Just before the embarkation, the army was divided into four corps, the commands of which were given to Generals Irvin McDowell, Edwin V. Sumner, Samuel P. Heintzelman, and Erasmus D. Keyes. High authorities say this was one of the causes of the failure of the campaign; for the army should have been divided into corps long before, when McClellan could have chosen his own lieutenants instead of having them chosen by the President. General Joseph Hooker said it was impossible for him to succeed with such corps commanders. But his near approach to success discredits this criticism.

Another element of the highest importance had also entered into the problem with which the nation was struggling. This was the appointment (January 21, 1862) of Edwin M. Stanton to succeed Simon Cameron as Secretary of War. Mr. Stanton, then forty-seven years of age, was a lawyer by profession, a man of great intellect, unfailing nerve, and tremendous energy. He had certain traits that often made him personally disagreeable to his subordinates; but it was impossible to doubt his thorough loyalty, and his determination to find or make a way to bring the war to a successful close as speedily as possible, without the slightest regard to the individual interests of himself or anybody else. He was probably the ablest war minister that ever lived—

with the possible exception of Carnot, the man to whom Napoleon said, "I have known you too late." It is indicative of Mr. Lincoln's sagacity and freedom from prejudice, that his first meeting with Mr. Stanton was when he went to Cincinnati, some years before the war, to assist in trying an important case. He found Mr. Stanton in charge as senior counsel, and Stanton was so unendurably disagreeable to him that he threw up the engagement and went home to Springfield. Yet he afterward gave that man the most important place in his Cabinet, and found him its strongest member.

One division of the army embarked on March 17th, and the others followed in quick succession. General McClellan reached Fort Monroe on April 2d, by which time fifty-eight thousand men and one hundred guns had arrived, and immediately moved with this force on Yorktown, the place made famous by the surrender of Cornwallis eighty years before. The Confederates had fortified this point, and thrown a line of earthworks across the narrow peninsula to the deep water of Warwick River. These works were held by General John B. Magruder with thirteen thousand effective men. General Johnston, who was in command of all the troops around Richmond, says he had no expectation of doing more than delaying McClellan at Yorktown till he could strengthen the defences of the capital and collect more men; and that he thought his adversary would use his transports to pass his army around that place by water, after destroying the batteries, and land at some point above.

McClellan, supposing that Johnston's entire army was in the defences of Yorktown, sat down before the place and constructed siege-works, approaching by regular parallels. As the remaining divisions of his army arrived at Fort Monroe, they were added to his besieging force; but McDowell's entire corps and General Louis Blenker's division had been detached at the last moment and retained at Washington, from fears on the part of the Administration that the capital was not sufficiently guarded, though McClellan had already left seventy thousand men there or within call. The fears were increased by the threatening movements of Stonewall Jackson in the Shenandoah Valley, where, however, he was defeated by General James Shields near Winchester, March 23d.

General Johnston had to contend with precisely the same difficulty that McClellan complained of. He wished to bring together before Richmond all the troops that were then at Norfolk and in the Carolinas and Georgia, and with the large army thus formed suddenly attack McClellan after he should have marched seventy-five miles up the peninsula from his base at Fort Monroe. But in a council of war General Robert E. Lee and the Secretary of War opposed this plan, and Mr. Davis adopted their views and rejected it. Johnston therefore undertook the campaign with the army that he had, which he says consisted of fifty thousand effective men.

McClellan spent nearly a month before Yorktown, and when he was ready to open fire with his siege-guns and drive out the enemy, May 3d, he found they had quietly departed, leaving "Quaker guns" (wooden logs on wheels) in the embrasures. There was no delay in pursuit, and the National advance came up with the Confederate rear-guard near Williamsburg, about twelve miles from Yorktown. Here, May 4th, brisk skirmishing began, which gradually became heavier, till reënforcements were hurried up on the one side and sent back on the other, and the skirmish was developed into a battle. The place had been well fortified months before. The action on the morning of the 5th was opened by the divisions of Generals Hooker and William F. Smith. They attacked the strongest of the earthworks, pushed forward the batteries, and silenced it. Hooker was then heavily attacked by infantry, with a constant menace on his left wing. He sustained his position alone nearly all day, though losing one thousand seven hundred men and five guns, and was at length relieved by the arrival of General Philip Kearny's division.

The delay was due mainly to the deep mud caused by a heavy rain the night before. Later in the day, General Winfield S. Hancock's brigade made a wide circuit on the right, discovered some unoccupied redoubts, and took possession of them. When the Confederates advanced their left to the attack, they ran upon these redoubts, which their commanding officers knew nothing about, and were repelled with heavy loss. Hancock's one thousand six hundred men suddenly burst over the crest of the works, and bore down upon the enemy with fixed bayonets, routing and scattering them. McClellan brought up reënforcements, and in the night the Confederates in front of him moved off to join their main army, leaving in Williamsburg four hundred of their wounded, because they had no means of carrying them away, but taking with them about that number of prisoners. The National loss had been about two thousand two hundred, the Confederate about one thousand eight hundred.

General Franklin's division of McDowell's corps had now been sent to McClellan, and immediately after the Battle of Williamsburg he moved it on transports to White House, at the head of York River, where it established a base of supplies. As soon as possible, also, the main body of the army was marched from Williamsburg to White House, reaching that place on May 16th. From this point he moved westward toward Richmond, expecting to be joined by a column of forty thousand men under McDowell, which was to move from Fredericksburg. On reaching the Chickahominy, McClellan threw his left wing across that stream, and sweeping around with his right fought small battles at Mechanicsville and Hanover Junction, by which he cleared the way for McDowell to join him. But at this critical point of time Stonewall Jackson suddenly made another raid down the Shenandoah Valley, and McDowell was called back to pursue him.

Johnston resolved to strike the detached left wing of the National army, which had crossed the Chickahominy and advanced within half a dozen miles of Richmond, and his purpose was seconded by a heavy rain on the night of May 30th, which swelled the stream and swept away some of the bridges, thus hindering reënforcement from the other wing. The attack, May 31st, fell first upon General Silas Casey's division of Keyes's corps, which occupied some half-finished works. It was bravely made and bravely resisted, and the Confederates suffered heavy losses before these works, where they had almost surprised the men with the shovels in their hands. But after a time a Confederate force made a détour and gained a position in the rear of the redoubts, when of course they could be held no longer. Reënforcements were very slow in coming up, and Keyes's men had a long, hard struggle to hold their line at all. They could not have done so if a part of Johnston's plan had not miscarried. He intended to bring in a heavy flanking force between them and the river, but was delayed several hours in getting it in motion.

Meanwhile McClellan ordered Sumner to cross the river and join in the battle. Sumner had anticipated such an order as soon as he heard the firing, and when the order came it found him with his corps in line, drawn out from camp, and ready to cross instantly. He was the oldest officer there (sixty-six), and the most energetic. There was but one bridge that could be used: many of the supports of this were gone, the approaches were under water, and it was almost a wreck. But he unhesitatingly pushed on his column. The frail structure was steadied by the weight of the men; and though it swayed and undulated with their movement and the rush of the water, they all crossed in safety.

Sumner was just in time to meet the flank attack, which was commanded by Johnston in person. The successive charges of the Confederates were all repelled, and at dusk a counter-charge cleared the ground in front and drove off the last of them in confusion. In this fight General Johnston received wounds that compelled him to retire from the field and laid him up for a long time. The battle—which is called both Fair Oaks and Seven Pines—cost the National army more than five thousand men, and the Confederate nearly seven thousand.

For some time after the Battle of Fair Oaks heavy rains made any movement almost impossible for either of the armies that confronted each other near Richmond. General Alexander S. Webb says: "The ground, which consisted of alternate layers of reddish clay and quicksand, had turned into a vast swamp, and the guns in battery sank into the earth by their own weight." McClellan kept his men at work, intrenching and strengthening his position, while he himself appears to have been occupied largely in writing despatches to the President and the Secretary of War, alternately promising an almost immediate advance on Richmond and calling for reënforcements. He wanted McDowell's corps of forty thousand men, and the authorities wished to give it to him if it could be sent by way of Fredericksburg and united with his right wing in such a way as not to uncover Washington. But in one despatch he declared he would rather not have it unless it could be placed absolutely under his command.

His position was in several respects very bad. The Chickahominy was bordered by great swamps, whose malarial influences robbed him of almost as many men as fell by the bullets of the enemy. His base was at White House; and the line thence over which his supplies must come, instead of being at right angles with the line of his front and covered by it, was almost a prolongation of it. It was impossible to maintain permanent bridges over the Chickahominy, and a rain of two or three days was liable at any time to swell the stream so as to sweep away every means of crossing. He could threaten Richmond only by placing a heavy force on the right bank of the river; he could render his own communications secure only by keeping a large force on the left bank. When it first occurred to him that his true base was on the James, or how long he contemplated its removal thither, nobody knows; but he received a startling lesson on June 12th, which appears to have determined him.

When General Joseph E. Johnston was wounded at Fair Oaks, the command devolved upon General G. W. Smith; but two days later General Robert E. Lee received the command of the Confederate forces in Virginia, which he retained continuously till his surrender brought the war to a close. The plan that he had opposed, and caused Mr. Davis to reject, when Johnston was in command—of bringing large bodies of troops from North Carolina, Georgia, and Southern Virginia, to form a massive army and fall upon McClellan—he now adopted and proceeded at once to carry out. Johnston enumerates reënforcements that were given to him aggregating fifty-three thousand men, and says he had then the largest Confederate army that ever fought. The total number is given officially at eighty thousand seven hundred sixty-two. This probably means the number of men actually carrying muskets, and excludes all officers, teamsters, musicians, and mechanics; for the Confederate returns were usually made in that way. McClellan's total effective force, including every man that drew pay the last week in June, was ninety-two thousand five hundred. His constant expectation of reënforcements by way of Fredericksburg was largely, if not wholly, what kept him in his false position, and it is fair to presume that but for this he would have swung across the peninsula to the new base on the James much sooner and under more favorable circumstances.

Wishing to know the extent of McClellan's earthworks on the right wing, Lee, on June 12th, sent a body of twelve hundred cavalry with two light guns, to reconnoitre. This was commanded by the dashing General J. E. B. Stuart, commonly called "Jeb Stuart," who used to dress in gay costume, with yellow sash and black plume, wore gold spurs, and rode a white horse. He was ordered to go only as far as Hanover Old Church; but at that point he had a fight with a small body of cavalry, and as he supposed dispositions would be made to cut him off, instead of returning, he kept on and made the entire circuit of McClellan's army, rebuilding a bridge to cross the lower Chickahominy, and reached Richmond in safety. The actual amount of damage that he had done was small; but the raid alarmed the National commander for the safety of his communications, and was perhaps what determined him to change his base.

Stonewall Jackson, if not Lee's ablest lieutenant, was considered his swiftest, and the one that threw the most uncertainty into the game by his rapid movements and unexpected appearances. At a later stage of the war his erratic strategy, if persisted in, would probably have brought his famous corps of "foot cavalry" (as they were called from their quick marches) to sudden destruction. An opponent like Sheridan, who knew how to be swift, brilliant, and audacious, without transgressing the fundamental rules of warfare, would have been likely to finish him at a blow. But Jackson did not live to meet such an opponent. At this time the bugbears that haunt imaginations not inured to war were still in force, and the massive thimble-rigging by which he was made to appear before Richmond, and presto! sweeping down the Shenandoah Valley, served to paralyze large forces that might have been added to McClellan's army.

The topography of Virginia is favorable to an army menacing Washington, and unfavorable to one menacing Richmond. The fertile valley of the Shenandoah was inviting ground for soldiers. A Confederate force advancing down the valley came at every step nearer to the National capital, while a National force advancing up the valley was carried at every step farther away from the Confederate capital. The Confederates made much of this advantage, and the authorities at Washington were in constant fear of the capture of that city.

Soon after Stuart's raid, Lee began to make his dispositions to attack McClellan and drive him from the peninsula. He wrote to Jackson: "Unless McClellan can be driven out of his intrenchments, he will move by positions, under cover of his heavy guns, within shelling distance of Richmond." To convey the impression that Jackson was to move in force down the valley, Lee drew two brigades from his own army, placed them on the cars in Richmond in plain sight of some prisoners that were about to be exchanged, and sent them off to Jackson. Of course the released prisoners carried home the news. But Jackson returned with these reënforcements and Ewell's division of his corps, joined Lee, and on June 25th concerted a plan for immediate attack. Secretary Stanton appears to have been the only one that saw through the game; for he telegraphed to McClellan that while neither Banks nor McDowell nor Frémont could ascertain anything about Jackson's movements, his own belief was that he was going to Richmond. Yet the impression was not strong enough in the mind of the Secretary of War (or else the Secretary could not have his own way) to induce the appropriate countermove of immediately sending McDowell's whole corps to McClellan. General George A. McCall's division of that corps, however, had been forwarded, and on the 18th took a strong position on McClellan's extreme right, near Mechanicsville.

On the 25th McClellan had pushed back the Confederates on his left, taken a new position there, and advanced his outposts to a point only four miles from Richmond. But he began his movements too late, for the Confederates were already in motion. Leaving about thirty thousand men in the immediate defences of Richmond, Lee crossed the Chickahominy with about thirty-five thousand under Generals Ambrose P. Hill, Daniel H. Hill, and James Longstreet, intending to join Jackson's twenty-five thousand, and with this enormous force make a sudden attack on the twenty thousand National troops that were on the north side of the river, commanded by General Fitz-John Porter, destroy them before help could reach them, and seize McClellan's communications with his base.

Jackson, who was to have appeared on the field at sunrise of the 26th, was for once behind time. The other Confederate commanders became nervous and impatient; for if the movement were known to McClellan, he could, with a little boldness and some fighting, have captured Richmond that day. Indeed, the inhabitants of the city expected nothing else, and it is said that the archives of the Confederate Government were all packed and ready for instant removal. At midday General A. P. Hill's corps drove the small National force out of Mechanicsville, and advanced to McCall's strong position on Beaver Dam Creek. This they dared not attack in front; but they made desperate attempts on both flanks, and the result was an afternoon of fruitless fighting, in which they were literally mowed down by the well-served artillery and lost more than three thousand men, while McCall maintained his position at every point and lost fewer than three hundred.

That night, in pursuance of the plan for a change of base, the heavy guns that had thwarted Lee in his first attack were carried across the Chickahominy, together with a large part of the baggage-train. On the morning of the 27th Porter fell back somewhat to a position on a range of low hills, where he could keep the enemy in check till the stores were removed to the other side of the river, which was now his only object. McClellan sent him five thousand more men in the course of the day, being afraid to send any greater number, because he believed that the bulk of the Confederate army was in the defences on his left, and a show of activity there still further deceived him.

On the morning of the 27th Porter had eighteen thousand infantry, two thousand five hundred artillerymen, and a small force of cavalry, with which to meet the attack of at least fifty-five thousand. Longstreet and the Hills had followed the retreat closely, but, warned by the experience of the day before, were not willing to attack until Jackson should join them. The fighting began about two o'clock in the afternoon, when A. P. Hill assailed the centre of Porter's position, and in a two-hours' struggle was driven back with heavy loss. Two attacks on the right met with no better success. The effect on the new troops that had been hurried up from the coast was complete demoralization. The Confederate General Whiting says in his report: "Men were leaving the field in every direction and in great disorder. Two regiments, one from South Carolina and one from Louisiana, were actually marching back from the fire. Men were skulking from the front in a shameful manner."

But at length Jackson's men arrived, and a determined effort was made on all parts of the line at once. Even then it seemed for a time as if victory might rest with the little army on the hills; and in all probability it would if they had had such intrenchments as the men afterward learned how to construct very quickly; but their breastworks were only such as could be made from hastily felled trees, a few rails, and heaps of knapsacks. The Confederates had the advantage of thick woods in which to form and advance. As they emerged and came on in heavy masses, with the Confederate yell, they were answered by the Union cheer. Volley responded to volley, guns were taken and retaken, and cannoneers that remained after the infantry supports retired were shot down; but it was not till sunset that the National line was fairly disrupted, at the left centre, when the whole gave way and slowly retired. Two regiments were captured, and twenty-two guns fell into the hands of the enemy. In the night Porter crossed the river with his remaining force and destroyed the bridges.

This was called by the Confederates the Battle of the Chickahominy; but it takes its better-known name from two mills (Gaines's) near the scene of action. The total National loss was six thousand men. The Confederate loss, never properly ascertained, was probably much larger. Some of the wounded lay on the field four days uncared for. This action is sometimes called the first battle of Cold Harbor. The armies under Grant and Lee fought on the same ground two years later.

Lee and Jackson believed that they had been fighting the whole of McClellan's forces, and another mistake that they made secured the safety of that army. They took it for granted that the National commander, driven from his base at White House, would retreat down the peninsula, taking the same route by which he had come. Consequently they remained with their large force on the left bank of the Chickahominy, and even advanced some distance down the stream, which gave McClellan twenty-four hours of precious time to get through the swamp roads with his immense trains. He had five thousand loaded wagons, and two thousand five hundred head of cattle. General Casey's division, in charge of the stores at White House, loaded all they could upon transports, and destroyed the remainder.

Trains of cars filled with supplies were put under full speed and run off the tracks into the river. Hundreds of tons of ammunition and millions of rations were burned or otherwise destroyed. At the last moment Casey embarked his men, and with what he had been able to save steamed down the Pamunkey and York Rivers and up the James to the new base. At the close of a long despatch to the Secretary of War on the 28th General McClellan said: "If I save this army now, I tell you plainly that I owe no thanks to you or to any other persons in Washington. You have done your best to sacrifice this army."

When General Magruder, who had been left in the defences of Richmond, found that the National army was retreating to the James, he moved out to attack it, and struck the rear-guard at Allen's farm. His men made three assaults, and were three times repelled. Magruder complained that he lost a victory here because Lee had left him but thirteen thousand men.

The National troops fell back to Savage's Station, where later in the day Magruder attacked them again. He had a rifled cannon mounted on a platform-car, with which he expected to do great execution. But there was an ample force to oppose him, and it stood unmoved by his successive charges. About sunset he advanced his whole line with a desperate rush in the face of a continuous fire of cannon and musketry; but it was of no avail, and half an hour later his own line was broken by a countercharge that closed the battle. He admitted a loss of four thousand men. Sumner and Franklin, at a cost of three thousand, had thus maintained the approach to the single road through White Oak Swamp, by which they were to follow the body of the army that had already passed. But it was found necessary to burn another immense quantity of food and clothing that could not be removed, and to leave behind two thousand five hundred sick and wounded men.

Jackson, after spending a day in building bridges, crossed the Chickahominy, and attempted to follow McClellan's rear-guard through White Oak Swamp; but when he got on the other side he found a necessary bridge destroyed and National batteries commanding its site, so that it was impossible for his forces to emerge from the swamp.

But meanwhile Hill and Longstreet had crossed the river farther up-stream, marched around the swamp, and struck the retreating army near Charles City Cross Roads on the 30th. There was terrific fighting all the afternoon. There were brave charges and bloody repulses, masses of men moving up steadily in the face of batteries that tore great gaps through them at every discharge, crossed bayonets, and clubbed muskets. Only on that part of the line held by McCall did the Confederates, with all their daring, succeed in breaking through. McCall, in his report, describes the successful charge: "A most determined charge was made on Randol's battery by a full brigade, advancing in wedge shape, without order, but in perfect recklessness. Somewhat similar charges had been previously made on Cooper's and Kern's batteries by single regiments, without success, they having recoiled before the storm of canister hurled against them. A like result was anticipated by Randol's battery, and the Fourth Regiment was requested not to fire until the battery had done with them. Its gallant commander did not doubt his ability to repel the attack, and his guns did indeed mow down the advancing host; but still the gaps were closed, and the enemy came in upon a run to the very muzzles of his guns. It was a perfect torrent of men, and they were in his battery before the guns could be removed." General McCall himself, endeavoring to rally his men at this point, was captured and carried off to Richmond. In Kearny's front a similar charge was made three times; but every time a steady musketry fire drove back the enemy that had closed up its gaps made by the artillery.

Darkness put an end to the fighting, and that night McClellan's army continued its retreat to Malvern Hill, where his advance-guard had taken up the strongest position he had yet occupied. The battle just described has several names—Glendale, Frayser's Farm, Charles City Cross Roads, Newmarket, Nelson's Farm. McClellan here lost ten guns. The losses in men cannot be known exactly, as the reports group the losses of several days together. Longstreet and the two Hills reported a loss of twelve thousand four hundred fifty-eight in the fighting from the 27th to the 30th.

The last stand made by McClellan for delivering battle was at Malvern Hill. This is a plateau near Turkey Bend of James River, having an elevation of sixty feet, and an extent of about a mile and a half in one direction and a mile in the other. It is so bordered by streams and swamps as to leave no practicable approach except by the narrow northwestern face. Here McClellan had his entire army in position when his pursuers came up. It was disposed in the form of a semicircle, with the right wing "refused" (swung back) and prolonged to Haxall's Landing, on the James. His position was peculiarly favorable for the use of artillery, and his whole front bristled with it. There were no intrenchments to speak of, but the natural inequalities of the ground afforded considerable shelter for the men and the guns. It was as complete a trap as could be set for an army, and Lee walked straight into it. Under ordinary circumstances both commander and men would properly hesitate to attack an enemy so posted. But to the confidence with which the Southerners began the war was now added the peculiar elation produced by a week's pursuit of a retreating army; and apparently it did not occur to them that they were all mortal.

In the first contact seven thousand Confederates, with six guns, struck the left of the position. They boldly advanced their artillery within eight hundred yards of the cliff; but before they could get at work a fire of twenty or thirty guns was concentrated upon their battery, which knocked it to pieces in a few minutes; and at the same time some huge shells from a gunboat fell among a small detachment of cavalry, threw it into confusion, and turned it back upon the infantry, breaking up the attack.

Lee was not ready to attack with his whole army till the afternoon of July 1st. An artillery duel was kept up during the forenoon; but the Confederate commander did not succeed in destroying the National batteries as he hoped to do; on the contrary, he saw his own disabled, one after another. The signal for the infantry attack was to be the usual yell, raised by Armistead's division on the right and taken up by the successive divisions along the line. But the Confederate line was separated by thick woods, there was long waiting for the signal, some of the generals thought they heard it, and some advanced without hearing it. The consequence was a series of separate attacks, some of them repeated three or four times, and every time a concentrated fire on the attacking column and a bloody repulse. The men themselves began to see the hopelessness of it, while their officers were still urging them to renewed efforts.

"Come on, come on, my men," said one Confederate colonel, with the grim humor of a soldier; "do you want to live forever?" There were some brief counter-charges, in one of which the colors were taken from a North Carolina regiment; but in general the National troops only maintained their ground, and though fighting was kept up till nine o'clock in the evening, the line—as General Webb, then assistant chief of artillery, tells us—was never broken or the guns in danger. This battle cost Lee five thousand men, and at its close he gave up the pursuit. The National loss was less than one-third as great. That night McClellan withdrew his army to Harrison's Landing, on the James, where he had fixed his base of supplies and where the gunboats could protect his position. This retreat is known as the Seven Days, and the losses are figured up at fifteen thousand two hundred forty-nine on the National side, and somewhat more than nineteen thousand on the Confederate.

From this time there was an angry controversy as to the military abilities of General McClellan and the responsibility for the failure of the campaign, and partisanship was never more violent than over this question. The General had won the highest personal regard of his soldiers, and they were mostly unwilling or unable to look at the matter in the cold light of the criticism that simply asks, What was required? and, What was accomplished? The truth appears to be that General McClellan, like most men, possessed some virtues and lacked others. He organized a great army, and to the end of its days it felt the benefit of the discipline with which he endowed it. But with that army in hand he did not secure the purpose of its creation. He was an accomplished engineer and a gigantic adjutant, but hardly the general to be sent against an army that could move and a commander that could think.

There can be no doubt that the Administration was over-anxious about the movements in the Shenandoah, and should have sent McDowell's corps to McClellan at once; but neither can there be much doubt that if Little Mac, the Young Napoleon, as he was fondly called, had been a general of the highest order, he would have destroyed Lee's army and captured the Confederate capital with the ample forces that he had.

EMANCIPATION IN THE UNITED STATES

A.D. 1862

ABRAHAM LINCOLN

From the very beginning of the Civil War there were committees and individuals who went to Washington to urge the President to exercise his war powers under the Constitution and proclaim the freedom of the slaves in the seceded States. Their argument was that the object of secession was to preserve and extend the system of bondage; and no peace, however obtained, could be permanent unless the cause of the war were destroyed. The most notable of these appeals was embodied in an open letter written by Horace Greeley, addressed to the President, and published in the New York *Tribune* August 19, 1862. Three days later Lincoln published an answer, in which he said: "As to the policy I 'seem to be pursuing,' as you say, I have not meant to leave anyone in doubt. I would save the Union. I would save it in the shortest way under the Constitution. If there be those who would not save the Union unless they could at the same time save slavery, I do not agree with them. If there be those who would not save the Union unless they could at the same time destroy slavery, I do not agree with them. My paramount object is to save the Union, and not either to save or to destroy slavery. What I do about slavery and the colored race I do because I believe it helps to save this Union; and what I forbear I forbear because I do not believe it would help to save the Union. I have here stated my purpose according to my views of official duty, and I intend no modification of my oft-expressed personal wish that all men everywhere could be free."

President Lincoln had several strong reasons for delaying emancipation. At the beginning of the war it would not have met with approval even by a considerable minority of the Northern people, and it would have hindered enlistments enormously. Later, as he himself pointed out, there were, in the National armies, fifty thousand bayonets from the border slave States, and he feared that a premature proclamation might send them over to the Confederacy, though this fear was probably not well founded. Finally, the Union arms met with a series of defeats early in the war, and, as he remarked, such a proclamation would appear impotent if it followed a Union defeat. The opportunity came, as he judged, after Antietam. The Army of Northern Virginia, commanded by General Robert E. Lee, set out on its first invasion of the North immediately after its victory at the Second Bull Run, or Groveton (August 30, 1862), and got as far as the village of Sharpsburg, Maryland, when, closely followed by the Army of the Potomac, commanded by General George

B. McClellan, it was obliged to stop and give battle. General Lee chose a strong position on the heights in the angle between the Potomac River and Antietam Creek, his left resting on the river, and his right on the creek. McClellan, coming through the passes of the South Mountain, from the east, crossed the creek and attacked in the morning of September 17th. The fight lasted almost till dark, and it was the bloodiest single day in the whole war, the losses on each side being more than twelve thousand. The Confederate army, leaving its dead unburied, retreated into Virginia; and as McClellan was left in possession of the field, and had not lost a gun or a color, the victory was fairly his, though he did not pursue the defeated enemy. Lincoln expressed a wish that the victory had been made more complete, but said it was sufficient to give character to a proclamation of emancipation. Five days later he issued the preliminary proclamation, and on January 1, 1863, the final proclamation, both of which are given herewith.

On October 12, 1864, the State of Maryland abolished slavery within her borders; and the Thirteenth Amendment to the National Constitution, abolishing slavery throughout the United States, was proclaimed adopted December 18, 1865.

THE PRELIMINARY PROCLAMATION

I, ABRAHAM LINCOLN, President of the United States of America, and Commander-in-Chief of the Army and Navy thereof, do hereby proclaim and declare that hereafter, as heretofore, the war will be prosecuted for the object of practically restoring the constitutional relation between the United States and each of the States and the people thereof in which States that relation is or may be suspended or disturbed.

That it is my purpose, upon the next meeting of Congress, to again recommend the adoption of a practical measure tendering pecuniary aid to the free acceptance or rejection of all slave States, so called, the people whereof may not then be in rebellion against the United States, and which States may then have voluntarily adopted, or thereafter may voluntarily adopt, immediate or gradual abolishment of slavery within their respective limits; and that the effort to colonize persons of African descent, with their consent, upon this continent or elsewhere, with the previously obtained consent of the governments existing there, will be continued.

That on the first day of January, in the year of our Lord one thousand eight hundred and sixty-three, all persons held as slaves within any State or designated part of a State the people whereof shall then be in rebellion against the United States, shall be then, thenceforward, and forever free; and the Executive Government of the United States, including the military and naval authority thereof, will recognize and maintain the freedom of such persons, and will do no act or acts to repress such persons, or any of them, in any efforts they may make for their actual freedom.

That the Executive will, on the first day of January aforesaid, by proclamation, designate the States and parts of States, if any, in which the people thereof respectively shall then be in rebellion against the United States; and the fact that any State or the people thereof shall on that day be in good faith represented in the Congress of the United States, by members chosen thereto at elections wherein a majority of the qualified voters of such State shall have participated, shall, in the absence of strong countervailing testimony, be deemed conclusive evidence that such State and the people thereof are not then in rebellion against the United States.

That attention is hereby called to an act of Congress entitled "An act to make an additional article of war," approved March 13, 1862, and which act is in the words and figures following:

"*Be it enacted by the Senate and House of Representatives of the United States of America in Congress assembled,* That hereafter the following shall be promulgated as an additional article of war for the government of the Army of the United States, and shall be obeyed and observed as such:

"Section 1. All officers or persons in the military or naval service of the United States are prohibited from employing any of the forces under their respective commands for the purpose of returning fugitives from service or labor who may have escaped from any persons to whom such service or labor is claimed to be due; and any officer who shall be found guilty by a court-martial of violating this article shall be dismissed from the service.

"Sec. 2. *And be it further enacted,* That this act shall take effect from and after its passage."

Also, to the Ninth and Tenth sections of an act entitled "An act to suppress insurrection, to punish treason and rebellion, to seize and confiscate property of rebels, and for other purposes," approved July 16, 1862, and which sections are in the words and figures following:

"Section 9. *And be it further enacted,* That all slaves of persons who shall hereafter be engaged in rebellion against the Government of the United States or who shall in any way give aid or comfort thereto, escaping from such persons and taking refuge within the lines of the army; and all slaves captured from such persons or deserted by them and coming under the control of the Government of the United States; and all slaves of such persons found *on* [or] being within any place occupied by rebel forces and afterward occupied by forces of the United States, shall be deemed captives of war, and shall be forever free of their servitude, and not again held as slaves.

"Sec. 10. *And be it further enacted,* That no slave escaping into any State, Territory, or the District of Columbia, from any other State, shall be delivered up or in any way impeded or hindered of his liberty except for crime or some offence against the laws, unless the person claiming said fugitive shall first make oath that the person to whom the labor or service of such fugitive is alleged to be due is his lawful owner and has not borne arms against the United States in the present rebellion, nor in any way given aid and comfort thereto; and no person engaged in the military or naval service of the United States shall, under any pretence whatever, assume to decide on the validity of the claim of any person to the service or labor of any other person, or surrender up any such person to the claimant, on pain of being dismissed from the service."

And I do hereby enjoin upon and order all persons engaged in the military and naval service of the United States to observe, obey, and enforce, within their respective spheres of service, the act and sections above recited.

And the Executive will in due time recommend that all citizens of the United States who shall have remained loyal thereto throughout the rebellion shall (upon the restoration of the constitutional relation between the United States and their respective States and people, if that relation shall have been suspended or disturbed) be compensated for all losses by acts of the United States, including the loss of slaves.

In witness whereof I have hereunto set my hand and caused the seal of the United States to be affixed.

[L.S.] Done at the city of Washington this twenty-second day of September, in the year of our Lord one thousand eight hundred and sixty-two, and of the Independence of the United States the eighty-seventh.

ABRAHAM LINCOLN.

By the President:
WILLIAM H. SEWARD, Secretary of State.

THE FINAL PROCLAMATION

Whereas, On the twenty-second day of September, in the year of our Lord one thousand eight hundred and sixty-two, a proclamation was issued by the President of the United States, containing, among other things, the following, to wit:

"That on the first day of January, in the year of our Lord one thousand eight hundred and sixty-three, all persons held as slaves within any State or designated part of a State the people whereof shall then be in rebellion against the United States, shall be then, thenceforward, and forever free; and the Executive Government of the United States, including the military and naval authority thereof, will recognize and maintain the freedom of such persons, and will do no act or acts to repress such persons, or any of them, in any efforts they may make for their actual freedom.

"That the Executive will, on the first day of January aforesaid, by proclamation, designate the States and parts of States, if any, in which the people thereof respectively shall then be in rebellion against the United States; and the fact that any State, or the people thereof, shall on that day be in good faith represented in the Congress of the United States, by members chosen thereto at elections wherein a majority of the qualified voters of such State shall have participated, shall, in the absence of strong countervailing testimony, be deemed conclusive evidence that such State, and the people thereof, are not then in rebellion against the United States."

Now, therefore, I, Abraham Lincoln, President of the United States, by virtue of the power in me vested as Commander-in-

Chief of the Army and Navy of the United States in time of actual armed rebellion against the authority and government of the United States, and as a fit and necessary war measure for suppressing said rebellion, do, on this first day of January, in the year of our Lord one thousand eight hundred and sixty-three, and in accordance with my purpose so to do, publicly proclaimed for the full period of one hundred days from the day first above mentioned, order and designate, as the States and parts of States wherein the people thereof respectively are this day in rebellion against the United States, the following, to wit:

Arkansas, Texas, Louisiana (except the parishes of St. Bernard, Plaquemines, Jefferson, St. John, St. Charles, St. James, Ascension, Assumption, Terre Bonne, Lafourche, Ste. Marie, St. Martin, and Orleans, including the city of New Orleans), Mississippi, Alabama, Florida, Georgia, South Carolina, North Carolina, and Virginia (except the forty-eight counties designated as West Virginia, and also the counties of Berkeley, Accomac, Northampton, Elizabeth City, York, Princess Anne, and Norfolk, including the cities of Norfolk and Portsmouth), and which excepted parts are for the present left precisely as if this proclamation were not issued.

And by virtue of the power and for the purpose aforesaid, I do order and declare that all persons held as slaves within said designated States and parts of States are, and henceforward shall be, free; and that the Executive Government of the United States, including the military and naval authorities thereof, will recognize and maintain the freedom of said persons.

And I hereby enjoin upon the people so declared to be free, to abstain from all violence, unless in necessary self-defence; and I recommend to them that, in all cases when allowed, they labor faithfully for reasonable wages.

And I further declare and make known that such persons, of suitable condition, will be received into the armed service of the United States, to garrison forts, positions, stations, and other places, and to man vessels of all sorts in said service.

And upon this act, sincerely believed to be an act of justice, warranted by the Constitution upon military necessity, I invoke the considerate judgment of mankind and the gracious favor of Almighty God.

In testimony whereof I have hereunto set my name and caused the seal of the United States to be affixed.

Done at the city of Washington this first day of January, in the year of our Lord one thousand eight hundred [L.S.] and sixty-three, and of the Independence of the United States the eighty-seventh.

ABRAHAM LINCOLN.

By the President:

WILLIAM H. SEWARD, Secretary of State.

THE BATTLE OF GETTYSBURG

A.D. 1863

ORVILLE J. VICTOR   EDWARD A. POLLARD
ABRAHAM LINCOLN

About midway on the ridge running south from the village of Gettysburg where the Army of the Potomac fought its greatest battle was a small, umbrella-shaped clump of trees, which is spoken of as the high-water mark of the Rebellion, since the centre of Pickett's column in the famous charge was directed toward that point, the battle culminated in that charge, and the military efforts of the Confederate Government culminated in that battle. It was the second attempt of their strongest army to invade the Northern States, both had failed, and it was also the last.

The full force of the event is realized only when it is considered in connection with the fall of Vicksburg. This great battle in the East was fought in the first three days of July, and on the fourth the Confederate stronghold at the West surrendered to General Grant with nearly thirty thousand prisoners.

Much has been written of Gettysburg, the later narratives abounding in criticism, controversy, and conjecture as to what might have been done. We have chosen to present the earlier accounts of Victor and Pollard (Federal and Confederate), which give all the essential facts with admirable clearness, and to add Lincoln's famous address at the dedication of the cemetery.

ORVILLE J. VICTOR

NEVER was a commander suddenly called to a graver responsibility than fell to the lot of General George G. Meade. A quiet, undemonstrative person, the contrast of Hooker in temper and personal bearing, his choice for the succession was surprising. Whatever the prompting motive, the selection was, to a certain degree, fortunate, since, with most of the corps commanders, his relations were those of professional confidence. Fewer personal animosities were excited by his promotion than had been caused by previous changes in the army's control. His assumption of command was followed by no change in Hooker's general disposition. On the contrary, having the power, he ordered the abandonment of Maryland

Heights, and French's brigades ere long contributed to his field strength. He was further sustained by having all forces operating against Lee made tributary to his orders. Even from the defences of Washington a few more men were spared to augment the efficiency of his columns.

His plan, as communicated to the General-in-Chief, was: "To move my army as promptly as possible on the main lines from Frederick to Harrisburg, extending my wings on both sides of that line as far as I could consistently with the safety and rapid concentration of that army, and to continue that movement until I either encountered the enemy or had reason to believe that the enemy was about to advance upon me; my object being at all hazards to compel him to loose his hold on the Susquehanna and meet me in battle at some point." Only a day was lost. On June 29th the columns were put in motion up the Monocacy Valley toward Gettysburg, preceded by Buford's and Kilpatrick's cavalry divisions, which Hooker, before retiring, had thrown forward, as a prelude to his advance on the same line.

On the same day the enemy released "his hold on the Susquehanna." Informed, on the 28th, of Hooker's intended descent on the line of his retreat, Lee suddenly changed his order of march upon Harrisburg to a retrograde; by securing a footing east of the South Mountain range, he hoped to keep open his imperilled communications. Ewell was then in occupancy of Carlisle and York; Longstreet and Hill were at or near Chambersburg. The three corps were directed to concentrate at Gettysburg; and on the 29th were *en route* to that important point.

Buford, reaching Gettysburg on the evening of the 30th, pushed out reconnoissances on the roads leading north and west. He then ascertained that the Confederates were marching toward that point, their columns having already reached Cashtown, on the Chambersburg road, and Heildersburg, on the Carlisle road. Of this Meade was at once informed. His advance, at that moment, had reached Taneytown and vicinity, though General Reynolds, with the First and Eleventh corps, had approached within four miles of Gettysburg, with orders to occupy the town on the following morning. Meade's want of correct knowledge, both of the topography of the country and of the enemy's designs, led him to locate a temporary line, stretching from Middle-burg to Manchester (Pipe Creek), considering it a good one for general battle, should it be Lee's design to advance upon him. Behind this line he ordered the trains, and the several corps were directed to be put in the lightest possible condition. The Federal disposition on the night of the 30th was: headquarters at Taneytown; Third Corps at Summitsburg; Second, at Taneytown; Fifth, at Hanover; Sixth, at Manchester; Twelfth, at Two Taverns; First and Eleventh, advanced upon Gettysburg, at Marsh Run. Kilpatrick's cavalry were observing on the east beyond Hanover Junction.

On the morning of July 1st the advance of Hill's corps struck Buford's lines at Willoughby Run, a mile or more northwest of Gettysburg. A sharp skirmishing fight at once followed, Buford resolving to hold the enemy there until the infantry should come up. Reynolds, hearing the sounds of battle, hurried forward the First division (Wadsworth's) of the First Corps, with orders for the other divisions of First and Eleventh corps to follow. The advancing division reached the point of conflict at 10 A.M. It was found that the enemy were still beyond the second of the two ridges lying west of Gettysburg; the first, or Seminary Ridge, being one-half mile, and the second one mile and a half, distant from the town. At the base of the second flowed Willoughby Run, along whose banks, and on the western declivity, Heth's division, of Hill's corps, was formed. Reynolds appears to have resolved upon delaying the Confederate advance at that point. As the Federal army lay from seven to thirty-two miles away, it was absolutely imperative, if the heights of Gettysburg were retained, that the Confederates should be held where they were for a day.

Wadsworth's two brigades were quickly disposed for action. Cutler's five regiments were on the right and left of the Chambersburg turnpike, as well as using for cover the embankment and "cuts" of a then unfinished railway running parallel with and close to the highway. Hall's Maine battery was placed between these roads, sustained by three regiments under Wadsworth's direct command, which constituted the extreme Federal right; while Reynolds in person directed the disposition of the other two regiments to the left of the road. The second brigade—Meredith's "Iron Brigade"—under General Doubleday's direction, was assigned to the Federal left, covering the road from Millerstown, and occupying a strip of woods into which the enemy already had penetrated.

The enemy opened fire sharply on the forming lines, and while directing the disposition on the right General Reynolds was killed. Davis's Mississippians, advancing over the run, turned Wadsworth's three regiments, which, after a severe fight, were withdrawn by way of the turnpike, to re-form under the lee of Seminary Ridge. This retirement left the battery unsupported, and it was retired after severe loss. The two regiments under Cutler were thus exposed to a flank assault. Seeing this, Doubleday ordered in his reserve regiment (Sixth Wisconsin), and the three regiments, facing about, charged upon the Mississippians, then forming along the railway for a charge. This movement, executed with celerity and intrepidity, was so much of a surprise to the enemy that, after a short conflict, nearly two entire regiments, with their colors, were captured.

Simultaneous with this charge Doubleday relieved the Iron Brigade from its too advanced position, turned it quickly upon its centre, and, sweeping down toward the right, caught a considerable number of the men of Archer's brigade, including Archer himself, who had advanced over the run upon Cutler's front.

These successes were now rapidly followed by an opening out of the respective battle lines. The arrival of Pender's division of Hill's corps as well as of the advance of Ewell, gave the enemy great additional strength, which was not fully counterbalanced by the coming up of the remaining divisions of the First Corps; and the Federals, therefore, fought at a disadvantage. Having re-formed his right brigade, Wadsworth moved still farther toward the right, to confront the increased strength of the enemy on his front, in that direction. Meredith's men still were firmly holding the left, under a scathing fire, in which the Confederate artillery made sad work with the lion-hearted men of that Iron Brigade, when the division of Rowley (Doubleday's old division) was put into the fight. With a wild cheer the columns moved forward, and soon the wood and hillsides became one blaze of musketry, while the several division batteries, getting at work, answered the enemy's guns, shot for shot. The Federal left, thus sustained, for the time being held its ground.

On the right, Wadsworth was so pressed that the remaining division of the First Corps (Robinson's), then in reserve, on Seminary Ridge, was sent to his support—two brigades (Baxter's and Paul's) getting into position on Cutler's right, covering the Mummasburg road, along which Rodes's division of Ewell's corps was advancing. The enemy, pressing his brigades too far forward, met a stunning fire, which, by throwing back his right, uncovered his left. Observing this, by a happy movement the bulk of Lawton's brigade was captured by the two fresh Federal commands. This second success was followed by the appearance, still farther on the right, of Early's division of Ewell's corps, just arrived from York. With his fine artillery Early soon so worried the Federal right as to compel it to give ground.

General Howard (Eleventh Corps) reached the field at noon, and as ranking officer he assumed command. Leaving one division (Steinwehr's) in town to occupy Cemetery Hill, which he perceived was the key to the Gettysburg ground, he threw the two divisions of Barlow and Schurz, of the Eleventh Corps, to the extreme right to confront Early's evident flanking advance. Thus posted he covered both the Carlisle and Harrisburg roads. This left a thin line, or, rather, no line at all, for a short distance between the Mummasburg and Carlisle roads; and while Barlow and Schurz were holding Early in check, Rodes pressed his brigades into the exposed section of the field. Doubleday detected the dangerous gap and tried to close it, by ordering in his last reserve brigade. This stayed the threatened perforation of the Federal line, and all again promised well. The battle raged with savage fury from one end to the other. About 3 P.M. the Eleventh Corps divisions opposed to Early fell away before his tremendous artillery fire. This was followed by a charge, beginning from their left column, when the entire Federal right was driven in, bearing with it the right division of the First Corps, which up to that time had held Rodes firmly at bay.

The First Corps division of Wadsworth fell back to Seminary Ridge, in fighting order, but the division of Robinson, and the two Eleventh Corps divisions were driven into the town, too disordered to offer any resistance. Once in the town this disorder was rendered complete by the dispersion of commands through the several streets; and the enemy, enveloping the northwest section of the village, succeeded in capturing a large portion of the disorganized ranks—about five thousand prisoners[1] and three guns falling into Ewell's hands. Wadsworth, with Buford's ever-ready cavalry, held Seminary Ridge till its abandonment became necessary, when he moved off, with all his guns and the reserve artillery, to Cemetery Hill, which Howard's forethought had secured against all comers. The play of Steinwehr's guns upon Ewell's ranks warned him off, and the fight was ended—Buford's command facing the foe to the last.

The news of this conflict borne to Meade had changed his whole prearranged order of battle. When informed of Reynolds's death he had despatched General Hancock to the field, giving him discretionary power to order the battle at Gettysburg if that place appeared to him propitious for the general conflict. Followed by General Warren, chief of engineers, Hancock reached the town at the moment of the Federal retreat. His opinion of the feasibility of the ground for Meade's operations already had been formed, and he so disposed the forces then available as to hold the commanding heights of Cemetery and Culp's hills. But, before receiving the reports of Hancock and Warren regarding the situation, Meade had ordered forward all the troops within ready call—the Twelfth and Second corps. The Fifth and Sixth corps were instructed by messengers to hasten to the same point. The Third, moving from Emmetsburg, was on the ground by 6 P.M. The Sixth, being at Manchester, had thirty miles to march, hence Sedgwick was instructed (at 7.30 P.M., July 1st) to make a forced march by the shortest route.

Lee's concentration was equally rapid. The fight of Wednesday had been, to him, a surprise. Moving his columns by easy marches, he expected to occupy Gettysburg unmolested, the absence of his cavalry, under Stuart, leaving him uninformed of Meade's advance upon the same point. When the booming of guns along Willoughby Run announced the Federal presence, the Confederate commander found his second projection impeded, and it remained for him at once to decide there to fight

[1] This number included all the wounded of the day, who had been borne to the town for care, as well as those left in the Seminary, too severely injured to be moved.

the decisive battle or to retire by Chambersburg and Fairfield to the Potomac. The choice, indeed, was made for him. He therefore ordered forward his commands, and during the night the divisions were getting into position.

The ground over which the conflict of July 2d was to rage may be thus described: Two roads coming into Gettysburg—one from Emmetsburg on the west and the Baltimore turnpike on the east—form the two sides of a Λ, their point of junction being on the south side of the village. Cemetery Ridge runs from near the point of junction directly south, dividing the Λ in two nearly equal divisions. Along this ridge runs the Taneytown road. Thus three roads converge at the point called Cemetery Hill, overlooking the town. Within the angles of these roads the main Union formation was made, on the night of July 1st and during the morning of the 2d. Culp's Hill, an important elevation, commanding Cemetery Hill, lay off to the right, between the Baltimore pike and Rock Creek. This was held as the Union extreme right. The general position was one of exceeding strength: the two roads from Taneytown and Emmetsburg, being almost wholly within the Federal lines, offered unusual facilities for rapid intercommunication, with commanding elevations for the artillery. Nor could the location be readily turned, for the two crests called Great and Little Round Top, lying south of Cemetery Ridge, about three miles away, acted as Malakoffs, whose proper armament would give the National army's left perfect security.

The enemy had Seminary Ridge, which, in its southerly extension, enveloped the Emmetsburg road, thus making it feasible to project their right out to Meade's left, and offering the natural line for a flank movement upon the Federal position. Or, if battle was declined by the Confederates, it gave them an open way to Emmetsburg and Frederick. Hence, while in a stronghold, if the enemy assailed, Meade was in no condition to "cover" Washington and Baltimore.

The morning of July 2d found the belligerents confronting each other nearly in full force. Lee's divisions were well on the ground. Of Meade's army, the Sixth Corps was not up until after noon; but, no assault being offered by Lee prior to that time, it was in season for duty. The Confederates passed the morning in determining their point of attack. Their line, forming a crescent five miles in length, swept around from Rock Creek, in front of Culp's Hill, through the town and along the western slope of Seminary Ridge, down to the Emmetsburg road; or, in this order by divisions: Johnson, Early, Rodes of Ewell's Corps constituting the left; Heth, Pender, and Anderson of A. P. Hill's corps constituting the centre; McLaws and Hood of Longstreet's corps constituting the right. Meade's assignment, as determined upon at noon, was: Twelfth Corps (Slocum's) on Culp's Hill; then Wadsworth's division of the First Corps; then what was left of Howard's Eleventh Corps occupying the cemetery, Doubleday's and Robinson's division acting as a reserve at that point; next Hancock's corps (Second) stretched along Cemetery Ridge; then Sykes's corps (Fifth) advancing to the Round Top hills, to be conjoined there with Sedgwick's Sixth Corps.

This gave the Union line a crescent shape, only broken by the elbow-like advance of Sickles's corps (Third) down to the Emmetsburg road, along which it was drawn to a point west of Round Top, where it was refused toward that height. Thus advanced, of course he offered the true point of attack, which Lee was not long in discovering. The attack was made about 4 P.M. of the 2d, at a moment when Meade was viewing the faulty and somewhat dangerous position. He said: "When I arrived on the ground, which I did a few minutes before 4 P.M., I found that General Sickles had taken up a position very much in advance of what it had been my intention that he should take—that he had thrown forward his right flank instead of connecting with the left of General Hancock, something like a half or three-quarters of a mile in front of General Hancock, thus leaving a large gap between his right and Hancock's left; and that his left, instead of being near the Round Top Mountain, was in advance of the Round Top; and that his line, instead of being a prolongation of Hancock's line, as I expected it would be, made an angle of about 45° with it. I told him that I was very fearful he would be attacked and would lose the artillery, which he had put so far in front, before I could support it, or that, if I undertook to support it, I would have to abandon all the rest of the line which I had adopted—that is, that I would have to fight the battle out there where he was. General Sickles expressed regret, and promptly said that he would withdraw his forces to the line which I had intended him to take. But I told him I was fearful that the enemy would not permit him to withdraw, and that there was no time for any further change of movement. And before I had finished that remark, the enemy's batteries opened upon him and the action began."

Referring to his order for attack, Lee said: "In front of General Longstreet the enemy held a position from which, if he could be driven, it was thought that our army could be used to advantage in assailing the more elevated ground beyond, and thus enable us to reach the crest of the ridge. That officer was directed to endeavor to carry the position, while General Ewell attacked directly the high ground on the enemy's right, which had been already partially fortified. General Hill was instructed to threaten the centre of the Federal line, in order to prevent reënforcements being sent to either wing, and to avail himself of any opportunity that might present itself for attack. After a severe struggle, Longstreet succeeded in getting possession of and holding the desired ground. Ewell also carried some of the strong positions which he assailed, and the result was such as to lead to the belief that he would be able ultimately to dislodge the enemy. The battle ceased at dark."

After twenty minutes of rapid and effective artillery fire, Hood's division of Longstreet's command pressed upon Sickles's extreme left. Two brigades of Birney's division—De Trobriand's and Ward's—held the refused line, from the Emmetsburg pike to the base of the Round Top Mountain. The Third Brigade (Graham's) faced the road and connected with the left of Sickles's second division (Humphreys's). The attack was, indeed, a flanking movement, for, while engaging Birney's two brigades, Hood swung his right around upon the ridge on whose length Meade's main line rested.

This effort to flank Sickles was successful, and only a happy circumstance averted the great calamity of the loss of Little Round Top. Chief of Engineers Warren, ascending to the crest of Little Round Top—then used as a signal station—arrived just in time to witness the flanking movement. His ready eye comprehended all in a moment, and he hastened down the rugged declivity for aid to hold the key to the ridge. Happily he encountered the Fifth Corps advance division (Barnes's), then marching to Sickles's aid. Assuming the responsibility of detaching Vincent's brigade, with Hazlett's battery, Warren led the men up the height, while the battery was literally lifted up by human hands. Not a moment too soon, for the enemy already were mounting the western slope, which commanded the crest, when Vincent's men came up from the east and north.

The two bodies rushed together like two athletes, Hood's Texans firing and then resorting to the bayonet, and Vincent's undaunted fellows using the bayonet or clubbed musket. Officers and men all fought like furies, and in thirty minutes the fray was ended by the appearance, on Vincent's right, of Weed's brigade, of Ayres's division (Fifth Corps). What was left of the Texan regiments retired sullenly to the valley below. There, reënforced, the regiments worked their way up the rocky defile between the two Round Top hills, and suddenly appeared on Vincent's flank. Only the bayonet could dislodge Hood's dogged men, and Colonel Chamberlain put his Maine men to the charge. The enemy again were driven back, and the hill was saved. Among the killed were both General Vincent and General Weed, Captain Hazlett, whose heroism was one of the marked features of that bloody contest, and Colonel O'Rourke, commanding the One Hundred Fortieth New York, which had carried Hazlett's battery up the hill. The dead lay scattered all over the rough, desolate spot; in many instances Confederate and Unionist were locked in a death embrace.

During this combat on the hill, the battle below was raging with great severity. Resolved to break Sickles's centre, and thus wrest the lower ridge (along the Emmetsburg road) from Meade, Longstreet threw McLaws upon the weak point where Birney's alignment bent from the road back toward Round Top. That section of the field became a vortex of fire. Meade, as seemed necessary, in order to maintain his left, put in reënforcements, but all to no purpose. De Trobriand's and Ward's brigades, terribly cut up, were forced in and lost as brigade formations. The brigades of Tilton and Sweitzer, of Barnes's division (Fifth Corps) passed to the front, on their line, and nobly stood their ground until McLaws, having penetrated the centre, took the brigades in flank, when Barnes withdrew his decimated column. To sustain the centre, Humphreys added one brigade from his division, but this reënforcement to Graham's four regiments could not resist the enemy's advance over the road and around his left. Humphreys, therefore, faced about his line, now taken in flank, retired his artillery, and fought, facing south, but still retaining his hold (on his right) on the Emmetsburg road. The contested field was then between himself and Round Top, where the antagonists still struggled.

Caldwell's division, from Hancock's corps, was put into action to stay the Confederate march, after Sickles's centre and left had given way. The two brigades of Cross and Kelly, first skirting the base of Little Round Top, pushed on through the woods into an open field beyond, whence, after a few moments' struggle, they were driven, broken and fearfully cut up. Colonel Cross—a man of astonishing bravery and a zealous soldier from love of his cause—was left dead on the field. Caldwell's second line, composed of the brigades of Brooke and Zook, then advanced and fell upon the enemy with such impetuosity as forced Hood's line back beyond the brook which flows a little to the west of the base of Round Top. It was but a momentary success, however, since, taken in flank by McLaws's advance, Caldwell had to retire. His brigades suffered dreadfully. The gallant Zook was killed and Brooke wounded. Nearly half of their brave fellows were left upon the blood-dyed field. Sweitzer's brigade, having preserved its formation, was pressed in to Caldwell's assistance, but it was hurled back with heavy loss. Ayres's division of regulars—less the brigade of Weed—also moving forward to Caldwell's aid, was met by a flank and front fire which fearfully riddled his ranks, and the regulars retired to their first battle line, well up the ridge, unable to hold the ground below them.

This strife, at the base of Round Top, momentarily ceased, for, having disposed of Sickles's entire left, Lee put Hill into the fight in the endeavor to advance his own centre. Humphreys's right and left, being uncovered, Hancock threw forward a brigade (Willard's) from Hays's division to Humphreys's left, and two regiments to his right. These were not fully in position when Hill's admirably timed attack was made. Taken on front and right flank by Hill, and on the left by McLaws, the division commander had no choice but to retire toward Cemetery Ridge. Sickles, steadying his lines, was stricken down about 6 P.M.—having, up to that moment, passed the day's dangers unscathed. The enemy pressed on, under a cutting fire from the ridge crest, but no storm of shot and shell could stay their advancing ranks. Humphreys fell away, contesting every rod of retreat, but leaving gun after gun on the ground with every horse and cannoneer shot away. Hancock, assuming command at Meade's order, directed the more rapid retirement of what was left of the division, and when it reached the cover of the ridge it was but a wreck of regiments—mere gatherings of battalions.

The Confederate leader had played a desperate but skilfully contrived and resolutely executed game. At seven o'clock he found his left and centre thundering at the base of Meade's main line. Could he push his advance further, and gain a lodgement on the ridge, he conceived the field his own and the Federal army defeated. But he was not to witness any further triumph. He had, after all that day's strife, won only a foothold; and though the Fifth Corps (Sykes's), on the extreme Federal left, and the Second Corps (Hancock's), on the centre, had been somewhat involved in the losses, Meade's advantages of concentration were so great that, when the final attempt was made by Lee to gain the crest, he found fresh troops there to meet him. Sedgwick's Corps was sent to the summit of Little Round Top, and to the north of it, to sustain Sykes. Meade, in person, led forward a section of the Twelfth Corps, to fill the weak spot in the line between Sykes and Hancock. Longstreet's column, attempting an advance, had made its way, under cover of woods, well up the ridge, when Hancock discovered the movement and the First Minnesotans were sent to the charge. The enemy broke and fell back in such haste as to lose their regimental colors.

Eight o'clock had now come. The enemy's attack had grown desultory and weak, evidently from exhaustion. Hancock, with a portion of his forces, including the gathered remnants of the Third Corps and the reënforcements from the right, made a charge to clear out what of the enemy still remained on his front. The Confederates fell back with but slight resistance, and Humphreys's men reclaimed all their abandoned guns. A similar charge was made on the left, by Crawford, who, with the Pennsylvania reserves, threw Longstreet's lines well back from the vicinity of Round Top; and the struggle ceased at dusk with the original Federal line unimpaired.

On the right a battle was fought, late in the day. Taking advantage of the detachment of reënforcements to the left, Ewell assaulted Slocum's lines on Cemetery and Culp's hills, hoping to carry them by storm. Early moved upon the former and Johnson upon the latter, after a furious cannonade, at sunset. Marching out from the town, Early encountered a withering fire from the guns on the heights, but, pushing forward his columns by brigades, the Confederates were quickly advanced up the slope. The artillery then fired shrapnel with such effect that Early's left and centre gave way and retired, but his right brigade, taking advantage of the ground and buildings, made its way up to the advanced batteries, over which a hand-to-hand struggle occurred, the artillerymen fighting for their guns with ramrods and handspikes. The infantry, Howard's (Eleventh Corps) troops, holding the field at that point, soon were closely engaged and the fight became severe. Howard despatched to Hancock for aid, and received Carroll's brigade, which, by its impetuous spirit, aided by the guns a little to the east, drove the enemy back. Their dead thickly strewed the ground. It was a perilous enterprise at best. Rodes's division, ordered to sustain Early's movement, as the exigencies should require, failed to reach the field on his right in season to stay the repulse.

The movement of Johnson's division against Culp's Hill was not without some success. Aided by the ravine of Rock Creek his column advanced steadily, and by enveloping the extreme Federal right gained a lodgement. The Twelfth Corps, first stationed at that point, had been drawn away to reënforce the left—only Green's brigade holding the line. Wadsworth's division (First Corps) stood upon Green's left. The Confederate advance was opposed with unflinching front, but Johnson, finding the lines on the extreme right deserted, took possession of the breastworks and there remained during the night, in spite of all efforts to drive him out.

It had been a sanguinary day for both contestants. To Meade it had brought more loss of men than could have been supposed possible—the ranks being reduced fully fifteen thousand, of whom about one-fourth were prisoners. Lee's casualties were reported at about ten thousand. His successes were such, he stated, as induced him to continue the assault the next day.

For that further trial of strength the Federal leader was prepared. A consultation of commanders, held on the evening of the 2d, decidedly expressed the feeling of the whole army to fight it out there. Orders were therefore issued by the generals of corps to strengthen their positions, as they were then held, by additional earthworks; the artillery was reorganized and redisposed in several particulars. Its losses in men had been considerable, and some guns were injured, but its largely effective force was unimpaired. The cavalry was thrown to the wings and also to the rear, to guard against any surprise from the Baltimore pike, and to cover the trains parked in its vicinity.

Lee's attack, on the morning of the 3d, was anticipated by Meade, who assumed the offensive on his right, where Johnson's division of Ewell's corps had made its lodgement. At daylight the Federal artillery opened on the enemy in a lively manner. Ewell having thrown considerable reënforcements into the position during the night, and strengthened the earthworks for a defensive fight, answered spiritedly, and the cannonade put the two armies on the alert. The troops whose withdrawal the previous day, to reënforce the left, had caused the loss of their line, were returned to the right and put to the assault. Assisted by a brigade (Shaler's) from the Sixth Corps, the Twelfth Corps divisions of Williams and Geary so pressed the enemy that a charge made by Geary, at eight o'clock, swept the enemy from Culp's Hill and restored the right to its entirety.

Losing this ground on his left, Lee had to change his programme of attack. A lull in operations therefore occurred, during which he rearranged his battle lines and concentrated his artillery with reference to a heavy assault upon the Federal centre and left. The strength of the National line, stretching along Cemetery Ridge, and out up to the Round Top fastness, Lee so well appreciated that he brought into requisition his every available gun. Before noon he had in place, beyond the Emmetsburg road on the extension of Seminary Ridge and to the south of it, about one hundred twenty-five guns, with which to demoralize the Union line preparatory to his final and most desperate effort to obtain a foothold on Cemetery Ridge. Pickett's division (Longstreet's corps) having reached the field too late for the previous day's battle, was assigned the post of honor, the van of the column of assault. It was strengthened by Wilcox's brigade of Anderson's division on its right, and Heth's division, commanded by Pettigrew, on the left.

Early in the afternoon the artillery from Seminary Ridge and Longstreet's centre opened with all the power of its metal. The outburst was so sudden and startling, and the shower of hurtled missiles so concentrated in range, that for a few minutes the Federal line was stunned, and the troops shrank away as from a sirocco, everywhere seeking the cover of rocks and the temporary fortifications. Eighty Federal guns answered, and the contest assumed sublime proportions. The hills seemed to tremble and rock. Shot and shell shrieked through the dun pall of sulphurous smoke which filled all the air; the ground was torn and seamed in the thousand places where the thunderbolts struck.[1] The Federal gunners, reeking with sweat as they worked beneath the half-suppressed blaze of a midsummer sun, grew more frenzied with every loss; and when ordered to the rear to make way for a fresh gun and men, left the charmed circle of fire and death with the reluctance of unsated vengeance.

This combat continued two hours, when, finding his ammunition running low, and it being too dangerous to bring forward more, Hunt ordered a gradual cessation of the fire along the line. This was regarded by the enemy as indicative of silenced power, and their own guns ceased, as if satisfied that their preliminary work was done. The assaulting column advanced to the edge of the woods covering the side of Seminary Ridge. The formation was in two battle lines, Kemper's and Garnett's brigades in front,

[1] Said Doubleday: "They had our exact range, and the destruction was fearful. Horses were killed in every direction. I lost two horses myself, while almost every officer lost one or more, and quite a large number of caissons were blown up." The ruin wrought in the cemetery was complete. That sacred resting-place became truly a city of the dead before nightfall of that momentous day. Said Hancock: "It was a most terrific and appalling cannonade, one possibly hardly ever paralleled. I doubt whether there have ever been more guns concentrated upon an equal space and opening at one time."

sustained by Armistead's regiments. This column was flanked by wings, composed, as already stated, of Wilcox's brigade on the right, and Heth's division, commanded by Pettigrew, on the left. As soon as it passed the Emmetsburg road the Federal artillery opened, and continued to play on the ranks, from Round Top to the cemetery, wherever the intervening woods permitted an aim. This fire told severely on the advance. When at length the column began to ascend the ridge's western slope, the musketry opened from sections of the Federal line, though the artillery never for a moment ceased to hurl destruction through and through the oncoming brigades. Only men used to death and to perfect submission to command could preserve ranks under such a fire. Great gaps, literal windrows, would follow a well-directed shot, only to be closed up again by the unflinching mass.

But, if the main column was schooled to fire, the supports were not; for, when about half way up the hill, the division of Pettigrew wavered, broke, and fell away before the fire on its front and flank, coming from Hays's division (Second Corps). The demoralization of the Confederate wing was complete, and two thousand prisoners with their colors fell into the National hands. The main lines dared not halt to steady the distempered mass, and thus the brigades of Heth, which had fought gallantly at Willoughby Run, were scattered, marking their advance and retreat by lines of killed and wounded. Pickett's brigades pushed on, until the first formation overleaped the barrier of stones and rails that constituted the outwork or advanced line of the Second Corps's central division. The line when struck was held by Webb's brigade of Pennsylvanians, two regiments at the barrier and one in reserve, lying behind a second barrier, sixty paces to the rear and fully on the crest. The two regiments gave way, but in no disorder, and, rallying at the second line, there held their own, while Hancock, with quick energy, threw into the fray regiment after regiment from his left and from Doubleday's command. Of the latter, Stannard's Vermont Brigade had been advanced to a grove on the slope. These, now covering the Confederate flank, poured in a scathing fire, before which the enemy shrank. Confronted thus by an impassable host on his front, with musketry and artillery cutting his ranks into shreds while Stannard scarred his flank, Pickett's veterans were only human to falter and fall away. To have stood there, gazing upon the crest which no sacrifice of theirs could win, was mere madness; and, without a brigade commander to direct, the remnant of that proud forlorn hope sought safety in flight, preserving no order in its retreat. Twenty-five hundred of them, with twelve battle-flags, were swooped up by the flanking Federal advance.

Wilcox's brigade, which was to have formed the right wing in the assault, did not move forward as appointed, but, witnessing the defeat, advanced to cover the broken lines, only to meet a sudden and disastrous repulse. Stannard's Vermonters took his line in flank, and Gibbon in front; and the last of the Confederate brigades vanished, strewing the way with its dead and disabled, and leaving behind a full regiment of prisoners in Stannard's hands.

A ghastly report the repulsed column had to make. Garnett was killed; Kemper badly wounded; Armistead mortally shot; fourteen of its field officers dead or left wounded on the hillside; while, of rank and file, only about one-fourth reported at roll-call that evening. As a division it had passed away, and a thousand Virginia homes were filled with mourning for brothers, sons, and fathers who would return no more.

The cavalry operations during these most momentous days were arduous and deserving of special notice. Buford's division, after its sanguinary resistance on the 1st, was ordered to Westminster, "to refit and guard the trains." Kilpatrick, in command of the Third Division Cavalry Corps, on the 30th, had a severe skirmish with Stuart's main body, which was then making its way from the Potomac, at Seneca to Carlisle, there to join Ewell. On the 30th, having reached Hanover, Kilpatrick sent Custer's brigade toward Abbottsville, while Farnsworth's brigade remained at Hanover. The enemy rode into Hanover on the charge—quite to the Federal General's surprise; he had no suspicion of Stuart's presence in that vicinity. The Fifth New York Cavalry, led by Farnsworth, received the brunt of the shock, and, in a fierce fight of two hours, sustained his hold upon the town, when, Custer's brigade returning, the enemy retired rapidly toward York, with a loss of ten killed, forty wounded, and forty prisoners. A dash made by the Confederate cavalry at Littletown, on the 30th, was repulsed by the Fifth and Sixth

Michigan Cavalry. July 1st Kilpatrick made a dash for Heildersburg, hoping to prevent Stuart's junction with Lee's army, but was a few hours too late. July 2d he moved his command to Hunterstown, where, on the previous day, General Gregg's cavalry division had a heavy skirmish and artillery fight with Ewell's left. Kilpatrick rode into the place named at 4 P.M., when the enemy retired toward Gettysburg. A "brush" followed, and the enemy were quickly sent back upon their main column.

During the 3d Gregg covered the Federal right. July 3d the Third Cavalry division, being ordered to the Federal extreme left, proceeded thither to threaten Longstreet's flank and, if possible, to reach his ammunition-trains. With the brigades of Farnsworth and Merritt, Kilpatrick struck the Confederate right at 2 P.M., so spiritedly as to render it necessary for the divisions of Hood to change front and face south, to meet the attack. Their line was flanked by two stone fences, some distance beyond which the ammunition-trains were supposed to be parked. To reach these Farnsworth's brigade (First Vermont, First Virginia, and Eighteenth Pennsylvania) was put to the charge, led by Farnsworth in person. The fences were scaled amid a deadly fire, and the daring Vermonters pressed on against odds which proved to be Hood's division, in line of battle. Farnsworth fell in passing the second stone wall, and his men, scattering, retired as best they could from a field where they were powerless. The brigade of Merritt, falling upon Longstreet's rear, kept the enemy well employed in that direction—a diversion which saved Farnsworth's men from greater loss.

Thus closed the mighty struggle at Gettysburg. On the 4th the combatants respectively awaited attack—Lee regarding it, apparently, as a military matter-of-course. Having decided to retreat, he dared not initiate it until another day should determine the fate in store for him. To meet Meade's expected assault the divisions were concentrated upon and fortified Seminary Ridge, so as to hold open the avenue of escape toward Hagerstown. All day long (of the 4th) the trains were being despatched, but there was no movement of the columns until the anxious day was past, and then, Meade having offered neither battle nor obstruction to the retirement, the Confederate divisions began to disappear, under the friendly cover of storm and darkness, along the road leading direct to Hagerstown, but it was not until daylight of the 5th that the rear-guard turned its face toward the Potomac.

Meade's operations on the 4th and 5th were confined chiefly to reconnoissances to determine Lee's purposes. Gregg, from the right, moved off toward Chambersburg, during the night of the 4th, and reported, on the morning of the 5th, that the enemy were in full retreat. He kept well up to their rear, making large captures of stragglers and abandoned *materiel.* The houses along the route were found to be hospitals—large numbers of the Confederate slightly as well as their badly wounded having been left to lighten their trains. Kilpatrick, on the 4th, was put out on the left, to move to the South Mountain, at Monterey Gap, through which to debouch on the Gettysburg and Hagerstown pike. Reaching the gap at dark (the 4th), the pass was found in possession of a small squad of the enemy, but a spirited charge, in the rain and gloom, cleared the way, and Kilpatrick precipitated his squadrons on the rear of Ewell's train. Extensive captures were made of men and property. The Eighteenth Pennsylvania Cavalry, barricading the road, held it against all comers, and numerous seizures of rear-guards and lagging officers were made—most of whom rode right into the Federal hands. Corralling his captures at the Monterey House, Kilpatrick, before daylight, had them *en route* down the mountain for Waterloo, but, in the excessive darkness and rain, many of the prisoners escaped. A conflagration of immovable wagons and stores was made on the pike. This reconnoissance having definitely determined the fact of Lee's flight, and located the route of his retreat, the victory was declared complete, and the Army of the Potomac began the pursuit early on the 5th.

Meade's summary of his losses and captures during this great three-days' conflict was as follows: "Our own losses were very severe, amounting to 2834 killed, 13,709 wounded, and 6643 missing—in all 23,186. The result of the campaign may be briefly stated in the defeat of the enemy at Gettysburg, their compulsory evacuation of Pennsylvania and Maryland, and withdrawal from the upper valley of the Shenandoah; and the capture of 3 guns, 41 standards, 13,621 prisoners, while 24,978 small-arms were collected on the field."

Lee's casualties, as in other great battles, never were reported.

He said in his preliminary report of July 31st: "It is not in my power to give a correct statement of our casualties, which were very severe, including many brave men and an unusual proportion of distinguished and valuable officers. Among them I regret to mention the following general officers: Major-Generals Hood, Pender, and Trimble, severely; and Major-General Heth, slightly. General Pender has since died. Brigadier-Generals Barksdale and Garnett were killed, and Semmes mortally wounded. Brigadier-Generals Kemper, Armistead, Scales, G. T. Anderson, Hampton, J. M. Jones, and Jennings were also wounded. Brigadier-General Archer was taken prisoner. General Pettigrew, though wounded at Gettysburg, continued in command until he was mortally wounded near Falling Waters." Their entire losses Swinton estimates at 30,000—these figures being obtained by Lee's own returns, which were, on May 31st, 68,352, and on July 31st, 41,135.

EDWARD A. POLLARD

The march toward Gettysburg was conducted slowly. At 10 A.M. on July 1, 1863, Heth's division, of Hill's corps, being ahead, encountered the enemy's advance line, the Eleventh Corps, about three miles west of Gettysburg. Here a sharp engagement ensued, our men steadily advancing and driving the enemy before them to the town, and to a range of hills or low mountains running out a little east of south from the town. General Reynolds, who commanded the enemy's advance, rode forward to inspect the ground and select a position for his line of battle. The Confederates, distinguishing him from his uniform to be an officer of high rank, opened upon him with heavy volleys of infantry fire. He was struck by several balls, and died instantly without uttering a word.

About an hour after the opening of the engagement, which was principally of artillery, General Ewell, who was moving from the direction of Carlisle, came up and took a position on our extreme left. Rodes came into the engagement on the flank of the enemy, who were confronting A. P. Hill, and occupied the most commanding point of the very ridge with artillery which the enemy were upon. This ridge runs in the shape of a crescent around Gettysburg, following the windings of a creek which is between it and the town.

After our artillery had been engaged for some half an hour, with admirable effect, the enemy were observed to be moving rapidly from Hill's front to that of Rodes, and to be advancing their new columns against Rodes from the town. Rodes, his dispositions having been made, advanced his whole line. It had first to cross a field, six hundred yards wide, and enter woods—immediately upon entering which it became hotly engaged.

The Alabama Brigade (Rodes's old command) advanced somewhat confusedly, owing, it is said, to a misconception as to the direction it should take, and, while confused, it became engaged, and was forced back with its lines broken, though reënforced by the Fifth Alabama, which uncovered Lawson's brigade. Two regiments of this brigade were almost entirely surrounded, in consequence of the giving way of the Alabama Brigade and the concentration of the enemy at that point, and were either killed or captured almost to a man. The gallant resistance, however, which they made is shown by a statement coming from General Rodes himself, that, riding along behind where their line had been, he thought he observed a regiment lying down as if to escape the Federal fire. On going up to force them into the fight, he found they were all corpses.

As the battle wavered, General Early came up, and got his artillery into position so as to enfilade and silence batteries which were then occupied in an attempt to enfilade Rodes's battery. As the enemy attempted a flank movement, Gordon's brigade of gallant Georgians was ordered to make a charge. They crossed a small stream and valley, and entered a long narrow strip of an opposite slope, at the top of which the enemy had a strong force posted. For five minutes nothing could be heard or seen save the smoke and roar proceeding from the heavy musketry and indicating a desperate contest; but the contest was not long or uncertain. The Federals were put to flight, and our men pressed them, pouring a deadly fire at the flying fugitives. Seeing a second and larger line near the town, General Early halted General Gordon until two other brigades (Hays's and Hoke's) could come up, when a second charge was made, and three pieces of artillery, besides several entire regiments of the enemy, were captured.

There should not be lost from the records of the individual

heroism of the Confederacy an incident of this battle. During a lull in the engagement, when the enemy were re-forming and awaiting reënforcements, Lieutenant Roberts, of the Second Mississippi, observing, some distance off, but nearer the enemy's than our own fires, two groups, each consisting of seven to ten men, and each guarding a stand of colors, called for volunteers to take them. Four gallant spirits from his own, and an equal number from the Forty-second Mississippi Regiment, readily responded, and soon a dash was made for the colors. A hand-to-hand fight ensued, in which all on both sides were either killed or wounded, except Private McPherson, who killed the last Federal color-bearer and brought off the colors, Lieutenant Roberts being killed just as he was seizing one of the colors.

The result of the day's fight may be summed up thus: We had attacked a considerable force; had driven it over three miles; captured five thousand prisoners, and killed and wounded many thousands. Our own loss was not heavy, though a few brigades suffered severely.

Unfortunately, however, the enemy, driven through Gettysburg, got possession of the high range of hills south and east of the town. Here was the fatal mistake of the Confederates. In the engagement of July 1st, the enemy had but a small portion of his force up, and if the attack had been pressed in the afternoon of that day there is little doubt that our forces could have got the heights and captured this entire detachment of Meade's army. But General Lee was not aware of the enemy's weakness on this day. In fact, he had found himself unexpectedly confronted by the Federal army. He never had intended to fight a general battle so far from his base. He was forced to deliver battle where prudence would have avoided it; he could obtain no certain information of the disposition of Meade's forces; and the inaction of an evening—the failure to follow up for a few hours a success—enabled the Federal commander to bring up his whole army, and post it on an almost impregnable line which we had permitted a routed detachment of a few thousand men to occupy.

During the night General Meade and staff came up to the front. Before morning all his troops but the Sixth Corps, commanded by General Sedgwick, arrived on the field. The forces of the enemy were disposed on the several hills or ridges, so as to construct a battle line in the form of a crescent.

The town of Gettysburg is on the northern slope of this ridge of hills or mountain range, and one and a half or two miles from its summit. The western slope of this range was in cultivation, except small patches, where the mountainside is so precipitous as to defy the efforts of the farmer to bring it into subjection to the ploughshare. At the foot of the mountain is a narrow valley, from a mile to two miles in width, broken in small ridges running parallel with the mountain. On the western side of the valley rises a long, high hill, mostly covered with heavy timber, but greatly inferior in altitude to the mountain range upon which the enemy had taken position, but running nearly parallel with it. The valley between this ridge and the mountain was in cultivation, and the fields were yellow with the golden harvest. About four or five miles south from Gettysburg the mountain rises abruptly to an altitude of several hundred feet. Upon this the enemy rested his left flank, his right being upon the crest of the range a mile or a mile and a half from Gettysburg.

Our line of battle was formed along the western slope of the second and inferior range described above, and in the following order: Ewell's corps on the left, beginning at the town with Early's division, then Rodes's division; on the right of Rodes's division was the left of Hill's corps, beginning with Heth's, then Pender's and Anderson's divisions. On the right of Anderson's division was Longstreet's left, McLaws's division being next to Anderson's, and Hood on the extreme right of our line, which was opposite the eminence upon which the enemy's left rested.

The preparations for attack were not completed until the afternoon of the 2d. Late in the afternoon an artillery attack was made by our forces on the left and centre of the enemy, which was rapidly followed by the advance of our infantry, Longstreet's corps on our side being principally engaged. A fearful but indecisive contest ensued, and for four hours the sound of musketry was incessant. The main object of the attack of the Confederates was the famous Cemetery Hill, the key of the enemy's position. The enemy's artillery replied vigorously. The roar and thunder and flame and smoke of artillery and the screech of shells so completely filled the heavens that all else seemed forgotten.

General Ewell had been ordered to attack directly the high ground on the enemy's right, which had already been partially fortified. It was half an hour of sunset when Johnson's infantry were ordered forward to the attack. In passing down the hill on which they had been posted, and while crossing the creek, they were much annoyed by the fire to which they were subjected from the enemy's artillery, which from Cemetery Hill poured nearly an enfilade fire upon them. The creek was wide and its banks were steep, so that our men had to break ranks to cross it. Having passed the creek, General Jones's brigade was thrown into disorder and retired a short distance.

On the extreme left General G. H. Steuart's brigade was more successful. Pushing around to the enemy's left, he enfiladed and drove the enemy from a breastwork which they had built in order to defend their right flank, and which ran at right angles to the rest of their lines up the mountainside. The enemy, however, quickly moved forward a force to retake it, but were repulsed, our troops occupying their own breastworks in order to receive their attack. General Steuart made no further effort to advance. Night had nearly fallen, and the ground was new to him.

General Early, upon hearing General Johnson's infantry engaged, sent forward Hays's Louisiana and Hoke's North Carolina brigades. The troops, advancing as a storming-party, quickly passed over a ridge and down a hill. In a valley below they met two lines of the Federals posted behind stone walls. These they charged. At the charge the Federals broke and fled up the hill closely pursued by our men. It was now dark; but Hays and Avery, still pursuing, pushed the enemy up the hill and stormed the Cemetery heights.

The contest here was intensely exciting and terrible. The gloom of the falling night was lighted up by the flashes of the enemy's guns. Thirty or forty pieces, perhaps more, were firing canister with inconceivable rapidity at Early's column. It must have been that they imagined this to be a general and simultaneous advance, for they opened on our men in three or four directions besides that which they were attacking.

Hays's and Hoke's brigades pressed on and captured two or

three lines of breastworks and three or four of their batteries of artillery. For a few moments every gun of the enemy on the heights was silenced; but, by the time General Hays could get his command together, a dark line appeared in front of them and on either flank a few yards off. The true situation soon became clear. The Federals were bringing up at least a division to retake the works. General Hays, being unsupported by the troops on his right (which were from Hill's corps), was compelled to fall back.

Major-General Rodes began to advance simultaneously with General Early. He had, however, more than double the distance of Early to go, and being unsupported by the troops on his right, who made no advance, he consequently moved slower than he would have moved had he been supported. Before reaching the enemy's works Early had been repulsed, and so General Rodes halted, thinking it useless to attack, since he was unsupported.

When the second day closed this was the position of Ewell's corps: Johnson's left had gained important ground, part of it being a very short distance from the top of the mountain, which, if once gained, would command the whole of the enemy's position; but his right had made no progress. Early's attack, almost a brilliant success, had produced no results, and he occupied nearly his former position. Rodes, having advanced nearly half way to the enemy's works, and finding there good cover for his troops, remained in his advanced position.

But we must take the reader's attention to another part of the field, where a more dramatic circumstance than Early's momentary grasp of victory had occurred. General Hill had been instructed to threaten the centre of the Federal line, in order to prevent reënforcements being sent to either wing, and to avail himself of any opportunity that might present itself to attack.

On the right of Hill's corps and the left of Longstreet, being joined on to Barksdale's brigade of McLaws's division, was Wilcox's brigade, then Perry's, Wright's, Posey's, Mahone's. At half-past five o'clock Longstreet began the attack, and Wilcox followed it up by promptly moving forward; Perry's brigade quickly followed, and Wright moved simultaneously with him. The two divisions of Longstreet's corps soon encountered the enemy, posted a little in rear of the Emmetsburg turnpike, which winds along the slope of the range upon which the enemy's main force was concentrated. After a short but spirited engagement the enemy was driven back upon the main line upon the crest of the hill. McLaws's and Hood's divisions made a desperate assault upon the main line, but, owing to the precipitate and rugged character of the slope, were unable to reach the summit.

After Barksdale's brigade, of McLaws's division, had been engaged for some time, Wilcox, Wright, and Perry were ordered forward, encountering a line of the enemy and soon putting them to rout. Still pressing forward, these three brigades met with another and stronger line of the enemy, backed by twelve pieces of artillery. No pause was made. The line moved rapidly forward and captured the artillery.

Another fresh line of battle was thrown forward by the enemy. Wright had swept over the valley under a terrific fire from the batteries posted upon the heights, had encountered the enemy's advance line, and had driven it across the Emmetsburg pike, to a position behind a stone wall or fence which runs parallel with the pike and sixty or eighty yards in front of the batteries on the heights and immediately under them. Here the enemy made a desperate attempt to retrieve his fortunes. The engagement lasted fifteen or twenty minutes. Charging up the steep sides of the mountains, the Confederates succeeded in driving the enemy from behind the wall at the point of the bayonet. Rushing forward with a shout, they gained the summit of the heights, driving the enemy's infantry in disorder and confusion into the woods beyond.

The key of the enemy's position was for a moment in our hands. But the condition of the brave troops who had wrested it by desperate valor had become critical in the extreme. Wilcox, Perry, and Wright had charged most gallantly over a distance of more than three-quarters of a mile, breaking two or three of the enemy's lines of battle and capturing two or three batteries of artillery. Of course our lines were greatly thinned, and our troops much exhausted. No reënforcements were sent to this column by the lieutenant-general commanding. The extent of the success was not instantly appreciated. A decisive moment was lost.

Wright's little brigade of Georgians had actually got into the enemy's intrenchments upon the heights. Perceiving, after getting possession of the enemy's works, that they were isolated —more than a mile from support—that no advance had been made on their left, and just then seeing the enemy's flanking column on their right and left flanks rapidly converging in their rear, these noble Georgians faced about, abandoning all the guns they had captured, and cut their way back to our main lines, through the enemy, who had now almost entirely surrounded them.

The results of the day were unfortunate enough. Our troops had been repulsed at all points save where Brigadier-General Steuart held his ground. A second day of desperate fighting and correspondingly frightful carnage was ended. But General Lee still believed himself and his brave army capable of taking these commanding heights, and thus able to dictate a peace on the soil of the free States.

The third day's battle was again to be begun by the Confederates. At midnight a council of war had been held by the enemy, at which it was determined that the Confederates would probably renew the attack at daylight on the following morning, and that for that day the Federals had better act purely on the defensive.

The enemy's position on the mountain was wellnigh impregnable, for there was no conceivable advance or approach that could not be raked and crossed with the artillery. All the heights and every advantageous position along the entire line where artillery could be massed or a battery planted frowned down on the Confederates through brows of brass and iron. On the slopes of the mountain was to occur one of the most terrific combats of modern times, in which more than two hundred cannon were belching forth their thunders at one time, and nearly two hundred thousand muskets were being discharged as rapidly as men hurried with excitement and passion could load them.

Early in the morning preparations were made for a general attack along the enemy's whole line, while a large force was to be concentrated against his centre, with the view of retaking the heights captured and abandoned the day before. Longstreet massed a large number of long-range guns (fifty-five) upon the crest of a slight eminence just in front of Perry's and Wilcox's brigades and a little to the left of the heights upon which they were to open. Hill massed some sixty guns along the hill in front of Posey's and Mahone's brigades and almost immediately in front of the heights. At twelve o'clock, while the signal-flags were waving swift intelligence along our lines, the shrill sound of a Whitworth gun broke the silence, and the cannonading began.

The enemy replied with terrific spirit, from their batteries posted along the heights. Never had been heard such tremendous artillery firing in the war. The warm and sultry air was hideous with discord. Dense columns of smoke hung over the beautiful valley. The lurid flame leaps madly from the cannon's mouth, each moment the roar grows more intense; now chime in volleys of small-arms. For one hour and a half this most terrific fire was continued, during which time the shrieking of shells, the crashing of falling timber, the fragments of rock flying through the air, shattered from the cliffs by solid shot, the heavy mutterings from the valley between the opposing armies, the splash of bursting shrapnel, and the fierce neighing of wounded horses made a picture terribly grand and sublime.

But there was now to occur a scene of moral sublimity and heroism unequalled in the war. The storming-party was moved up—Pickett's division in advance, supported on the right by Wilcox's brigade, and on the left by Heth's division, commanded by Pettigrew. With steady measured tread the division of Pickett advanced upon the foe. Never did troops enter a fight in such splendid order. Their banners floated defiantly in the breeze as they pressed across the plain. The flags which had waved amid the wild tempest of battle at Gaines's Mill, Frayser's Farm, and Manassas never rose more proudly. Kemper, with his gallant men, leads the right; Garnett brings up the left; and the veteran Armistead, with his brave troops, moves forward in support. The distance is more than half a mile. As they advance, the enemy fire with great rapidity—shell and solid shot give place to canister—the very earth quivers beneath the heavy roar—wide gaps are made in this regiment and that brigade. The line moves onward, cannons roaring, shells and canister plunging and ploughing through the ranks, bullets whizzing as thick as hailstones in winter, and men falling as leaves fall in the blasts of autumn.

As Pickett got well under the enemy's fire, our batteries ceased firing, for want, it is said, of ammunition. It was a fearful moment, one in which was to be tested the pride and mettle of glorious Virginia. Into the sheets of artillery fire advanced the unbroken lines of Pickett's brave Virginians. They have reached the Emmetsburg road, and here they meet a severe fire from heavy masses of the enemy's infantry, posted behind the stone fence, while their artillery, now free from the annoyance of our artillery, turn their whole fire upon this devoted band. Still they remain firm. Now again they advance. They reach the works—the contest rages with intense fury—men fight almost hand to hand—the Red Cross and the Stars and Stripes wave defiantly in close proximity. A Federal officer dashes forward in front of his shrinking columns, and with flashing sword urges them to stand. The noble Garnett is dead, Armistead wounded, and the brave Kemper, with hat in hand, still cheering on his men, falls from his horse. But Kemper and Armistead have already planted their banners in the enemy's works. The glad shout of victory is already heard.[1]

[1] A correspondent of a Northern paper thus alludes to the traces of the struggle at the cemetery: "Monuments and headstones lie here and there overturned. Graves, once carefully tended by some loving hand, have been trampled by horses' feet until the vestiges of verdure have disappeared. The neat and well-trained shrubbery has vanished, or is but a broken and withered mass of tangled brushwood. On one grave lies a dead artillery horse fast decomposing under a July sun. On another lie the torn garments of some wounded soldier, stained and saturated with his blood. Across a small headstone bearing the words 'To the memory of our beloved child Mary' lie the fragments of a musket, shattered by a cannon-shot. In the centre of the space enclosed by an iron fence and containing a half-dozen graves, a few rails are still standing where they were erected by our soldiers and served to support the shelter tents of a bivouacking squad. A family shaft has been broken to fragments by a shell, and only the base remains, with a portion of the inscription thereon. Stone after stone felt the effect of the *feu d'enfer* that was poured upon the crest of the hill. Cannon thundered, and foot and horse soldiers trampled over the sleeping-places of the dead. Other dead were added to those who are resting there, and many a wounded soldier still lives to remember the contest above those silent graves."

But where is Pettigrew's division? where are the supports? The raw troops had faltered and the gallant Pettigrew himself had been wounded in vain attempts to rally them. Alas, the victory was to be relinquished again. Pickett is left alone to contend with the masses of the enemy now pouring in upon him on every side. Now the enemy move around strong flanking bodies of infantry, and are rapidly gaining Pickett's rear. The order is given to fall back, and our men begin the movement, doggedly contesting for every inch of ground. The enemy press heavily our retreating line, and many noble spirits who had passed safely through the fiery ordeal of the advance and charge now fall on the right and on the left.

This division of Virginia troops, small at first, with ranks now torn and shattered, most of the officers killed or wounded, no valor able to rescue victory from such a grasp, annihilation or capture inevitable, slowly, reluctantly fell back. It was not given to these few remaining brave men to accomplish human impossibilities. The enemy dared not follow them beyond their works. But the day was already lost. The field was covered with Confederates slowly and sulkily retiring in small parties under a heavy fire of artillery. There was no panic.

Never did a commanding general behave better in such trying circumstances than did Lee. He was truly great in disaster. An English colonel who witnessed the fight says: "I joined General Lee, who had in the mean while come to the front on becoming aware of the disaster. General Lee was perfectly sublime. He was engaged in rallying and encouraging the broken troops, and was riding about a little in front of the wood quite alone—the whole of his staff being engaged in a similar manner farther to the rear. His face, which is always placid and cheerful, did not show signs of the slightest disappointment, care, or annoyance, and he was addressing to every soldier he met a few words of encouragement, such as, 'All this will come right in the end; we'll talk it over afterward; but in the mean time all good men must rally. We want all good and true men just now.' He spoke to all the wounded men that passed him, and the slightly wounded he exhorted 'to bind up their hurts and take up a musket' in this emergency. Very few failed to answer his appeal, and I saw many badly wounded men take off their hats and cheer him."

At night the Confederate army held the same position from which it had driven the enemy two days previous. The starry sky hung over a field of hideous carnage. In the series of engagements a few pieces of artillery were captured by the Confederates and nearly seven thousand prisoners taken, two thousand of whom were paroled on the field. Pickett's division had been engaged in the hottest work of the day, and the havoc in its ranks was appalling. Its losses on this day are famous, and should be commemorated in detail. Every brigadier in the division was killed or wounded. Out of twenty-four regimental officers, only two escaped unhurt. The Ninth Virginia went in two hundred fifty strong, and came out with only thirty-eight men. Conspicuous in our list of casualties was the death of Major-General Pender. He had borne a distinguished part in every engagement of this army, and was wounded on several occasions while leading his command with admirable gallantry and ability. Brigadier-Generals Barksdale and Garnett were killed, and Brigadier-General Semmes mortally wounded, while leading their troops with the courage that had always distinguished them. The brave and generous spirit of Barksdale had expired, where he preferred to die, on the ensanguined field of battle.

The fearful trial of a retreat from a position far in the enemy's country was now reserved for General Lee. Happily he had an army with zeal unabated, courage intrepid, devotion unchilled, with unbounded confidence in the wisdom of that great chieftain who had so often led them to victory. The strength of the enemy's position, the reduction of our ammunition, the difficulty of procuring supplies—these left no choice but retreat.

On the night of the 4th, General Lee's army began to retire by the road to Fairfield, without any serious interruption on the part of the enemy. In passing through the mountains, in advance of the column, the great length of the trains exposed them to attack by the enemy's cavalry, which captured a number of wagons and ambulances; but they succeeded in reaching Williamsport without serious loss.

They were attacked at that place on the 6th, by the enemy's cavalry, which was gallantly repulsed by General Imboden.

The attacking force was subsequently encountered and driven off by General Stuart, and pursued for several miles in the direction of Boonsboro. The army, after an arduous march, rendered more difficult by the rains, reached Hagerstown on the afternoon of July 6th and morning of the 7th.

Any comment on Gettysburg must necessarily be a tantalizing one for the South. The Pennsylvania campaign had been a series of mishaps. General Lee was disappointed of half of his plan, in the first instance, on account of the inability or unwillingness of the Richmond authorities to assemble an army at Culpeper Court House under General Beauregard, so as to distract the enemy and divide his force by a demonstration upon Washington. Johnston was calling for reënforcements in Mississippi; Bragg was threatened with attack; Beauregard's whole force was reported to be necessary to cover his line on the seacoast; and the force in Richmond and in North Carolina was very small. Yet with what force Lee had, his campaign proposed great things—the destruction of his adversary, which would have uncovered the Middle and Eastern States of the North; for, behind Meade's array, there was nothing but militia mobs and home-guards incapable of making any resistance to an army of veterans. It was in anticipation of this great stake that Richmond was on the tiptoe of expectation. For once in the Confederate capital gold found no purchasers, prices declined, speculation was at its wits' end, and men consulted their interests as if on the eve of peace. The recoil at Gettysburg was fatal, perhaps not necessarily, but by the course of events, to General Lee's campaign, and the return of his army to its defensive lines in Virginia was justly regarded in the South as a reverse in the general fortunes of the contest.

But news of an overshadowing calamity, undoubtedly the greatest that had yet befallen the South, accompanied that of Lee's retreat, and dated a second period of disaster more frightful than that of Donelson and New Orleans. The same day that Lee's repulse was known in Richmond, came the astounding intelligence of the fall of Vicksburg. In twenty-four hours two calamities changed all the aspects of the war, and brought the South from an unequalled exaltation of hope to the very brink of despair.

ABRAHAM LINCOLN

[Soon after the Battle of Gettysburg a piece of ground about seventeen acres in extent, a part of the battle-field, was purchased for a national cemetery. This was dedicated on November 19th with imposing ceremonies, and President Lincoln's brief address on the occasion has become one of the classics of our literature. —EDITOR.]

Fourscore and seven years ago our fathers brought forth upon this continent a new nation, conceived in liberty, and dedicated to the proposition that all men are created equal. Now we are engaged in a great civil war, testing whether that nation, or any nation so conceived and so dedicated, can long endure. We are met on a great battle-field of that war. We have come to dedicate a portion of that field as a final resting-place for those who here gave their lives that that nation might live. It is altogether fitting and proper that we should do this. But in a larger sense we cannot dedicate, we cannot consecrate, we cannot hallow this ground. The brave men, living and dead, who struggled here have consecrated it far above our power to add or detract. The world will little note, nor long remember, what we say here, but it can never forget what they did here. It is for us, the living, rather to be dedicated here to the unfinished work which they who fought here have thus far so nobly advanced. It is rather for us to be here dedicated to the great task remaining before us, that from these honored dead we take increased devotion to that cause for which they gave the last full measure of devotion; that we here highly resolve that these dead shall not have died in vain; that this nation, under God, shall have a new birth of freedom, and that government of the people, by the people, and for the people shall not perish from the earth.

THE FALL OF VICKSBURG

A.D. 1863

CHARLES A. DANA AND JAMES H. WILSON

Vicksburg had a double importance for the Confederacy. Its height, at a bend of the Mississippi, gave its guns command of the river, so that the National vessels could not pass up or down. Even more important than this was the fact that a large part of the supplies for the Confederate armies was drawn from the country west of the Mississippi. These were brought by rail to a point opposite Vicksburg, ferried across, and again loaded upon rail-cars and carried to the east. The capture of the city, therefore, would rob the Confederacy of both these advantages. Grant first approached the place from the north, but found that the natural protection of swamps and a network of bayous made capture from that side impossible. He then crossed the Mississippi with his entire army, marched down the west side to a point below the city, recrossed to the eastern shore, and then moving northward and eastward fought the battles and began the siege that are so clearly described in the narrative of Dana and Wilson that here follows.

AFTER Beauregard's retirement, the Richmond authorities put the control of all their military operations in the Southwest into the hands of Joseph E. Johnston, who made his headquarters with Bragg, receiving daily reports from all parts of his extensive command. Pemberton gave him the impression that Grant would relinquish the campaign against Vicksburg, but he sadly misconceived the temper of his adversary.

During the progress of the battle near Port Gibson, Johnston ordered reënforcements from Tennessee, South Carolina, and Georgia, and directed Pemberton to gather all his forces and "drive Grant into the river"; but that officer was not only incapable of doing this, but of understanding the principles of warfare upon which the order was based. Instead of abandoning Vicksburg at once and concentrating his entire force in the direction of Jackson—a railroad centre—he collected his troops within the fortifications that had already shown their inutility, and waited for the blow that was menacing him.

In pursuance of Grant's instructions, Hurlbut sent out from

West Tennessee, in the latter part of April, a detachment of cavalry under Colonel Grierson, with instructions to ride through Mississippi for the purpose of destroying Confederate property, breaking the railroads, and scattering Confederate conscripts, and finally joining either Grant or Banks, as circumstances should determine. This raid proved to be eminently successful, demonstrating clearly to the country that the Confederacy was but a shell—empty within, and strong only on the outside—a piece of information upon which Grant was by no means slow to act.

Sherman, with the Fifteenth Corps, joined the army on May 8th; wagons and supplies had been brought forward in the mean while, and definite information obtained touching the enemy's movements. Grant's force was now not far from forty-five thousand men, and everything was in excellent condition when the word for the advance was given. His plan was to sweep around to the eastward of the Big Black, with Sherman's and McClernand's corps, marching by the roads toward Edwards's Depot and Bolton, on the Vicksburg and Jackson Railroad, while McPherson was to be thrown well out toward the interior—if necessary, as far as Jackson—by the way of Raymond. Rations of sugar, coffee, and salt, together with "three days of hard bread to last five," were issued to the troops; everything else was to be gathered from the country. In pursuance of these instructions, the different corps pushed forward, encountering little or no resistance.

On May 12th McPherson's leading division, under command of the gallant and irrepressible Logan, encountered the enemy in strong force under Gregg and Walker, recently arrived from Port Gibson and Georgia, posted on the north side of Fondreau's Creek, near Raymond, and after a brilliant combat of several hours, in which a part of Crocker's division became finally engaged, drove them from the field, with the loss of 120 killed and 750 wounded and prisoners. Our losses were 69 killed (from Colonel Richards's Twentieth Illinois Infantry and Major Kaga's Twentieth Ohio), 341 wounded, and 32 missing. The Confederate force was about 6000 strong, and fought well. McPherson and Logan behaved with great gallantry and displayed excellent generalship in this affair, while Stevenson, Dennis, Lieutenant-Colonel Sturgis of the Eighth Illinois, and all the officers and men showed the highest soldierly qualities.

This battle, in which a second detachment of the enemy had been routed, gave Grant great confidence in the following steps of the campaign. Instead of pushing McClernand and Sherman, who had both crossed Fourteen-mile Creek and got within seven miles of Edwards's Depot, directly upon the latter place, he determined to make sure of Jackson first, and to scatter the force now known to be assembling there under Johnston in person. To this end McPherson was pushed toward that place by the Clinton road; Sherman was ordered to move rapidly by the way of Raymond and Mississippi Springs, to the same place; while McClernand was directed to withdraw by his right flank from his menacing position in front of Edwards's Depot, and to march to Raymond, whence he could support either McPherson or Sherman. These movements were made with precision and celerity, and on the 14th Grant entered Jackson in triumph, after a sharp fight of several hours between McPherson's leading division under Crocker and a force under Johnston. The latter, finding that the city could not be held, had posted guns in front of Sherman and thrown this force out upon the Clinton road for the purpose of resisting McPherson's advance long enough to permit the evacuation of the city by the Canton road. Large quantities of military stores, including six or eight guns and an abundant supply of sugar, fell into Federal hands. Grant was one of the first to perceive the ruse which his wily antagonist had adopted, and at once galloped into the town, followed by the troops.

Charging Sherman with the demolition of the bridge across Pearl River, and the destruction of Confederate military property not needed by the army—not forgetting the railroads north, south, east, and west—Grant apprised McClernand that evening of his success, and directed him to move Carr, Osterhaus, and Hovey, the next morning, toward Bolton Station, and A. J. Smith toward Edwards's Depot. General Francis P. Blair, commanding a division of Sherman's troops, not yet arrived, and Ransom, with a brigade of McPherson's corps, were also directed to move upon the same point. Soon after arriving at Jackson, Grant learned that Johnston had sent, the night before, three different couriers with positive orders for Pemberton, requiring him to march out and fall upon the rear of the National army. Without giving McPherson an hour's rest, Grant directed him to countermarch his corps and push with all possible haste toward Bolton, for the purpose of uniting with McClernand's corps and anticipating the attack. Sherman was left to finish the work which he had so thoroughly begun, and then to follow the main body of the army by the Clinton road.

Grant in person left Jackson on the morning of the 15th, and encamped that night at Clinton. Before daylight on the 16th he was informed by two citizens just from Vicksburg that they had passed Pemberton's entire army, estimated at twenty-five or thirty thousand men, the evening before, at Baker's Creek, and still marching toward Bolton. Their information was so explicit and circumstantial that Grant despatched a staff officer at once to McPherson and McClernand with orders to prepare for a general battle, but not to bring on the action till all the troops were thoroughly in hand. A short time afterward he rode rapidly to the front himself, arriving on the field about ten o'clock. He found Hovey's division with artillery posted and drawn out in line of battle at Champion's plantation, on the Edwards Depot road, two miles east of Baker's Creek; McPherson's corps was in readiness to support Hovey; McClernand, with Carr and Osterhaus, occupied a position on the same line, on the middle road from Raymond to Edwards's Depot, but about a mile and a half to the left of Hovey; while Blair and A. J. Smith were still farther to the left, converging on the same point. Sherman at the same time was well on the way from Jackson.

Grant threw forward Logan's division to the right of Hovey, and gave the latter orders to advance. The skirmishing had already become pretty hot, and by twelve o'clock the troops of both armies were in full battle array. A prelude of sharp skirmishing, with an occasional shot from the cannon of either side, introduced the terrible shock of arms that followed. The Confederates held the advantage in position, their lines being formed along the heavily wooded ridges lying in the bend of Baker's Creek. Their centre on the main road held Champion's Hill, the key-point of the field. Upon this point Hovey impelled his enthusiastic men with terrible vigor, and by two o'clock had carried it in the handsomest manner, capturing four guns and several hundred prisoners. The enemy did all in his power to withstand the onset, but was steadily pressed back. Logan advanced almost simultaneously with Hovey, pushing through an open field, along the northern slopes of Champion's Hill, and also driving back the enemy in his front. In the mean time the enemy had rallied in Hovey's front and, being strongly reënforced, threw themselves upon him with great determination, in their turn pressing him back and threatening to wrest from him the heights he had gained at such a fearful cost.

At this critical juncture McPherson, who had fortunately brought forward Crocker's division and posted it behind the interval between Hovey and Logan, under Grant's direction, ordered it at once to the support of Hovey, whose hard-pressed regiments were now greatly fatigued and some of them entirely out of ammunition. Boomer's brigade, on the left, was marched rapidly by the flank to the top of the hill, and reached it just in time to catch the full force of the Confederate onset. For fifteen minutes the rattle of musketry was incessant. At the same time several batteries had been collected near Grant's headquarters, and converging their fire upon the woods from which the enemy was emerging, Boomer was enabled to drive them back with great loss. McPherson and Logan were meanwhile swinging the right of the line well forward, steadily driving the enemy, and finally overlapping his left and striking him in the flank and rear, capturing two batteries and nearly a thousand prisoners. This movement, in connection with Boomer's splendid assault, resulted in driving the enemy from the field, broken and routed. By four o'clock they were fleeing in confusion rapidly toward Vicksburg. McClernand, although frequently ordered, did not succeed in getting either Carr or Osterhaus heavily engaged. Smith and Blair were too far to the left to produce any decided effect, although their artillery and skirmishers were engaged with Loring's division for a short time. Ransom marched across the country toward the heaviest firing and joined McPherson after the action had ceased.

The victory could scarcely have been more complete, and, as has been seen, it was gained almost entirely by three divisions—Hovey's, Logan's, and Crocker's—not exceeding fifteen thousand men in all, while the Confederates could not have been fewer than twenty-five thousand. The Southern historians excuse this defeat also on the ground that they were vastly outnumbered; and it is true that Grant had in the short space of twenty-four hours transformed the rear of his army into the full front of it, concentrating about thirty-five thousand men in all within supporting distance of each other, but it is also true that he won the battle with less than one-half of this force. His combinations were admirable; nothing in warfare was ever more praiseworthy, and had McClernand forced the fighting in his immediate front, as did Hovey, Boomer, and Logan, under Grant's immediate supervision, it is difficult to see how any part of the enemy's forces could have escaped. As it was, they lost about 500 killed, including General Tilghman, 2200 wounded, and 2000 prisoners, besides 18 guns and a large number of small arms. Grant's loss (mostly in Hovey's division and Boomer's brigade) was 426 killed, 1842 wounded, and 189 missing; total, 2457.

The pursuit was continued to Edwards's Depot that night, the leading troops capturing at that place an ammunition-train of ten or twelve railroad-cars. At dawn of the 17th the pursuit was renewed in the direction of Vicksburg; and by seven o'clock McClernand's advance, under Osterhaus and Carr, came up with the Confederate rear-guard posted in strong intrenchments nearly a mile in extent, covering the railroad and military bridges across the Big Black. These divisions were developed without delay under a strong fire from the Confederate artillery, during which Osterhaus was wounded. Carr held the right, his right brigade, commanded by General Lawler, resting upon the Big Black. After some desultory artillery firing and skirmishing, Lawler found a weak place on the extreme left of the enemy's works, and lost no time in leading his brigade, composed of Iowa and Wisconsin men, to the assault. Advancing across an open field several hundred yards in width, they received a deady fire, but without faltering they rushed gallantly through the ditch and over the breastworks, sweeping away all opposition and capturing eighteen guns and nearly two thousand prisoners. In this gallant affair Colonel Kinsman of the Twenty-third Iowa was killed, and Colonel Merrill of the Twenty-first was wounded—both, while cheering forward their men in the most conspicuous manner.

This put an end to the campaign in the open field. Pemberton immediately abandoned his camp on the Big Black, and retreated in disorder to Vicksburg. Johnston had gone in the direction of Canton, but did not attempt a diversion in Pemberton's favor, though he might have fallen upon Sherman's flank and harassed him considerably.

During the night four floating bridges were built across the Big Black by the troops under the direction of the engineer officers. McClernand built one out of the ruins of the railroad bridge, near the railroad crossing; McPherson built two farther up the river, one of timber obtained by pulling down cotton-gin houses, the other of cotton-bales rafted together; while Sherman made his of the india-rubber pontoons. After nightfall Grant rode up the river to see Sherman, whom he found at Bridgeport engaged in crossing his command. The two commanders crossed the bridge and seated themselves on a fallen tree, in the light of a pile of burning fence-rails, and had a friendly conference, while the eager and swift-marching men of the Fifteenth Corps filed by them and disappeared in the darkness. Grant recounted the results of the campaign and detailed his plans for the next day, after which he returned through the forest to his own headquarters.

On the next day, May 18th, the army marched by the various roads to the rear of Vicksburg, and after slight skirmishing drove the Confederate pickets inside of their works. Communication by signal was opened at once with the gunboats and transports lying above Vicksburg, and measures were taken to establish communications with Yazoo River. The enemy had already evacuated Haines's Bluff, and the navy took possession of the place, and proceeded to burn the gun-carriages, camps, and stores, and to blow up the magazines. This, however, was done in mistaken zeal, and inflicted an actual damage upon the Federal army rather than upon the enemy.

Within these eighteen days Grant had won five battles; taken 40 field-guns, many colors and small arms, and nearly 5000 prisoners; killed or wounded 5200 of the enemy; separated their armies, in the aggregate nearly 60,000 strong; captured one fortified capital city; compelled the abandonment of the strong positions of Grand Gulf and Haines's Bluff, with their armament of 20 heavy guns; destroyed the railroads and bridges; and made the investment of Vicksburg complete. In doing this

McPherson's and McClernand's corps had marched an average of 156 miles, while Sherman's had marched 175 miles. During this time the united strength of these three corps did not exceed 45,000 men. There is nothing in history since Hannibal invaded Italy to compare with the surpassing boldness and vigor of the generalship displayed by Grant in conducting this campaign.

The Confederates, though badly beaten, were at last concentrated within the fortifications of Vicksburg, and availing themselves of its great advantages they were enabled to make a protracted and desperate defence. In order that the reader may have a definite understanding of this position and the difficulties that still remained for the Union army to overcome, let him imagine a plateau two hundred fifty feet above the surface of the Mississippi, originally level, or sloping off gently toward the Big Black, but now cut and seamed in all directions by ravines from eighty to a hundred feet deep, with steep sides made more difficult by a heavy growth of fallen timber, which the Confederates had cut down for the purpose of encumbering the ground and giving them fair range upon troops trying to advance over it. These ravines leading into three creeks flowing into the Mississippi, one just above Vicksburg, another within its limits, and the third entirely below it, were divided by high and difficult ridges, along which had been thrown up a series of open and closed redoubts, armed with artillery and connected by single and double lines of well-constructed rifle-trench for infantry. The entire line, including three miles of river front, was nearly eight miles in extent, for the defence of which the Confederate General had something more than twenty thousand effective men.

Grant's army was posted in the following order: Sherman's corps, composed of Steele's, Blair's, and Tuttle's divisions, held the right, extending from the ridge road around to the river; McPherson, with Logan's, Crocker's, and Quinby's divisions, held the centre on both sides of the Jackson road; while McClernand, with Carr's, A. J. Smith's, Osterhaus's, and Hovey's divisions, held the left, extending well around to the south side of the city. The ground had been reconnoitred in front of the different divisions, and although seen to be exceedingly difficult it was not regarded as impassable. Grant had been informed by his cavalry that Johnston was gathering a strong force on the east side of the Big Black with which to fall upon his rear, and knowing that Pemberton's army must still be in considerable disorder, if not actually too much demoralized to make a determined resistance, he decided upon an assault of the enemy's line.

Accordingly he issued orders for all the field-batteries to open fire upon the enemy's works at half-past one, and that at precisely two o'clock the entire army should move to the attack. These orders were promptly obeyed; the batteries poured forth an incessant fire for more than a half-hour at close range, dismounting and silencing nearly all the enemy's guns; and promptly at the time appointed the infantry sprang cheerfully forward, confident of sweeping over the works as they had done at the Big Black bridge. Steele, Blair, Logan, and Carr made fair headway, but the Confederates replied with spirit and with deadly effect. The ground was too much broken and encumbered with fallen timber and regular abattis; no order could be maintained among the troops, though every effort was made to carry them forward even in disarray; but it was impossible. The Thirteenth Regulars, Eighty-third Indiana, and One Hundred and Twenty-seventh Illinois planted their colors on the parapet, but officers and men alike perceived their inability to do more, and suspended the attack. The National loss was considerable, with no adequate gain except a more advanced position and a better understanding of the ground in front of the works.

The failure of this attempt did not, however, cut off all hope of carrying the place without resorting to the laborious process of a siege. The troops were permitted to rest for a while; roads were opened along the lines of investment, and to the new bases of supplies at Chickasaw Landing and Warrenton; provisions and ammunition were brought forward, and everything was got in readiness for a new trial. At 6 P.M. of the 21st Grant issued orders directing that at 10 A.M. the next day a general attack should be made along the entire line and particularly on all the roads leading into Vicksburg. In pursuance of these instructions the troops moved forward at the appointed time, but, owing to the broken ground over which they were compelled to march, it was soon found to be impossible to move either in well-ordered lines or in weighty effective columns.

As before, officers and men from right to left did their best. Sherman's troops reached the parapet of the works in their front, and planted their colors upon them, but could not cross. Logan's division of McPherson's corps, headed by Stevenson's brigade, made a gallant and orderly advance, but the position they assailed was the strongest part of the line, and they were compelled to fall back, after losing heavily. Lawler's brigade of McClernand's corps, remembering their success at Big Black River bridge, dashed forward in handsome style, and at one time seemed about to add a new victory to the number already inscribed upon their tattered colors. Sergeant Griffith, with a handful of men from the leading regiment, actually crossed the parapet and captured a number of prisoners, but the regiment found it impossible to follow him. After holding on at the ditch of the works for several hours, they were compelled to fall back.

This partial success was magnified by McClernand into the capture of "several points of the enemy's intrenchments." He therefore called upon Grant for reënforcements, expressing his confidence that with them he could take the city. Grant, from his headquarters, had witnessed the attack along McClernand's front, and therefore doubted the propriety of sending reënforcements, but, fearing that he might underestimate the advantages which had been gained, he reluctantly consented to send one of McPherson's divisions, and instructed that officer accordingly. He also informed him and Sherman of what McClernand claimed to have done, and directed them to renew the attack. McPherson sent Quinby's division from his left, Boomer's brigade leading. The attack was renewed again, and this time with still more disastrous results. The gallant Boomer was killed, and the list of casualties throughout the army largely increased. Simultaneously with the land attack Admiral Porter attacked the river-front, both from above and below, but, although he used ammunition without stint, he could not silence the enemy's guns.

It had now become apparent that the Confederates could not be dislodged except by a siege or starvation. Grant therefore determined to try both. He sent to West Tennessee for all the troops that could be spared there. Halleck, with great alacrity, gathered all that could be dispensed with in West Virginia, Kentucky, and Missouri, and sent them forward. Herron's division of the Thirteenth, Lauman's of the Seventeenth, Kimball's and Sooy Smith's of the Sixteenth Corps under Washburn, and the Ninth Corps under Parke, were brought forward in succession as fast as steamboats could be found to transport them; so that within a fortnight the besieging army was more than seventy-five thousand effective men. In order to prevent the escape of the garrison, Grant completed the investment of the lines, established batteries on the peninsula in front of the city, and stationed a force at Milliken's Bend. For the purpose of rendering his own lines secure, he caused all the roads leading toward the Big Black to be obstructed by felling trees in them.

Sherman with a corps of observation, consisting of about twenty thousand men, drawn from the investing force, and further strengthened by the Ninth Corps, was thrown out to the northeastward for the purpose of watching the movements of Johnston, now threatening the line of the Black River with more than twenty thousand men. Sherman established a strong line of detached works, extending from a point near Bridgeport on the Big Black, by the way of Tiffinton and Milldale, to the Yazoo; Osterhaus kept watch over the Big Black below the railroad crossing; while Washburn established a strongly fortified camp on Sherman's left, at Haines's Bluff.

During all this time the siege operations were pushed steadily forward night and day; parallels and trenches were opened at every favorable point; batteries were built and cavaliers erected; heavy guns were borrowed from the navy and mounted on commanding points; roads were made; siege materials were prepared; mines were sunk; towers for sharpshooters were built; every means that ingenuity could devise was brought to bear upon the work in hand. Wooden mortars were made for throwing grenades and small shells; and sharpshooters were kept constantly on the watch for the luckless Confederates who might show themselves above their works. So accurate and destructive was their fire that after the first four or five days every Confederate gun was silenced, and, when the place was finally taken, hundreds of men were found in the hospitals, who had been wounded in their hands and arms while raising them above the parapet to ram cartridges.

Immediately after the assault of May 22d McClernand issued a bombastic order of congratulation to his command, claiming for them most of the honor of the campaign, and indirectly censuring Grant and casting unjust reflections upon Sherman and McPherson. These officers protested to Grant, sending him a copy of the order, which they had cut from a newspaper. This was the first information Grant had received of the existence of such an order, McClernand having failed to transmit directly to him a copy as required by regulations. Grant inquired of McClernand whether the newspaper copy was correct, and, if so, why he had not complied with the rules of the service in forwarding it to army headquarters. McClernand's answer was defiant in the extreme. Grant, therefore, relieved him from command, and assigned Ord to the Thirteenth Corps. This secured entire harmony throughout the army.

McPherson's mine in front of Logan's division was exploded at 4 P.M. on June 26th, throwing a number of Confederates and a large column of earth high into the air, shaking the ground for several hundred yards like an earthquake and levelling the salient of Fort Hill. In anticipation of this effect Grant had issued orders for a demonstration along the lines, with an immediate assault upon that part of the front shaken by the explosion. The assault was made by John E. Smith's brigade, but was unsuccessful, and after suffering severe loss the troops were withdrawn.

By this time the heads of saps at various points had been pushed close up to the enemy's works, and in several instances even into the very ditches. Orders were issued that they should be widened and connected so as to permit them to be used for the protection of troops for a general and final assault.

It was known from deserters, and confirmed by voluntary information from the Confederate pickets, that their provisions were nearly exhausted. Having completed all the necessary arrangements, Grant directed that the attack should be made on the morning of July 5th; but early in the morning of the 3d the Confederate General sent out a flag of truce with a proposition for the appointment of commissioners to arrange the terms of capitulation. Grant declined to leave the matter to commissioners or to allow any other terms than those of "unconditional surrender" and humane treatment to all prisoners of war, but signified his willingness to meet and confer with General Pemberton in regard to the arrangement of details. This meeting took place between the lines, in front of McPherson's corps, and gave rise to the following ultimatum, submitted in writing by General Grant:

"In conformity with the agreement of this afternoon, I will submit the following propositions for the surrender of the city of Vicksburg, public stores, etc. On your accepting the terms proposed, I will march in one division as a guard, and take possession at 8 A.M. to-morrow. As soon as paroles can be made out and signed by the officers and men, you will be allowed to march out of our lines; the officers taking with them their regimental clothing, and staff, field, and cavalry officers one horse each. The rank and file will be allowed all their clothing, but no other property. If these conditions are accepted, any amount of rations you may deem necessary can be taken from the stores you now have, and also the necessary cooking-utensils for preparing them, and thirty wagons also, counting two two-horse or -mule teams as one. You will be allowed to transport such articles as cannot be carried along. The same conditions will be allowed to all sick and wounded officers and privates as fast as they become able to travel. The paroles of these latter must be signed, however, while officers are present authorized to sign the roll of prisoners." Pemberton answered as follows:

"GENERAL: I have the honor to acknowledge the receipt of your communication of this date, proposing terms for the surrender of this garrison and post. In the main, your terms are accepted; but, in justice both to the honor and spirit of my troops, manifested in the defence of Vicksburg, I have the honor to submit the following amendments, which, if acceded to by you, will perfect the agreement between us. At ten o'clock to-morrow I propose to evacuate the works in and around Vicksburg, and to surrender the city and garrison under my command, by marching out with my colors and arms and stacking them in front of my present lines—after which you will take possession; officers to retain their side-arms and personal property, and the rights and property of citizens to be respected."

Grant rejoined, declining to fetter himself by any stipulations in regard to citizens; limiting Confederate officers to their private baggage, side-arms, and one horse each to mounted officers, and giving him till nine o'clock to consider the matter.

On these terms the surrender took place early on July 4th. By three o'clock our troops had taken possession of the city and all public stores, the gunboats and transports had landed at the levee, and the troops charged with keeping order had gone into their camps. The Confederates were retained as prisoners for six or eight days, till their paroles could be made out and properly delivered, during which time they drew their subsistence from the National stores.

Grant's losses during the entire campaign were 943 killed, 7095 wounded, and 537 missing; total, 8575, of whom 4236 were killed or wounded before Vicksburg. The Confederates surrendered 21,000 effective men, and 6000 wounded in hosipital, besides more than 120 guns of all calibres, with many thousand small-arms.

As soon as it was known that Vicksburg would surrender, Grant reënforced Sherman, and sent him to drive off Johnston. The march was begun promptly, and pushed with celerity to Jackson, whither Johnston fled. He was dislodged from there, however, in a short time, and continued his retreat toward Meridian. Sherman did not follow him further, on account of the exceedingly hot weather and the great scarcity of water in the country east of Pearl River. Grant, therefore, permitted Sherman to return to the Black River, and to go into camp with his own corps, sending the rest of his forces to their respective corps.

Immediately after the fall of Vicksburg, Grant sent Herron's division to reënforce Banks at Port Hudson, which surrendered on July 8th; thus gaining ten thousand more prisoners and fifty guns. These were also fruits of the great campaign which Grant had just finished, and should be credited to him almost as much as to Banks.

Ransom was sent to Natchez to break up the business of bringing cattle from Texas for the support of the Confederate army. That active officer did his duty admirably, capturing about five thousand head, two thousand of which were sent to Banks, and the others issued to the Army of the Tennessee.

DESTRUCTION OF THE ALABAMA

A.D. 1864

JOHN ANCRUM WINSLOW RAPHAEL SEMMES

After the memorable victory of the Monitor over the Merrimac (March 9, 1862), there was no naval duel of like importance in the American Civil War until that which resulted in the sinking of the Confederate steam-sloop Alabama by the United States corvette Kearsarge, off Cherbourg, France, June 19, 1864. The Alabama was built and equipped for the Confederate Government, at Birkenhead, England, under the name (or number) of the 290, May 15, 1862. She was commanded by Captain Raphael Semmes, of the Confederate Navy, and carried an English crew. From the time that Semmes assumed command of her (August, 1862) to the day of her fatal encounter with the Kearsarge, the Alabama inflicted great damage upon United States commerce. In various waters she captured or sank sixty-five merchant-vessels, and before her career was ended United States shipowners saw nearly all their craft driven from the ocean or transferred to the protection of foreign flags.

In June, 1864, the Alabama, cruising homeward from India, arrived at Cherbourg, where she put in for repairs. Lying off the harbor was the Kearsarge. This vessel was launched at Portsmouth, New Hampshire, in 1861. Her commander was Captain John Ancrum Winslow, who was born in Wilmington, North Carolina, November 19, 1811, and entered the navy in 1827. Semmes might have avoided a fight with the Kearsarge, but he was desirous to increase the prestige of the Confederacy and to secure recognition of its independence by European powers.

In the two accounts here presented, the story of the famous combat is told by the rival commanders, upon whose reports historians have drawn for their narratives. With these opposing records before him, the reader may view the battle from both sides.

JOHN ANCRUM WINSLOW

ON the morning of June 19, 1864, the day being fine, with a hazy atmosphere, wind moderate from the westward, at ten o'clock was near the buoy which marks the line of shoals to the eastward of Cherbourg, and distant about three miles from the eastern entrance, which bore to the southward and westward. At twenty minutes after ten o'clock the Alabama was descried coming out of the western entrance, accompanied by the Couronne (ironclad). I had, in an interview with the Admiral at Cherbourg, assured him that in the event of an action occurring with the Alabama the position of the ships should be so far off shore that no question could be advanced about the line of jurisdiction. Accordingly, to perfect this object, and with the double purpose of drawing the Alabama so far off shore that, if disabled, she could not return, I directed the ship's head seaward and cleared for action with the battery pivoted to starboard. Having attained a point about seven miles from the shore, the head of the Kearsarge was turned short round, and the ship steered directly for the Alabama; my purpose being to run her down, or, if circumstances did not warrant it, to close in with her. Hardly had the Kearsarge come round before the Alabama sheered, presented her starboard battery, and slowed her engines. On approaching her at long range of about a mile, she opened her full broadside, the shot cutting some of our rigging, and going over and alongside of us.

Immediately I ordered more speed, but in two minutes the Alabama had loaded and again fired another broadside, and followed it with a third, without damaging us except in rigging. We had now arrived within about nine hundred yards of her, and I was apprehensive that another broadside, nearly raking as it was, would prove disastrous. Accordingly I ordered the Kearsarge sheered, and opened on the Alabama. The position of the vessels was now broadside and broadside, but it was soon apparent that Captain Semmes did not seek close action. I became then fearful lest, after some fighting, he would again make for the shore. To defeat this, I determined to keep full speed on, and, with a port helm, to run under the stern of the Alabama and rake, if he did not prevent it by sheering and keeping his broadside to us. He adopted this mode as a preventive, and, as a consequence, the Alabama was forced, with a full head of steam, into a circular track during the engagement.

The effect of this manœuvre was such that at the last of the action, when the Alabama would have made off, she was near five miles from the shore; and had the action continued from the first, in parallel lines, with her head in-shore, the line of jurisdiction would no doubt have been reached.

The firing of the Alabama from the first was rapid and wild; toward the close of the action her firing became better. Our men, who had been cautioned against rapid firing without direct aim, were much more deliberate, and the instructions given to point the heavy guns below rather than above the water-line, and clear the deck with the lighter ones, were fully observed.

I had endeavored with a port helm to close in with the Alabama, but it was not until just before the close of the action that we were in position to use grape. This was avoided, however, by her surrender. The effect of the training of our men was evident, nearly every shot from our guns telling fearfully on the Alabama; and on the seventh rotation on the circular track, she winded, setting fore-trysail and two jibs, with head in-shore.

Her speed was now retarded, and, by winding, her port broadside was presented to us, with only two guns bearing, not having been able, as I learned afterward, to shift over but one. I saw now that she was at our mercy, and a few more guns, well directed, brought down her flag. I was unable to ascertain whether it had been hauled down or shot away, but a white flag having been displayed over the stern, followed by two guns fired to leeward, our fire was reserved. Not more than two minutes had elapsed before she again opened on us with the two guns on the port side. This drew our fire again, and the Kearsarge was immediately steamed ahead and laid across her bows for raking. The white flag was still flying, and our fire was again reserved. Shortly after this her boats were seen to be lowering, and an officer in one of them came alongside and informed us that the ship had surrendered and was fast sinking. In twenty minutes from this time the Alabama went down, her mainmast, which had received a shot, breaking near the head as she sank, and her bow rising high out of the water as her stern rapidly settled.

Our two boats not disabled were at once lowered, and, as it was apparent the Alabama was settling, this officer was permitted to leave in his boat to afford assistance. An English yacht, the Deerhound, had approached near the Kearsarge at this time, when I hailed and begged the commander to run down to the Alabama, as she was fast sinking, and we had but two boats, and assist in picking up the men. He consented to do so, and steamed toward the Alabama, but the latter sank almost immediately. The Deerhound, however, sent her boats and was actively engaged, aided by several others which had come from shore. These boats were busy in bringing the wounded and others to the Kearsarge, whom we were trying to make as comfortable as possible, when it was reported to me that the Deerhound was moving off. I could not believe that the commander of that vessel could be guilty of so disgraceful an act as taking our prisoners off, and therefore took no means to prevent it, but continued to keep our boats at work rescuing the men in the water. I am sorry to say that I was mistaken. The Deerhound made off with Captain Semmes and others, and also the very officer who had come on board to surrender.

The fire of the Alabama, though it is said that she discharged three hundred seventy or more shell and shot, was not of serious damage to the Kearsarge. Thirteen or fourteen of these had taken effect in and about the hull, and sixteen or seventeen about the mast and rigging. The casualties were small, only three persons having been wounded, yet it is a matter of surprise that so few were injured, considering the number of projectiles that came aboard. Two shots passed through the port in which the thirty-twos were placed, with men stationed thickly around them, one taking effect in the hammock-netting, and the other going through the port on the opposite side; yet no one was hit, the captain of one of the guns being only knocked down by the wind of the shot, as was supposed. The fire of the Kearsarge, although only one hundred seventy-three projectiles had been discharged, according to the prisoners' accounts, was terrific. One shot alone had killed or wounded eighteen men and disabled the gun; another had entered the coal-bunkers, exploding, and completely blocked up the engine-room; and Captain Semmes says that shot and shell had taken effect in the sides of his vessel, tearing large holes by explosion, and his men were everywhere knocked down.

Of the casualties on the Alabama no correct account can be given. One hundred fifteen persons reached the shore, either in England or in France, after the action. It is known that the Alabama carried a crew, officers and men, of about one hundred fifty into Cherbourg, and that while in the Southern Ocean her complement was about one hundred seventy, but desertions had reduced this figure.

The prisoners say that a number of men came on board at Cherbourg; and, the night before the action, boats were going to and fro, and in the morning strange men were seen, who were stationed as captains of the guns. Among these there was one lieutenant (Sinclair), who joined her at Cherbourg.

The Alabama had been five days in preparation; she had taken in three hundred fifty tons of coal, which brought her down into the water. The Kearsarge had only one hundred twenty tons in; but, as an offset to this, her sheet-chains were stowed outside, stopped up and down, as an additional preventive and protection to her more empty bunkers. The number of the crew of the Kearsarge, including officers and sick men, was one hundred sixty-three, and her battery numbered seven guns —two 11-inch, one 30-pounder rifle, and four light 32-pounder guns. The battery of the Alabama numbered eight guns. In the engagement the Alabama fought seven guns, and the Kearsarge five, both exercising the starboard battery, until the Alabama winded, using her port battery, with one gun, and another, shifted over.

RAPHAEL SEMMES

It has been denied that the captain of the Kearsarge sent a challenge to the Alabama. Captain Semmes,[1] indeed, says nothing of it himself. What the Kearsarge did—and with a particular object, there cannot be a doubt—was, as recorded, to enter the breakwater at the east end, and "at about 11 A.M. on Tuesday she *passed through the west end without anchoring*." These are the words of a French naval captain, who speaks of what he saw. Few will deny that among brave men this would be considered something equivalent to a challenge. It was more than a challenge—it was a defiance. The officer we have quoted adds that "anyone could then see her outside protection."

It is easy to see everything after the event. The Kearsarge looked bulky in her middle section to an inspecting eye; but she was very low in the water, and that she was armed to resist shot

[1] Semmes, in this account, speaks of himself in the third person.—ED.

and shell it was impossible to discern. It is distinctly averred by the officers of the Alabama that from their vessel the armor of the Kearsarge could not be distinguished. There were many reports abroad that she was protected on her sides in some peculiar way; but all were various and indistinct, and to a practical judgment untrustworthy. Moreover, a year previous to this meeting, the Kearsarge had lain at anchor close under the critical eye of Captain Semmes. He had on that occasion seen that his enemy was not artifically defended. He believes now that the reports of her plating and armor were so much harbor gossip, of which during his cruises he had experienced enough.

Now the Kearsarge was an old enemy, constantly in pursuit, and her appearance produced, as Captain Semmes has written, great excitement on board the Alabama. For two years the officers and men of the Alabama had been homeless, and without a prospect of reaching home. They had been constantly crowded with prisoners, who devoured their provender—of which they never had any but a precarious supply. Their stay in any neutral harbor was necessarily short. They were fortified by the assurance of a mighty service done to their country. They knew that they inflicted tremendous damage upon their giant foe. But their days were wretched; their task was sickening. In addition, they read of the reproaches heaped upon them by comfortable shoremen. They were called pirates. The execrations of certain of the French and English and of all the United States press sounded in their ears across the ocean; but from their own country they heard little. The South was a sealed land in comparison with the rest of the world. Opinion spoke loudest in Europe; and though they knew that they were faithfully and gallantly serving their country in her sore need, the absence of any immediate comfort, physical or moral, made them keenly sensitive to virulent criticism.

It was this state of mind through the whole crew which caused the excitement on board the Alabama when the Kearsarge steamed in and out of the breakwater. Now, and at last, our day of action has come! was the thought of every man on board. They trusted for victory; but defeat itself was to be a vindication of their whole career, and they welcomed the chances gladly.

The application for coal at a neutral port was in itself a renunciation of any further hospitality from the harbor, as Captain Semmes was aware. The port-admiral contented himself with pointing it out to him. The prospective combat of two apparently equally matched ships-of-war would have been sufficient to melt any scruples entertained by Frenchmen in authority. French officers agreed with Captain Semmes in thinking that there was marked offence and defiance in the manœuvres of the Kearsarge, and that he could hardly do less than go out and meet her. The Captain, whether in his heart he felt the mere chances to be equal or not, was desirous to persuade himself that they were so. He knew his opponent to be the heavier in ship, battery, and crew, but "I did not know that she was also ironclad," he says. Personally he desired the battle; the instigations of an enthusiastic crew, unanimous for action, as also of friendly foreign officers, are to be taken into account.

On Sunday, in the morning, being June 19th, the Alabama steamed out of Cherbourg harbor and steered straight to meet the Kearsarge, accompanied by the French ironclad La Couronne. The late foul weather had given way to a gentle breeze, and the subsiding swell of the Atlantic wave under a clear sky made the day eminently favorable for the work in hand. All Cherbourg was on the heights above the town and along the bastions and the mole. It chanced fortunately that an English steam-yacht, the Deerhound, with its owner, Mr. John Lancaster, and his family on board, was in harbor at the time. The Deerhound followed the Alabama at a respectful distance, and was the closest witness of the fight. Some French pilots-boat hung as near as they considered prudent. At the limit of neutral waters the Alabama parted company with her escort, and La Couronne returned to within a league of the shore.

Left to herself at last, the Alabama made her final preparations for the coming struggle. Mustering all his ship's company upon the deck, Captain Semmes addressed them as follows:

"You have at length another opportunity of meeting the enemy—the first that has been presented to you since you sunk the Hatteras![1] In the mean time you have been all over the world, and it is not too much to say that you have destroyed, and driven

[1] The Alabama sunk the Federal gunboat Hatteras off Galveston January 11, 1863.—ED.

for protection under neutral flags, one-half of the enemy's commerce, which, at the beginning of the war, covered every sea. This is an achievement of which you may well be proud; and a grateful country will not be unmindful of it. The name of your ship has become a household word wherever civilization extends. Shall that name be tarnished by defeat? The thing is impossible! Remember that you are in the English Channel, the theatre of so much of the naval glory of our race, and that the eyes of all Europe are at this moment upon you. The flag that floats over you is that of a young republic, which bids defiance to her enemy's whenever and wherever found. Show the world that you know how to uphold it. Go to your quarters."

It took three-quarters of an hour for the Alabama to come within range of the Kearsarge. At the distance of one mile the Alabama opened fire with solid shot. The Kearsarge took time to reply. After ten minutes the firing was sharp on both sides.

According to the statement of the Captain of the Kearsarge, her battery consisted of seven guns, to wit: two 11-inch Dahlgrens (very powerful pieces of ordnance), four 32-pounders, one light rifled 30-pounder. She went into action with a crew of one hundred sixty-two officers and men.

The armament of the Alabama consisted of one 7-inch Blakeley rifled gun, one 8-inch smooth-bore pivot gun, six 32-pounders, smooth-bore, in broadside. The Alabama's crew numbered not more than one hundred twenty. On this head Captain Winslow speaks erroneously. He sets down the Alabama's crew at one hundred fifty officers and men. The Alabama had a formidable piece in the Blakeley rifled gun, but she was destitute of steel shot.

It will thus be seen that there was inequality between the antagonists. Captain Winslow speaks of the Alabama having "one gun more" than the Kearsarge. His two great Dahlgrens gave the balance altogether in his favor. But in an estimate of the rival capabilities of the two vessels, the deteriorated speed of the Alabama should be considered as her principal weakness. Cherbourg had done little to repair the copper of her bottom, which spread out in broad fans and seriously impeded her cutting of the water; and it had been found impossible to do more than to patch up the boilers for the day's business. They were not in a state to inspire the engineers with confidence. The Kearsarge, on the other hand, was in first-rate condition and well in hand. She speedily showed that she could overhaul the Alabama. In fact, the Alabama entered the lists when she should have been lying in dock. She fought with an exhausted frame. She had the heroism to decide upon the conflict, without the strength to choose the form of it. After some little manœuvring this became painfully evident to Captain Semmes. The Kearsarge selected her distance at a range of five hundred yards, and being well protected she deliberately took time and fired with sure effect.

Captain Semmes had great confidence in the power of his Blakeley rifled gun, and we believe it is a confidence not shaken by its failure to win the day for him. He wished to get within easy range of his enemy, that he might try this weapon effectively; but any attempt on his part to come to closer quarters was construed by the Kearsarge as a design to bring the engagement between the ships to a hand-to-hand conflict between the men. Having the speed, she chose her distance, and made all thought of boarding hopeless. It was part of the plan of Captain Semmes to board, if possible, at some period of the day, supposing that he could not quickly decide the battle with artillery. It was evidently Captain Winslow's determination to avoid the old-fashioned form of a naval encounter, and to fight altogether in the new style; his superior steam-power gave him the option. When the Alabama took her death-wound she was helpless.

The crew of the Alabama, seamen and officers, were in high spirits throughout the engagement, though very early the slaughter set in and the decks were covered with blood. Their fire was rapid and admirable. It has been said in the House of Lords by no less a person than the Duke of Somerset that her firing was positively bad and that she hit the Kearsarge only three times during the action. By Captain Winslow's own admission the Kearsarge was hit twenty-eight times by shot and shell—or once to every fifth discharge. No seaman knowing anything of an actual engagement on the deep will object to the accuracy of such an aim. Had the Kearsarge shown the same blank sides as the Alabama another tale might have been told. Captain Semmes, however, perceived that his shell rebounded after striking her, and exploded harmlessly. This led him to rely upon solid shot. The Alabama, not being thus or in any way shielded, was pierced with shell, and soon showed vast rents in her afterpart. Her pivot-gun was a distinct mark for the enemy, and a single shell exploding near it killed and wounded half the number of men by whom it was worked. Each ship fought her starboard broadside, and steamed in a circle to keep that side to the enemy. So for an hour this, to a distant spectator, monotonous manœuvre continued, without perceptibly narrowing the range. Captain Semmes was standing on the quarter-deck when the chief engineer sent word to say that the ship was endangered by leakage. The first lieutenant, Mr. Kell, was sent below to inspect the damage. He returned with word that the ship was sinking. Captain Semmes at once ordered the ship to be put about and steered toward shore. But the water was rising in her: the fires were speedily extinguished. The Alabama's shot, from slackening, had now ceased. It was evident to all on board that she was doomed. Captain Semmes's thoughts were directed toward saving the lives of his crew. He gave command for the Confederate flag to be hauled down. The flag came down quietly and decorously. All on board perceived that there was no help for it, and that it would be a shocking breach of humanity to imperil the lives of the wounded men.

The general detestation of the Yankee was yet more strongly instanced when the men were struggling for life in the water. The head of every man was pointed away, as if instinctively, from the vessel that stood nearest to rescue him. One who was hailed from the Kearsarge with the offer of a rescue, declined it civilly, and made his way for the neutral flag. The men swam as if they had still an enemy behind them, and not one that was ready to save. Tardy as were the boats of the Kearsarge in descending to perform this office, they found many of the poor fellows still painfully supporting themselves above the surface. Of these, both men and officers, when, after being hauled into the boats, they had dashed the blinding salt water from their eyes and discovered among whom they were, many sprang overboard again, preferring any risk to the shelter of the Federalists. Hatred to the flag of the old Union and love of their Captain appear to have been their chief active passions. When taken on board the Deerhound, the question as to the safety of Captain Semmes was foremost in every mouth.

Captain Semmes asserts that shots were fired at the Alabama after the signal of surrender. We will not attempt to substantiate a charge like this: but French officers maintain it to be an undeniable fact that, after the Confederate flag had been lowered, the Kearsarge fired no less than five shots into her. We believe that Captain Winslow does not deny the charge; but asserts that he was unaware of the act of surrender.

The master's mate of the Alabama, Mr. Fullam, was despatched in the dingey to the Kearsarge with a request that assistance might immediately be given in rescuing the lives of the wounded men. During Mr. Fullam's absence the Alabama had gone down stern foremost. All the wounded had been stretched in the whale-boat for transmission to the Kearsarge. The surgeon of the Alabama, an Englishman, Mr. David Herbert Llewellyn, was offered a place in this boat. He refused it, saying that he would not imperil the wounded men, and he sank with the Alabama. The rest of the crew, with their captain, were already in the waves. Mr. Lancaster meantime had steamed up to the Kearsarge, requesting permission to assist in saving life, and he was soon among them, throwing lines from the yacht, and picking up many exhausted men in his boats. The loss of men by drowning was nineteen, including an officer (Mr. Llewellyn), carpenter, and assistant engineer. The loss in killed or wounded was twenty-eight, of whom seven were killed. Not a wrack of the Alabama was secured by the victors in this memorable sea-fight. The captain and his officers dropped their swords into the deep; the men drove their oars into the bottoms of the boats. Not a man who was able to support himself in the water swam toward the Kearsarge.

SHERMAN'S MARCH TO THE SEA

A.D. 1864

ROSSITER JOHNSON[1]

In May, 1864, when General Grant, with the Army of the Potomac, began his campaign in Virginia, General William T. Sherman at the same time, with an army of ninety-eight thousand men, set out from Chattanooga, Tennessee, on a campaign toward Atlanta, Georgia. He was stoutly opposed at every step by a Confederate army that was ably commanded by General Joseph E. Johnston, until they were within sight of the spires of Atlanta. Then Johnston was superseded by General John B. Hood, who differed from Johnston in being a furious and sometimes reckless fighter. After one or two bloody battles, Sherman gained possession of Atlanta, September 1st, and his army remained there two months, before it set out for the sea. Sherman's march from Atlanta to the sea was one of the least bloody and most picturesque of the great operations of the Civil War. Its importance lay, first, in the fact that it cut through the heart of the Confederacy and revealed the state of exhaustion to which it had been reduced; and, second, in bringing a powerful veteran army to the Atlantic seaboard, where it could coöperate with the Army of the Potomac in the final destruction of the forces that defended the Confederate capital. It was bold in conception, but not very difficult of execution. In fact, Sherman's march northward through the Carolinas was a much harder and more hazardous task; for in Georgia he moved in lines parallel with the streams, and was opposed only by a not very large body of Confederate cavalry, while in the Carolinas he had to cross the streams and to meet opposition from a considerable force of Confederate infantry commanded by his old and able antagonist, General Joseph E. Johnston.

GENERAL SHERMAN thought he conceived of the march to the sea some time in September; the first definite proposal of it was in a telegram to General Thomas on October 9th, in which he said: "I want to destroy all the road below Chattanooga, including Atlanta, and to make for the seacoast. We cannot defend this long line of road." In various despatches be-

[1] From Rossiter Johnson's *History of the War of Secession* (New York: Bryan, Taylor and Company), by permission.

tween that date and November 2d Sherman proposed the great march to Grant and to the President. Grant thought Hood's army should be destroyed first, but finally said: "I do not see that you can withdraw from where you are, to follow Hood, without giving up all we have gained in territory. I say, then, go on as you propose." This was on the understanding, suggested by Sherman, that Thomas would be left with force enough to take care of Hood. Sherman sent him the Fourth and Twenty-third Corps, commanded by Generals David S. Stanley and John M. Schofield, and further reënforced him with troops that had been garrisoning various places on the railroad, while he also received two divisions from Missouri and some recruits from the North. These, when properly organized, made up a very strong force; and, with Thomas at its head, neither Sherman nor Grant felt any hesitation about leaving it to take care of Tennessee.

Sherman rapidly sent north all his sick and disabled men, and all baggage that could be spared. Commissioners came and took the votes of the soldiers for the Presidential election, and departed. Paymasters came and paid off the troops, and went back again. Wagon-trains were put in trim and loaded for a march. Every detachment of the army had its exact orders what to do; and as the last trains whirled over the road to Chattanooga, the track was taken up and destroyed, the bridges were burned, the wires torn down, and all the troops that had not been ordered to join Thomas concentrated in Atlanta. From November 12th nothing more was heard from Sherman till Christmas.

The depot, machine-shops, and locomotive-house in Atlanta were torn down, and fire was set to the ruins. The shops had been used for the manufacture of Confederate ammunition, and all night the shells were exploding in the midst of the ruin, while the fire spread to a block of stores, and finally burned out the heart of the city.

With every unsound man and every useless article sent to the rear, General Sherman now had fifty-five thousand three hundred twenty-nine infantrymen, five thousand sixty-three cavalrymen, and eighteen hundred twelve artillerymen, with sixty-five guns. There were four teams of horses to each gun, with its caisson and forge; six hundred ambulances, each drawn by two horses; and twenty-five hundred wagons, with six mules to each. Every soldier carried forty rounds of ammunition, while the wagons contained an abundant additional supply and twelve hundred thousand rations, with oats and corn enough to last five days. Probably a more thoroughly appointed army never was seen, and it is difficult to imagine one of equal numbers more effective. Every man in it was a veteran, was proud to be there, and felt the most perfect confidence that under the leadership of "Uncle Billy" it would be impossible to go wrong.

On November 15th they set out on the march to the sea, nearly three hundred miles distant. The infantry consisted of four corps. The Fifteenth and Seventeenth formed the right wing, commanded by General Oliver O. Howard; the Fourteenth and Twentieth the left, commanded by General Henry W. Slocum. The cavalry was under the command of General Judson Kilpatrick. The two wings marched by parallel routes, usually a few miles apart, each corps having its own proportion of the artillery and trains. General Sherman issued minute orders as to the conduct of the march, which were systematically carried out. Some of the instructions were these:

"The habitual order of march will be, wherever practicable, by four roads, as nearly parallel as possible. The separate columns will start habitually at 7 A.M., and make about fifteen miles a day. Behind each regiment should follow one wagon and one ambulance. Army commanders should practise the habit of giving the artillery and wagons the road, marching the troops on one side. The army will forage liberally on the country during the march. To this end each brigade commander will organize a good and sufficient foraging party, who will gather corn or forage of any kind, meat of any kind, vegetables, cornmeal, or whatever is needed by the command, aiming at all times to keep in the wagons at least ten days' provisions. Soldiers must not enter dwellings or commit any trespass; but, during a halt or camp, they may be permitted to gather turnips, potatoes, and other vegetables, and to drive in stock in sight of their camp. To corps commanders alone is intrusted the power to destroy mills, houses, cotton-gins, etc. Where the army is unmolested, no destruction of such property should be permitted; but should guerillas or bushwhackers molest our march, or should the inhabitants burn bridges, obstruct roads, or otherwise manifest local hostility, then army commanders should order and enforce a devastation more or less relentless, according to the measure of such hostility. As for horses, mules, wagons, etc., belonging to the inhabitants, the cavalry and artillery may appropriate freely and without limit; discriminating, however, between the rich, who are usually hostile, and the poor and industrious, usually neutral or friendly. In foraging, the parties engaged will endeavor to leave with each family a reasonable portion for their maintenance."

Thus equipped and thus instructed, the great army moved steadily, day after day, cutting a mighty swath, from forty to sixty miles wide, through the very heart of the Confederacy. The columns passed through Rough and Ready, Jonesboro, Covington, McDonough, Macon, Milledgeville, Gibson, Louisville, Millen, Springfield, and many smaller places.

The wealthier inhabitants fled at the approach of the troops. The negroes in great numbers swarmed after the army, believing the long-promised day of jubilee had come. Some of them appeared to have an intelligent idea that the success of the National forces meant destruction of slavery, while most of them had but the vaguest notions as to the whole movement. One woman, with a child in her arms, walking along among the cattle and horses, was accosted by an officer, who asked her, "Where are you going, aunty?" "I's gwine whar you's gwine, massa." One party of black men, who had fallen into line, called out to another who seemed to be asking too many questions, "Stick in dar! It's all right. We's gwine along; we's free." Major George Ward Nichols describes an aged couple whom he saw in a hut near Milledgeville. The old negress, pointing her long finger at the old man, who was in the corner of the fireplace, hissed out: "What fer you sit dar? You s'pose I wait sixty years for nutten? Don't yer see de door open? I's follow my child, I not stay, I walks till I drop in my tracks."

The army destroyed nearly the whole of the Georgia Central Railroad, burning the ties and heating and twisting the rails. As they had learned that a rail merely bent could be straightened and used again, a special tool was invented with which a red-hot rail could be quickly twisted like an auger, and rendered forever useless. They also had special appliances for tearing up the track methodically and rapidly. All the depot buildings were in flames as soon as the column reached them. As the bloodhounds had been used to track escaped prisoners, the men killed all that they could find.

The foraging parties—or "bummers," as they were popularly called—went out for miles on each side, starting in advance of the organizations to which they belonged, gathered immense quantities of provisions, and brought them to the line of march, where each stood guard over his pile till his own brigade came along. The progress of the column was not allowed to be interrupted for the reception of the forage, everything being loaded upon the wagons as they moved. The "flankers" were thrown out on either side, passing in thin lines through the woods to prevent any surprise by the enemy, while the mounted officers went through the fields to give the road to the troops and trains.

The only serious opposition came from Wheeler's Confederate cavalry, which hung on the flanks of the army and burned some bridges, but was well taken care of by Kilpatrick's, who usually defeated it when brought to an encounter. There was great hope that Kilpatrick would be able to release the prisoners of war confined in Millen, but when he arrived there he found that they had been removed to some other part of the Confederacy. When the advance-guard was within a few miles of Savannah, there was some fighting with infantry, and a pause before the defences of the city.

Fort McAllister, which stood in the way of communication with the blockading fleet, was elaborately protected with ditches, palisades, and *chevaux-de-frise;* but General William B. Hazen's division made short work with it, going straight over everything and capturing the fort on December 13th, losing ninety-two men in the assault, and killing or wounding about fifty of the garrison. That night General Sherman, with a few officers, pulled down the river in a yawl and visited the fleet in Ossabaw Sound.

Four days later, having established full communication, Sherman demanded the surrender of the city of Savannah, which General William J. Hardee, who was in command there with a considerable force, refused. Sherman then took measures to make its investment complete; but on the morning of the 21st it was found to be evacuated by Hardee's forces, and General John W. Geary's division of the Twentieth Corps marched in.

The next day Sherman wrote to the President: "I beg to present you as a Christmas gift the city of Savannah, with one hundred fifty heavy guns and plenty of ammunition, also about twenty-five thousand bales of cotton." Sherman's entire loss in the march had been seven hundred sixty-four men.

That phase of war which reaches behind the armies in the field and strikes directly at the sources of supply, bringing home its burdens and its hardships to men who are urging on the conflict without participating in it, was never exhibited on a grander scale or conducted with more complete success. This in fact is the most humane kind of war, since it accomplishes the purpose with the least destruction of life and limb. Sherman's movement across Georgia naturally brings to mind another famous march to the sea; but that was a retreat of ten thousand, while this was a victorious advance of sixty thousand, and it was only in their shout of welcome, *Thalatta! thalatta!* ("The sea! the sea!") that the weary and disheartened Greeks resembled Sherman's triumphant legions.

CAREER OF THE INTERNATIONAL

A.D. 1864–1873

THOMAS KIRKUP

No concerted movement of men in various countries has been more distinctly modern in spirit and method than that out of which came the organization of the International Workingmen's Association, commonly called "The International," and sometimes "The Red International," on account of its sympathy with the "Reds" or Communists. This was a union designed to embrace the workingmen of all countries, with the object of advancing industrial and social reform through political action. The movement may be said to have originated with certain thinkers and writers representing the socialistic theory of civil polity. This "scientific socialism," as its advocates call it, is the direct outcome of modern views on the practical solidarity of human society and its interests; and in its specializations it has taken many forms of endeavor, independent or co-operative, to readjust the relations and improve the condition of what are called the "working classes."

It is said by socialistic writers that this movement has its historical antecedents in the special international sympathy that has always existed among nations participating in the inheritance of Greek and Roman culture, and of the spirit of Christianity, breaking down the walls of national exclusiveness. Feudalism, chivalry, and the crusades, we are told, were mediums of the same fraternal influences. The spread of the Protestant movement and of revolutionary ideas of the eighteenth century led to a further growth of the spirit that heralded the coming internationalism. Modern inventions—the steam-engine, the telegraph, etc.—and the new agencies of commerce and industry have become the bearers of a still more widening international movement.

Yet in spite of this growing community of mankind, labor and capital, the great industrial partners, are brought into frequent antagonism. This and various economic questions that equally concern capital and labor have led to organizations representing each interest, and such organization on the side of labor has its earliest example on a large scale in the International. Of this organization a small prototype existed in Paris in 1836, when a group of German exiles formed themselves into a secret communistic society called the "League of the Just." In 1839 its members removed to London, and the League began to spread through Northern Europe. Adopting the principles of the German socialist leader, Karl Marx (1818–1883), these men entered upon a propaganda for the ' social revolution." In 1847 they reorganized under the name of the "Communist League." The principles of this organization were set forth by Karl Marx and his associate, Friedrich Engels (1820–1896), sometimes called the founder of scientific socialism. It was held by them that "human society more and more divides itself into two great conflicting classes, *bourgeoisie* and proletariat," and the league aimed to deliver the proletariat from the exploiting rule of the bourgeoisie, to abolish the old society resting on class antagonisms, and to found "a new society without classes and without private property."

With the ending of the Communist League, and a survey of the conditions preparatory to the rise of its famous successor, begins this narrative of the birth and career of the International, by Thomas Kirkup, the historian of socialism.

THE Revolution of 1848 was a rising of the people in France, Italy, Germany, Austria, and Hungary against antiquated political arrangements and institutions. It was partly an interruption to the operations of the Communist League, as it was far too weak to exercise any great influence on the course of events; but it was also an opportunity, as its members found access to the land of their birth, and in many parts of Germany formed the most resolute and advanced wing of the struggling democracy during that troubled period.

After the triumph of the reaction it became clear that the hope of effective revolutionary activity had again for a time passed away. A period of unexampled industrial prosperity set in. Capitalism was about to enter a far wider phase of development than it had yet seen, a fact which abundantly showed that the time was not favorable for an active propaganda in the interests of the proletariat. When capitalism has become a hinderance to progressive social development, when it is obviously too weak and narrow a framework for further evolution, only then is there hope of successful effort against it. So reasoned Marx and his associates. He withdrew, therefore, from the scene of action to his study in London. In 1852 the first international combination of workingmen came to a close, and observers who could not reasonably be considered superficial thought that the movement had died without hope of resurrection.

But the triumph of reactionary governments in 1849 was not a settlement of the great questions that had been raised during that period of revolution; it was only a postponement of them.

Before many years had passed, the peoples of Europe again began to move uneasily under the yoke of antiquated political forms. The rising of Italy against Austria in 1859; the struggle of Prussian Liberals against the ministry; the resolve of Bismarck and his sovereign to have the Prussian army ready for action in the way of reconstituting a united Germany on the ruins of the old federation—these were only different symptoms of a fresh advance. They were ere long to be followed by similar activity in France, Spain, and Eastern Europe, all proving that the history of European communities is an organic movement, the reach and potency of which often disturb the forecast of the politician. In the generation after 1848 the governments were everywhere constrained to carry out the political programme that the people had drawn for them during the revolution.

The social question may appear to have only a remote connection with the political movements just mentioned, and yet the revival of the social question was but another sign of the new life in Europe, which could not be repressed. The founding of the social-democracy of Germany by Ferdinand Lassalle, and the appearance of the International on a wider and worthier scale under the auspices of Marx, were a clear proof that the working classes of the most advanced countries of Europe now meant to claim a better share in the moral and material inheritance of the human race.

Appropriately enough, the event that gave the first occasion for the founding of the International Workingmen's Association was the International Exhibition of London in 1862. The workmen of France sent a deputation to visit the exhibition. This visit had the approval and even pecuniary support of the Emperor, Napoleon III, and it was warmly commended by some of the Parisian journals as a means not only of acquainting the workmen with the industrial treasures of the exhibition, but of removing from the relations of the two countries the old leaven of international discord and jealousy. In the course of their visit the French delegates were entertained by some of their English brethren at the Freemasons' Tavern, where views as to the identity of the interests of labor, and the necessity for common action in promoting them, were interchanged.

In the following year a second deputation of French workmen crossed the Channel. Napoleon was interested in the Polish insurrection of 1863, and it was part of his policy to encourage the expression of opinion in favor of an intervention in Poland by the Western Powers. At this visit wishes for the restoration of Poland and for general congresses in the interest of labor against capital were expressed. Nothing decisive, however, was done till 1864, when on September 28th a great public meeting of workingmen of all nations was held in St. Martin's Hall, London. Professor Beesly presided, and Karl Marx was present. The meeting resulted in the appointment of a provisional committee to draw up the constitution of the new association. This committee consisted of fifty representatives of different nations, the English forming about half of its number.

The work of writing the constitution was first of all undertaken by Mazzini, but the ideas and methods of the Italian patriot were not suited to the task of founding an international association of labor. The statutes he drew up were adapted to the political conspiracy, conducted by a strong central authority, in which he had spent his life; he was strongly opposed to the antagonism of classes, and his economic ideas were vague. Marx, on the other hand, was in entire sympathy with the most advanced labor movement; indeed, he had already done much to mould and direct it; to him, therefore, the duty of drawing up a constitution was transferred, and the inaugural address and the statutes drawn up by him were adopted by the committee.

In the inaugural address three points were particularly emphasized. First, Marx contended that, notwithstanding the enormous development of industry and of national wealth since 1848, the misery of the masses had not diminished. Secondly, the successful struggle for the ten-hour working-day meant the breakdown of the political economy of the middle classes, the competitive operation of supply and demand requiring to be regulated by social control. Thirdly, the productive association of a few daring "hands" had proved that industry on a great scale, and with all the appliances of modern science, could be carried on without the existence of capitalist masters; and that wage-labor, like slave-labor, was only a transitory form, destined to disappear before associated labor, which gives to the workman a diligent hand, a cheerful spirit, and a joyful heart.

The numbers of the workmen gave them the means of success, but it could be realized only through union. It was the task of the International to bring about such an effective union, and for this end the workmen must take international politics into their own hands, must watch the diplomacy of their governments, and uphold the simple rules of morality in the relations of private persons and nations. "The struggle for such a policy forms part of the struggle for the emancipation of the working class. Proletarians of all lands, unite!"

The preamble to the statutes contains implicitly the main principles of international socialism. The economic subjection of the workmen to the appropriator of the instruments of labor—that is, of the sources of life—is the cause of servitude in all its forms, of social misery, of mental degradation and of political dependence; the economic emancipation of the working class is neither a local nor a national, but a social, problem, to be solved only by the combined efforts of the most advanced nations.

For these reasons the International Workingmen's Association has been founded. It declares: "That all societies and individuals who adhere to it recognize truth, justice, and morality as the rule of their conduct toward one another and to all men without distinction of color, faith, or nationality. No duties without rights; no rights without duties."

Such are the leading ideas of the preamble; we have only to develop them, and we have the programme of international socialism. Whatever opinion we may hold of the truth and practicability of the theories set forth in it, we must respect the lucid and masterly form in which Marx has presented them. It is seldom, in the history of the world, that talents and learning so remarkable have been placed at the service of an agitation that was so wide and far-reaching.

The International Workingmen's Association was founded for the establishment of a centre of union and of systematic co-operation between the workingmen's societies, which have the same aim, viz., the protection, the progress, and the complete emancipation of the working class. It would be a mistake to regard its organization as one of excessive centralization and dictatorial authority. It was to be a means of union, a centre of information and of initiative, in the interests of labor; but the existing societies that should join it were to retain their organization intact.

A general council, having its seat in London, was appointed. While the president, treasurer, and general secretary were to be Englishmen, each nation was to be represented in the council by a corresponding secretary. The general council was to summon annual congresses and exercise an effective control over the affairs of the association, but local societies were to have free play in all local questions. As a further means of union it was recommended that the workmen of the various countries should be united in national bodies, represented by national central organs, but no independent local society was to be excluded from direct correspondence with the general council. It will be seen that the arrangements of the association were so made as to secure the efficiency of the central directing power on the one hand, and on the other to allow local and national associations a real freedom and abundant scope for adapting themselves to the peculiar tasks imposed by their local and national position.

As in founding, so in conducting, the International, Marx took the leading part. The proceedings of the various congresses might be described as a discussion, elucidation, and filling-up of the programme sketched by him in the inaugural address and in the statutes of the association. Men representing the schools of Proudhon (who died in 1865), of Blanqui, and of Bakunin also exercised considerable influence; but the general tendency was in accordance with the views of Marx.

It was intended that the first congress for finally arranging the constitution of the association should be held at Brussels in 1865, but the Belgian Government forbade the meeting, and the council had to content itself with a conference in London. The first congress was held at Geneva in September, 1866, sixty delegates being present. Here the statutes as drawn by Marx were adopted. Among other resolutions it decided on an agitation in favor of the gradual reduction of the working-day to eight hours, and it recommended a most comprehensive system of education, intellectual and technical, which should raise the working people above the level of the higher and middle classes. Socialistic principles were set forth only in the most general terms. With regard to labor, the International did not seek to enunciate a *doctrinaire* system, but only to proclaim general principles. They must aim at free cooperation; and for this end the decisive power in the State must be transferred from the capitalists and landlords to the workers.

The proposal of the French delegates for the exclusion of the intellectual proletariat from the association led to an interesting discussion. Was this proletariat to be reckoned among the workers? Ambitious talkers and agitators belonging to this class had done much mischief. On the other hand, their exclusion from socialistic activity would have deprived the laborers of the services of most of their greatest leaders, and the intellectual proletariat suffered from the pressure of capital quite as much as any other class of workers. The proposal for their exclusion was rejected.

The second congress, held at Lausanne in 1867, made considerable progress in the formulating of the socialistic theories. It was resolved that the means of transport and communication should become the property of the state, in order to break the mighty monopoly of the great companies, under which the subjection of labor does violence to human worth and personal freedom. The congress encouraged cooperative associations and efforts for the raising of wages, but emphatically called attention to the danger lest the spread of such associations should be found compatible with the existing system, thus resulting in the formation of a fourth class and of an entirely miserable fifth. The social transformation can be radically and definitely accomplished only by working on the whole of society in thorough accordance with reciprocity and justice.

In the third congress, held at Brussels in September, 1868, the socialistic principles that had been implicitly contained in the aims and utterances of the International received most explicit statement. Ninety-eight delegates—representing England, France, Germany, Belgium, Italy, Spain, and Switzerland—assembled at this congress. It resolved that mines and forests and the land, as well as all the means of transport and communication, should become the common property of society or of the democratic state; and that they should by the state be handed over to associations of workers, who should utilize them under rational and equitable conditions determined by society. It was further resolved that the producers could gain possession of the machines only through cooperative societies and the organization of the mutual credit system, the latter clause being a concession apparently to the followers of Proudhon.

After proposing a scheme for the better organizing of strikes, the congress returned to the question of education, particularly emphasizing the fact that an indispensable condition toward a thorough system of scientific, professional, and productive instruction was the reduction of the hours of labor.

The fundamental principle, "To labor the full product of labor," was recognized in the following resolution: "Every society founded on democratic principles repudiates all appropriation by capital, whether in the form of rent, interest, profit, or in any other form or manner whatsoever. Labor must have its full right and entire reward."

In view of the struggle imminent between France and Germany, the congress made an emphatic declaration denouncing it as a civil war in favor of Russia, and calling upon the workers to resist all war as systematic murder. In case of war the congress recommended a universal strike. It reckoned on the solidarity of the workers of all lands for this strike of the peoples against war.

At the Congress of Basel, in 1869, little remained for the International to accomplish in further defining the socialistic position. The resolution for transforming land from private to collective property was repeated. A proposal to abolish the right of inheritance failed to obtain a majority; for while thirty-two delegates voted for the abolition, twenty-three were against it, and seventeen declined to vote.

If we now turn from the congresses of the International to consider the history of its influence in Europe, we shall see that its success was very considerable. It gained its first triumph in the effectual support of the bronze-workers at Paris during their lockout in 1867; and it repeatedly gave real help to the English trades-unionists by preventing the importation of cheap labor from the Continent. At the beginning of 1868 one hundred twenty-two workingmen's societies of South Germany, assembled at Nuremberg, declared their adhesion to the International. In 1870 Cameron announced himself as the representative of eight hundred thousand American workmen who had adopted its principles.

It soon spread as far east as Poland and Hungary; it had affiliated societies, with journals devoted to its cause, in every country of Western Europe. The European press became more than interested in its movements, and the London *Times* published four leaders on the Brussels Congress. It was supposed to be concerned in all the revolutionary movements and agitations of Europe, thus gaining a world-historic notoriety as the rallying-point of social overthrow and ruin. Its prestige, however, was always based more on the vast possibilities of the cause it represented than on its actual power. Its organization was loose, its financial resources insignificant; the Continental unionists joined it more in the hope of borrowing than of contributing support.

In 1870 the International resolved to meet at the old hearth of the revolutionary movement by holding its annual congress in Paris, but this plan was rendered abortive by the Franco-Prussian War. The war, however, helped to bring the principles of the association more prominently before the world. During the Austro-German struggle of 1866 the International had declared its emphatic condemnation of war, and now the affiliated societies of France and of Germany, as well as the general council at London, uttered a solemn protest against a renewal of the scourge. Some of its German adherents likewise incurred the wrath of the authorities by venturing to protest against the annexation of Alsace and Lorraine.

All will agree that it is a happier omen for the future that the democracy of labor as represented by the International was so prompt and courageous in its denunciation of the evils of war. It gives us ground to hope that as the influence of the democracy prevails in the council of nations the passion for war may decline. On this high theme no men have a better right to speak than the workers, for they have, in all ages, borne the heaviest of the burden of privation and suffering imposed on the world by the military spirit, and have had the least share in the miserable glories which victory may obtain.

The relation of the International to the rising of the Commune at Paris in 1871 is often misunderstood. It is clear that the International, as such, had no part in either originating or conducting the Commune. Some of the French members joined it, but only on their individual responsibility. Its complicity after the event is equally clear. After the fall of the Commune, Karl Marx, in the name of the general council, wrote a long and trenchant manifesto commending it as substantially a government of the working class, whose measures tended really to advance the interests of the working class. "The Paris of the workers, with its Commune, will ever be celebrated as the glorious herald of a new society. Its martyrs will be enshrined in the great heart of the working class. History has already nailed its destroyers in the pillory, from which all the prayers of their priests are impotent to deliver them."

The Commune was undoubtedly a rising for the autonomy of Paris, supported chiefly by the lower classes. It was a protest against excessive centralization, raised by the democracy of Paris, which has always been far in advance of the provinces, and which found itself in possession of arms after the siege of the city by the Germans. But while it was prominently an assertion of local self-government, it was also a revolt against the economic oppression of the moneyed classes. Many of its measures were what we should call social-radical.

In two important points, therefore, the communal rising at Paris had a very close affinity with socialism. In the first place, it was a revolutionary assertion of the Commune or local unit of self-government as the cardinal and dominating principle of society over against the state or central government. That is to say, the Commune was a vindication of the political form that is necessary for the development of socialism, the self-governing group of workers. And, in the second place, the Commune was a rising chiefly of the proletariat, the class of which socialism declares itself the special champion, which in Paris only partially saw the way of deliverance, but was weary of oppression and full of indignation against the middle-class adventurers that, on the fall of the empire, had seized the central government of France.

It would, however, be a mistake to assume for the Commune a clearness and comprehensiveness of aim which it did not really possess. We should not be justified in saying that the Commune had any definite consciousness of such a historical mission as has been claimed for it. The fearful shock caused by the overwhelming events of the Franco-Prussian War had naturally led to widespread confusion and uncertainty in the French mind; and those who undertook to direct it, whether in Paris or elsewhere, had painfully to grope their way toward the renovation of the country. At a time when it could hardly be said that France had a regular government, the Commune seized the opportunity to make a new political departure. The story of its rise and fall was only one phase of a sad series of troubles and disasters, which happily do not often overtake nations in a form so terrible.

From this point the decline and fall of the association must be dated. The English trades-unions, intent on more practical concerns at home, never took a deep interest in its proceedings; the German socialists were disunited among themselves, lacking in funds, and hampered by the police.

It found its worst enemies, perhaps, in its own household. In 1869 Bakunin, with a following of anarchists, had joined the International, and from the first they found themselves at variance with the majority led by Marx. It can hardly be maintained that Marx favored a very strongly centralizing authority, yet, as his views and methods were repugnant to the anarchists, a breach was inevitable.

The breach came at The Hague congress in September, 1872. Sixty-five delegates were present, including Marx himself, who, with his followers, after animated discussion, expelled the anarchist party, and then removed the seat of the general council to New York. The congress concluded with a meeting at Amsterdam, of which the chief feature was a remarkable speech from Marx. "In the eighteenth century," he said, "kings and potentates used to assemble at The Hague to discuss the interests of their dynasties. At the same place we resolved to hold the assize of labor"—a contrast which with world-historic force did undoubtedly mark the march of time. "I cannot deny that there are countries like the United States, England, and, as far as I know its institutions, Holland also, where workmen can attain their goal by peaceful means; but in most European countries force must be the lever of revolution, and to force we must appeal when the time comes."

Thus it was a principle of Marx to prefer peaceful methods where peaceful methods are permitted, but resort to force must be made when necessary. Force also is an economic power. He concluded by expressing his resolve that in the future, as in the past, his life should be consecrated to the triumph of the social cause.

The transfer of the general council of the Marx International from London to New York was the beginning of the end. It survived just long enough to hold another congress at Geneva in 1873, and then quietly expired.

THE SURRENDER OF LEE

A.D. 1865

ULYSSES S. GRANT[1]

As the Civil War progressed through its first three years, it developed the fact that the most successful commander at the West was the Federal General Ulysses S. Grant; at the East, the Confederate General Robert E. Lee. It was therefore apparent, at the beginning of the fourth year, when Grant was transferred to the East and placed in command of all the Federal armies, that the most terrific struggle of the war was at hand. The characters of the two commanders were very different, and there was a corresponding difference in their achievements. Grant invariably assumed the offensive, never took a step backward, and obtained everything that he went for at the West. Lee was more cautious, stood mainly on a skilful and stubborn defensive, and was criticised for not following up his successes. When Grant, on May 5, 1864, crossed the Rapidan and plunged into the Wilderness, two veteran armies confronted each other in that gloomy region, whose broken ground and tangled thickets formed perhaps the worst battle-field that ever was chosen for civilized warfare. Grant's object was to place his army between the Confederate army and its capital, Richmond, and compel the Confederate army to fight where it might be captured or destroyed; for, as he announced at the outset, his objective was not Richmond, but Lee's army, which it was his duty to fight wherever he found it. Lee's object was to prevent Grant from getting between him and Richmond, and to hold a defensive that should make every step costly for his antagonist. Indeed, at the outset he assumed the tactical offensive and struck the Army of the Potomac in the Wilderness, hoping that after a heavy blow it would recross the river, since it had done this under its other commanders. But Grant never turned back, and high military authority has said that when, after that battle, he issued the order "Forward by the left flank," he practically determined what the end of the contest should be. Lee, partly because he had the shorter lines to traverse, and partly for other reasons, kept his army, at every move, between his capital and his antagonist, while Grant, after every contest in that fearful battle-summer, still marched forward by the left flank, until the armies were brought to a final stand at Petersburg, the junction of the Southern

[1] From General Grant's *Memoirs* (New York : The Century Company), by permission of General Frederick D. Grant and the publishers.

railroads that lead to Richmond. Here Lee occupied strong intrenchments surrounding the city, and Grant, constructing equally strong ones, established a siege that lasted through the autumn and winter with processes of destruction never intermitted day or night. By a series of engagements and movements westward, Grant cut off one after another of the roads by which Lee drew his supplies from the south; and when, on April 1, 1865, Lee could no longer hold his lines, he drew his army out of them and marched toward Lynchburg, hoping to elude Grant. But the Army of the Potomac was close after him and close beside him in a running fight of six days, and when he arrived at Appomattox Court House he found that a strong detachment was in his front as well, and there he was obliged to stop and surrender the remnant of his once powerful army. The final scenes in this campaign are told better by General Grant himself than by any other writer.

ON April 8th [1865] I had followed the Army of the Potomac in rear of Lee. I was suffering very severely with a sick-headache, and stopped at a farmhouse on the road, some distance in rear of the main body of the army. I spent the night in bathing my feet in hot water and mustard, and putting mustard-plasters on my wrists and the back part of my neck, hoping to be cured by morning. During the night I received Lee's answer to my letter of the 8th, inviting an interview between the lines on the following morning. But it was for a different purpose from that of surrendering his army, and I answered him as follows:

"HEADQUARTERS
"ARMIES OF THE UNITED STATES, April 9, 1865.

"GENERAL R. E. LEE, *Commanding Confederate States Armies:*

"Your note of yesterday is received. I have no authority to treat on the subject of peace; the meeting proposed for 10 A.M. to-day could lead to no good. I will state, however, General, that I am equally anxious for peace with yourself, and the whole North entertains the same feeling. The terms upon which peace can be had are well understood. By the South laying down their arms they will hasten that most desirable event, save thousands of human lives and hundreds of millions of property not yet destroyed. Sincerely hoping that all our difficulties may be settled without the loss of another life, I subscribe myself, etc., U. S. GRANT, Lieutenant-General."

I proceeded at an early hour in the morning, still suffering with the headache, to get to the head of the column. I was not more than two or three miles from Appomattox Court House at the time; but to go direct I would have to pass through Lee's army or a portion of it. I had therefore to move south in order to get upon a road coming up from another direction.

When the white flag was put out by Lee, as already described, I was in this way moving toward Appomattox Court House, and consequently could not be communicated with immediately and be informed of what Lee had done. Lee, therefore, sent a flag to the rear to advise Meade, and one to the front to Sheridan, saying that he had sent a message to me for the purpose of having a meeting to consult about the surrender of his army, and asked for a suspension of hostilities until I could be communicated with. As they had heard nothing of this until the fighting had got to be severe and all going against Lee, both of these commanders hesitated very considerably about suspending hostilities at all. They were afraid it was not in good faith, and we had the Army of Northern Virginia where it could not escape except by some deception. They, however, finally consented to a suspension of hostilities for two hours, to give an opportunity of communicating with me in that time, if possible. It was found that, from the route I had taken, they would probably not be able to communicate with me and get an answer back within the time fixed unless the messenger should pass through the Confederate lines.

Lee, therefore, sent an escort with the officer bearing this message through his lines to me:

"April 9, 1865.

"GENERAL: I received your note of this morning on the picket-line, whither I had come to meet you and ascertain definitely what terms were embraced in your proposal of yesterday, with reference to the surrender of this army. I now ask an interview, in accordance with the offer contained in your letter of yesterday, for that purpose. R. E. LEE, General.

"Lieutenant-General U. S. GRANT, Commanding United States Armies."

When the officer reached me I was still suffering with the sick-headache; but the instant I saw the contents of the note I was cured. I wrote the following note in reply and hastened on:

"April 9, 1865.

"GENERAL R. E. LEE, *Commanding Confederate States Armies:*

"Your note of this date is but this moment (11.50 A.M.) received, in consequence of my having passed from the Richmond and Lynchburg road to the Farmville and Lynchburg road. I am at this writing about four miles west of Walker's Church, and will push forward to the front for the purpose of meeting you. Notice sent to me on this road where you wish the interview to take place will meet me.

"U. S. GRANT, Lieutenant-General."

I was conducted at once to where Sheridan was located with his troops drawn up in line of battle facing the Confederate army near by. They were very much excited, and expressed their view that this was all a ruse employed to enable the Confederates to get away. They said they believed that Johnston was marching up from North Carolina now, and Lee was moving to join him; and they would whip the rebels where they now were in five minutes if I would only let them go in. But I had no doubt about the good faith of Lee, and pretty soon was conducted to where he was. I found him at the house of a Mr. McLean, at Appomattox Court House, with Colonel Marshall, one of his staff-officers, awaiting my arrival. The head of his column was occupying a hill, on a portion of which was an apple-orchard, beyond a little valley which separated it from that on the crest of which Sheridan's forces were drawn up in line of battle to the south.

Before stating what took place between General Lee and myself, I will give all there is of the story of the famous apple-tree. Wars produce many stories of fiction, some of which are told until they are believed to be true. The War of the Rebellion was no exception to this rule, and the story of the apple-tree is one of those fictions based on a slight foundation of fact. As I have said, there was an apple-orchard on the side of the hill occupied by the Confederate forces. Running diagonally up the hill was a wagon-road, which at one point ran very near one of the trees, so that the wheels of vehicles had on that side cut off the roots of this tree, leaving a little embankment. General Babcock, of my staff, reported to me that when he first met General Lee he was sitting upon this embankment with his feet in the road below and his back resting against the tree. The story had no other foundation than that. Like many other stories, it would be very good if it were only true.

I had known General Lee in the old army, and had served with him in the Mexican War, but did not suppose, owing to the difference in our age and rank, that he would remember me; while I would more naturally remember him distinctly, because he was the chief of staff of General Scott in the Mexican War.

When I had left camp that morning I had not expected so soon the result that was then taking place, and consequently was in rough garb. I was without a sword, as I usually was when on horseback in the field, and wore a soldier's blouse for a coat, with the shoulder-straps of my rank to indicate to the army who I was. When I went into the house I found General Lee. We greeted each other, and after shaking hands took our seats. I had my staff with me, a good portion of whom were in the room during the whole of the interview.

What General Lee's feelings were, I do not know. As he was a man of much dignity, with an impassable face, it was impossible to say whether he felt inwardly glad that the end had finally come, or felt sad over the result and was too manly to show it. Whatever his feelings, they were entirely concealed from my observation; but my own feelings, which had been quite jubilant on the receipt of his letter, were sad and depressed. I felt like anything rather than rejoicing at the downfall of a foe who had fought so long and valiantly and had suffered so much for a cause, though that cause was, I believe, one of the worst for which a people ever fought, and one for which there was the least excuse. I do not question, however, the sincerity of the great mass of those who were opposed to us.

General Lee was dressed in a full uniform which was entirely new, and was wearing a sword of considerable value, very likely the sword which had been presented by the State of Virginia; at all events, it was an entirely different sword from the one that would ordinarily be worn in the field. In my rough travelling suit, the uniform of a private with the straps of a lieutenant-general, I must have contrasted very strangely with a man so handsomely dressed, six feet high, and of faultless form. But this was not a matter that I thought of until afterward.

We soon fell into a conversation about old army times. He remarked that he remembered me very well in the old army; and I told him that as a matter of course I remembered him perfectly, but from the difference in our rank and years (there being about sixteen years difference in our ages) I had thought it very likely that I had not attracted his attention sufficiently to be remembered by him after such a long interval.

Our conversation grew so pleasant that I almost forgot the object of our meeting. After the conversation had run on in this style for some time, General Lee called my attention to the object of our meeting, and said that he had asked for this interview for the purpose of getting from me the terms I proposed to give his army. I said that I meant merely that his army should lay down their arms, not to take them up again during the continuance of the war unless duly and properly exchanged. He said that he had so understood my letter.

Then we gradually fell off again into conversation about matters foreign to the subject which had brought us together. This continued for some little time, when General Lee again interrupted the course of the conversation by suggesting that the terms I proposed to give his army ought to be written out. I called to General Parker, secretary of my staff, for writing materials, and commenced writing out the following terms:

"APPOMATTOX C. H., Virginia, April 9, 1865.

"GENERAL R. E. LEE, *Commanding Confederate States Armies:*

"GENERAL: In accordance with the substance of my letter to you of the 8th instant, I propose to receive the surrender of the Army of Northern Virginia on the following terms, to wit:

"Rolls of all the officers and men to be made in duplicate, one copy to be given to an officer designated by me, the other to be retained by such officer or officers as you may designate. The officers to give their individual paroles not to take up arms against the Government of the United States until properly exchanged, and each company or regimental commander to sign a like parole for the men of their commands.

"The arms, artillery, and public property to be parked and stacked, and turned over to the officer appointed by me to receive them. This will not embrace the side-arms of the officers, nor their private horses or baggage. This done, each officer and man will be allowed to return to their homes, not to be disturbed by United States authority so long as they observe their parole and the laws in force where they may reside.

"Very respectfully,

"U. S. Grant, Lieutenant-General."

When I put my pen to the paper I did not know the first word that I should make use of in writing the terms. I only knew what was in my mind, and I wished to express it clearly, so that there could be no mistaking it. As I wrote on, the thought occurred to me that the officers had their own private horses and effects, which were important to them, but of no value to us; also that it would be an unnecessary humiliation to call upon them to deliver their side-arms.

No conversation—not one word—passed between General Lee and myself, either about private property, side-arms, or kindred subjects. He appeared to have no objections to the terms first proposed; or, if he had a point to make against them, he wished to wait until they were in writing to make it. When he read over that part of the terms about side-arms, horses, and private property of the officers, he remarked, with some feeling, I thought, that this would have a happy effect upon his army.

Then, after a little further conversation, General Lee remarked to me again that their army was organized a little differently from the army of the United States (still maintaining by implication that we were two countries); that in their army the cavalrymen and artillerists owned their own horses; and he asked if he was to understand that the men who so owned their horses were to be permitted to retain them. I told him that as the terms were written they would not; that only the officers were permitted to take their private property. He then, after reading over the terms a second time, remarked that that was clear.

I then said to him that I thought this would be about the last battle of the war. I sincerely hoped so; and I said, further, I took it that most of the men in the ranks were small farmers. The whole country had been so raided by the two armies that it was doubtful whether they would be able to put in a crop to carry themselves and their families through the next winter without the aid of the horses they were then riding. The United States did not want them, and I would therefore instruct the officers I left behind to receive the paroles of his troops to let every man of the Confederate army who claimed to own a horse or mule take the animal to his home. Lee remarked again that this would have a happy effect. He then sat down and wrote out the following letter:

"HEADQUARTERS
"ARMY OF NORTHERN VIRGINIA, April 9, 1865.

"GENERAL: I have received your letter of this date containing the terms of the surrender of the Army of Northern Virginia as proposed by you. As they are substantially the same as those expressed in your letter of the 8th instant, they are accepted. I will proceed to designate the proper officers to carry the stipulations into effect. R. E. LEE, General.

"Lieutenant-General U. S. GRANT."

While duplicates of the two letters were being made, the Union Generals present were severally presented to General Lee.

The much-talked-of surrendering of Lee's sword and my handing it back—this and much more that has been said about it—is the purest romance. The word "sword" or "side-arms" was not mentioned by either of us until I wrote it in the terms. There was no premeditation, and it did not occur to me until the moment I wrote it down. If I had happened to omit it, and General Lee had called my attention to it, I should have put it in the terms precisely as I acceded to the provision about the soldiers retaining their horses.

General Lee, after all was completed, and before taking his leave, remarked that his army was in a very bad condition for want of food, and that they were without forage; that his men had been living for some days on parched corn exclusively; and that he would have to ask me for rations and forage. I told him, "Certainly," and asked for how many men he wanted rations. His answer was, "About twenty-five thousand"; and I authorized him to send his own commissary and quartermaster to Appomattox Station, two or three miles away, where he could have, out of the trains we had stopped, all the provisions wanted. As for forage, we had ourselves depended almost entirely upon the country for that.

Generals Gibbon, Griffin, and Merritt were designated by me to carry into effect the paroling of Lee's troops before they should start for their homes—General Lee leaving Generals Longstreet, Gordon, and Pendleton for them to confer with in order to facilitate this work. Lee and I then separated as cordially as we had met, he returning to his own lines; and all went into bivouac for the night at Appomattox.

Soon after Lee's departure I telegraphed to Washington as follows:

"HEADQUARTERS,
"APPOMATTOX COURT HOUSE, VA.,
"April 9, 1865, 4.30 P.M.

"HON. E. M. STANTON, *Secretary of War, Washington:*

"General Lee surrendered the Army of Northern Virginia this afternoon on terms proposed by myself. The accompanying additional correspondence will show the conditions fully.

"U. S. GRANT, Lieutenant-General."

When news of the surrender first reached our lines our men commenced firing a salute of a hundred guns in honor of the victory. I at once sent word, however, to have it stopped. The Confederates were now our prisoners, and we did not want to exult over their downfall.

I determined to return to Washington at once, with a view to putting a stop to the purchase of supplies and what I now deemed other useless outlay of money. Before leaving, however, I thought I would like to see General Lee again; so next morning I rode out beyond our lines toward his headquarters, preceded by a bugler and a staff-officer carrying a white flag.

Lee soon mounted his horse, seeing who it was, and met me. We had there between the lines, sitting on horseback, a very pleasant conversation of over half an hour, in the course of which Lee said to me that the South was a big country, and that we might have to march over it three or four times before the war entirely ended, but that we would now be able to do it, as they could no longer resist us. He expressed it as his earnest hope, however, that we would not be called upon to cause more loss and sacrifice of life; but he could not foretell the result. I then suggested to General Lee that there was not a man in the Confederacy whose influence with the soldiery and the whole people was as great as his; and that if he would now advise the surrender of all the armies I had no doubt his advice would be followed with alacrity. But Lee said he could not do that without consulting the President first. I knew there was no use to urge him to do anything against his ideas of what was right.

I was accompanied by my staff and other officers, some of whom seemed to have a great desire to go inside the Confederate lines. They finally asked permission of Lee to do so for the purpose of seeing some of their old army friends, and the permission was granted. They went over, had a very pleasant time with their old friends, and brought some of them back with them when they returned.

When Lee and I separated he went back to his lines and I returned to the house of Mr. McLean. Here the officers of both armies came in great numbers, and seemed to enjoy the meeting as much as if they had been friends separated for a long time while fighting battles under the same flag. For the time being, it looked very much as if all thought of the war had escaped their minds. After an hour pleasantly passed in this way, I set out on horseback, accompanied by my staff and a small escort, for Burkesville Junction, up to which point the railroad had by this time been repaired.

THE AUSTRO-PRUSSIAN WAR

A.D. 1866

CHARLES A. FYFFE

This conflict, called also the Seven Weeks' War, was productive of results not to be measured by the duration of the struggle in the field—the total exclusion of Austria from political control in Germany, and the rise of Prussia to a position of primacy among the German States. The annexation of Schleswig-Holstein to Prussia, as a consequence of the war, not only aggrandized that kingdom, but made an important change in the relations of the duchies so annexed.

The "Schleswig-Holstein question" was the cause of the war—that and the ancient rivalry between Austria and Prussia. The Schleswig-Holstein question is one of the most complicated matters in modern history. The two duchies had been long united under a single duke. When ducal heirs failed, Denmark undertook the government of both duchies, which were "never to be separated." Schleswig was a vassal State of Denmark, and Holstein of Germany. When in 1846 the duchies demanded local independence, Denmark attempted to absorb them, and German troops were sent to their assistance. Denmark secured a provisional triumph, and adhered to her purpose of incorporating the duchies with her own territory. In 1864 Schleswig and Holstein were occupied by the allied forces of Austria and Prussia, and the "Danish War" ensued, in which the duchies were quickly wrested from Denmark to be disposed of by the other two Powers. This war furnished a notable example of the fact that royal alliances no longer control the fate of nations. Only the year before the Prince of Wales had wedded the Crown Princess of Denmark, yet Denmark was robbed of territory with no protest from England.

For many years Austria had been dominant in Germany and had subjected Prussia to her will. On the accession of William I, in 1861, Prussia began to assert her independence, and this new policy was aggressively pursued by Count Otto von Bismarck, the King's minister. He strengthened the army, and directed his schemes against Austria. It had been agreed that Prussia should govern Schleswig, while Holstein was to be ruled by Austria. Bismarck accused Austria of violating this agreement, and, after various moves by both sides, warlike preparations were begun. In April, 1866, a treaty of alliance was signed between Prussia and Italy, while several German States took the part of Austria.

ON March 16, 1866, the Austrian Government announced that it should refer the affairs of Schleswig-Holstein to the Federal Diet. This was a clear departure from the terms of the Convention of Gastein,[1] and from the agreement made between Austria and Prussia before entering into the Danish War in 1864 that the Schleswig-Holstein question should be settled by the two Powers independently of the German Federation. King William was deeply moved by such a breach of good faith; tears filled his eyes when he spoke of the conduct of the Austrian Emperor, Francis Joseph; and though pacific influences were still active around him, he now began to fall in more cordially with the warlike policy of his minister. The question at issue between Prussia and Austria expanded from the mere disposal of the duchies to the reconstitution of the federal system of Germany. In a note laid before the Governments of all the minor States, Bismarck declared that the time had come when Germany must receive a new and more effective organization, and inquired how far Prussia could count on the support of allies if it should be attacked by Austria or forced into war. Immediately after this reopening of the whole problem of federal reform in Germany the draft of the treaty with Italy was brought to its final shape by Bismarck and the Italian envoy, and sent to the Ministry at Florence for its approval.

Bismarck had now to make the best use of the three-months' delay that was granted to him. On the day after the acceptance of the treaty by the Italian Government the Prussian representative at the Diet of Frankfort handed in a proposal for the summoning of a German parliament, to be elected by universal suffrage. Coming from the minister who had made parliamentary government a mockery in Prussia, this proposal was scarcely considered as serious. Bavaria, as the chief of the secondary States, had already expressed its willingness to enter upon the discussion of federal reform, but it asked that the two leading Powers should in the mean time undertake not to attack each other. Austria at once acceded to this request, and so forced Bismarck into giving a similar assurance. Promises of disarma-

[1] A treaty concluded between Austria and Prussia at Wildbad Gastein, August 14, 1865, by which the duchies conquered from Denmark were disposed of.—ED.

ment were then exchanged; but as Austria declined to stay the collection of its forces in Venetia against Italy, Bismarck was able to charge his adversary with insincerity in the negotiation, and preparations for war were resumed on both sides. Other difficulties now came into view. The treaty between Prussia and Italy had been made known to the Court of Vienna by Napoleon, whose advice La Marmora, the Italian minister, had sought before its conclusion, and the Austrian Emperor had thus become aware of his danger. He now determined to sacrifice Venetia if Italy's neutrality could be so secured. On May 5th the Italian ambassador at Paris, Count Nigra, was informed by Napoleon that Austria had offered to cede Venetia to him in behalf of Victor Emmanuel if France and Italy would not prevent Austria from indemnifying itself at Prussia's expense in Silesia.

Without a war, at the price of mere inaction, Italy was offered all that it could gain by a struggle which was likely to be desperate and which might end in disaster.

La Marmora was in sore perplexity. Though he had formed a juster estimate of the capacity of the Prussian army than any other statesman or soldier in Europe, he was thoroughly suspicious of the intentions of the Prussian Government; and in sanctioning the alliance of the previous month he had done so half expecting that Bismarck would through the prestige of this alliance gain for Prussia its own objects without entering into war, and then leave Italy to reckon with Austria as best it might. He would gladly have abandoned the alliance and have accepted Austria's offer if Italy could have done this without disgrace. But the sense of honor was sufficiently strong to carry him past this temptation. He declined the offer made through Paris, and continued the armaments of Italy, though still with a secret hope that European diplomacy might find the means of realizing the purpose of his country without war.

The neutral Powers were now, with various objects, bestirring themselves in favor of a European congress. Napoleon believed the time to be come when the treaties of 1815 might be finally obliterated by the joint act of Europe. He was himself ready to join Prussia with three hundred thousand men if the King would transfer the Rhenish Provinces to France. Demands, direct and indirect, were made on Count Bismarck in behalf of the Tuileries for cessions of territory of greater or less extent. These demands were neither granted nor refused. Bismarck procrastinated; he spoke of the obstinacy of the King his master; he inquired whether parts of Belgium or Switzerland would not better assimilate with France than a German Province; he put off the Emperor's representatives by the assurance that he could more conveniently arrange these matters with the Emperor when he should himself visit Paris. On May 28th invitations to a congress were issued by France, England, and Russia jointly, the objects of the congress being defined as the settlement of the affairs of Schleswig-Holstein, of the differences between Austria and Italy, and of the reform of the Federal Constitution of Germany, in so far as these affected Europe at large. The invitation was accepted by Prussia and by Italy; it was accepted by Austria only under the condition that no arrangement should be discussed which should give an increase of territory or power to one of the States invited to the congress.

This subtly worded condition would not indeed have excluded the equal aggrandizement of all. It would not have rendered the cession of Venetia to Italy or the annexation of Schleswig-Holstein to Prussia impossible; but it would either have involved the surrender of the former Papal territory by Italy in order that Victor Emmanuel's dominions should receive no increase, or, in the alternative, it would have entitled Austria to claim Silesia as its own equivalent for the augmentation of the Italian Kingdom. Such reservations would have rendered any efforts of the Powers to preserve peace useless, and they were accepted as tantamount to a refusal on the part of Austria to attend the congress. Simultaneously with its answer to the neutral Powers Austria called upon the Federal Diet to take the affairs of Schleswig-Holstein into its own hands, and convoked the Holstein Estates. Bismarck thereupon declared the Convention of Gastein to be at an end, and ordered General Manteuffel to lead his troops into Holstein. The Austrian commander, protesting that he yielded only to superior force, withdrew through Altona into Hanover.

Austria at once demanded and obtained from the Diet of Frankfort the mobilization of the whole of the federal armies. The representative of Prussia, declaring that this act of the Diet had made an end of the existing federal union, handed in the plan of his Government for the reorganization of Germany, and quitted Frankfort. Diplomatic relations between Austria and Prussia were broken off on June 12th, and on the 15th Count Bismarck demanded of the sovereigns of Hanover, Saxony, and Hesse-Cassel that they should on that very day put a stop to their military preparations and accept the Prussian scheme of federal reform. Negative answers being given, Prussian troops immediately marched into these territories, and war began. Weimar, Mecklenburg, and other petty States in the north took part with Prussia; all the rest of Germany joined Austria.

The goal of Bismarck's desire, the end he had steadily set before himself since entering upon his ministry, was attained; and, if his calculations as to the strength of the Prussian army were not at fault, Austria was at length to be expelled from the German Federation by force of arms. But the process by which Bismarck had worked up to this result had ranged against him the almost unanimous opinion of Germany outside the military circles of Prussia itself. His final demand for the summoning of a German parliament was taken as mere comedy. The guiding star of his policy had hitherto been the dynastic interest of the house of Hohenzollern; and now, when the Germans were to be plunged into war with one another, it seemed as if the real object of the struggle was no more than the annexation of the Danish duchies and some other coveted territory to the Prussian Kingdom. The voice of protest and condemnation rose loud from every organ of public opinion. Even in Prussia itself the instances were few where any spontaneous support was tendered to the Government.

The Parliament of Berlin, struggling up to the end against the all-powerful minister, had seen its members prosecuted for speeches made within its own walls, and had at last been prorogued in order that its insubordination might not hamper the Crown in the moment of danger. But the mere disappearance of Parliament could not conceal the intensity of ill-will which the minister and his policy had excited. The author of a fratricidal war of Germans against Germans was in the eyes of many the greatest of all criminals; and on May 7th an attempt was made by a young fanatic to kill Bismarck in the streets of Berlin. The minister owed the preservation of his life to the feebleness of his assailant's weapon and to his own vigorous arm. But the imminence of the danger affected King William far more than Bismarck himself. It spoke to his simple mind of supernatural protection and aid; it stilled his doubts and confirmed him in the belief that Prussia was in this crisis the instrument for working out the Almighty's will.

A few days before the outbreak of hostilities the Emperor Napoleon gave publicity to his own view of the European situation. He attributed the coming war to three causes: To the faulty geographical limits of the Prussian State, to the desire for a better federal system in Germany, and to the necessity felt by the Italian nation for securing its independence. These needs would, he conceived, be met by a territorial rearrangement in the north of Germany consolidating and augmenting the Prussian Kingdom; by the creation of a more effective federal union between the secondary German States; and finally, by the incorporation of Venetia with Italy, Austria's position in Germany remaining unimpaired.

Only in the event of the map of Europe being altered to the exclusive advantage of one great Power would France require an extension of frontier. Its interests lay in the preservation of the equilibrium of Europe, and in the maintenance of the Italian Kingdom. These had already been secured by arrangements which would not require France to draw the sword; a watchful but unselfish neutrality was the policy which its Government had determined to pursue. Napoleon had in fact lost all control over events, and all chance of gaining the Rhenish Provinces, from the time when he permitted Italy to enter into the Prussian alliance without any stipulation that France should at its option be admitted as a third member of the coalition. He could not ally himself with Austria against his own creation, the Italian Kingdom; on the other hand, he had no means of extorting cessions from Prussia when once Prussia was sure of an ally who could bring two hundred thousand men into the field. His diplomacy had been successful in so far as it had assured Venetia to Italy whether Prussia should be victorious or overthrown, but as regarded France it had landed him in absolute powerlessness. He was unable to act on one side; he was not wanted on the other. Neutrality had become a matter, not of choice, but of necessity;

and until the course of military events should have produced some new situation in Europe, France might well be watchful, but it could scarcely gain much credit for its disinterested part.[1]

Assured against an attack from the side of the Rhine, Bismarck was able to throw the mass of the Prussian forces southward against Austria, leaving in the north only the modest contingent that was necessary to overcome the resistance of Hanover and Hesse-Cassel. Through the precipitancy of a Prussian general, who struck without waiting for his colleagues, the Hanoverians gained a victory at Langensalza on June 27th; but other Prussian regiments arrived on the field a few hours later, and the Hanoverian army was forced to capitulate the next day. The King made his escape to Austria; the Elector of Hesse-Cassel, less fortunate, was made a prisoner of war. Northern Germany was thus speedily reduced to submission, and any danger of a diversion in favor of Austria in this quarter disappeared.

In Saxony no attempt was made to bar the way to the advancing Prussians. Dresden was occupied without resistance, but the Saxon army marched southward in good time, and joined the Austrians in Bohemia. The Prussian forces, about two hundred fifty thousand strong, now gathered on the Saxon and Silesian frontier, covering the line from Pirna to Landshut. They were composed of three armies: the first, or central, army under Prince Frederick Charles, a nephew of the King; the second, or Silesian, army under the Crown Prince; the westernmost, known as the Army of the Elbe, under General Herwarth von Bittenfeld. Against these were ranged about an equal number of Austrians, led by Benedek, a general who had gained great distinction in the Hungarian and Italian campaigns. It had at first been thought probable that Benedek, whose forces lay about

[1] On May 11th Nigra, Italian ambassador at Paris, reported that Napoleon's ideas on the objects to be attained by a congress were as follows: Venetia to Italy; Silesia to Austria; the Danish duchies and other territory in North Germany to Prussia; the establishment of several small States on the Rhine under French protection; the dispossessed German princes to be compensated in Roumania. Napoleon III was pursuing in a somewhat altered form the old German policy of the republic and the empire—namely, the balancing of Austria and Prussia against each other, and the establishment of a French protectorate over the group of secondary States.

Olmuetz, would invade Southern Silesia, and the Prussian line had therefore been extended far to the east. Soon, however, it appeared that the Austrians were unable to take up the offensive, and Benedek moved westward into Bohemia. The Prussian line was now shortened, and orders were given to the three armies to cross the Bohemian frontier and converge in the direction of the town of Gitschin. General Moltke, chief of staff, directed their operations from Berlin by telegraph.

The combined advance of the three armies was executed with extraordinary precision; and in a series of hard-fought combats, extending from June 26th to the 29th, the Austrians were driven back upon their centre, and effective communication was established between the three invading bodies. On the 30th the King of Prussia, with General Moltke and Count Bismarck, left Berlin; on July 2d they were at headquarters at Gitschin. It had been Benedek's design to leave a small force to hold the Silesian army in check, and to throw the mass of his army westward upon Prince Frederick Charles and overwhelm him before he could receive help from his colleagues. This design had been baffled by the energy of the Crown Prince's attack, and by the superiority of the Prussians in generalship, in the discipline of their troops, and in the weapon they carried; for though the Austrians had witnessed in the Danish campaign the effects of the Prussian breechloading rifle (called the needle-gun), they had not thought it necessary to adopt a similar arm.

Benedek, though no great battle had yet been fought, saw that the campaign was lost, and wrote to the Emperor on July 1st recommending him to make peace, for otherwise a catastrophe was inevitable. He then concentrated his army on high ground a few miles west of Koeniggraetz, and prepared for a defensive battle on the grandest scale. In spite of the losses of the past week he could still bring about two hundred thousand men into action. The three Prussian armies were now near enough to one another to combine in their attack, and on the night of July 2d the King sent orders to the three commanders to move against Benedek before daybreak.

Prince Frederick Charles, advancing through the village of Sadowa, was the first in the field. For hours his divisions sustained an unequal struggle against the assembled strength of the

Austrians. Midday passed; the defenders now pressed down upon their assailants; and preparations for a retreat had been begun, when the long-expected message arrived that the Crown Prince was close at hand. The onslaught of the army of Silesia on Benedek's right, which was accompanied by the arrival of Hewarth at the other end of the field of battle, at once decided the day. With difficulty the Austrian commander prevented the enemy from seizing the positions that would have cut off his retreat. He retired eastward across the Elbe with a loss of eighteen thousand killed or wounded and twenty-four thousand prisoners. His army was ruined; and ten days after the Prussians had crossed the frontier the war was practically at an end.

The disaster of Koeniggraetz was too great to be neutralized by the success of the Austrian forces in Italy. La Marmora, who had given up his place at the head of the Government in order to take command of the army, crossed the Mincio at the head of a hundred twenty thousand men, but was defeated by inferior numbers on the fatal ground of Custozza, and compelled to fall back on the Oglio. This gleam of success, which was followed by a naval victory at Lissa off the Istrian coast, made it easier for the Austrian Emperor to face the sacrifices that were now inevitable. Immediately after the Battle of Koeniggraetz he invoked the mediation of Napoleon III, and ceded Venetia to him in behalf of Italy. Napoleon at once tendered his good offices to the belligerents, and proposed an armistice. His mediation was accepted in principle by the King of Prussia, who expressed his willingness also to grant an armistice as soon as preliminaries of peace should be recognized by the Austrian Court.

In the mean time, while negotiations passed between all four Governments, the Prussians pushed forward until their outposts came within sight of Vienna. If in pursuance of General Moltke's plan the Italian generals had thrown a corps northeastward from the head of the Adriatic, and so struck at the very heart of the Austrian monarchy, it is possible that the victors of Koeniggraetz might have imposed their own terms without regard to Napoleon's mediation, and, while adding the Italian Tyrol to Victor Emmanuel's dominions, have completed the union of Germany under the house of Hohenzollern at one stroke. But with Hungary still intact, and the Italian army paralyzed by the dissensions of its commanders, prudence bade the great statesman of Berlin content himself with the advantages he could reap without prolongation of the war, and without the risk of throwing Napoleon into the enemy's camp. He had at first required, as conditions of peace, that Prussia should be left free to annex Saxony, Hanover, Hesse-Cassel, and other North German territory; that Austria should wholly withdraw from German affairs; and that all Germany, less the Austrian Provinces, should be united in a federation under Prussian leadership.

To gain the assent of Napoleon to these terms, Bismarck hinted that France might by accord with Prussia annex Belgium. Napoleon, however, refused to agree to the extension of Prussia's ascendency over all Germany, and presented a counter-project, which in its turn was rejected by Bismarck. It was finally settled that Prussia should not be prevented from annexing Hanover, Nassau, and Hesse-Cassel, as conquered territory that lay between its own Rhenish Provinces and the rest of the Kingdom; that Austria should completely withdraw from German affairs; that Germany north of the Main, together with Saxony, should be included in a federation under Prussian leadership; and that for the States south of the Main the right of entering into a national bond with the Northern League should be reserved.

Austria escaped without loss of any of its non-Italian territory; it also succeeded in preserving the existence of Saxony, which, as in 1815, the Prussian Government had been most anxious to annex.

Napoleon, in confining the Prussian Federation to the north of the Main, and in securing by a formal stipulation in the treaty the independence of the South German States, imagined himself to have broken Germany into halves, and to have laid the foundation of a South German League that should look to France as its protector. On the other hand, Bismarck by his annexation of Hanover and neighboring districts had added a population of four millions to the Prussian Kingdom, and given it a continuous territory; he had forced Austria out of the German system; he had gained its sanction to the federal union of all Germany north of the Main, and had at least kept the way open for the later extension of this union to the South German States.

Preliminaries of peace embodying these conditions and recognizing Prussia's sovereignty in Schleswig-Holstein were signed at Nicolsburg on July 26th, and formed the basis of the definitive treaty of peace, which was concluded at Prague on August 23d. An illusory clause, added at the instance of Napoleon, provided that if the population of the northern districts of Schleswig should by a free vote express the wish to be united with Denmark, these districts should be ceded to the Danish Kingdom.

Bavaria and the southwestern allies of Austria, though their military action was ineffective, continued in arms for some weeks after the Battle of Koeniggraetz, and the suspension of hostilities arranged at Nicolsburg did not come into operation in their behalf till August 2d. Before that date their forces were dispersed and their power of resistance broken by the Prussian generals Falckenstein and Manteuffel in a series of unimportant engagements and intricate manœuvres. The city of Frankfort, against which Bismarck seems to have borne some personal hatred, was treated for a while by the conquerors with extraordinary and most impolitic harshness; in other respects the action of the Prussian Government toward these conquered States was not such as to render future union and friendship difficult.

All the South German Governments, with the single exception of Baden, appealed to the Emperor Napoleon for assistance in the negotiations they had opened at Berlin. But at the very moment when this request was made and granted Napoleon was himself demanding from Bismarck the cession of the Bavarian Palatinate and of the Hessian districts west of the Rhine. Bismarck had only to acquaint the King of Bavaria and the South German ministers with the designs of their French protector in order to reconcile them to his own chastening but not unfriendly hand. The grandeur of a united "Fatherland" flashed upon minds hitherto impenetrable by any national ideal, when it became known that Napoleon was bargaining for Oppenheim and Kaiserslautern. Not only were the insignificant questions as to the war indemnities to be paid to Prussia and the frontier villages to be exchanged promptly settled, but by a series of secret treaties all the South German States entered into an offensive and defensive alliance with the Prussian King, and engaged in case of war to place their entire forces at his disposal and under his command.

The diplomacy of Napoleon III had in the end effected for Bismarck almost more than his earlier intervention had frustrated, for it had made the South German courts the allies of Prussia, not through conquest or mere compulsion, but out of regard for their own interests. It was said by the opponents of the Imperial Government in France, and scarcely with exaggeration, that every error which it was possible to commit had, in the course of the year 1866, been committed by Napoleon III. One crime, one act of madness, remained open to the Emperor's critics, to lash him and France into a conflict with the power whose union he had not been able to prevent.

THE LAYING OF THE ATLANTIC CABLE

A.D. 1866

CYRUS W. FIELD

Twenty-two years after the completion of the first telegraph line—between Washington and Baltimore, in 1844—came the greatest triumph in the history of telegraphy. The first successful laying of an ocean telegraph, the Atlantic cable of 1866, marked the beginning of a new era in human intercourse, for the first achievement has been followed by others of like magnitude in various parts of the world. It is said that the first experiments for demonstrating the practicability of a submarine telegraph were made by Samuel F. B. Morse, under whose direction the Washington and Baltimore telegraph line was opened.

The successful demonstration of submarine telegraphy was made through the work of Cyrus W. Field and his associates. He was the son of David Dudley Field, who also had several other sons distinguished in American history. Cyrus W. Field was born in Stockbridge, Massachusetts, in 1819. In 1853 he retired from business in New York with a fortune, and devoted himself to the enterprise that gave him his fame. About this time Peter Cooper, Moses Taylor, Marshall O. Roberts, Chandler White, Robert W. Lowber, and David Dudley Field, brother of Cyrus, met at the residence of the last-named on "four successive evenings, and, around a table covered with maps and charts and plans and estimates, considered a project to extend a line of telegraph from Nova Scotia to St. John's, in Newfoundland, thence to be carried across the ocean." The undertaking appeared to the projectors to be much less difficult than it actually proved. They thought it might be accomplished from New York to St. John's "in a few months," but it took two years and a half to lay this line. Few persons had any faith in the scheme, and the money for this great initial step was all furnished by Field and his friends mentioned above.

The development and carrying out of the enterprise to its transatlantic completion are here related in the words of its leading promoter, to whom the chief honors of this inestimable service to mankind are universally ascribed. The account was written in 1866.

AT first the Atlantic-cable project was wholly an American enterprise. It was begun, and for two years and a half was carried on, solely by American capital. Our brethren across the sea did not even know what we were doing away in the forests of

Newfoundland. Our little company raised and expended over a million and a quarter of dollars before an Englishman paid a single pound sterling. Our only support outside was in the liberal character and steady friendship of the Government of Newfoundland, for which we were greatly indebted to Mr. E. M. Archibald, then Attorney-General of that colony. In preparing for an ocean cable, the first soundings across the Atlantic were made by American officers in American ships. Our scientific men—Morse, Henry, Bache, and Maury—had taken great interest in the subject. The United States ship Dolphin discovered the telegraphic plateau as early as 1853, and the United States ship Arctic sounded across from Newfoundland to Ireland in 1856, a year before Her Majesty's ship Cyclops, under command of Captain Dayman, went over the same course. This I state, not to take aught from the just praise of England, but simply to vindicate the truth of history.

It was not till 1856 that the enterprise had any existence in England. In that summer I went to London, and there, with Mr. John W. Brett, Mr. (now Sir) Charles Bright, and Doctor Whitehouse, organized the Atlantic Telegraph Company. Science had begun to contemplate the necessity of such an enterprise; and the great Faraday cheered us with his lofty enthusiasm. Then, for the first time, was enlisted the support of English capitalists; and then the British Government began that generous course which it has continued ever since—offering us ships to complete soundings across the Atlantic and to assist in laying the cable, and an annual subsidy for the transmission of messages. The expedition of 1857 and the two expeditions of 1858 were joint enterprises, in which the Niagara and the Susquehanna took part with the Agamemnon, the Leopard, the Gordon, and the Valorous; and the officers of both navies worked with generous rivalry for the same great object. The capital—except one-quarter which was taken by myself—was subscribed wholly in Great Britain. The directors were almost all English bankers and merchants, though among them was one gentleman whom we are proud to call an American—Mr. George Peabody, a name honored in two countries, since he has showered his princely benefactions upon both.

After two unsuccessful attempts, on the third trial we gained a brief success. The cable was laid, and for four weeks it worked—though never very brilliantly. It spoke, though only in broken sentences. But while it lasted no less than four hundred messages were sent across the Atlantic. Grèat was the enthusiasm it excited. It was a new thing under the sun, and for a few weeks the public went wild over it. Of course, when it stopped, the reaction was very great. People grew dumb and suspicious. Some thought it was all a hoax; and many were quite sure that it never had worked at all. That kind of odium we have had to endure for eight years, till now, I trust, we have at last silenced the unbelievers.

After the failure of 1858 came our darkest days. When a thing is dead, it is hard to galvanize it into life. It is more difficult to revive an old enterprise than to start a new one. The freshness and novelty are gone, and the feeling of disappointment discourages further effort.

Other causes delayed a new attempt. The United States had become involved in a tremendous war; and while the nation was struggling for life, it had no time to spend in foreign enterprises. But in England the project was still kept alive. The Atlantic Telegraph Company kept up its organization. It had a noble body of directors, who had faith in the enterprise and looked beyond its present low estate to ultimate success. Our chairman, the Right Honorable James Stuart Wortley, did not join us in the hour of victory, but in what seemed the hour of despair, after the failure of 1858, and he has been a steady support through all these years.

All this time the science of submarine telegraphy was making progress. The British Government appointed a commission to investigate the whole subject. It was composed of eminent scientific men and practical engineers—Galton, Wheatstone, Fairbairn, Bidder, Varley, and Latimer and Edwin Clark—with the secretary of the company, Mr. Saward—names to be held in honor in connection with this enterprise, along with those of other English engineers, such as Stephenson and Brunel and Whitworth and Penn and Lloyd and Joshua Field, who gave time and thought and labor freely to this enterprise, refusing all compensation. This commission sat for nearly two years, and spent many thousands of pounds in experiments. The result was a clear conviction in every mind that it was possible to lay a telegraph across the Atlantic. Science was also being all the while applied to practice. Submarine cables were laid in different seas—in the Mediterranean, in the Red Sea, and the Persian Gulf. The last was laid by my friend Sir Charles Bright.

When the scientific and engineering problems were solved, we took heart again and began to prepare for a fresh attempt. This was in 1863. In the United States—though the war was still raging—I went from city to city, holding meetings and trying to raise capital, but with poor success. Men came and listened and said it was all very fine and hoped I would succeed, but did nothing. In one of the cities they gave me a large meeting and passed some beautiful resolutions and appointed a committee of "solid men" to canvass the city, but I did not get a solitary subscriber! In New York city I did better, though money came by the hardest effort. By personal solicitations, encouraged by good friends, I succeeded in raising three hundred fifty thousand dollars. Since not many had faith, I must present one example to the contrary, though it was not till a year later. When almost all deemed it a hopeless scheme, one gentleman came to me and purchased stock of the Atlantic Telegraph Company to the amount of one hundred thousand dollars. That was Mr. Loring Andrews. But at the time I speak of, it was plain that our main hope must be in England, and I went to London. There, too, it dragged heavily. There was a profound discouragement. Many had lost before, and were not willing to throw more money into the sea. We needed six hundred thousand pounds, and with our utmost efforts we had raised less than half, and there the enterprise stood in a deadlock. It was plain that we must have help from some new quarter. I looked around to find a man who had broad shoulders and could carry a heavy load and who would be a giant in the cause.

At this time I was introduced to a gentleman, whom I would hold up to the American public as a specimen of a great-hearted Englishman, Mr. Thomas Brassey. In London he is known as one of the men who have made British enterprise and British capital felt in all parts of the earth. I went to see him, though with fear and trembling. He received me kindly, but put me through such an examination as I never had before. I thought I was in the witness-box. He asked me every possible question, but my answers satisfied him, and he ended by saying it was an enterprise that should be carried out, and that he would be one of ten men to furnish the money to do it. This was a pledge of sixty thousand pounds sterling! Encouraged by this noble offer, I looked around to find another such man, though it was almost like trying to find two Wellingtons. But he *was* found in Mr. John Pender, of Manchester. I went to his office in London one day, and we walked together to the House of Commons, and before we got there he said he would take an equal share with Mr. Brassey.

The action of these two gentlemen was a turning-point in the history of our enterprise; for it led shortly after to a union of the well-known firm of Glass, Elliot and Company with the Gutta-percha Company, making of the two one concern known at The Telegraph Construction and Maintenance Company, which included not only Mr. Brassey and Mr. Pender, but other men of great wealth, such as Mr. George Elliot and Mr. Barclay of London, and Mr. Henry Bewley of Dublin, and which, thus reënforced with immense capital, took up the whole enterprise in its strong arms. We needed, I have said, six hundred thousand pounds, and with all our efforts in England and America we raised only two hundred eighty-five thousand pounds. This new company now came forward, and offered to take the whole remaining three hundred fifteen thousand pounds, besides one hundred thousand pounds of the bonds, and to make its own profits contingent on success. Mr. Richard A. Glass was made managing director and gave energy and vigor to all its departments, being admirably seconded by the secretary, Mr. Shuter.

A few days after, half a dozen gentlemen joined together and bought the Great Eastern to lay the cable; and at the head of this company was placed Mr. Daniel Gooch, a member of Parliament, and chairman of the Great Western Railway, who was with us in both the expeditions which followed. His son, Mr. Charles Gooch, a volunteer in the service, worked faithfully on board the Great Eastern.

The good-fortune which favored us in our ship favored us also in our commander, Captain Anderson, who was for years in the Cunard Line. How well he did his part in two expeditions the result has proved, and it was just that a mark of royal favor should fall on that manly head. Thus organized, the work of making a new Atlantic cable was begun. The core was prepared with infinite care, under the able superintendence of Mr. Chatterton and Mr. Willoughby Smith, and the whole was completed in about eight months. As fast as ready, it was taken on board the Great Eastern and coiled in three enormous tanks, and on July 15, 1865, the ship sailed.

I will not stop to tell the story of that expedition. For a week all went well; we had paid out one thousand two hundred miles of cable, and had only six hundred miles farther to go, when, hauling in the cable to remedy a fault, it parted and went to the bottom. That day I never can forget—how men paced the deck in despair, looking out on the broad sea that had swallowed up their hopes; and then how the brave Canning for nine days and nights dragged the bottom of the ocean for our lost treasure, and, though he grappled it three times, failed to bring it to the surface. The story of that expedition, as written by Doctor Russell, who was on board the Great Eastern, is one of the most marvellous chapters in the whole history of modern enterprise. We returned to England defeated, yet full of resolution to begin the battle anew. Measures were at once taken to make a second cable and fit out a new expedition; and with that assurance I came home to New York in the autumn.

In December I went back again, when lo! all our hopes had sunk to nothing. The Attorney-General of England had given his written opinion that we had no legal right, without a special act of Parliament (which could not be obtained under a year), to issue the new 12 per cent. shares, on which we relied to raise our capital. This was a terrible blow. The works were at once stopped, and the money which had been paid in returned to the subscribers. Such was the state of things when I reached London on December 24, 1865, and the next day was not a "merry" Christmas to me. But it was an inexpressible comfort to have the counsel of such men as Sir Daniel Gooch and Sir Richard A. Glass, and to hear stout-hearted Mr. Brassey tell us to go ahead, and, if need were, he would put down sixty thousand pounds more. It was finally concluded that the best course was to organize a new company, which should assume the work; and so originated the Anglo-American Telegraph Company. It was formed by ten gentlemen who met around a table in London and put down ten thousand pounds apiece. The great Telegraph Construction and Maintenance Company, undaunted by the failure of last year, answered us with a subscription of one hundred thousand pounds. Soon after the books were opened to the public, through the eminent banking-house of J. S. Morgan and Company, and in fourteen days we had raised the six hundred thousand pounds. Then the work began again, and went on with speed. Never was greater energy infused into any enterprise. It was only the last day of March that the new company was formed, and it was registered as a company the next day; and yet such was the vigor and despatch that in five months from that day the cable had been manufactured, shipped on the Great Eastern, stretched across the Atlantic, and was sending messages, literally swift as lightning, from continent to continent.

Yet this was not "a lucky hit"—a fine run across the ocean in calm weather. It was the worst weather I ever knew at that season of the year. The despatch that appeared in the New York papers read, "The weather has been most pleasant." I wrote it "unpleasant." We had fogs and storms almost the whole way. Our success was the result of the highest science combined with practical experience. Everything was perfectly organized to the minutest detail. We had on board an admirable staff of officers, such men as Halpin and Beckwith; engineers long used to this business, such as Canning and Clifford and Temple; and electricians such as Professor Thomson of Glasgow and Willoughby Smith and Laws. Mr. C. F. Varley, our companion of the year before, remained with Sir Richard Glass at Valentia, to keep watch at that end of the line, and Mr. Latimer Clark, who was to test the cable when done.

But our work was not over. After landing the cable safely at Newfoundland, we had another task—to return to mid-ocean and recover that lost in the expedition of last year. This achievement has perhaps excited more surprise than the other. Many even now "don't understand it," and every day I am asked "How it was done"? Well, it does seem rather difficult to fish for a jewel at the bottom of the ocean two and a half miles deep. But it is not so very difficult when you know how. You may be sure we did not go fishing at random, nor was our success mere "luck." It was the triumph of the highest nautical and engineering skill. We had four ships, and on board of them some of the best seamen in England—men who knew the ocean as a hunter knows every trail in the forest. There was Captain Moriarty, who was in the Agamemnon in 1857–1858. He was in the Great Eastern in 1865, and saw the cable when it broke; and he and Captain Anderson at once took observations so exact that they could go right to the spot. After finding it, they marked the line of the cable by buoys; for fogs would come, and shut out sun and stars, so that no man could take an observation.

These buoys were anchored a few miles apart, they were numbered, and each had a flagstaff on it so that it could be seen by day, and a lantern by night. Having thus taken our bearings, we stood off three or four miles, so as to come broadside on, and then, casting over the grapnel, drifted slowly down upon it, dragging the bottom of the ocean as we went. At first it was a little awkward to fish in such deep water, but our men got used to it, and soon could cast a grapnel almost as straight as an old whaler throws a harpoon. Our fishing-line was of formidable size. It was made of rope, twisted with wires of steel, so as to bear a strain of thirty tons. It took about two hours for the grapnel to reach bottom, but we could tell when it struck. I often went to the bow, and sat on the rope, and could feel by the quiver that the grapnel was dragging on the bottom two miles under us. But it was a very slow business. We had storms and calms and fogs and squalls.

Still we worked on day after day. Once, on August 17th, we got the cable up, and had it in full sight for five minutes, a long, slimy monster, fresh from the ooze of the ocean's bed, but our men began to cheer so wildly that it seemed to be frightened and suddenly broke away and went down into the sea. This accident kept us at work two weeks longer, but, finally, on the last night of August we caught it. We had cast the grapnel thirty times. It was a little before midnight on Friday night that we hooked the cable, and it was a little after midnight Sunday morning when we got it on board. What was the anxiety of those twenty-six hours! The strain on every man was like the strain on the cable itself. When finally it appeared, it was midnight; the lights of the ship, and those in the boats around our bows, as they flashed in the faces of the men, showed them eagerly watching for the cable to appear on the water.

At length it was brought to the surface. All who were allowed to approach crowded forward to see it. Yet not a word was spoken save by the officers in command who were heard giving orders. All felt as if life and death hung on the issue. It was only when the cable was brought over the bow and on to the deck that men dared to breathe. Even then they hardly believed their eyes. Some crept toward it to feel of it, to be sure it was there. Then we carried it along to the electricians' room, to see if our long-sought-for treasure was alive or dead. A few minutes of suspense, and a flash told of the lightning current again set free. Then did the feeling long pent up burst forth. Some turned away their heads and wept. Others broke into cheers, and the cry ran from man to man, and was heard down in the engine-rooms, deck below deck, and from the boats on the water, and the other ships, while rockets lighted the darkness of the sea. Then with thankful hearts we turned our faces again to the west.

But soon the wind rose, and for thirty-six hours we were exposed to all the dangers of a storm on the Atlantic. Yet in the very height and fury of the gale, as I sat in the electricians' room, a flash of light came up from the deep, which having crossed to Ireland, came back to me in mid-ocean, telling that those so dear to me, whom I had left on the banks of the Hudson, were well and following us with their wishes and their prayers. This was like a whisper of God from the sea, bidding me keep heart and hope. The Great Eastern bore herself proudly through the storm, as if she knew that the vital cord, which was to join two hemispheres, hung at her stern; and so, on Saturday, September 7th, we brought our second cable safely to the shore.

But the Great Eastern did not make her voyage alone. Three other ships attended her across the ocean—the Albany, the Medway, and the Terrible—the officers of all of which exerted themselves to the utmost. The Queen of England showed her appreciation of the services of some of those more prominent in the expedition, but if it had been possible to do justice to all, honors would have been bestowed upon many others. If this cannot be, at least their names live in the history of this enterprise, with which they will be forever associated.

When I think of them all, not only of those on the Great Eastern, but of Captain Commerill of the Terrible, and his first officer, Mr. Curtis (who with their ship came with us not only to Heart's Content, but afterward to the Gulf of St. Lawrence, to help in laying the new cable), and of the officers of the other ship, my heart is full. Better men never trod a deck. If I do not name them all it is because they are too many, their ranks are too full of glory. Even the sailors caught the enthusiasm of the enterprise, and were eager to share in the honor of the achievement. Brave, stalwart men they were, at home on the ocean and in the storm, of that sort that have carried the flag of England around the globe. I see them now as they dragged the shore end up the beach at Heart's Content, hugging it in their brawny arms as if it were a shipwrecked child whom they had rescued from the dangers of the sea.

THE VICTORY[1]

ROSSITER JOHNSON

When Man, in his Maker's image, came
  To be the lord of the new-made earth,
To conquer its forests, its beasts to tame,
  To gather its treasures and know their worth,
All readily granted his power and place
Save the Ocean, the Mountain, and Time, and Space;
And these four sneered at his puny frame,
  And made of his lordship a theme for mirth.

Whole ages passed while his flocks he tended,
  And delved and dreamed, as the years went by
Till there came an age when his genius splendid
  Had bridged the river and sailed the sky,
And raised the dome that defied the storm,
And mastered the beauties of color and form;
But his power was lost, his dominion ended,
  Where Time, Space, Mountain, or Sea was nigh.

[1] When Samuel F. B. Morse died, in 1872, memorial services were held in many cities, and full reports of the meetings were printed in a handsome volume, by order of Congress. At Concord, N. H., were displayed portraits that Morse had painted when, a young artist, he had sojourned there, and this poem was a part of the memorial exercises.—ED.

The Mountains rose in their grim inertness
  Between the peoples, and made them strange,
Save as in moments of pride or pertness
  They climbed the ridge of their native range,
And, looking down on the tribe below,
Saw nothing there but a deadly foe,
Heard only a war-cry, long and shrill,
In echoes leaping from hill to hill.

The Ocean rolled in its mighty splendor,
  Washing the slowly wasting shore,
And the voices of nations, fierce or tender,
  Lost themselves in its endless roar.
With frail ships launched on its treacherous surge,
And sad eyes fixed on its far blue verge,
Man's hold of life seemed brittle and slender,
  And the Sea his master forevermore.

And Space and Time brought their huge dimensions
  To separate man from his brother man,
And sowed between them a thousand dissensions,
  That ripened in hatred and caste and clan.
So Sea and Mountain and Time and Space
Laughed again in his lordship's face,
And bade him blush for his weak inventions
  And the narrow round his achievements ran.

But one morning he made him a slender wire,
  As an artist's vision took life and form,
While he drew from heaven the strange, fierce fire
  That reddens the edge of the midnight storm;
And he carried it over the Mountain's crest,
And dropped it into the Ocean's breast;
And Science proclaimed, from shore to shore,
That Time and Space ruled man no more.

Then the brotherhood lost on Shinar's plain
Came back to the peoples of earth again.
"Be one!" sighed the Mountain, and shrank away.
"Be one!" murmured Ocean, in dashes of spray.
"Be one!" said Space; "I forbid no more."
"Be one!" echoed Time, "till my years are o'er."
"We are one!" said the nations, as hand met hand
In a thrill electric from land to land.

THE FALL OF MAXIMILIAN

A.D. 1867

CHARLES A. FYFFE PRINCE SALM-SALM

Compared with the Civil War in the United States, the contemporary French intervention in Mexico seems but a slight episode, little more than an eddy in the tremendous current of greater events. But as a unique passage in the diversified history of Mexico, no less than in its bearings upon European attitudes toward the United States at a critical time, the story of Maximilian's ill-starred empire, and of his own fate, possesses a distinct interest.

The French expedition against Mexico had at first the backing of England and Spain. Its professed object was "to demand from the Mexican authorities more efficacious protection for the persons and properties" of the subjects of England, France, and Spain in Mexico, and fulfilment of the obligations contracted toward the sovereigns of the three former countries by the latter. Finding that France wished to go beyond this design in Mexico, and failing to agree with her upon a plan of action, England and Spain withdrew from the undertaking. But Napoleon himself was determined to establish "a sort of feudatory monarchy" in Mexico. How he went about the accomplishment of this purpose is well shown, in few words, by Fyffe, the excellent historian of modern Europe. The tragic ending of this enterprise is described by a prominent participant in the events here narrated, Prince Felix Salm-Salm. He was a German soldier of fortune who came to the United States in 1861, entered the Union army, and rose to the rank of brevet brigadier-general of volunteers. In 1866 he entered Maximilian's service in Mexico, and, as aide-de-camp to the Emperor and chief of the imperial household, shared intimately in his experiences. After the execution of Maximilian, Salm-Salm entered the Prussian army, and was killed at the battle of Gravelotte, August 18, 1870.

CHARLES A. FYFFE

THERE were in Napoleon III, as a man of state, two personalities, two mental existences, which blended but ill with each other. There was the contemplator of great human forces, the intelligent, if not deeply penetrative, reader of the signs of the times, the brooder through long years of imprisonment and exile, the child of Europe, to whom Germany, Italy, and England had all in turn been nearer than his own country; and there was the crowned adventurer, bound by his name and position to gain for France something that it did not possess, and to regard the greatness of every other nation as an impediment to the ascendency of his own.

Napoleon correctly judged the principle of nationality to be the dominant force in the immediate future of Europe. He saw in Italy and in Germany races whose internal divisions alone had prevented them from being the formidable rivals of France, and yet he assisted the one nation to effect its union, and was not indisposed, within certain limits, to promote the consolidation of the other. That the acquisition of Nice and Savoy, and even of the Rhenish Provinces, could not in itself make up to France for the establisment of two great nations on its immediate frontiers Napoleon must have well understood: he sought to carry the principle of agglomeration a stage further in the interests of France itself, and to form some moral, if not political, union of the Latin nations, which should embrace under his own ascendency communities beyond the Atlantic as well as those of the Old World. It was with this design that in the year 1862 he made the financial misdemeanors of Mexico the pretext for an expedition to that country, the object of which was to subvert the native republican Government, and to place the Hapsburg Maximilian, as a vassal prince, on its throne.

The design of Napoleon to establish French influence in Mexico was connected with his attempt to break up the United States by establishing the independence of the Southern Confederacy, then in rebellion, through the mediation of the great Powers of Europe. So long as the Civil War in the United States lasted, it seemed likely that Napoleon's enterprise in Mexico would be successful. Maximilian was placed upon the throne, and the republican leader, Juarez, was driven into the extreme north of the country. But with the overthrow of the Southern Confederacy and the restoration of peace in the United States in 1865 the prospect totally changed. The Government of Washington refused to acknowledge any authority in Mexico but that of Juarez, and informed Napoleon in courteous terms that his troops must be withdrawn. Napoleon had bound himself by treaty to keep twenty-five thousand men in Mexico for the protection of Maximilian. He was, however, unable to defy the order of the United States.

Early in 1866 he acquainted Maximilian with the necessities of the situation, and with the approaching removal of the force which alone had placed him and could sustain him on the throne. The unfortunate Prince sent his consort, Carlotta, daughter of the King of the Belgians, to Europe to plead against this act of desertion; but her efforts were vain, and her reason sank under the just presentiment of her husband's ruin. The utmost on which Napoleon could venture was the postponement of the recall of his troops till the spring of 1867. He urged Maximilian to abdicate before it was too late; but the Prince refused to dissociate himself from his counsellors who still implored him to remain.

Meanwhile the Juarists pressed back toward the capital from north and south. As the French detachments were withdrawn toward the coast the entire country fell into their hands. The last French soldiers quitted Mexico at the beginning of March, 1867, and on May 15th Maximilian, still lingering at Queretaro, was made prisoner by the Republicans. He had himself while in power ordered that the partisans of Juarez should be treated, not as soldiers, but as brigands, and that when captured they should be tried by court-martial and executed within twenty-four hours. The same severity was applied to himself. He was sentenced to death and shot at Queretaro on June 19th.

Thus ended the attempt of Napoleon III to establish the influence of France and of his dynasty beyond the seas. The doom of Maximilian excited the compassion of Europe; a deep, irreparable wound was inflicted on the reputation of the man who had tempted him to his treacherous throne, who had guaranteed him protection, and at the bidding of a superior power had abandoned him to his ruin. From this time, though the outward splendor of the Empire was undiminished, there remained scarcely anything of the personal prestige which Napoleon had once enjoyed in so rich a measure. He was no longer in the eyes of Europe or of his own country the profound, self-contained statesman in whose brain lay the secret of coming events; he was rather the gambler whom Fortune was preparing to desert, the usurper trembling for the future of his dynasty and his crown.

PRINCE SALM-SALM

In the morning of June 16th, at eleven o'clock, Colonel Miguel Palacios came, accompanied by General Refugio Gonzales, with a detachment of soldiers, and the latter read the death-warrant to the Emperor and the two generals. The Emperor heard it with a calm smile, and, looking at his watch, he said to Doctor Basch: "Three o'clock is the hour; we still have more than three hours, and can easily finish all."

The fatal hour came, and the three condemned waited in the passage for the officer charged with their execution. They waited a whole hour, and the Emperor conversed as usual with his confessor and two of his counsellors. At last came, at four o'clock, Colonel Palacios with a telegram from San Luis Potosi, ordering the postponement of the execution until June 19th. This news produced a most disagreeable impression upon the Emperor, for he had done with life, and looked on this delay rather as a cruelty, knowing the Mexicans too well to believe in grace. The troops who had been placed near the Alameda, to be marched thence to the Cerro de la Campaña, where the execution was to take place, were discontented also, fearing that they might be deprived of their victim. They had arrived with merry music, but returned home silent and sullen.

When the Colonel left me, I abandoned myself to unrestrained joy. I ordered a bottle of wine, to drink good luck to the Emperor, and smoking my cigar and humming a tune I paced my chapel, and even the horrid faces of the martyrs on the wall seemed to smile. The sentinel stared at me with his mouth wide open, probably thinking me mad. To give him a better idea of my wits, I presented him with four reals, but as he could not see any more reason for my present than for my good humor, I am afraid I only confirmed his bad opinion of the state of my brain.

On June 17th I awoke in very good spirits. I had slept excellently on my hard couch, and across my dreams I heard continually the joyful news, "The Emperor is saved."

Colonel Villanueva had promised to come at one o'clock; but I waited in vain for him all day, and my doubts returned. What has happened? Should the bloody Indian, Juarez, or his Mephistopheles, Lerdo, the minister with the false, sarcastic mouth, dare still to commit the refined cruelty of murdering my Emperor, after making him pass through all the bitterness of death? Maybe he offended their low souls by the nobleness of his demeanor. It would be an infamous cruelty; but what might not be expected from Mexicans?

On the morning of June 18th Lieutenant-Colonel Pitner came for a moment into the little yard and whispered that things went very badly for the Emperor; and soon afterward Colonel Villanueva came. He was greatly excited and told me that he had been cruelly disappointed; Maximilian was lost, without any hope; the execution would take place at eight o'clock next morning. "I am ashamed," he said, "that so many bad elements are among us. I hoped still that the Moderate party would conquer, and the life of the Emperor be saved. I feel grieved that my poor country, hated and despised by all the world, must be stained again in this manner."

The Emperor had taken leave of his officers on the 17th, in Queretaro, in the following letter:

"QUERETARO,
"PRISON DE LOS CAPUCINOS, June 17, 1867.

"*To the Generals and Field Officers, prisoners in this city:*

"At this solemn moment I address to you the present lines, in order both to acknowledge the loyalty with which you have served me and to give you a token of the true regard which I feel for you. Your affectionate

"MAXIMILIAN."

As I was separated from the rest of the prisoners, I saw this letter only later, and therefore my name, as that of some other generals, is wanting under the reply.

The Emperor ordered Doctor Basch to make a list of persons to whom he desired to leave some little keepsake. To me he bequeathed his beloved perspective glass, which he held almost constantly in his hand during the entire siege of Queretaro, and to the Princess the fan which he had used in prison during his last days. The Emperor went to bed at half past eight, and was already asleep when he was disturbed by a visit from Escobedo, at 11 P.M.

Captain Enking, who accompanied the General at this improper visit, noticed that the Emperor looked with an expression of intense expectation on the entrance of the General, as if expecting to hear news of his pardon from him. Had the Captain observed correctly, the look of the Emperor would have been very explicable and natural. He could not, indeed, expect from Escobedo a visit of friendly sympathy, or believe that he only came to enjoy the sight of his foe conquered solely by vile treason. A visit from the Commander-in-Chief under these circumstances was solely justifiable if, disturbing the last sleep of his prisoner, he came to announce life to him.

From the Emperor, Escobedo went to see Mejia, who saved him once when he was condemned to be shot. Mejia recommended his children to him, and Escobedo promised to take care of them. He sent later an aide-de-camp to the General's widow, and offered her his assistance for her children; but the noble woman spurned with scorn the assistance of the murderer of her husband, and said that she was young and strong, and could work for her children.

In the afternoon of the 18th the Emperor telegraphed to Juarez: "I would desire that M. Miguel Miramon and Thomas Mejia, who suffered all the tortures and bitterness of death the day before last, might be spared, and that I, as I have already said when taken prisoner, may be the only victim."

This request was refused, and the same fate attended the request of the same date of Baron Magnus, addressed to the minister Lerdo de Tejada, which thus concluded: "I implore you, in the name of humanity and of Heaven, not to make any further attempt against his life, and repeat how certain I am that my sovereign His Majesty the King of Prussia, and all the monarchs of Europe, who are related to the imprisoned Prince, his brother the Emperor of Austria, his cousin the Queen of Great Britain, his brother-in-law the King of Belgium, and his cousin the Queen of Spain, as also the Kings of Italy and Sweden, will readily agree to give all possible guarantee that none of the prisoners shall ever return to Mexican territory." The Emperor addressed letters of thanks to his four advisers, and wrote the following letter to Juarez, which is dated June 19th, as it was to be delivered on that day:

"QUERETARO, June 19, 1867.

"M. BENITO JUAREZ: On the point of suffering death because I desired to try whether new institutions would enable me to put an end to the bloody war which for so many years has been causing ruin to this unhappy country, I will yield up my life with satisfaction if this sacrifice can contribute to the welfare of my adopted country. Being fully convinced that nothing durable can be produced on a soil soaked in blood and moved by violent agitations, I implore you in the most solemn manner, and with that sincerity which is peculiar to moments like those in which I find myself, that my blood may be the last that may be spilled, and that the same perseverance, which I appreciated when in the midst of prosperity, and with which you defended the cause that conquers now, might be applied to the most noble end—to reconcile all hearts, and to rebuild on a durable, firm foundation the peace and order of this unhappy country.

"MAXIMILIAN."

In the morning of the 19th, at four o'clock, all were up in our convent, for the disposable part of the battalion Supremos Poderes marched out at half past four. Soon after six o'clock Lieutenant-Colonel Pitner came into the room adjoining the chapel, and called out, "They have already led him away!"

We now listened with breathless anxiety; but nothing betrayed what had happened, when on a sudden all the bells of the city began ringing after seven o'clock. Pitner called out, "He is dead now!" and, not caring for the sentinel at my door, he rushed into the chapel, and in a mute embrace our tears fell in memory of the much beloved, noble dead. Toward eight o'clock the troops returned from the execution.

The last moments of the Emperor have been frequently described; but all these descriptions differ from one another. Though it was not my lot to assist my Emperor in his last moments, I shall write down what eight or ten Liberal officers, among whom was Colonel Villanueva, concurred in saying.

The Emperor rose as early as half past three, and made a very careful toilet. He wore a short dark (blue or black) coat, black trousers and waistcoat, and a small felt hat. At four o'clock Pater Soria came, from whom the Emperor had already received

the last sacraments. At five o'clock a mass was celebrated, for which purpose an altar had been placed in a convenient niche. The Emperor gave to Doctor Basch several commissions and greetings to his friends, among whom he did not forget to mention me. He then breakfasted at a quarter to six. The people in the city were much excited, and this excitement was even noticeable among some portion of the troops. Escobedo was afraid of demonstrations, and even of a riot, and to baffle such attempts the execution was ordered to take place an hour sooner.

With the stroke of six o'clock the Liberal officer came to take the Emperor. Before he had yet spoken, the Emperor said, "I am ready," and came from his cell, where he was surrounded by his few servants, who wept and kissed his hands. He said: "Be calm; you see I am so. It is the will of God that I should die, and we cannot act against that."

The Emperor then went toward the cells of his two generals, and said: "Are you ready, gentlemen? I am ready." Miramon and Mejia came forward, and he embraced his companions in death. Mejia, the brave, daring man, who hundreds of times had looked smilingly into the face of grim Death, was weakened by sickness and very low-spirited. All three went down the staircase, the Emperor in advance with a firm step. On arriving at the street before the convent he looked around, and, drawing a deep breath, he said: "Ah, what a splendid day! I always wished to die on such a day." He then stepped with Pater Soria into the next carriage waiting for him, the *fiacre* No. 10; for the republican Government probably thought it below its dignity to provide a proper carriage for a fallen Emperor. Miramon entered the *fiacre* No. 16, and Mejia, No. 13, and the mournful procession moved. At its head marched the Supremos Poderes. The carriages were surrounded by the Cazadores de Galeano, and the rear was brought up by the battalion Nueva Leon, which was ordered for the execution.

Though the hour had been anticipated, the streets were crowded. Everybody greeted the Emperor respectfully, and the women cried aloud. The Emperor responded to the greetings with his heart-winning smile, and perhaps compared his present march with his entrance and reception into Queretaro four months ago. What a contrast! However, the people kept quiet, and could not muster courage for any demonstration; only the soldiers were favored with odious names and missiles.

On their arrival at the Cerro de la Campaña, the door of the Emperor's *fiacre* could not be opened. Without waiting for further attempts to do so, the Emperor jumped to the ground. At his side stood his Hungarian servant, Tudos. On looking around he asked the servant, "Is nobody else here?" In his fortunate days everybody strove to be near him, but now on the way to his untimely grave only a single person was at his side. However, Baron Magnus and Consul Bahnsen were present, though he could not see them.

Pater Soria dismounted as well as he could. But the comforter required comfort from the condemned. He felt sick and faint, and with a compassionate look the Emperor drew from his pocket a smelling-bottle (which my wife had given him, and which is said to be now in the possession of the widowed Empress of Brazil), and held it under his nose.

The Emperor, followed by Miramon, and Mejia, who had to be supported, now moved toward the square of soldiers, which was open toward the *cerro*. The troops for the execution were commanded by General Jesus Diaz de Leon. Where the square was open, a wall of *adobe* had been erected. In the middle, where the Emperor was to stand, who was taller than his two companions, the wall was somewhat higher. On the point of taking their respective positions, the Emperor said to Miramon: "A brave soldier must be honored by his monarch even in his last hour: therefore, permit me to give you the place of honor," and Miramon had to place himself in the middle.

An officer and seven men now stepped forward, until within a few yards of each of the three condemned. The Emperor went up to those before him, gave each soldier his hand and a maximilian d'or [three dollars twenty-seven cents], and said, "*Muchachos* ['boys'], aim well, aim right here," pointing to his heart. Then he returned to his stand, took off his hat, and wiped his forehead with his handkerchief. This and his hat he gave to Tudos, with the order to take them to his mother, the Archduchess Sophia. Then he spoke with a clear and firm voice the following words:

"MEXICANS: Persons of my rank and origin are destined by

God to be either benefactors of the people or martyrs. Called by a great part of you, I came for the good of the country. Ambition did not bring me here; I came animated with the best wishes for the future of my adopted country, and for that of my soldiers, whom I thank, before my death, for the sacrifices they made for me. Mexicans, may my blood be the last that shall be spilled for the welfare of the country; and if it should be necessary that its sons shall still shed theirs, may it flow for its good, but never by treason. *Viva* independence! *Viva* Mexico!"

Looking around, the Emperor noticed, not far from him, a group of men and women who sobbed aloud. He looked at them with a mild and friendly smile, then he laid both his hands on his breast and looked forward. Five shots were fired, and the Emperor fell on his right side, whispering slowly the word, "*Hombre!*" ("O Man!"). All the bullets had pierced his body, and each of them was deadly; but the Emperor still moved slightly. The officer laid him on his back, and pointed with the point of his sword on the Emperor's heart. A soldier then stepped forward, and sent another bullet into the spot indicated.

Neither the Emperor nor Miramon nor Mejia had his eyes bandaged. Miramon, not addressing the soldiers, but the citizens assembled, said: "Mexicans: my judges have condemned me to death as a traitor to my country. I never was a traitor, and request you not to suffer this stain to be affixed to my memory, and still less to my children. *Viva* Mexico! *Viva* the Emperor!" When the shots hit him he died instantly.

Mejia only said, "*Viva* Mexico! *Viva* the Emperor!" He lived after the firing, and two more bullets were necessary to despatch him. All the three condemned were shot at the same moment.

CANADIAN CONFEDERATION

A.D. 1867

J. EDMUND COLLINS

The demand in Upper Canada for representation in Parliament in proportion to population, early in the 'sixties, met with bitter opposition in Lower Canada, and along with other causes threatened the permanence of the existing union between the two Provinces. Party strife increased these discords; and the far-seeing began to look in other directions for a solution of the difficulties that now pressed heavily on both sections of the community. Then was revived the suggestion, made at an earlier period in the country's history, of a more extended union among the British Provinces of North America. At this period there were seven distinct colonies in North America owning allegiance to Britain, each—if we except the two Canadas—having its own political system and separate government. These were the Provinces of Nova Scotia, New Brunswick, Prince Edward Island, the two Canadas, and the Crown colonies of Newfoundland and British Columbia.

In 1860 two resolutions were moved in Parliament, which met that year in Quebec, affirming "that the existing legislative union of the Provinces (Upper and Lower Canada) had failed to realize the anticipations of its promoters," and recommending "the formation of two or more local governments, to which should be committed all matters of a sectional character, and the erection of some joint authority to dispose of the affairs common to all." These resolutions were at the time defeated; but two years later the "joint authority" scheme was acted upon, and a coalition government was formed, which warmly advocated a confederation of all the British American Provinces, and held a series of conferences with the view to bringing about the desired measure. As the project continued to engage the attention of Canadian statesmen, a convention of representatives from the various Provinces met in 1864, first in Charlottetown, Prince Edward Island, and then in Quebec, to discuss the feasibility of the scheme and finally to arrange the terms of the contemplated union. Next year, the Canadian Legislature adopted the union resolutions, which by this time had received the hearty support of the Imperial authorities; but in the Maritime Provinces the confederation scheme as yet failed to meet the approval of the people. Prince Edward Island and Newfoundland withdrew from the negotiations; and the latter colony still maintains its separate political existence. In spite of dissensions and opposition, the project gained way, and delegates from the various Provinces finally met in London to arrange with the Home Government a formal basis of union. The result was the passing in the Imperial Parliament of the British North America Act, and the ratifying of the Confederation of the British American Provinces. Effect was duly given in Canada to the measure, as will be seen from the following article, which narrates the details of the confederation movement that created the Dominion of Canada.

THE idea of a federation of the colonies had been mooted many times. Indeed, so early as the time when the New England colonies separated from the empire, an article was introduced into the constitution of the new confederacy authorizing the admission of Canada to the union, should the latter seek such alliance. In 1810 an enterprising colonist put forward the federation scheme, but political opinion was in a crude state, and nothing more was heard of the proposition till four years later, when Chief Justice Sewell, of Quebec, submitted a plan of confederation to the Duke of Kent. The Duke, in a very cordial note, agreed with the suggestions. In 1827 the Legislative Council of Upper Canada originated resolutions aiming at a union of the two Canadian Provinces, suggesting likewise a "union of the whole four Provinces of North America under a viceroyalty, with a *facsimile* of the British Constitution."

Nothing more was heard of the scheme in public places till Lord Durham had been disgraced and had presented his report. From that hour the question engrossed the public mind, and in 1849 the North American League met in Toronto and discussed the question, though the immediate object of the gathering was an application of the federal principle to the two Provinces of Canada. In 1854 the Legislature of Nova Scotia adopted resolutions recommending a closer union of the British North American colonies. From this period statesmen warmly recommended the measure in the House of Commons, and the foremost newspapers took up a similar tone. But the plan approved by the Nova Scotia Legislature was not for a federation of all the Provinces, but a maritime union, comprehending under one government Nova Scotia, New Brunswick, and Prince Edward Island. In 1864 the Legislatures of these Provinces passed resolutions authorizing the appointment of delegates to meet in the autumn, to discuss the project of maritime union.

At once it occurred to the Premier, Mr. [afterward Sir] John A. Macdonald, that the meeting could be turned to account by the Government of Canada in promoting the general-confederation scheme. The Maritime Province delegates were to meet in September at Charlottetown, and thither repaired eight members of the Canadian Administration.

The Canadian ministers, not having been appointed to confer respecting legislative union, had no official standing at the Island conference, but they were invited to join in the discussion, of which courtesy they vigorously availed themselves. "The Canadians descended upon us," said one of the Islanders; "and before they were three days among us we forgot our own scheme and thought only about theirs." No longer did anyone speak of maritime union; all were absorbed by the greater project of a general federation, guaranteeing local and joint control. So completely did the general-confederation scheme absorb the maritime idea that the convention closed only to reassemble at Quebec, on a date to be fixed by the Governor-General of Canada.

On October 10th, the day named by the Governor-General for the meeting of the conference in Quebec, the delegates had assembled in that quaint city. The number of delegates had been increased by the presence of Hon. (now Sir) Frederick B. T. Carter, Speaker of the Newfoundland House of Assembly; Hon. Ambrose Shea, leader of the opposition in the same chamber; and Sir Etienne P. Taché, A. Campbell, Oliver Mowat, James Cockburn, and J. C. Chapais, from the Canadian Cabinet. The conference was organized by the election of Sir E. P. Taché to the chair. Then the doors of the conference-chamber were closed, and the discussion went on, without anyone raising his voice to say nay. Before the delegates dispersed, they paid a visit to the capital of this new dominion, of which, it might be said, they were now wildly dreaming. Leaving Ottawa, the party proceeded westward through the Province, receiving cordial welcome and lavish hospitality at Kingston, Toronto, Hamilton, and other cities. The delegates then returned to their homes, eager to get before the Legislatures and propose the scheme that had filled them with such high hope.

Parliament met on February 19th, and in the Ministry's opening speech, which the Governor read, the confederation scheme was warmly recommended to the House. The union question absorbed the attention of Parliament. Some of the ablest speeches ever delivered in a Canadian legislature were heard during the session. On the Ministerial side, Messrs. John A. Macdonald, Brown, Cartier, and McGee supported the question with marked ability, while with scarcely less skill and power Messrs. John Sandfield Macdonald, Huntington, Dorion, Holton, and Dunkin opposed it. All that careful research and skilful manipulation of fact and figures could urge against the scheme was put forward with impassioned force by these gentlemen. "All that a well-read public man," says the Hon. John H. Gray, in his work *Confederation*, "all that a thorough sophist, a dexterous logician, a timid patriot, or a prophet of evil could array against the project was brought up and pressed against the scheme." On Friday, March 10th, the discussion had ended, and Attorney-General Macdonald, rising, offered the following motion, "That an humble address be presented to her Majesty praying that she may be graciously pleased to cause a measure to be submitted to the Imperial Parliament for the purpose of uniting the colonies of Canada, Nova Scotia, New Brunswick, Prince Edward Island, and Newfoundland in one government, with provisions based on certain resolutions, which were adopted at a conference of delegates from the said colonies, held at the city of Quebec, on October 10, 1865." This resolution, after some discussion, was carried by a vote of ninety-one to thirty-three. Of the minority, four were from the Upper Province, and of the majority fifty-four. The question might not have fared so well in the Lower Province but that M. Cartier was an enthusiastic champion of union and was supported by the priests almost to a man. A motion similar to that carried in the House of Commons had been introduced in the Legislative Council by the Premier, Sir E. P. Taché, and carried by a vote of three to one. Parliament was prorogued on March 18th, and in the month following Messrs. John A. Macdonald, Galt, Brown, and Cartier went to England, to confer with the Imperial Government and to promote the scheme of confederation.

These Canadian delegates had several long conferences with the Imperial ministers on the proposed constitutional changes, on treaties and legislation, the defences of Canada, the settlement of the Northwest Territories, the Hudson Bay Company's claim, and other subjects. The confederation scheme having attracted much favorable attention in England, the emissaries were received with marked cordiality by the Ministry as well as by the Queen and the royal family. Hon. John A. Macdonald pressed upon the home Government the expediency of making known to the recalcitrant colonies that the Imperial authorities desired to see a union consummated; for one of the weapons used against the project in Nova Scotia and New Brunswick was that the aim of the confederation was separation from the empire and the assumption of independent nationality. Such an intention at that day was regarded as a public offence. If it is an offence for the son, approaching the years and the strength of manhood, to turn his thoughts to separation from the homestead under whose jurisdiction and shelter he has lived during his infancy and boyhood, to sketch out a manly and independent career of his own, plan to build his own house, conduct his own business, and carve out his own fortune—then was it an offence for those Canadians, if there were at that time any such, who on the eve of union dreamt of nationality, of a time when Canada should have passed the years of boyhood, and be brave and strong enough to stand forth among the independent nations.

After the despatches of the Colonial Secretary had reached the Provincial Government, some of those who had opposed union on the ground of loyalty now began with much consistency to inveigh against the alleged "undue pressure" of the Imperial Government; while many declared that "an atrocious system for the coercion of the colonies into the hateful bond" had been inaugurated in the Home Office. The truth is, neither pressure nor coercion was exercised from the Colonial Office, since no proceeding could have been more fatal to the prospects of the confederation. The home Ministry had grown to be enthusiastic supporters of the "new dominion" scheme, and stated their views at much length in their despatches to the colonial governors, whom they wished to give to the project every possible proper support at their command; but that was all. On the one hand, Mr. John A. Macdonald and his colleagues avouched the loyalty of the Provinces to the Crown, and declared that the colonists would spend their only dollar and shed the last drop of their blood in maintaining connection with the mother-land. The parent was much moved at these earnest and lavish protestations of the child, and in token of her appreciation and gratitude guaranteed a loan for the construction of an intercolonial railway, admitted her obligation to defend the colonies with all the resources at her command, and consented to strengthen the fortifications at Quebec, and provide armaments. Among other things, the home Government undertook to ascertain what were the rights of the Hudson Bay Company, with a view to the cession of the Northwest Territory to the Dominion.

A meeting of the Canadian Parliament to discuss the report of the delegates was called for August 8th. The chief work of the session was a consideration of the report of the delegates to England. The Government carried its measures by overwhelming majorities, and there appeared to be no disposition to tolerate the obstruction of the small band of opposition. The result of the labors of the commission, appointed in 1857, to frame a civil code for Lower Canada was presented to the Legislature, and M. Cartier introduced a bill to carry it into effect. The code went into operation on August 1st in the following year. The House rose after a six-weeks' session; and in the autumn the public offices were removed to the new capital in the wilderness, one hundred twenty miles up the Ottawa River. During the summer, for the sake of convenience, the cabinet meetings were held in Montreal.

The last session of the Provincial Parliament met at Ottawa on June 8th. The Ministry's speech expressed the hope that the union scheme would soon be *un fait accompli*, and that the next Parliament would embrace an assemblage not only of the federate representatives of Canada, but of every colony in British North America. There was brisk discussion upon some of the Government measures, but the opposition found themselves, in comparison with their opponents, as "that small infantry warred on by cranes," and hence, as the session wore on, learned not to offer opposition where nothing was to be gained. A series of resolutions defining the Constitution of Upper and Lower Canada under the proposed confederation, which subsequently were, in great measure, incorporated in the Imperial act, was passed.

In 1866 the Legislature of New Brunswick met under exciting circumstances. Governor Gordon, in his speech, announced that it was the earnest wish of the Queen that the Provinces should unite in one confederacy, and strongly urged the question upon the Legislature. The Smith-Hatheway Administration was willing to meet the royal wish half-way, provided that New Brunswick obtained better terms in the compact than those offered in the Quebec scheme. But the public were not disposed to abide by the half-way marches of the Ministry or even to tolerate its existence. The Legislative Council passed an address expressing the desire that the Imperial Government might unite New Brunswick and the other Provinces in a federative union. The Ministry were obliged to resign, and the Governor called on Mr. [now Sir] Leonard Tilley to form an administration. A dissolution followed, and to the same length which the Province had before gone in opposing confederation it now went in supporting the scheme. This election had a marked influence on the fortunes of confederation in other quarters. "The destiny of British North America, indeed," says Mr. Archer, "was decided in New Brunswick." Nova Scotia appointed delegates to London to perfect a measure of union. Meanwhile the little Province in the Gulf [Prince Edward Island] remained refractory, while her more rugged sister out on the edge of the Atlantic [Newfoundland] was listless. The little meadow Province afterward fell before the wooer, but the "ancient colony" chose, as it seems, perpetual celibacy.

In November, 1866, the Canadian delegation, consisting of Messrs. John A. Macdonald, George E. Cartier, A. T. Galt, W. P. Howland, William McDougall, and H. L. Langevin, went to England, where they were to meet the Nova Scotia and New Brunswick delegates to discuss the confederation plan. The Nova Scotia delegates were Messrs. Tupper, Archibald, Henry, McCully, and Ritchie; those of New Brunswick were Messrs. Tilley, Mitchell, Fisher, Johnson, and Robert Duncan Wilmot. The delegates met at Westminister palace on December 4th, and, by preëminence, the chair was given to the Hon. John A. Macdonald during the conference. The conference sat till December 24th, after which the assemblage were in a position to proceed with the structure of a constitution. Though some of the ablest men the colonies ever produced were instrumental in framing the new charter, Mr. Macdonald, it was readily admitted, was the master-head. Many a time during the progress of the negotiations conflicting interests arose, which, but for careful handling, might have wrecked the scheme; and here the matchless tact of the Attorney-General of Canada West preëminently asserted itself.

Several concessions were made to the Maritime Provinces, and a more uniform and equitable feature was given to the whole. The Nova Scotia delegates were confronted by the colossal figure of Joseph Howe, who poured out a stream of fiery eloquence against the confederation; but those who were present say that Doctor Tupper turned the orator's arguments back with such force and clearness that the Imperial Government never for a moment wavered in concluding what was its duty to Nova Scotia. After the conclusion of the discussion on the general scheme, the conference, in conjunction with the Imperial law officers, prepared certain draft bills, which were afterward fused into a harmonious whole, and submitted to the Imperial Parliament on February 5th following. On March 29th the amalgamated bill received the royal assent; and on April 12th another Imperial act was passed, authorizing the commissioners of the treasury to guarantee interest on a loan not to exceed three million pounds sterling, which sum was to be appropriated to the construction of an intercolonial railway between Halifax and the St. Lawrence. The union was not considered perfected by the constitutional ceremony, and needed a firmer linking by the bonds of iron. On May 22d a royal proclamation was issued giving effect to "The British North America Act," and appointing the first day of July following as the date on which it should come in force.

Briefly, the act provided that the Provinces of Canada, New Brunswick, and Nova Scotia should be one dominion, under the name of Canada. This dominion was to be divided into four Provinces—Ontario, Quebec, New Brunswick, and Nova Scotia; the boundaries of the former two to be the same as those of the old Provinces of Upper and Lower Canada; the boundaries of the two Maritime Provinces remaining unchanged. The executive authority, and the command of the naval and military forces, were vested in the Imperial Sovereign, represented by a governor-general or other executive officer for the time being. The city of Ottawa was declared the seat of government during the sovereign's pleasure. The legislative machinery was to consist of a viceroy or his deputy, and a ministerial council, to be styled the Queen's Privy Council of Canada, the members of which body were to be chosen by the Governor-General and to hold office during his pleasure. The legislative power was vested in a parliament to consist of the Queen, the Senate, and the House of Commons. It was provided that a parliament should be held at least once in each year, so that not more than a twelvemonth might elapse between session and session. The system of election to the political dead-house [the Senate] was abolished—though the thing itself was maintained—and it was provided instead that the Senate should consist of seventy-two life members, twenty-four for Ontario, twenty-four for Quebec—an apportionment which, in view of the disparity of population and the outlook of increased inequality, would have been a rank injustice, but that the members so distributed are but the shadows in an institution which in practice is a myth—and twelve for each of the Maritime Provinces; the members to possess certain property qualifications, to be appointed by the Crown, and to retain their seats for life unless guilty of gross misbehavior. Provision was made for increasing the membership of the body, but the number (as finally arranged) was not to exceed eighty-two, or to reach that limit unless upon the entry of Newfoundland into the Confederation. The principle of representation by population was established for the House of Commons, the basis adopted for the original adjustment being the census of 1861. It was declared, however, that an adjustment should take place every ten years, upon a census of population being obtained. The representation of Quebec was permanently fixed at sixty-five members, while that of each of the other Provinces was to bear the same relation to the population thereof that sixty-five should from time to time bear to the population of Quebec.

The duration of the House of Commons was not to exceed five years. Constitutions were likewise given to the four Provinces embraced in the union. Each comprised a lieutenant-governor who was to be appointed by the Governor-General, paid out of the general treasury, and to hold office for five years;

an executive council which was to be appointed by the lieutenant-governor, who had the power of dismissal; a legislative council to be nominated by the Lieutenant-Governor and to hold their seats for life; and the House of Assembly. Such Legislature was to have control over local affairs, all questions of a character affecting the Dominion at large falling within the jurisdiction of the General Government. Provision was made, likewise, in the British North America Act, for the admission into the Confederation of any colony that had so far refused to be a party to the compact. The royal proclamation announced the names of seventy-two senators, thirty-six of whom were conservatives and thirty-six reformers; so that when the date that was to witness the birth of the Dominion came round, the machinery was in readiness to set in motion.

THE PURCHASE OF ALASKA

A.D. 1867

CHARLES SUMNER

One need not be old at this date to remember that in his school-days the geographies labelled as "Russian Possessions" a great country in the northwest corner of North America. It was one of those unexplored and mysterious regions to which the poets and romancers were at liberty to attribute almost any imaginable wild beast, natural feature, or action of the elements; and Campbell utilized it in his famous lines

> "Waft across the waves' tumultuous roar
> The wolf's long howl from Oonalaska's shore,"

which became so familiar to almost every class of readers that few thought of Alaska as anything but a desolate land of ice and wolves, with the pitiful cry of the famishing animals almost heard across the wide Pacific. When the United States bought the country, in 1867, it was a favorite expression with those who opposed the purchase to allude to it as "Seward's icebergs," and to say that seven million dollars was a large ice-bill for a single summer. It is now known that Alaska is a land of gold, a land of furs, a land of fish, a land with a mighty river, a land that has the highest mountain on the continent and the greatest glacier in the world, a land that attracts the same class of tourists that have heretofore gone to Norway for its wild fiords and the midnight sun. Moreover, it was not altogether a land of desolation; for it had native inhabitants, and they had their own literature—prose and poetry—rude, but picturesque and interesting. When it was purchased it added almost half as much territory as the United States already possessed; the chain of Aleutian Islands stretches far toward the Orient; and with the subsequent acquisition of Guam and the Philippines, we may almost paraphrase a famous saying and declare that the stroke of the American hammer and scream of the American whistle are heard round the globe.

The chapter that follows is the main part of a speech delivered in the United States Senate by Charles Sumner when the treaty was under consideration. It is especially interesting in view of the recent controversy over the boundary between Alaska and British America, which was amicably settled by arbitration.

YOU have just listened to the reading of the treaty by which Russia cedes to the United States all her possessions on the North American continent in consideration of seven million two hundred thousand dollars, to be paid by the United States. On the one side is the cession of a vast country, with its jurisdiction and its resources of all kinds; on the other side is the purchase-money. Such is this transaction on its face.

In endeavoring to estimate its character I am glad to begin with what is clear and beyond question. I refer to the boundaries fixed by the treaty. Beginning at the parallel of 54° 40′ north latitude, so famous in our history, the line ascends Portland Channel to the mountains, which it follows on their summits to the point of intersection with 141° west longitude, which line it ascends to the frozen ocean, or, if you please, to the North Pole. This is the eastern boundary, separating this region from the British possessions, and it is borrowed from the treaty between Russia and Great Britain in 1825, establishing the relations between those two Powers on this continent.

It will be seen that this boundary is old; the rest is new. Starting from the frozen ocean the western boundary descends Bering Strait, midway between the two islands of Krusenstern and Ratmanov, to the parallel of 65° 30′, just below the point where the continents of America and Asia approach each other the nearest; and from this point it proceeds in a course nearly southwest through Bering Strait, midway between the island of St. Lawrence and Cape Chonkotski, to the meridian of 172° west longitude, and thence, in a southwesterly direction, traversing Bering Sea, midway between the island of Atton on the east and Copper Island on the west, to the meridian of 193° west longitude, leaving the prolonged group of the Aleutian Islands in the possessions now transferred to the United States, and making the western boundary of our country the dividing-line that separates Asia from America.

Look at the map and see the configuration of this extensive region, whose estimated area is more than five hundred seventy thousand square miles. Including the Sitkan Archipelago at the south, it takes a margin of the mainland, fronting on the ocean, thirty miles broad and three hundred miles long, to Mount St. Elias, the highest peak of the continent, when it turns with an elbow to the west, and then along Bering Strait northerly, when it rounds to the east along the frozen ocean. Here are more than four thousand statute miles of coast, indented by capacious bays and commodious harbors without number, embracing the

Peninsula of Alaska, one of the most remarkable in the world, fifty miles in breadth, and three hundred miles in length; piled with mountains, many volcanic and some still smoking; penetrated by navigable rivers, one of which is among the largest of the world; studded with islands that stand like sentinels on the coast; and flanked by that narrow Aleutian range which, starting from Alaska, stretches far away to Japan, as if America were extending a friendly hand to Asia.

This is the most general aspect. There are details specially disclosing maritime advantages and approaches to the sea which properly belong to this preliminary sketch. According to accurate estimates the coast-line, including bays and islands, is not less than eleven thousand two hundred seventy miles. In the Aleutian range, besides innumerable islets and rocks, there are not fewer than fifty-five islands exceeding three miles in length; there are seven exceeding forty miles, with Ounimak, which is the largest, exceeding seventy-three miles. In one part of Bering Sea there are five considerable islands, the largest of which is St. Lawrence, more than ninety-six miles long. Add to all these the group south of the Peninsula of Alaska, including the Shumagins and the magnificent island of Kodiak, and then the Sitkan group—archipelago added to archipelago—and the whole constitutes the geographical complement to the West Indies.

The title of Russia to all these possessions is derived from prior discovery, which is the admitted title by which all European powers have held in North and South America, unless we except what England acquired by conquest from France; and here the title of France was derived from prior discovery. Russia, shut up in a distant interior and struggling with barbarism, was scarcely known to the other powers at the time they were lifting their flags in the western hemisphere. At a later day the same powerful genius that made her known as an empire set in motion the enterprise by which these possessions were opened to her dominion. Peter the Great, himself a shipbuilder and a reformer, who had worked in the shipyards of England and of Holland, was curious to know whether Asia and America were separated by the sea or constituted one undivided body with different names, like Europe and Asia. To obtain this information, he wrote with his own hand the following instructions, and ordered his chief admiral to see them executed:

"One or two boats with decks to be built at Kamchatka, or at any other convenient place, with which inquiry should be made with relation to the northerly coasts, to see whether they were not contiguous with America, since their end was not known: and, this done, they should see whether they could not somewhere find a harbor belonging to Europeans or a European ship. They should likewise set apart some men who should inquire after the name and situation of the coasts discovered. Of all this an exact journal should be kept, with which they should return to Petersburg."

The Czar died in the winter of 1725; but the Empress Catharine, faithful to the desires of her husband, did not allow this work to be neglected. Vitus Bering, a Dane by birth and a navigator of some experience, was made commander. The place of embarkation was on the other side of the Asiatic continent. Taking with him officers and shipbuilders, the navigator left St. Petersburg by land on February 5, 1725, and began the preliminary journey across Siberia, and the Sea of Okhotsk to the coast of Kamchatka, which they reached after infinite hardships and delays, sometimes with dogs for draft, and sometimes supporting life by eating leather bags, straps, and shoes. More than three years were passed in this toilsome and perilous journey to the place of embarkation. At last, on July 20, 1728, the party was able to set sail in a small vessel, called the Gabriel, described as "like the packet-boats used in the Baltick." Steering in a northeasterly direction, Bering passed a large island, which he called St. Lawrence, for the saint on whose day it was seen. This island, which is included in the present cession, may be considered the first point in Russian discovery, as it is also the first outpost of the North American continent. Continuing northward, and hugging the Asiatic coast, Bering turned back only when he thought he had reached the northeastern extremity of Asia, and was satisfied that the two continents were separated from each other. He did not go farther north than 67° 30′.

In his voyage Bering was struck by the absence of such great and high waves as in other places are common to the open sea, and he observed fir-trees floating in the water, although they were unknown on the Asiatic coast. Relations of inhabitants, in harmony with these indications, pointed to a "country at no great distance toward the east." His work was still incomplete, and the navigator, before returning home, put forth again for this discovery, but without success. By another dreary land journey he made his way back to St. Petersburg in March, 1730, after an absence of five years.

The spirit of discovery continued at St. Petersburg. A Cossack chief, undertaking to conquer the obstinate natives on the northeastern coast, proposed also "to discover the pretended country on the frozen sea." But he was killed by an arrow before his enterprise was completed. Little is known of the result; but it is said that the navigator whom he had selected, by name Gwosdew, in 1730 succeeded in reaching a "strange coast" between 65° and 66° of north latitude, where he saw persons, but could not speak with them for want of an interpreter. This must have been the coast of North America, not far from the group of islands in Bering Strait through which the present boundary passes.

The desire of the Russian Government to get behind the curtain increased. Bering volunteered to undertake the discoveries that remained to be made. He was created a commodore, and his old lieutenants were made captains. Several academicians were appointed to report on the natural history of the coasts visited, among whom was Steller, the naturalist. All these, with a numerous body of officers, journeyed across Siberia (northern Asia) and the Sea of Okhotsk, to Kamchatka, as Bering had journeyed before. Though ordered in 1738, the expedition was not able to leave the western coast until June 4, 1741, when two well-appointed ships set sail in company "to discover the continent of America." One of these, called the St. Paul, was under Commodore Bering; the other, called the St. Peter, was under Captain Tschirikoff. For some time the two kept together; but in a violent storm and fog they were separated, when each continued the expedition alone.

Bering first saw the continent of North America on July 18, 1741, in latitude 58° 28′. Looking at it from a distance "the country had terrible high mountains that were covered with snow." Two days later he anchored in a sheltered bay near a point which he called, for the saint day on which he saw it, Cape St. Elias. He was in the shadow of Mount St. Elias. On landing he found deserted huts, fireplaces, hewn wood, household furniture, an arrow, edge-tools of copper, with "store of red salmon." Here also several birds unknown in Siberia were noticed by the faithful Steller. Steering northward, Bering found himself constrained by the elbow in the coast to turn westward, and then in a southerly direction. Hugging the shore, his voyage was arrested by islands without number, among which he zigzagged to find his way. Several times he landed, and on one of these occasions he saw natives, who wore upper garments of whales' guts, breeches of sealskins, caps of the skins of sea-lions, adorned with various feathers, especially those of hawks." These "Americans," as they are called, were fishermen, without bows and arrows. This was on one of the Shumagin Islands, near the southern coast of the Peninsula of Alaska.

Meanwhile, the other solitary ship, proceeding on its way, had sighted the same coast, July 15, 1741, in latitude 56°. Anchoring at some distance from the steep and rocky cliffs before him, Tschirikoff sent his mate with the long-boat and ten of his best men, provided with small arms and a brass cannon, to inquire into the nature of the country and to obtain fresh water. The long-boat disappeared in a small wooded bay, and was never seen again. The captain sent his boatswain, with the small boat and carpenters, well armed, to furnish assistance. But the small boat disappeared also, and was never seen again. At the same time a great smoke was observed continually ascending from the shore. Shortly afterward two boats filled with natives sallied forth and lay at some distance from the vessel, when, crying "*Agai! Agai!*" they put back to the shore. Sorrowfully the Russian navigator turned away, not knowing the fate of his comrades and unable to help them. This was not far from Sitka.

Such was the first discovery of these northwestern coasts, and such are the first recorded glimpses of the aboriginal inhabitants. Tschirikoff, deprived of his boats, and therefore unable to land, hurried home.

During this time, Bering was driven, like Ulysses, on the uncertain waves. A single tempest raged for seventeen days. Scurvy came with its disheartening horrors, and the Commodore himself was a sufferer. Rigging broke, cables snapped. Anchors were lost. At last the tempest-tossed vessel was cast upon a desert island, where the Commodore, sheltered in a ditch and half covered with sand as a protection against cold, died, December 8, 1741. His body after his decease was "scraped out of the ground" and buried on this island, which is called by his name, and constitutes an outpost of the Asiatic continent.

For some time after these expeditions, by which Russia achieved the palm of discovery, imperial enterprise slumbered in those seas. The knowledge already acquired was continued and confirmed only by private individuals, who were led there in quest of furs. In 1745 the Aleutian Islands were discovered by an adventurer in search of sea otter. In successive voyages all these islands were visited for similar purposes. Among them was Oonalaska, the principal of the group of Fox Islands, which consitute a continuation of the Aleutian Islands, whose inhabitants and productions were minutely described. In 1768 private enterprise was superseded by an expedition ordered by the Empress Catharine, which, leaving Kamchatka, explored this whole archipelago and the Peninsula of Alaska, which to the islanders stood for the whole continent. Shortly afterward all these discoveries, beginning with those of Bering and Tschirikoff, were verified by the great English navigator Captain James Cook. In 1778 he sailed along the northwestern coast, and his report shed a flood of light upon the geography of that region.

Such from the beginning is the title of Russia, dating at least from 1741. The coast of British Columbia, next below, was discovered by George Vancouver, in 1790, and that of Oregon, still farther down, by Robert Gray, who, sailing from Boston in 1789, entered the Columbian River in 1790; so that the title of Russia is the earliest on the northwestern coast.

There were at least four other Russian expeditions by which this title was confirmed, if it needed any confirmation. The first was ordered by the Empress Catharine in 1785. It was under the command of Commodore Billings, an Englishman in the service of Russia, and was narrated from the original papers by Martin Sauer, secretary of the expedition. In the instructions from the Admiralty at St. Petersburg the Commodore was directed to take possession of "such coasts and islands as he shall first discover, whether inhabited or not, but cannot be disputed, and are not yet subject to any European Power, with consent of the inhabitants, if any," and this was to be accomplished by setting up "posts marked with the arms of Russia, with letters indicating the time of sovereignty, a short account of the people, and their voluntary submission to the Russian sovereignty; and that this was done under the glorious reign of the great Catharine the Second." The next was in 1803, in the interest of the Russian-American Company. There were two ships, one under the command of Captain Lisiansky, and the other of Captain Krusenstern, of the Russian navy. It was the first voyage round the world ordered by the Russian Government, and it lasted three years. These ships visited separately the northwest coast of America, and especially Sitka and the island of Kodiak. Still another enterprise organized by the celebrated minister Count Romanzoff, and at his expense, left Russia, in 1815, under the command of Lieutenant Kotzebue, an officer of the Russian navy, and son of the German dramatist whose assassination darkened the return of the son from his long voyage. There remains the enterprise of Luetke, at the time captain and afterward admiral in the Russian navy, which was a voyage round the world, embracing especially the Russian possessions, begun in 1826.

Turning from this question of title, which time and testimony have already settled, I meet the inquiry, Why does Russia part with possessions thus associated with the reign of her greatest emperor and filling an important chapter of geographical history? On this head I have no information that is not open to others. But I do not forget that the First Napoleon, in parting with Louisiana, was controlled by three several considerations: First, he needed the purchase-money for his treasury; secondly, he was unwilling to leave this distant unregarded territory a prey to Great Britain in the event of hostilities which seemed at hand; and thirdly, he was glad, according to his own remarkable language, "to establish forever the power of the United States and give to England a maritime rival destined to humble her pride."

Such is the record of history. Perhaps a similar record may be made hereafter with regard to the present cession. It is sometimes imagined that Russia, with all her great empire, is financially poor, so that these few millions may not be unimportant to her.

These general considerations are reënforced when we call to mind the little influence which Russia has thus far been able to exercise in this region. Though possessing dominion over it for more than a century, this gigantic Power has not been more genial or productive there than the soil itself.

So little were those possessions regarded during the last century that they were scarcely recognized as a component part of the empire. I have now before me an authentic map, published by the Academy of Sciences at St. Petersburg in 1776, and reproduced at London in 1787, entitled "General Map of the Russian Empire," where you will look in vain for Russian America, unless we except that link of the Aleutian chain nearest to Asia, which appears to have been incorporated under the Empress Anna at the same time with Siberia. Alexander Humboldt, whose insight into geography was unerring, in his great work on New Spain, published in 1811, after saying that he is able from official documents to give the position of the Russian factories on the American continent, says that they are "nothing but sheds and cabins employed as magazines of furs." He remarks further that "the larger part of these small Russian colonies do not communicate with each other except by sea."

I am not able to say when the idea of this cession first took shape. I have heard that it was as long ago as the administration of President Polk. It is within my knowledge that the Russian Government was sounded on the subject during the administration of President Buchanan. This was done through Mr. Gwin, at the time Senator from California, and Mr. Appleton, Assistant Secretary of State. For this purpose the former had more than one interview with the Russian Minister at Washington some time in December, 1859, in which, while professing to speak for the President unofficially, he represented "that Russia was too far off to make the most of these possessions; and that, as we are near, we can derive more from them." In reply to an inquiry of the Russian Minister, Mr. Gwin said that "the United States could go as high as five million dollars for the purchase," on which the former made no comment. Mr. Appleton, on another occasion, said to the Minister that "the President thought that the acquisition would be very profitable to the States on the Pacific; that he was ready to follow it up, but wished to know in advance whether Russia was ready to cede; that if she were, he would confer with his Cabinet and influential members of Congress." All this was unofficial; but it was promptly communicated to the Russian Government, who seem to have taken it into careful consideration. Prince Gortschakoff, in a despatch that reached Washington early in the summer of 1860, said that "the offer was not what might have been expected, but it merited mature reflection; that the Minister of Finance was about to inquire into the condition of these possessions, after which Russia would be in a condition to treat." The Prince added for himself that he was "by no means satisfied personally that it would be for the interest of Russia politically to alienate these possessions; that the only consideration which could make the scales incline that way would be the prospect of great financial advantages; but the sum of five million dollars does not seem in any way to represent the real value of these possessions"; and he concluded by asking the Minister to tell Mr. Appleton and Senator Gwin that the sum offered was not considered "an equitable equivalent." The subject was submerged by the approaching Presidential election and then by the Civil War.

After the Civil War had been brought to an end, peaceful enterprise was renewed, which on the Pacific coast was directed toward the Russian possessions. Our people there, wishing new facilities to obtain fish, fur, and ice, sought the intervention of the National Government. The Legislature of Washington Territory, in the winter of 1866, adopted a memorial to the President of the United States, entitled "In reference to the cod and other fisheries," in which they said: "Your memorialists, the Legislative Assembly of Washington Territory, beg leave to show that abundance of codfish, halibut, and salmon of excellent quality has been found along the shores of the Russian possessions. Your memorialists respectfully request your Excellency to obtain such rights and privileges of the Government of Russia as will enable our fishing-vessels to visit the ports and harbors of its possessions, to the end that fuel, water, and provisions may be easily obtained; that our sick and disabled fishermen may obtain sanitary assistance, together with the privilege of curing fish and repairing vessels in need of repairs. Your memorialists further request that the Treasury Department be instructed to forward to the collector of customs of this Puget Sound district such fishing-licenses, abstract journals, and log-books as will enable our hardy fishermen to obtain the bounties now provided and paid to the fishermen in the Atlantic States. Your memorialists finally pray your Excellency to employ such ships as may be spared from the Pacific naval fleet in exploring and surveying the fishing-banks known to navigators to exist along the Pacific coast from the Cortes bank to Bering Strait, and as in duty bound your memorialists will ever pray."

This memorial, on its presentation to the President in February, 1866, was referred to the Secretary of State, by whom it was communicated to Mr. De Stoeckl, the Russian Minister, with remarks on the importance of some early and comprehensive arrangement between the two Powers in order to prevent the growth of difficulties, especially from the fisheries in that region.

Shortly afterward another influence was felt. Mr. Cole, who had recently been elected to the Senate from California, acting in behalf of certain persons in that State, sought to obtain from the Russian Government a license or franchise to gather furs in a portion of its American possessions. The charter of the Russian-American Company was about to expire. This company had already underlet to the Hudson Bay Company all its franchise on the mainland between 54° 40′ and Mount St. Elias; and now it was proposed that an American company, holding direct from the Russian Government, should be substituted for the latter. The mighty Hudson Bay Company, with its headquarters in London, was to give way to an American company, with its headquarters in California. Among the letters on this subject addressed to Mr. Cole and now before me is one dated at San Francisco, April 10, 1866, in which this scheme is developed as follows:

"There is at the present time a good chance to organize a fur-trading company to trade between the United States and the Russian possessions in America, and, as the charter formerly granted to the Hudson Bay Company has expired, this would be the opportune moment to start in. . . . I should think that by a little management this charter could be obtained from the

Russian Government for ourselves, as I do not think they are very willing to renew the charter of the Hudson Bay Company, and I think they would give the preference to an American company, especially if the company should pay to the Russian Government 5 per cent. on the gross proceeds of their transactions, and also aid in civilizing and ameliorating the condition of the Indians by employing missionaries, if required by the Russian Government. For the faithful performance of the above we ask a charter for a term of twenty-five years, to be renewed for the same length of time if the Russian Government finds the company deserving. The charter to invest us with the right of trading in all the country between the British-American line and the Russian Archipelago. . . . Remember, we wish for the same charter as was formerly granted to the Hudson Bay Company, and we offer in return more than they did."

The Russian Minister at Washington, whom Mr. Cole saw, was not authorized to act, and the Department of State was induced to address Mr. Clay, Minister of the United States at St. Petersburg, who laid the application before the Russian Government. This was an important step. A letter from Mr. Clay, dated at St. Petersburg February 1, 1867, makes the following revelation:

"The Russian Government has already ceded away its rights in Russian America for a term of years, and the Russo-American Company has also ceded the same to the Hudson Bay Company. This lease expires in June next, and the president of the Russo-American Company tells me that they have been in correspondence with the Hudson Bay Company about a renewal of the lease for another term of twenty-five or thirty years. Until he receives a definite answer he cannot enter into negotiations with us or your California company. My opinion is that if he can get off with the Hudson Bay Company he will do so, when we can make arrangements with the Russo-American Company."

In October, 1866, Mr. De Stoeckl, who had long been the Russian Minister at Washington, and who enjoyed in a high degree the confidence of our Government, returned home on leave of absence, promising his best exertions to promote good relations between the two countries. While he was at St. Petersburg the applications from the United States were under consideration; but the Russian Government was disinclined to any minor arrangement of the character proposed. Obviously something like a crisis was at hand with regard to these possessions. The existing government was not adequate. The franchises granted there were about to terminate. Something must be done. As Mr. De Stoeckl was leaving in February to return to his post, the Archduke Constantine, brother and chief adviser of the Emperor, handed him a map with the lines in our treaty marked upon it, and told him he might treat for this cession. The Minister arrived in Washington early in March, and a negotiation was opened at once with our Government. Final instructions were received by the Atlantic cable from St. Petersburg on March 29th, and at four o'clock on the morning of March 30th this important treaty was signed by Mr. Seward on the part of the United States and by Mr. De Stoeckl on the part of Russia.

Few treaties have been conceived, initiated, prosecuted, and completed in so simple a manner without protocols or despatches. The whole negotiation will be seen in its result, unless we except two brief notes, which constitute all that passed between the negotiators. These have an interest general and special, and I conclude the history of this transaction by reading them:

"Department of State,
"Washington, March 23, 1867.

"Sir: With reference to the proposed convention between our respective Governments for a cession by Russia of her American territory to the United States, I have the honor to acquaint you that I must insist upon that clause in the sixth article of the draft which declares the cession to be free and unencumbered by any reservations, privileges, franchises, grants, or possessions by any associated companies, whether corporate or incorporate, Russian or any other, etc., and must regard it as an ultimatum. With the President's approval, however, I will add two hundred thousand dollars to the consideration-money on that account.

"I avail myself of this occasion to offer to you a renewed assurance of my most distinguished consideration.

"William H. Seward.

"Mr. Edward de Stoeckl, etc., etc., etc."

"WASHINGTON, March 17/29, 1867.

"MR. SECRETARY OF STATE: I have the honor to inform you that by a telegram dated 16/28th of this month from St. Petersburg, Prince Gortschakoff informs me that his majesty the Emperor of All the Russias gives his consent to the cession of the Russian possessions on the American continent to the United States for the stipulated sum of seven million two hundred thousand dollars in gold, and that his majesty the Emperor invests me with full powers to negotiate and sign the treaty.

"Please accept, Mr. Secretary of State, the assurance of my very high consideration. STOECKL.

"To Honorable WILLIAM H. SEWARD,
"Secretary of State of the United States."

The treaty begins with the declaration that "the United States of America and his majesty the Emperor of All the Russias, being desirous of strengthening, if possible, the good understanding which exists between them," have appointed plenipotentiaries, who have proceeded to sign articles wherein it is stipulated in behalf of Russia that "his majesty the Emperor of All the Russias agrees to cede to the United States by this convention, immediately upon the exchange of the ratifications thereof, all the territory and dominion now possessed by his said majesty on the continent of America and in the adjacent islands, the same being contained within the geographical limits herein set forth"; and it is stipulated in behalf of the United States that "in consideration of the cession aforesaid the United States agree to pay, at the Treasury in Washington, within ten months after the ratification of this convention, to the diplomatic representative or other agent of his majesty the Emperor of All the Russias duly authorized to receive the same, seven million two hundred thousand dollars in gold." The ratifications are to be exchanged within three months from the date of the treaty, or sooner, if possible.

Beyond the consideration founded on the desire of "strengthening the good understanding" between the two countries, there is the pecuniary consideration already mentioned, which underwent a change in the progress of the negotiation. The sum of seven millions was originally agreed upon; but when it was understood that there was a fur company and also an ice company enjoying monopolies under the existing government, it was thought best that these should be extinguished, in consideration of which our Government added two hundred thousand dollars to the purchase money, and the Russian Government in formal terms declared "the cession of territory and dominion to be free and unencumbered by any reservations, privileges, franchises, grants, or possessions, by any associated companies, whether corporate or incorporate, or by any parties, except merely private individual property-holders."

The treaty proceeds to say that "the cession hereby made conveys all the rights, franchises, and privileges now belonging to Russia in the said territory or dominion, and appurtenances thereto."

There are questions not unworthy of attention, which arise under the treaty between Russia and Great Britain, fixing the eastern limits of these possessions, and conceding certain privileges to the latter power. By this treaty, signed at St. Petersburg February 28, 1825, after fixing the boundaries between the Russian and British possessions, it is provided that "for the space of ten years the vessels of the two Powers, or those belonging to their respective subjects, shall mutually be at liberty to frequent, without any hinderance whatever, all the inland seas, gulfs, havens, and creeks on the coast, for the purpose of fishing and trading with the natives"; and also that "for the space of ten years the port of Sitka, or Novo Archangelsk, shall be open to the commerce and vessels of British subjects." In the same treaty it is also provided that "the subjects of his Britannic majesty, from whatever quarter they may arrive, whether from the ocean or from the interior of the continent, shall forever enjoy the right of navigating freely and without any hinderance whatever all the rivers and streams which in their course toward the Pacific ocean may cross the line of demarcation." Afterward a treaty of commerce and navigation between Russia and Great Britain was signed at St. Petersburg, January 11, 1843, subject to be terminated on notice from either party at the expiration of ten years, in which it is provided that "in regard to commerce and navigation in the Russian possessions on the northwest coast of America the convention of February 28, 1825, continues in force."

Then ensued the Crimean War between Russia and Great Britain, effacing or suspending treaties. Afterward another treaty of commerce and navigation was signed at St. Petersburg, January 12, 1859, subject to be terminated on notice from either party at the expiration of ten years, which repeats the last provision.

Thus we have three different stipulations on the part of Russia: one opening seas, gulfs, and havens on the Russian coast to British subjects for fishing and trading with the natives; the second making Sitka a free port to British subjects; and the third making British rivers that flow through the Russian possessions forever free to British navigation. Do the United States succeed to these stipulations?

Among these I make a distinction in favor of the last, which by its language is declared to be "forever," and may have been in the nature of an equivalent at the settlement of the boundaries between the two Powers. While pleading with Great Britain in 1826 for the free navigation of the St. Lawrence, Mr. Clay, who was at that time Secretary of State, said that "the American Government did not mean to contend for any principle the benefit of which, in analogous circumstances, it would deny to Great Britain." In the same year Mr. Gallatin, our Minister in London, when negotiating with Great Britain for the adjustment of our boundaries on the Pacific, proposed that "if the line should cross any of the branches of the Columbia at points from which they are navigable by boats to the main stream, the navigation of both branches and of the main stream should be perpetually free and common to the people of both nations."

The two other stipulations are different in character. They are not declared to be "forever" and do not stand on any principle of public law.

From this survey of the treaty, as seen in its origin and the questions under it, I might pass at once to a survey of the possessions that have been conveyed, but there are other matters of a more general character which present themselves at this stage and challenge the judgment. These concern nothing less than the unity, power, and grandeur of the republic, with the extension of its dominion and its institutions.

Foremost in order, if not in importance, I put the desires of our fellow-citizens on the Pacific coast, and the special advantages that they will derive from this enlargement of boundary. They were the first to ask for it, and will be the first to profit by it. While others knew the Russian possessions only on the map, they knew them practically in their resources. While others were still indifferent, they were planning how to appropriate Russian peltries and fisheries.

These well-known desires were founded, of course, on supposed advantages; and here experience and neighborhood were prompters. Since 1854 the people of California have received their ice from the fresh-water lakes in the island of Kodiak, not far westward from Mount St. Elias. Later still their fishermen have searched the waters about the Aleutians and Shumagins, beginning a promising fishery. Others have proposed to substitute themselves for the Hudson Bay Company in their franchise on the coast. But all were looking to the Orient, as in the time of Columbus, although like him they sail to the west. To them China and Japan, those ancient realms of fabulous wealth, are the Indies. To draw this commerce to the Pacific coast is no new idea.

For a long time most, if not all, the sea-otter skins of this coast found their way to China, excluding even Russia herself. China was the best customer, and therefore Englishmen and Americans followed the Russian company in carrying these furs to her market.

To unite the east of Asia with the west of America is the aspiration of commerce. Of course, whatever helps this result is an advantage. This treaty is another advantage, for nothing can be clearer than that the western coast must exercise an attraction that will be felt in China and Japan just in proportion as it is occupied by a commercial people communicating readily with the Atlantic and with Europe. This cannot be done without consequence not less important politically than commercially. Owing so much to the union, the people there will be bound to it anew, and the national unity will receive another confirmation. Thus the whole country will be a gainer.

The extension of dominion is another consideration, calculated to captivate the public mind. Few are so cold or so philosophical as to regard with insensibility a widening of the bounds of country. Our territorial acquisitions are among the landmarks of our history. If the United States have from time to time added to their dominion they have only yielded to the universal passion for annexation, although I do not forget that the late Theodore Parker was accustomed to say that among all people the Anglo-Saxons were remarkable for "a greed of land." It was land, not gold, that aroused the Anglo-Saxon phlegm. I doubt, however, whether this passion is stronger with us than with other nations, except, perhaps, that in a community where all participate in government national sentiments are more active.

More than the extension of dominion is the extension of republican institutions, which is a traditional aspiration. In this spirit independence was achieved. In the name of human rights our fathers overthrew the kingly power, whose representative was George III. They set themselves openly against this form of government. They were against it for themselves, and offered their example to mankind.

John Adams, in the preface to his *Defence of the American Constitution*, written in London, where he resided as Minister, and dated January 1, 1787, at Grosvenor Square, the central seat of aristocratic fashion, after exposing the fabulous origin of the kingly power in contrast with the simple origin of our republican constitutions, thus for a moment lifts the curtain of the future: "Thirteen governments, thus founded on the natural authority of the people alone, and without any pretence of miracle or mystery, and which are destined to spread over the northern part of that whole quarter of the globe, is a great point gained in favor of the rights of mankind." Thus, according to this prophetic Minister, even at that early day was the destiny of the republic manifest. It was to spread over the northern part of the American quarter of the globe; and it was to be a support to the rights of mankind.

By the text of our Constitution, the United States are bound to guarantee a republican form of government to every State in this Union; but this obligation, which is only applicable at home, is an unquestionable indication of the national aspiration everywhere. The republic is something more than a local policy; it is a general principle, not to be forgotten at any time, especially when the opportunity is presented of bringing an immense region within its influence. Elsewhere it has for the present failed; but on this account our example is more important.

The present treaty is a visible step in the occupation of the whole North American continent. As such it will be recognized by the world and accepted by the American people. But the treaty involves something more. By it we dismiss one more monarch from this continent. One by one they have retired; first France, then Spain, then France again; and now Russia—all giving way to that absorbing unity which is declared in the national motto: *E pluribus unum.*

THE DISCOVERY OF DIAMONDS IN AFRICA

A.D. 1867

GARDNER F. WILLIAMS, M.A.[1]

The story of the Kimberley diamond-field is one of the romances of the industrial world. Any chemist can tell us that the diamond is pure crystallized carbon; but the wisest geologist cannot make even a reasonable conjecture as to its origin or say how it came to be where it is found. By a bold figure the diamond might be called the comet of the mineral kingdom. The most experienced prospector cannot count upon any "indications," and the child of an ignorant herder may pick up a gem that would found a college. The great production of diamonds in recent years has not diminished their market value—partly because there is an increased demand for them in some of the mechanic arts, but more because human vanity of adornment may always be trusted to grow by what it feeds on.

In the volume from which this chapter is taken, Mr. Williams has produced not only the most complete and interesting account of diamonds generally and of the great African diamond discovery and the resulting camps and mining operations, but one of the most beautifully and profusely illustrated books of the season.

NEARLY two hundred years had passed since the memorable expedition of Van der Stel made known to geographers the Groote River, which, a hundred years later, was christened the Orange. Before Great Britain took the Cape, the daring Van Reenen had penetrated to Modder Fontein, unconsciously skirting the rim of a marvellous diamond-field. Since the beginning of the century scores of roving hunters had chased their game over a network of devious tracks, traversing every nook of the land between the Orange and the Vaal, and often camping for days upon their banks. Then the trekking pioneer graziers and farmers plodded on after the hunters, sprinkling their huts and kraals over the face of the Orange Free State, but naturally squatting first on the arable lands and grazing-ground nearest the water-courses. So, in the course of years, in the passage of

[1] From Gardner F. Williams's *The Diamond Mines of South Africa* (New York: B. F. Buck and Company), by permission.

the Great Trek, thousands of men, women, and children had passed across the Orange and Vaal, and up and down their winding valleys, and hundreds, at least, had trodden the river-shore sands of the region in which the most precious gems were lying.

On the Orange River, thirty miles above its junction with the Vaal, was the hamlet of Hopetown, one of the most thriving of the little settlements; and farms dotted the angle between the rivers. Along the line of the Vaal, for some distance above its entry into the Orange, were some ill-defined reservations occupied by a few weak native tribes—Koranas and Griquas—for whose instruction there were mission-stations at Pniel and Hebron.

After the discovery there arose, it is true, an imposing tale of an old mission-map of the Orange River region, drawn as early as the middle of the eighteenth century, across whose worn and soiled face was scrawled: "Here be diamonds." Even if this report were true, there was no evidence to determine the date of the scrawl, which might more credibly be a crude new record than a vague old one. In any event, it does not appear that there was even a floating rumor of the probable existence of a South African diamond-field at the time of the actual discovery of the first identified gem.

There is nothing surprising in this oversight. When a spectator beholds a great semicircle of artfully cut gems sparkling on the heads, necks, and hands of fair women massed in superb array and resplendent in the brilliant lights of an opera-house, or when one views the moving throng glittering with jewels in grand court assemblies, it is hard for him to realize how inconspicuous a tiny crystal may be in the richest of earth-beds. No spot in a diamond-field has the faintest resemblance to a jeweller's show-tray. Here is no display of gems blazing like a mogul's throne or a queen's tiara or the studded cloak of a Russian noble. Only in the marvellous valley of Sindbad are diamonds strewn on the ground in such profusion that they are likely to stick in the toes of a barefooted traveller, and can be gathered by flinging carcasses of sheep from surrounding precipices to tempt eagles to serve as diamond-winners.

It needs no strain of faith to credit the old Persian tale of the discontented Ali Hafed roaming far and wide from his charming home on the banks of the Indus in search of diamonds, and, finally, beggared and starving, casting himself into the river that flowed by his house, while the diamonds of Golconda were lying in his own garden-sands. It is probable that the diamonds of India were trodden under foot for thousands of years before the first precious stone of the Deccan was stuck in an idol's eye or a raja's turban. It is known that the Brazilian diamond-fields were washed for many years by gold-placer diggers without any revelation of diamonds to the world, although these precious stones were often picked up and so familiarly handled that they were used by the black slaves in the fields as counters in card-games.

If this be true of the most famous and prolific of all diamond-fields before the opening of the South African placers and mines, any delay in the revelation of the field in the heart of South Africa may be easily understood. For it was not only necessary to have eyes bright and keen enough to mark one of the few tiny precious crystals that were lying on the face of vast stretches of pebbles, bowlders, and sand, but the observer must prize such a crystal enough to stoop to pick it up if it lay plainly before his eyes.

Nobody that entered the Vaal River region conceived it to be a possible diamond-field or thought of searching for any precious stones. Probably, too, there was not a person in the Orange Free State, and few in the Cape Colony, able to distinguish a rough diamond if he found one by chance, or likely to prize such a crystal. For the discovery of diamonds under such conditions it was practically necessary that prospectors should enter it who would search the gravel-beds often and eagerly for the prettiest pebbles. Were such collectors at work in the field?

One of the trekking Boers, Daniel Jacobs, had made his home on the banks of the Orange River near the little settlement of Hopetown. He was one of the sprinkling of little farmers who were content with a bare and precarious living on the uncertain pasture-lands of the veld. Here his children grew up about him with little more care than the goats that browsed on the kopjes.

His boys and girls had never seen a doll or a toy of any kind; but the instinct of childhood will find playthings on the face of the most barren karroo, and the Jacobs children were luckily close to the edge of a river that was strewn with uncommonly beautiful pebbles, mixed with coarser gravel.

Here were garnets with their rich carmine flush, the fainter rose of the carnelian, the bronze of jasper, the thick cream of chalcedony, heaps of agates of motley hues, and many shining rock-crystals. From this party-colored bed the children picked whatever caught their eye and fancy, and filled their pockets with their chosen pebbles. So a poor farmer's child found scattered on a river-bank playthings that a little prince might covet, and the boy might have skimmed the face of the river with one little white stone that was worth more than his father's farm. Fortunately for the future of South Africa, he did not play ducks and drakes with this particular stone, which he found one day in the early spring of 1867, but carried it home in his pocket and dropped it with a handful of other pebbles on the floor.

A heap of these party-colored stones was so common a sight in the yard or on the floor of a farmhouse on the banks of the Orange and the Vaal that none of the plodding Boers gave it a second glance. But when the children tossed the stones about, the little white pebble sparkling in the sunlight caught the eye of the farmer's wife. She did not care enough for it to pick it up, but spoke of it as a curious stone to a neighbor, Schalk van Niekerk. Van Niekerk asked to see it, but it was not in the heap. One of the children had rolled it away in the yard. After some little search it was found in the dust, for nobody on the farm would stoop for such a trifle.

When Van Niekerk wiped off the dust, the little stone glittered so prettily that he offered to buy it. The good vrouw laughed at the idea of selling a pebble. "You can keep the stone if you want it," she said. So Van Niekerk put it into his pocket and carried it home. He had only a vague notion that it might have some value, and put it in the hands of a travelling trader, John O'Reilly, who undertook to find out what kind of stone the little crystal was and whether it could be sold. He showed the stone to several Jews in Hopetown, and in Colesberg, a settlement farther up the Orange River Valley. No one of these would give a penny for it. "It is a pretty stone enough," they said, "probably a topaz, but nobody would pay anything for it."

Perhaps O'Reilly would have thrown the pebble away if it had not come under the eye of the acting Civil Commissioner at Colesberg, Lorenzo Boyes. Mr. Boyes found on trial that the stone would scratch glass. "I believe it to be a diamond," he observed gravely. O'Reilly was greatly cheered up. "You are the only man I have seen," he said, "who says it is worth anything. Whatever it is worth you shall have a share in it." "Nonsense," broke in Dr. Kirsh, a private apothecary of the town, who was present; "I'll bet Boyes a new hat it is only a topaz." "I'll take the bet," replied Mr. Boyes, and at this suggestion the stone was sent for determination to the foremost mineralogist of the Colony, Dr. W. Guybon Atherstone, residing at Grahamstown. It was so lightly valued that it was put into an unsealed envelope and carried to Grahamstown in the regular post-cart.

When the post-boy handed the letter to Dr. Atherstone the little river stone fell out and rolled away. The doctor picked it up and read the letter of transmission. Then he examined the pebble expertly and wrote to Mr. Boyes: "I congratulate you on the stone you have sent me. It is a veritable diamond, weighs twenty-one and a quarter carats, and is worth five hundred pounds. It has spoiled all the jewellers' files in Grahamstown, and where that came from there must be lots more. May I send it to Mr. Southey, Colonial Secretary?"

This report was a revelation that transformed the despised karrooland as the grimy Cinderella was transfigured by the wand of her fairy godmother. The determination was so positive and the expertness of the examiner so well conceded that Sir Philip Wodehouse, the Governor at the Cape, bought the rough diamond at once, at the value fixed by Dr. Atherstone and confirmed by the judgment of M. Henriette, the French consul in Cape Town. The stone was sent immediately to the Paris Exhibition, where it was viewed with much interest, but its discovery, at first, did not cause any great sensation. The occasional finding of a diamond in a bed of pebbles had been reported before from various parts of the globe, and there was no assurance in this discovery of any considerable diamond-deposits.

Meanwhile Mr. Boyes hastened to Hopetown and to Van Niekerk's farm, to search along the river-shore where the first diamond was found. He prodded the phlegmatic farmers and their black servants and raked over many bushels of pebbles for two weeks, but no second diamond repaid his labor. Still, the news of the finding of the first stone made the farmers near the river look more sharply at every heap of pebbles in the hope of finding one of the precious *blink klippe* ("bright stones"), as the Boers named the diamond, and many bits of shining rock-crystal were carefully pocketed in the persuasion that the glittering stones were diamonds. But it was ten months from the time of the discovery at Hopetown before a second diamond was found, and this was in a spot more than thirty miles away, on the bank below the junction of the Vaal and the Orange rivers. Mr. Boyes again hastened to the place from which the diamond had been taken, but he again failed to find companion stones, though he reached the conclusion that the diamond had been washed downstream by the overflowing Vaal.

From the Orange River the search passed up the Vaal, where the beds of pebbles were still more common and beautiful. The eyes of the native blacks were much quicker and keener in such a quest than those of the Boer, who scarcely troubled himself to stoop for the faint chance of a diamond. But no steady or systematic search was undertaken by anybody, and it was not until the next year, 1868, that a few more diamonds were picked up on the banks of the Vaal by some sharp-sighted Koranas. The advance of discovery was so slow and disappointing that there seemed only a faint prospect of the realization of the cheering prediction of Dr. Atherstone, which was scouted by critics who were wholly incompetent to pass upon it. Even the possibility of the existence of diamond-deposits near the junction of the Orange and Vaal rivers was denied by a pretentious examiner who came from England to report on the Hopetown field. It was gravely asserted that any diamonds in that field must have been carried in the gizzards of ostriches from some far-distant region, and any promotion of search in the field was pronounced a bubble scheme.

To this absurd and taunting report Dr. Atherstone replied with marked force and dignity, presenting the facts indicating the existence of diamond-bearing deposits, and adding: "Sufficient has been already discovered to justify a thorough and extensive geological research into this most interesting country, and I think for the interest of science and the benefit of the Colony a scientific examination of the country will be undertaken. So far from the geological character of the country making it impossible, I maintain that it renders it probable that very extensive and rich diamond-deposits will be discovered on proper investigation. This, I trust, the home Government will authorize, as our colonial exchequer is too poor to admit of it."

There was no official response to this well-warranted suggestion, for it had hardly been penned when the news of a great discovery aroused such excitement, followed by such a rush to the field, that no government exploration was needed. In March, 1869, a superb white diamond, weighing 83.5 carats, was picked up by a Griqua shepherd-boy on the farm Zendfonstein, near the Orange River. Schalk van Niekerk bought this stone for a monstrous price in the eyes of the poor shepherd—500 sheep, 10 oxen, and a horse—but the lucky purchaser sold it easily for 11,200 pounds to Lilienfeld Brothers, of Hopetown, and it was subsequently purchased by Earl Dudley for 25,000 pounds. This extraordinary gem, which soon became famous as "the Star of South Africa," drew all eyes to a field that could yield such products, and the existence and position of diamond-beds were soon further assured and defined by the finding of many smaller stones in the alluvial gravel on the banks of the Vaal.

Alluvial deposits form the surface on both sides of this river, stretching inland for several miles. In some places the turns of the stream are frequent and abrupt, and there are many dry water-courses, which were probably old river-channels. The flooding and winding of the river partly account for the wide spreading of the deposits, but there had been a great abrasion of the surface of the land, for the water-worn gravel sometimes covers even the tops of the ridges and kopjes along the course of the river.

This gravel was a medley of worn and rolled chips of basalt, sandstone, quartz, and trap, intermingled with agates, garnets, peridot, and jasper, and other richly colored pebbles, lying in and on a bedding of sand and clay. Below this alluvial soil was in some places a calcareous tufa, but usually a rock of melaphyse or a clayey shale varying in color. Scattered thickly through the gravel and the clay along the banks were heavy bowlders of basalt and trap which were greatly vexing in after-days to the diamond-diggers.

For a stretch of a hundred miles above the mission-station at Pniel the river flows through a series of rocky ridges, rolling back from either bank to a tract of grassy, undulating plains. Fancy can scarcely picture rock-heaps more contorted and misshapen. Only prodigious subterranean forces could have so rent the earth's crust and protruded jagged dikes of metamorphic, conglomerate, and amygdaloid rocks, irregularly traversed by veins of quartz, and heavily sprinkled with big bare bowlders of basalt and trap. Here the old lacustrine sedimentary formation of the South African high veld north of the Zwarte Bergen and Witte Bergen ranges has plainly been riven by volcanic upheaval. The shale and sandstone of the upper and lower karroo beds have been washed away down to an igneous rock lying between the shale and the sandstone. Along this stretch of the river the first considerable deposit of diamonds in South Africa was uncovered.

For more than a year since the discovery of the first diamond there had been some desultory scratching of the gravel along the Vaal by farmers and natives in looking for blink klippe, and a few little diamonds had been found by the Hottentots, as before noted. But the first systematic digging and sifting of the ground were begun by a party of prospectors from Natal at the mission-station of Hebron. This was the forerunner of the second great trek to the Vaal from the Cape — a myriad of adventurers that spread down the stream like a locust swarm, amazing the natives, worrying the missionaries, and agitating the pioneer republics on the north and the east.

The first organized party of prospectors at Hebron on the Vaal was formed at Maritzburg in Natal, at the instance of Major Francis, an officer in the English Army Service, then stationed at that town. Captain Rolleston was the recognized leader, and after a long plodding march over the Drakensberg and across the veld, the little company reached the valley of the Vaal in November, 1869. Up to the time of its arrival there had been no systematic washing of the gravel edging the river. Two experienced gold-diggers from Australia, Glenie and King, and a trader, Parker, had been attracted to the field, like the Natalians, by the reported discoveries, and were prospecting on the line of the river when Captain Rolleston's party reached Hebron.

Their prospecting was merely looking over the surface gravel for a possible gem, but the wandering Koranas were more sharp-sighted and lucky in picking up the elusive little crystals that occasionally dotted the great stretches of alluvial soil.

It was determined by Captain Rolleston to explore the ground as thoroughly as practicable from the river's edge for a number of yards up the bank, and the washing began on a tract near the mission-station. The Australian prospectors joined the party, and their experience in placer-mining was of service in conducting the search for diamonds. The workers shovelled the gravel into cradles, like those used commonly in Australian and American placer-washing, picked out the coarser stones by hand, washed away the sand and lighter pebbles, and saved the heavier mineral deposit, hoping to find some grains of gold as well as diamonds above the screens of their cradles. But the returns for their hard labor for many days were greatly disappointing. They washed out many crystals and brilliant pebbles, but never a diamond nor an atom of gold-dust. Then they passed down the river more than twenty miles to another camp at Klip-drift, opposite the mission-station at Pniel. Here, too, they washed the ground for days without finding even the tiniest gem, and were almost on the point of abandoning their disheartening drudgery when, finally, on January 7, 1870, the first reward of systematic work in the field came in the appearance of a small diamond in one of the cradles.

This little fillip of encouragement determined their continuance of the work, and a party from the British Kaffraria joined them in washing the gravel in places that seemed most promising along the line of the river. It was agreed that the first discovery of rich diamond-bearing ground should be shared alike by both parties, but there was nothing to share for some weeks. Then some native Koranas were induced to point out to the Natalians a gravel-coated hummock or kopje near the Klip-drift camp, where they had picked up small diamonds. When the prospectors began the washing of the gravel on this kopje, it was soon apparent that a diamond-bed of extraordinary richness had been reached at last. Good faith was kept with the company from King William's Town, and the combined parties worked to the top of their strength in shovelling and washing the rich bed. The lucky men kept their mouths closed, as a rule, and did not intend to make known their good fortune; but such a discovery could not long be concealed from visiting traders and roaming prospectors, and before three months had passed some prying eye saw half a tumblerful of the white sparkling crystals in their camp, and the news spread fast that the miners had washed out from two hundred to three hundred stones ranging in size from the smallest gems to diamonds of thirty carats or more.

Then a motley throng of fortune-hunters began to pour into the valley of the Vaal. The first comers were those living nearest to the new diamond-field—farmers and tradesmen from the cattle-ranges and little towns of the Orange Free State. Some of these were Boers, drawn to the fields as to a novel and curious spectacle, but disdaining the drudgery of shovelling and washing from morning till night for the chance of a tiny bright stone. They stared for a while at the laboring diamond-seekers, and then turned their backs on the field contemptuously, and rode home sneering at the mania that was dragging its victims hundreds of miles, over sun-cracked and dusty karroos, to hunt for white pebbles in a river-bed. Still there were many poor farmers who caught the infectious diamond-fever at sight of the open field and a few sparkling stones, and they camped at Klip-drift or went on farther up or down the river, to join, as well as they knew how, in the search for diamonds.

Following this influx from the Free State came swarming in men of every class and condition from the southern English Colony and from the ships lying in the coast ports. The larger number were of English descent, but many were Dutch, and hardly a nation in Europe was unrepresented. Black grandsons of Guinea-coast slaves and natives of every dusky shade streaked the show of white faces. Butchers, bakers, sailors, tailors, lawyers, blacksmiths, masons, doctors, farmers, carpenters, clerks, gamblers, sextons, laborers, loafers—men of every pursuit and profession, jumbled together in queerer association than the comrades in the march to Finchley—fell into line in a straggling procession to the diamond-fields. Army officers begged furloughs to join the motley troops, schoolboys ran away from school, and women even of good families could not be held back from joining their husbands and brothers in the long and wearisome journey to the banks of the Vaal.

There was the oddest medley of dress and equipment: shirts of woollen—blue, brown, gray, and red—and of linen and cotton —white, colored, checked, and striped; trim jackets, cord riding-breeches, and laced leggings and "hand-me-downs" from the cheapest ready-made-clothing shops; the yellow oilskins and rubber boots of the sailor; the coarse brown corduroy and canvas suits, and long-legged stiff leather boots of the miner; the ragged, greasy hats, tattered trousers or loin-cloths of the native tribesmen; jaunty cloth caps, broad-brimmed felt, battered straw, garish handkerchiefs twisted close to the roots of stiff black crowns, or tufts of bright feathers stuck in a wiry mat of curls; such a higgledy-piggledy as could only be massed in a rush from African coast towns and native kraals to a field of unknown requirements, in a land whose climate swung daily between a scorch and a chill, where men in the same hour were smothered in dust and drenched in a torrent.

It is doubtful whether a single one of this fever-stricken company ever had seen a diamond-field or had had the slightest experience in rough-diamond winning, but no chilling doubt of themselves or their luck restrained them from rushing to their fancied Golconda. Their ideal field was much nearer a mirror of the valley of Sindbad than the actual African river-bank, and it was certain that many would be as bitterly disappointed by the rugged stretch of gravel at Klip-drift as the gay Portuguese cavaliers were at the sight of the Manica gold-placers.

Everything in the form of a carriage, from a chaise to a buck-wagon, was pressed into service, but the best available transport was the big trekking ox-wagon of the Boer pioneer. This was a heavily framed, low-hung wagon, about twenty feet long and five and a half feet broad. In this conveyance more than a dozen men often packed themselves and their camping outfit and food. An exceptionally well-equipped party carried bacon, potatoes, onions, tea, coffee, sugar, condensed milk, flour, biscuits, dried pease, rice, raisins, pickles, and Cape brandy. The total weight of load allowed, including the living freight, was limited to seven thousand pounds.

East London, the nearest port, was more than four hundred miles from the diamond-field, and Cape Town nearly seven hundred. Durber, Port Alfred, and Port Elizabeth were almost equally distant, as the crow flies, approximately four hundred fifty miles; but the length of the journey to the Vaal could not be measured by any bare comparison of air-line distances. The roads, at best, were rough trampled tracks, changing after a rainfall to beds of mire. Their tortuous courses rambled from settlement to settlement, or from one farmhouse to another, over the veld, and often were wholly lost in the shifting sands of the karroo. It was a tedious and difficult journey by land even from one seacoast town to another, and fifty miles from the coast the traveller was fortunate if his way was marked by even a cattle-path.

When the rain fell in torrents, with the lurid flashes and nerve-shaking crash of South African thunder-storms, the diamond-seekers huddled under the stifling cover of their wagons, while fierce gusts shook and strained every strip of canvas, and water-drops spurted through every crevice. In fair weather some were glad to spread their blankets on the ground near the wagon, and stretch their limbs, cramped by their packing like sardines in a box. On the plains they had no fuel for cooking except what they could gather of dry bullock's dung. Sometimes no headway could be made against the blinding dust-storms, that made even the tough African cattle turn tail to the blasts, and clogged the eyes and ears and every pore of exposed skin with irritating grit and powder. Sometimes the rain fell so fast that the river-beds were filled in a few hours with muddy torrents, which blocked any passage by fording for days and even weeks at a time, and kept the impatient diamond-seekers fuming in vain on their banks. Payton's party was forty-six days in its passage from Port Elizabeth to the diamond-fields without meeting with any serious delays, and journeys lasting two months were not uncommon.

Still, in spite of all obstacles, privations, and discomforts, the long journey to the fields was not wholly monotonous and unpleasant. As there was no beaten way, the prospectors chose their own path, riding by day and camping at night as their fancy led them. In ascending to the table-land of the interior from Natal, there were shifting and stirring visions of mountain-peaks, terraces, gorges, and valleys.

Throughout the Orange Free State, but especially in the neighborhood of the valleys of the Orange and Vaal, volcanic-rock elevations are common, sometimes massed in irregular rows and often rising in the most jagged and fantastic shapes. "When we see them at the surface," wrote the geologist Wyley in 1856, "they look like walls running across the country, or more frequently from a narrow, stony ridge like a wall that has been thrown down. The rock of which they are composed, greenstone or basalt, is known by the local name of iron-stone, from its great hardness and toughness and from its great weight. The origin of these dikes is well known. They have been produced by volcanic agency, which, acting from below upon horizontal beds of stratified rock, has cracked and fissured them at right angles to their planes of stratification, and these vertical cracks have been filled up with the melted rock or lava from below. The perpendicular fissures through which it has found its way upward are seldom seen, nor should we expect to see much of them, for along the line of these the rocks have been most broken up and shattered and the denudation has been greatest."

Even in traversing the karroos there were curious and awesome sights to attract and impress the mind of a traveller beholding for the first time these desert wastes so widely spread over the face of South Africa. They differ little in appearance except in size. The Great or Central Karroo, which lies beneath the foothills of the Zwarte Bergen range, has a sweep to the north of more than three hundred miles in a rolling plateau ranging in elevation from two to three thousand feet. Day after day, as the diamond-seekers from Cape Town plodded on with their creaking wagons, the same purpled brown face was outspread before them of the stunted flowering shrub which has given its name to the desert, spotted with patches of sun-cracked clay or hot red sand. To some of the Scotchmen this scrub had the cheery face of the heather of their own Highlands, and homesick Englishmen would ramble far through the furze to pick the bright yellow flowers of plants that recalled the gorse of their island homes. These common bushes, rarely a foot in height, and the thick, stunted camel-thorn were almost the only vegetable coating of the desert.

Straggling over this plain ran the quaint ranges of flat-topped hummocks and pointed spitz-kopjes, streaked with ragged ravines torn by the floods, but utterly parched for most of the year. Shy meerkats (*Cynictis penicillata*), weasel-like creatures with furry coats, peered cautiously from their burrows at the strange procession of fortune-hunters, and from myriads of the mammoth ant-hills that dot the face of the desert innumerable legions of ants swarmed on the sand along the track of the wagons. Sometimes at nightfall the queer aard-vark lurked upon the ant-heap and licked up the crawling insects by thousands. Far over the heads of the travellers soared the predatory eagles and swooping hawks, harrying the pigeons and dwarf doves that clustered at daybreak to drink at the edge of every stagnant pool.

Even in the earliest years of the Dutch advance into South Africa, when wild beasts browsed in troops on every grassy plain and valley, and the poorest marksman could kill game almost at will, the karroo was shunned by almost every living creature except in the fickle season of rainfall. The lion skirted the desert-edge warily, unwilling to venture far from a certain water-brook or pool. There was nothing on the bare karroo to tempt the rhinoceros from his bed in green-leaved thickets, and only the wild-roaming antelopes (trekbok) rambled for pasturage far over the sparsely coated and parched desert waste. If this was true in the days when the tip of Africa was swarming with animal life, it is not surprising that the diamond-seekers in 1869 and 1870 rarely saw any living mark for their rifles when they journeyed over the desert. Rock-rabbits, akin to the scriptural coney, scampering to their holes, were often the largest game in sight for days at a time, and it was counted remarkable luck when any hunter put a bullet through a little brown antelope, a grysbok or springbok. The springboks still haunted the Great Karroo, for they were particularly fond of its stunted bush-growth, and in the rainy season many droves of these antelopes could be seen browsing warily or flying in panic from the spring of the cheetah, the African hunting leopard; but most of the bigger game, blesbok, hartebeest, koodoo, and wildebeest, that used to feed greedily on the same pasture, had been killed or driven away by the keen hunting of the years that followed the taking of the Cape by the English.

Sometimes the clear sky of the horizon was blurred by the advancing of monstrous swarms of locusts, the "black snowstorms" of the natives, sweeping over the face of the land like the scourge of devouring flames, chased by myriads of locust-birds, and coating the ground for miles around at nightfall with a crawling, heaving coverlet. Then might be heard the hoarse trump of the cranes winging their way over the desert and dropping on the field strewn with locusts to gorge on their insect prey. Or the travellers saw the slate-white secretary bird, stalking about with his self-satisfied strut and scraping up mouthfuls with his eagle-like bill.

More marvellous than the locust clouds were the amazing mirages that deceived even the keen-eyed ostriches with their counterfeit lakes and wood-fringed streams, so temptingly near, but so provokingly receding, like the fruits hanging over Tantalus. Sometimes hilltops were reared high above the horizon, distorted to mountainous size and melting suddenly in thin air or a flying blur. Now a solitary horseman was seen to swoop over the desert in the form of a mammoth bird, or a troop of antelopes were changed to charging cavalry. No trick of illusion and transformation was beyond the conjuring power of the flickering atmosphere charged with the radiating heat of the desert.

When the prospectors crossed the karroo and entered the stretches of pasture-land which the Dutch called veld, the scenes of their marches were much more lively and cheery. Little farm-houses dotted the plains and valleys, rude cottages of clay-plastered stones or rough timbers, but hospitable with fires blazing on open hearths, big iron pots hanging from cranes and simmering with stews; and broad-faced, beaming vrouws and clusters of chunky boys and girls greeted the arrival of an ox-wagon from the coast as a welcome splash in the stagnant stream of their daily life.

At some of the halting-places on the banks of streams, or where plentiful water was stored in natural pans or artificial ponds, the extraordinary fertility of the irrigated soil of South Africa was plainly to be seen in luxuriant gardens, with brilliant flower-beds and heavy-laden fruit trees and vines. Here figs, pomegranates, oranges, lemons, and grapes ripened side by side, and hung more tempting than apples of Eden in the sight of the thirsting, sunburnt, dust-choked men who had plodded so far over the parched karroos. They stretched their cramped legs and aching backs in the grateful shade of spreading branches, and watched with half-shut eyes the white flocks nibbling on the pasture-land, and the black and red cattle scattered as far as the eye could see over the veld. Tame ostriches stalked fearlessly about them, often clustering like hens at the door of the farm-house to pick up a mess of grain or meal, apparently heedless of any approach, but always alert and likely to resent familiarity from a stranger with a kick as sharp and staggering as any dealt by a mule's hind leg.

The interior of the homes in these oases was not so inviting, for the rooms, at best, were small and bare to the eye of a townsman. But some were comparatively neatly kept, with smoothly cemented floors, cupboards of quaintly figured china and earthenware, hangings and rugs of leopard, fox, jackal, and antelope skins, and brackets of curving horns loaded with hunting-arms and garnished with ostrich-feathers. For the guests there was probably the offer of a freshly killed antelope or sheep; but the farmer's family was often content with "biltong," the dried meat that hung in strips or was piled in stacks under his curing-shed.

When a settler was fortunate in getting a tract of land with a pan or a water-spring, he almost invariably gave the name to his farm, as Dutoitispan, Dorstfontein, Jagersfontein, Bultfontein—names of inconsiderable little patches on the face of South Africa, which were destined to become memorable by approaching revelations.

Attracted by the good pasturage and water and the sight of flowers, fruits, and birds, even the eager diamond-seekers were not loath to linger for a day at one of these oases and rest themselves and their cattle before pushing on to the Vaal. As they drew near to their goal the face of the country began to change. After passing the Modder River, the grassy plains stretched out wider and longer and more gently undulating, and the mirage was more greatly magnifying and illusive. Herds of wild game, chiefly springbok, blesbok, hartebeest, wildebeest, and koodoo, were now frequently seen, and the ears of the travellers were tickled with the cheery "karack-karack" of flying korhaan and the pipes of red-legged plover.

There were great numbers, too, of the paauw (or Cape bustard) near the Modder River, and red-winged partridges and

Guinea fowl that gave a welcome variety to the meals of the travellers.

Over the rolling ground the prospectors pressed rapidly to the diamond-fields and soon reached the river-border where the plains ran into the barrier of ridges of volcanic rocks. Jolting heavily over these rough heaps and sinking deeply in the red sand-wash of the valleys, the heavy ox-wagons were slowly tugged to the top of the last ridge above Pniel, opposite the opened diamond-beds of Klip-drift, where the anticipated Golconda was full in sight. Here the Vaal River winds with a gently flowing stream, two hundred yards or more in width, through a steeply shelving oblong basin something over a mile and a half in length and a mile across. A thin line of willows and cotton-woods marked the edge of the stream on both banks. On the descending slope toward the river stood the clustering tents and wagons of the pilgrims waiting to cross the stream.

In the dry season the Vaal was easily fordable by ox-wagons at a point in this basin, and the ford, which the Boers call "drift," gave the name to the shore and camp opposite Pniel—"Klip-drift" ("Rockyford").

How stirring were the sights and sounds from the ridge at Pniel to every newcomer while the swarming diamond-seekers were crossing the river and spreading out over the northern bank — the confused clustering at the ford — the rambling of stragglers along the shore—the gravel cracking and grinding under the hoofs of the horses and ponies racing along the bank and rearing, plunging, and bucking at the check of the bits and prick of the spurs—the outspanning and inspanning of hundreds of oxen—the swaying and creaking wagons—the writhing, darting lash of the cracking whips of the drivers—the sulking, balking oxen, driven into long, straining lines that dragged the ponderous canvas-arched "prairie-schooners" through the turbid water and over the quaking sands—the whistling, shouting, yelling, snoring, neighing, braying, squeaking, grinding, splashing babel—the scrambling up the steep Klip-drift bank—the scattering of the newcomers—the perching of the white-topped wagons and the camp-tents like monstrous gulls on every tenable lodging-place on bank, gully, and hillside—the scurrying about for wood and water—the crackling, smoking, flaming heaps of the camp-fires—

the steaming pots and kettles swinging on cranes—the great placer-face, pockmarked with holes and heaps of reddish sand, clay, and gravel—the long stretches of the miners' rockers and troughs at the water's edge—and chief of all in interest, the busy workmen, sinking pits and throwing out shovelfuls of earth, filling buckets and hauling them up with ropes, loading and shaking the rockers, driving carts full of heavy gravel to the water-troughs, returning for new loads, scraping and sorting the fine, heavy pebbles on tables or flat rocks or boards spread on the ground!

No labored, crawling recital can compass and picture in print any approach to the instant impress on the eye and ear of the moving drama on the banks of the Vaal. Observer after observer groped vainly for graphic comparison. "Klip-drift is a swarm of bees whose hive is upset," said one; "a bank lined with ant-hills," wrote another, prosily; "a wild-rabbit warren scurried by a fox," ventured a third; "an insane-asylum turned loose on a beach," sneered a fourth. It was a mushroom growth of a seething placer-mining camp in the heart of the pasture-lands of South Africa. To old Australian and American miners it had a patent likeness to familiar camps and diggings, but its local coloring was glaringly vivid and unique.

REVOLUTION IN SPAIN

A.D. 1868

WILLIAM I. KNAPP

From the time of the Carlist uprising (1833–1840), the history of Spain has been full of vicissitudes, with frequent political and military crises. Among the changes that have taken place in the Kingdom since 1840 none is more important than that brought about by the Revolution of 1868, which resulted in the deposition and banishment of Queen Isabella II. Under the regency of her mother, Maria Christina, Isabella succeeded her father, Ferdinand VII, in 1833, the child-Queen being then but three years old. Ten years afterward she assumed personal control of the Government, but by marrying her cousin, Francisco de Assisi (1846), and especially by permitting her sister to marry the Duke of Montpensier, son of Louis Philippe, King of France, she weakened her position in Spain, where it was the object of the French monarch to secure a lasting influence for his house. The reign of Isabella was troubled by the frequent rise and fall of ministries, by rebellion in Cuba, complicated with filibustering movements from the United States, by war with Peru, and by many other disturbances at home and abroad. From 1864 to 1868 the annals of Spain record an uninterrupted series of popular conspiracies and military insurrections. But more than anything else the personal vices and misgovernment of Isabella operated against her and at last precipitated the revolution that drove her from her throne and her country. The events of this upheaval are recounted here with dramatic and picturesque effect by Knapp, an enthusiastic yet judicial historian.

IN 1864 the well-known orator Don Emilio Castelar published a strong article in a Madrid journal satirizing a recent gift. Queen Isabella had presented to the Premier, Narvaez, three-fourths of her income for one year for his eminent services to the dynasty. There was no doubt as to the service, but the cause was not popular. So Castelar headed his article *El Rasgo* ("the stroke of generosity"), and Narvaez expelled him from his chair of history in the university. The students, joined by the masses, made a demonstration in the Central Plaza—the Puerta del Sol. The troops were ordered to fire on the defenceless people. Hundreds were killed, and the Queen was compelled by public indignation to dismiss Narvaez. The alternate, Leopoldo O'Donnell, was called, and the incident ended.

In January, 1866, Don Juan Prim made his unlucky *coup* at Aranjuez. O'Donnell was on the alert, for both men were veterans in conspiracy. Suspecting that Prim might be meditating another station in the long *via crucis* of retribution, he had sent the suburban garrisons travelling about by rail, as they do in Spain when it is convenient to occupy idle elements of danger. So Prim rose with his troops at Aranjuez, but his confederates at Alcala made no sign. As usual, he called it a betrayal and fled over the neighboring border. A few shots early in the dawn against a dead wall in Madrid, a thousand exiles for France, and the dupes of Prim had paid the debt of their temerity.

But Prim was no common conspirator. From the frontier of Portugal he addressed a word to the nation: "Because I tread foreign soil, is the work thus to end? No, a thousand times, no! The external obstacles that keep me at bay for a moment will soon be removed. The forces of revolution are the same as before, the necessity the same. Even though I should not share its glories, the revolution will come. But I shall be at my post. Courage, Spaniards, the day of retribution draws nigh. We have opened the campaign for the people, and the people never die. Our foes, of themselves, can do nothing; their hope lies in our despair. They cannot afford to risk an encounter; a single blow will achieve our triumph."

This attempt of Prim in January was but one of a series that fill up the remaining months. Isabella II was encircled by the ever-narrowing bond of fate; by a hedge of bristling steel. The notes of that swan-song of 1856 echoed in the corridors of the palace; the "Dance of Death" clattered on the marble floor of her alcove. On June 22d it sounded again; this time close by her mansion, in the barracks she had reared to protect her.

San Gil, or St. Giles, is a large *caserne*, or military depot, like those buildings that Napoleon III set up over Paris. The garrison rose in San Gil on that day and slaughtered their chiefs in cold blood. The populace, forewarned and forearmed, poured into the streets and there were a rush and roar and barricade. An insurrection in Madrid is a sight to see, but not to be forgotten. At the first note of alarm, there are shrieks and running, the ponderous siege-doors of shop, hotel, and *cafe* are shut with an ominous crash, and the street exits of private houses are secured by mediæval bolts and bars. An affair like this is put down—if put down at all—by occupying the plazas and corners with artillery. Then the cavalry parade the streets, and the warfare of small arms begins.

More than eight hundred bodies lay dead in the streets on that day; but the Government triumphed. Both Narvaez and Serrano fought well, and for the nonce aided the Premier. But it was that kind of support which is soon coined to profit. When order was restored, the country was placed in a state of siege and the work of vengeance began. More than threescore and ten were led to the wall beyond the perimeter of the town and there shot. The most eminent statesmen and writers fell under the ban, and thousands followed their comrades to exile. But it was the final blow; at the next, the nation and the world will assist.

O'Donnell had again saved the Bourbon monarchy, and as a consequence Isabella, always short-sighted, always acting under the impulse of a personal bias for the *Moderados*, dismissed him on July 10th. "She has sent me off," said he, "like the meanest of her servants; but I will never again be a minister under that woman." The same day Narvaez, the champion of despotism, was installed in the presidency, and O'Donnell took the way to Biarritz—to die.

One bright afternoon in the autumn of 1867 I first saw Isabella in the presence of her people. I was standing on the edge of the grand square of the town. A picturesque throng of strangely dressed humanity was slowly moving along in the direction of the gossiping Prado. Of the women, some had black veils on their heads, some silk kerchiefs; none wore the bonnet of Europe. The men walked mincingly beside their women, their arms hidden beneath the folds of the graceful *capa*. I thought how little Romanic they seemed who had suffered six centuries of Rome. Their gait, the wary eye, the solemn, eager manner, savored more of Judea than of Latium. The political captivity in which they then groaned added a still deeper shade to their traditional gloom. Since those terrible days in June of the previous year there was nothing more to be done but to watch and wait. The walls of the public buildings were riddled and scarred by the missiles of recent combat. The point of most desperate resistance, the course of attack and defence, could be read on the walls and traced from St. Giles to Atocha, the opposite extremes of the city.

O'Donnell had but just died in France as we crossed the frontier. When Isabella heard of this she coldly remarked, "Well, he said in July he would never serve 'that woman' again; he has kept his word."

While we stood gazing and thinking on the Puerta del Sol a company of cavalry rode in from the farther end of the square, by the street that leads to the palace. Then an open landau drawn by six sleek and well-sheared mules advanced toward the spot where we stood. Mounted officers in showy uniform rode after on either side of the carriage. In it were Isabella and the Prince Consort on their way to the suburban church of Atocha. The royal pair sat with faces partly averted, and that of the Queen was the picture of hate and revenge. Not a soul of all the large company gathered on the great forum uncovered or uncloaked as she passed. Each one gazed steadily upon her in the provoking attitude of contempt. Ours were the only friendly manifestations, and they were justly interpreted as the neutrality of strangers.

We were again in Madrid at the opening of the historic year 1868. The month of January began with a public renewal of reaction. Her Majesty had resolved to support the temporal power of Rome against the encroachments of Italy and the contingencies of the hour. As an illustration of the mediæval sort of eloquence indulged in by Congress, we will give an extract from the session of January 3d. The question was on the reply to the usual Crown message. A man with a foxlike countenance arose and said:

"I wish to say that we shall transmit to the throne of our august sovereign the expression of our profoundest satisfaction at the magnificent words by which she has exalted the sublime position she occupies; by which she reminds Europe that she is proud to wear the glorious epithet of Catholic Queen; by which she reminds Spain and the universe entire that she is seated on the throne of St. Ferdinand, of Isabella I, and of the great Philip, that right arm of Christianity." This effort of the respectable academician, Don Candido Nocedal, drew from the members present fervent cries of "Hear! Hear!" Poor Spain! she will never get over those one hundred years of prosperity she had from 1492 to 1598, the period when her chains were forged.

We have said that O'Donnell died at Biarritz the previous November. In April an event occurred that gave a new impulse to Spanish politics and startled the palace more than the nation. Narvaez, the Boanerges of the retrograde party, was no more! The arm on which mother and daughter had leaned for a quarter of a century, was withdrawn from the living.

The Cortes met and delivered their jeremiad over the remains of their fallen chieftain. In amount it was a sarcasm and a challenge; in fact, it was a confession of defeat. "We shall retire from his coffin," said one, "impressed with this single patriotic idea, that if the school of anarchy and tumult is eager to show its hand once more, in the conviction that, because there is no longer an O'Donnell or a Narvaez, the breach lies open and triumph secure, we shall be found standing shoulder to shoulder under the banner of order, liberty, and the throne."

All through the speeches of that day the veteran Premier was represented as the type of moderation and the stanch protagonist of progress. He had even been heard to say a few days before that order had become so deeply inracinated, and its enemies been taught such severe lessons, he was intending ere long "to abandon the repressive policy, and allow some slack to the tight rope."

"Yes," cried Castelar from his exile at Brussels, "for ye cannot long pull on a rotten cord." The climax was reached by another speaker, who remarked that everybody knew Narvaez was a liberal man, and no one could deny it. No one was present to deny it, for the truly liberal parties had long since abstained from the national councils.

The supports on which Isabella II had rested for so many years had vanished from her grasp in five short months, and sunk into the mould of the tomb. The political situation demanded generals, not the routine parasites of a court. As her friends had been growing into age, her foes had been ripening into manhood. The surviving military men were not on the side of the Crown. Prim was now in London; Topete at Cadiz; Serrano in Madrid, abiding his time. All was calm on the surface, but it was the sinister calm of foreboding.

Gonzalez Bravo was fixed on to succeed the Duke of Valencia—a politician, after all, of the school of the stalwart *Moderado*. It was a fitting choice, for it was both natural and convenient that the first conservative Prime Minister of the Queen's majority in 1843 should now come forward to witness the work of his party and attend the victim to exile. Isabella, bred in despotism and intrigue, knew not how to enter on a period of righteous government, or she knew it was too late. She had pledged her Crown to sustain the Holy Father against the cry of her people, and she resolved to stand by her traditional policy. Having chosen this ground before Narvaez's death, she refused to yield a tittle to the new situation.

In the mean time a spirit of conciliation pervaded all parties outside the immediate *entourage* of the palace. Suddenly, on July 7th, a detonation fell on the summer air, and a strong arm intervened. All the leading generals of the confederated parties, all over Spain, were arrested at break of day and thrown into prison. At the same time the Duke and Duchess of Montpensier were invited to proceed at once to Lisbon. The prisoners, among whom were Serrano, Caballero de Rodas, Cordova, and Dulce, were soon hurried off to Cadiz, and thence to the Canary Islands, or to other remote fortresses of the realm.

The Montpensiers were slow to leave their pleasant palace of St. Elmo and the cool shades of their gardens by the Guadalquivir, within sight of the Alcazar, the Cathedral, and the graceful Giralda. But the order was peremptory, and on the 16th they were transported to Lisbon on a ship-of-war.

This vigorous action was not inopportune. The conspiracy, brought to naught by the Cabinet, five days after the departure of the court for the country, involved a serious programme. It was no less an affair than the abduction of the royal family by night, and the proclamation of Montpensier as King. This scheme had only the Union Liberal with it—men like Serrano and Topete; and it is probable that the authorities obtained the clue to the project from disaffected "Progressists." Thus the new Government was inaugurated. At the moment the preparations were complete and the tocsin about to sound, the hand that was to be smitten smote, and all was changed.

July 3d the court had left Madrid as usual for the season. First they repaired to La Granja, officially called San Ildefonso. This is a Crown domain with palace and park and fountains, about forty miles northwest of the capital. It was established by Philip V, the first Bourbon King (1700–1746), to replace his accustomed Versailles. Frenchmen still call it *Le petit Versailles*. In August, Isabella left La Granja, with her ministers and suite, and passed over the mountain to the Escorial. Flitting messengers of evil seemed brooding over this retreat, and the *manes* of her fathers lurking in the dismal halls.

From this point the royal company moved quickly forward to the Cantabrian coast. In this same month of August a similar scene was taking place in the Imperial Court of France. As Isabella travelled northward to her frontiers, so Napoleon III travelled southward to his. From Biarritz and from San Sebastian the two sovereigns could sit in their doors and survey each other's dominions.

There was to be an alliance and a banquet. Intent on her policy, renewed at the opening of the year, Isabella was to agree to send to Rome thirty thousand Spanish troops, so that Napoleon might recall his army of occupation at the "opportune moment." The opportune moment was to attack Germany. For this purpose the Emperor, Empress, and Prince Imperial were to accept a banquet at San Sebastian, in the Province of Guipuzcoa, on September 18th.

The energetic action of the Government in July was received in Spain with smiles of derision. For the first time the country perceived that O'Donnell and Narvaez were dead, and the Queen bereft indeed. By the moderation of Gonzalez Bravo the plans of the confederates had only been disturbed, not foiled. New ones had been concerted on the way to exile, under the very eyes and in the very ears of their captors.

The principals in the movement were now widely scattered. Serrano and other leading generals were on the islands of Teneriffe and the Grand Canary, four days' sail from the Peninsula. Prim was in London, Topete in Cadiz, Malcampo on the Bay of

Biscay, attending the Queen with the fleet. The first step of all was to gather in the Bay of Cadiz.

On September 6th and 8th, respectively, two swift steamers sailed, the one from Gravesend, England, and the other from Cadiz, bound for the group of islands lying off the west coast of Africa. Both had regular clearance as trading-vessels. On board the one was the brisk old General Milans del Bosch; and on the other, Lopez de Ayala, the speaker of the Spanish Assembly. Again, on the evening of the 10th a travelling carriage, emblazoned with a ducal coronet, might have been seen to dash down the Strand, in London, and, turning at the Somerset House, cross the Waterloo Bridge, whence it plunged into the South-Western Railway station. A valet descended from the box, opened the door of the carriage, and guided his master and mistress to the waiting train. He was a short, wiry man of medium build, about fifty-three or fifty-four years of age. He was dressed in the full livery of an English servant, and though there was a foreign savor about his manner, he seemed at home in his *role*. He accommodated himself in a second-class coach, as became his caste, and the door was closed and locked by the guard. It was the last Indian mail, and the train flew over the fields and bridges of pleasant England, to the town of Southampton. It was the same at which Philip II had landed in 1554 when he came to marry Mary Tudor ["Bloody Mary"]. But now our travellers, arrived at the wharf, soon disappeared from the deck of a large Peninsular and Oriental steamer about to cast off for Bombay. The names of the noble master and mistress need not be told; the valet was Don Juan Prim, Count of Reus and Marquis of Los Castillejos. The party was booked for Gibraltar.

The next morning an official-looking gentleman called at the residence of Prim in London. "Can I see the General?" said he to the servant. "You can, sir; be so good as to step into the library." Presently the servant returned with the message that his master had gone out to the club to read the foreign journals. Satisfied, the emissary took his leave. That same day a cipher telegram was despatched to the Spanish Government couched in in these words: "Prim is here."

The three swift-winged messengers were on their way. Two, with their singular freight, were battling with the billows of the ocean, and one was skirting the sunny Andalusian shore between the white Chiclana and the foreland of Trafalgar.

The Delta arrived at Gibraltar on the evening of the 16th. Three men rowed to the shore and concealed themselves in a coal-barge. They were Prim, Sagasta, and Ruiz Zorrilla. In twenty-two days they were to be the Government of Spain. A fourth man (Angulo) appeared on the barge and received his instructions. The next morning he entered the office of a well-known shipper and desired to charter a small steamer.

"What is the service?" demanded Mr. B.

"Secret service."

"I cannot accommodate you without further explanations."

"Well, then, I am authorized to say that General Prim is here, and to-morrow the squadron will rise at Cadiz."

"Not a steamer only, but my person and my fortune are at your disposal," responded the delighted son of the Rock.

The evening of September 17, 1868, was dark and threatening on the southern coast of Spain. The sun had slipped beneath the troubled clouds into the bosom of the Atlantic, casting back fitful glories against the towers and belvederes of the ancient city. The castle had fired the signal gun, and the echo of answering shots had slowly died away. Flag after flag had settled from the bastions, the forts, and the shipping in the harbor. The public promenades run along the broad sea-wall, and at eventide the traditional beauty and chivalry of Cadiz are there in picturesque type and costume. Here and there in the gloaming rise the shapeless hulks of monster war-ships. They have just arrived from the Biscay shore. From the side of one of them a bronze-hued light still throws a dim glow over the rising vapor of the funnel. The squadron is here. The Admiral is at his post, and seems to be anxiously waiting. The expected guests are nearing. There is a strange admixture of heroism and treason abroad in the night air—heroism and honor and popular acclaim, if all succeed; treason and obloquy and death, if all fail.

Suddenly four colored rockets shot across the sky in the offing and burst into a thousand stars. It was the preconcerted signal; Topete and Malcampo saw it from the pilot-house of the Zaragoza. Then there was a light at the ladder, and the measured music of the oarsmen blended with the moaning of the waves. A solitary steam-whistle was heard, and the rattle of a chain. Presently a steam-launch glided along like a shadow out into the unseen beyond. An inbound vessel rounded to and hailed the launch: "Which is the Zaragoza?" cried a voice.

"Follow us."

"Who are you?"

"The commander of the Zaragoza; who are you?"

"We are all friends."

Arrived on board the flagship, Prim and Admiral Topete held a long conference. The latter was pledged to the Duke of Montpensier, as the Liberal Union candidate to the throne. The motto of Prim was that of the Progressists—"The nation shall decide." Topete, anxious to gain over the General, had sent a steamer for him to England, together with a large sum of money from Montpensier. Prim had returned both unused. Hence the long struggle between the Unionist and Progressist, which only ceased two years after, when Topete, standing at the couch of his dying opponent, "saw the revolution and the honor of his country wounded and bleeding." Now, however, the first step was to achieve what all were united in desiring—the ejection of the Queen of Spain. In this there was no division.

Early the next morning, September 18th, a dozen ships-of-war were drawn up in line of battle in the inner bay. At a signal from the Zaragoza the air seemed filled with gay bunting of every hue, which suddenly shrouded the frigates, alow and aloft, as with butterfly clouds. The yards and rigging were peopled with marines as by magic. The decks sparkled with the instruments of music and flashed with gorgeous uniforms. From the flanks protruded grim messengers of death in long dark parallels. At last a half-dozen signal-flags fluttered at the spanker peak of the Admiral's ship. The screws revolved; the procession moved. Past Puntales and the historic Trocadero the squadron curved in front of the astonished city. Then arose the thunder of revolt; eight thousand voices, blended with the crash of ordnance, pealed forth the cry of freedom and the chorus of the national anthem.

The population, wild with enthusiasm, poured forth from the narrow streets and thronged the sea-wall. The flat roofs of the white houses were swarming with agitated life. The proclamations of Topete and Prim were being read aloud to excited groups, and the placards of the Governor denouncing the treason were repeated with the sarcasms of savage triumph. Bands of young men paraded the thoroughfares singing the "Hymn of Riego" and the forbidden ballads of Fernande's time.

Meanwhile the stirring words of Prim were producing their effect on the garrison. "To arms, citizens, to arms! Enough of patient waiting. The crisis of humiliation has been reached, the hour for revolution has come! Let the war-cry be the only cry of all good Spaniards to-day. Let every Liberal forget his discords and lay the strife of parties on his country's altar! Throughout the wide family of freedom let there be but one ambition, war; one aim, victory; one banner, the regeneration of our country. Spaniards, soldiers, countrymen, the *patria* needs your help! Forget not the cries of your fathers, your sons, your brothers. To arms with the weapons you have; wait not to look for better, for all are good when they are borne for our country's honor.

"And so let us regain our trampled liberties. Let us recover the traditional pride of our ancient character. Let us once more excite the admiration of the world, and prove ourselves to be worthy sons of noble Spain! Spaniards, liberty forever! The sovereignty of the nation forever!" These and such words, added to other arguments that appealed to the public consciousness, produced the desired effect. The shouts of the army in revolt burst on the air amid the enthusiasm of the populace.

The news of the uprising of Cadiz and the return of Serrano and Prim flew over the land. The entire Province of Andalusia adhered to the movement on the 19th and 20th. General Serrano, who in the mean time had arrived, took immediate steps to organize an army and march toward Madrid. Juntas or local committees were formed in the revolted districts, and men and money were not wanting. Prim sailed away with the fleet to support the uprising along the Mediterranean coast, while confederates were moving in Galicia and the North.

By September 26th the new army of liberation had advanced beyond Cordova, at a place called the Bridge of Alcolea. There the forces of the Government awaited them for the decisive combat. Queen Isabella in August was on the Cantabrian coast, preparing for the imperial visit, but that visit was never paid. Napoleon III heard of the uprising and returned silently to his home.

The union of the two great Liberal parties as represented in Serrano and Prim was too significant not to augur triumph from the start. Besides it was patent to all that the monarchy was in a deplorable state of abandonment. The most distinguished statesmen, ambassadors, and generals had thrown up their commissions and retired to voluntary exile. The leading provincial governors were absent on leave from their respective charges. Most of the Cabinet officers, foreseeing the end, had accompanied the court. The Minister of Public Works had gone to Aragon to inaugurate an industrial exhibition. The Department bureaus in Madrid were in the hands of subordinates. Gonzalez Bravo had resigned twice since they had left the capital; once in July at La Granja, and again at the Escorial in August. Worried with the rumors of seditious measures in preparation, and incapable of averting them, he wrote in despair to a friend: "This petty police warfare is killing me. I am tired of squibs; let big shot come, and I shall know where to strike." He wanted "big shot." Topete furnished it.

On the first vibration of the fatal wires, Isabella knew her doom was sealed. The cloud that had hung over the throne vanished and disclosed vacuity. Smarting under the wounds of ingrates; writhing under the silent contempt of the "Parvenu of Biarritz"; anticipating the sentence of a merciless world, and dreading its cruel decrees more than those of a merciful God, she summoned her expiring Cabinet. The session was stormy; it lasted all that night, until the dawn of the 19th. No one can report in our day all the ravings and recriminations that passed in that council.

Isabella II raved and wept before her astonished Cabinet. She had forgotten the divorce from the Crown pronounced by her people in 1856, and renewed in the last three years. So, blinded by ambition, she cast away the lessons of her father, confounding partial duty with treason.

The rest is soon told. The ministers resigned and Manuel Concha became Dictator of the realm. He divided the land, as the augurs of old divided the sky, into four zones, over each of which loyal men were set. He put the country under the law of the sword and hastened to the swaying capital.

On the 29th it was all over. The field of Alcolea, on the banks of the Guadalquivir, had been the valley of decision to the sovereign. Her best friends had done for her all that duty and honor could demand. Their mission was discharged with her reign; fifteen thousand had poured out their precious lives in either cause. Her General had been loyal to his trust and sealed his valor with his blood.

September 29, 1868, the date of the Spanish Revolution, was a bitter day to Isabella. It was a twofold anniversary. Thirty-five years before, on that same day, her father, Ferdinand VII, had breathed out his troubled spirit. Thirty-five years before, on that same day, she became the Queen of the Spains. And now in eleven short days she had been despoiled of her ancestral throne by that same Spanish people whose attachment to the native monarchy had ever been proverbial. The hitherto secret committees now became provisional governments. To them the dependents of the late situation handed over their powers. No telegrams, no reports, no bulletins came to Isabel now. Her very name reverted to the simplicity of private life. Henceforth she was known as "Doña Isabel de Borbon." The sceptre slipped from her grasp, her crown was an empty jewel.

The Central Junta of Madrid telegraphed to "know why San Sebastian hesitates to join the nation." The Governor informed the wretched Queen, as the executioner reminds the condemned. "Oh, yes! she would go to-morrow:" she could not go that day. The people of San Sebastian were too gallant, the Spanish people too chivalrous, not to comprehend. The nation could afford to wait a little over a history, an agony, like this.

The next morning, the 30th, the ex-Queen emerged from her lodgings at about ten o'clock. Her attire was neglected, her hands ungloved. She wore a gray impermeable cloak and a French straw bonnet garnished with a crimson plume. Her face was ruddy and swollen; a forced smile lingered on her lips. Her consort followed, pale and haggard. He was plainly dressed in black without insignia. As they passed to a carriage a group of Frenchmen cried feebly, but politely, "*Hommage a la*

Reine!" She turned and said, "To the Frenchmen, thanks for their courtesy."

At the door of the station there was still the faded trumpery of a floral arch crowned by two Spanish flags. Within were a guard of soldiers and a waiting crowd. No bustling inspectors flourished as usual their lace and gold. The engine slowly backed to the train, which pointed toward France. At five minutes past ten came the roll of a drum. The soldiers presented arms. The eager crowd looked up; many whispered, "*Jes ella!*" ("It is she!").

Father Claret led her in. Nervously he held out his fingers. Nobody wanted the proffered blessing; not one advanced to receive it. The Archbishop of Cuba forgot that it was a judgment day. The Prince Consort followed next, never so insignificant as now; then Don Sebastian and the Princess. Alfonso, though a child of only eleven years, bustled about to hide his emotion, as if he fully comprehended the sad situation. The three little infantas ran up to the train enchanted at the prospect of a ride in the cars. Their innocent jubilee forced the tear from the eyes of many who saw it. The mother appeared resigned now, but it was the resignation of a dream. Her eyes wandered or glistened with a filmy stare. At one time she turned to the crowd on the platform, as if they could save her now. They were the same that in 1840 took her in their arms, while they drove her mother to exile. But to-day Isabella stands before them as Maria Christina did then. Those October days in Valencia call to these September days in Guipuzcoa. "With fate," says the Arab poet, "it is idle to reason." So the convoy moved away from the station, and the people cried, "Long live Spain!"

The fall of Isabella in 1868 was an imperious necessity. Her reign had come to be incompatible with the honor and aspirations of her country. By a series of arbitrary measures she had divorced herself from her people; she had chilled the national heart. Her expulsion was not the catastrophe of a plot; she was not the victim of a conspiracy. It was not the work of Topete, Serrano, or Prim, of army or navy, of party or banner. Public opinion, the latent instinct of Spain, arose after the long probation, and thrust out the unworthy sovereign. Questionable means were of course employed, but underneath lay the pressure of an inexorable law.

In Madrid the first days passed in a prolonged outburst of joy. The elasticity of freedom expanded to its utmost tension. The populace filled the *fora*—those breathing-places in the dense purlieus of ancient cities—but there was no panic, no apprehension of disorder. Fraternization and conciliation were the order of the day. The throng moved along the streets demolishing the emblems of Bourbon rule. On the Ministry of Finance, or the Exchequer building, they set up this apocalyptic inscription: "The spurious race of the Bourbons is fallen, is fallen forever!"

THE ABOLITION OF THE FUR COMPANIES

A.D. 1869

G. MERCER ADAM

The fur-trade of Canada, once large and lucrative, has of recent years been much diminished by colonization and the opening up of the country by the railways. In its prime, vast was the industry at the great entrepôts of the Hudson Bay Company, at the Moose River and York factories, on the shores of the great inland sea discovered by Henry Hudson, as well as at Fort William, on Lake Superior, the headquarters of its chief rival, the Northwest Company. To-day the peltry trade is greatly reduced, and what remains is mainly shipped by the railway companies at Montreal, Winnipeg, and Victoria, B. C., instead of by the sailing-vessels that used to come annually to the exporting-posts on Hudson Bay. The value of the season's catch is estimated at about two and a half million dollars; while its bulk is still large and varied, though consisting chiefly now of beaver, mink, musquash, and marten. In the early days of Canada, the fur-trade was obviously very helpful in opening up the country for settlement and civilization, especially along the great waterways; though that was not to its advantage, nor was it the ostensible purpose of the fur companies, in their trade relations with the Indian and white trappers of the region, or with the French *voyageurs* and *coureurs de bois*. Their interest manifestly lay in keeping the country a vast, silent, and unsettled preserve of game.

Long and keen, as will be seen from the following article, was the rivalry that existed between the two chief fur-trading companies engaged in the industry, though the adventurous life their employés led was fascinating in spite of the loneliness and the isolation from their kin and kind in the far-off and widely scattered posts of the companies. Each at length was the gainer by the amalgamation that ensued in 1821; while the British Government was the gainer, on the expiration of the trading-charters, by the purchase and taking over of the joint companies' rights and privileges in 1869, and their transfer, for the compensation of one million five hundred thousand dollars, to the Canadian Dominion. Nor have the joint companies been much the losers by the transaction, since, besides the money payment, they received a grant of three and a half million acres of land in the fertile belt of the great Canadian Northwest, which, in the altered economic conditions of the region, must be of vast and increasing value in the era of settlement and enormous wheat-raising that has now in great measure displaced the old and profitable fur-trade.

WE should be glad if we could say that the world has outgrown monopolies. One monopoly on this continent, however, it has outgrown. A great fur-trading corporation that had seen ten British sovereigns come and go while it held sway over the territories once ceded to his Serene Highness Rupert, Prince Palatine of the Rhine, yielded up its proprietary interests to the Government of a young and lusty nation. In 1869 the rule over the "Great Lone Land" of the Honorable Company of Merchant Adventurers trading to Hudson Bay ceased, and the Dominion of Canada took over almost its entire interests. With the relinquishment of its rights and privileges, though it stipulated for the retention of some of its trading-posts and a certain portion of land, the company parted with not a few of the factors, trappers, *voyageurs*, and laborers that had grown gray in its service. It parted with its millions of acres of territory, some of its isolated posts, and their treasuries of fox-skin, marten, mink, musk-rat, and otter. It parted with the traditions and associations of centuries of traffic, and all the pretensions that adhere to absolute power in the hands of an old and wealthy corporation and a long-established monopoly. So scattered and distant were the possessions of the company that many moons rose and waned ere the news reached the secluded inmates of its lonely stockaded posts that the great trading company had transferred its interests to the British Government, and from that to the Canadian people. The price of the transfer was a million and a half of dollars.

The cession of the interests of the Hudson Bay Company in the vast tract of country known as Rupert's Land set at rest the long-vexed question of the right of that corporation to the lordship of the region known as the Hudson Bay Territories. It set at rest, also, not only the validity of the company's title to the territory, but the equally delicate question of the area over which the company was supposed to rule. Both questions often disturbed the councils of the company, and at successive periods were the subjects of contemplated Parliamentary inquiry.

Not only was it held that the company, in the course of time, had extended its territorial claims much further than the charter or any sound construction of it would warrant, but the charter itself was repeatedly called in question. In 1670, when the company was founded, it seems clear that the English sovereign, Charles II, had no legal right to the country, for it was then and long afterward the possession of France. By the treaty of St. Germain-en-Laye (1632) the English had resigned to the French Crown all interest in New France. The Treaty of Ryswick (1697), moreover, confirmed French right to the country. Hence Charles's gift to his cousin, Prince Rupert, and to those associated with him in the organization of the Hudson Bay Company, was gratuitous, if not illegal. The subsequent retransfer of the country to Britain by the Treaty of Utrecht (1713) may be said, however, to have given the company a right to its possessions, a right that was practically confirmed by the Conquest, and by the Treaty of Paris, in 1763. But, conceding this, there arose the other question, namely, To what extent of territory, by the terms of the original charter, was the company entitled? The text of the charter conveys only those lands whose waters drain into Hudson Bay, or, more specifically, "all the lands and territories upon the countries, coasts, and confines of the seas, etc., that lie within Hudson Straits." This very materially limited the area of the company's sway in the Northwest, and nullified its claim over the country that drains into the St. Lawrence, into the Atlantic, the Pacific, and the Arctic oceans. The company, of course, never acknowledged this view of the matter; but had its title been tested in a court of law, its territorial assumptions would doubtless have been greatly abridged.

In 1666 two French Huguenots made their way round Lake Superior, ascended the Kaministiquia River, and following the waterway, subsequently known as the Dawson route, reached Winnipeg River and Lake, and probed a route for themselves down the Nelson to the sea discovered by Henry Hudson. In process of time they returned to Quebec, and proceeded to France, where they endeavored to interest capitalists in opening up the fur-bearing regions of Hudson Bay to commerce. But French enterprise was then looking to the East rather than to the West, to the extension of trade in the rich archipelago of the East Indies, rather than to that in the frozen seas of the North. Silks and spices and the diamonds of the Orient were more attractive just then to the Gallic sense than the skins of wild beasts. The two French explorers we have referred to were thus foiled in the attempt to enlist French capital in their enterprise. But one of them, M. de Grosseliez, was not to be balked. He went to England, and there met with the retired student-soldier Prince Rupert, whose head was filled with curious schemes of enterprise; and his imagination was readily fired with the story that M. de Grosseliez had to tell.

The result was the forming of the English Hudson Bay Company, and the grant of Charles II over the region in which the company intended to operate. A New England captain connected with the Newfoundland trade was the first to sail to Hudson Bay to further the interests of the new-formed company. Presently a governor was despatched to establish and take charge of a fort on the Rupert River and one on the Nelson. By the year 1686 the Hudson Bay Company had organized five trading-posts round the shores of James Bay and Hudson Bay. These were known as the Albany, the Moose, the Rupert, the Nelson, and the Severn factories. The right to establish these posts was actively combated by the French, who sent contingents from Quebec, by the Ottawa and by Lake Superior, to harass the English in their possession of them. For several years a keen conflict was maintained between the two races, and the forts successively changed hands as Fortune happened to favor the one or the other. Possession was further varied by the treaties of Ryswick and Utrecht.

Meanwhile the French were active in the lower waters of the continent; for in 1672 La Salle had discovered the Mississippi, Joliet and Marquette had traced the outline of the Georgian Bay and Lake Superior, and Father Hennepin had seen and made a chart of the Falls of Niagara. Afterward M. Du Luth and M. De la Vérendrye penetrated into all the bays of Lake Superior, and the latter, in 1632, constructed a fort on the Lake of the Woods. At the period of the Conquest the French had done far more to discover and open up what is now the Canadian Northwest than the English. Up to 1763 they had gone as far west as the Assiniboine and the Saskatchewan. They had established Fort Maurepas on the Winnipeg, Fort Dauphin on Lake Manitoba, Fort Bourbon on Cedar Lake, and Fort a la Corne below the forks of the Saskatchewan. The Hudson Bay Company, on the contrary, had done little to invade the continent. The trade of the company hardly extended beyond the shores of Hudson Bay, or, at most, a short distance down the Albany River and the Churchill. They were inactive in their work, and for a time found their charter ineffectual to prevent interlopers from sharing the profits of the growing fur-trade. Petitioning Parliament, they now and again got a confirmation of their title and increased powers of trade; though one of the objects for which the company had originally secured its charter, the prosecution of discovery in the Arctic regions, had been little promoted. Hence enemies in Parliament repeatedly tried to limit the company's privileges and to annul its charter. Instigated by these enemies rival traders fitted out expeditions to Hudson Bay to embarrass the company and seize some portion of its trade. The fate of these expeditions was, however, adverse to rivalry; for no better sport was found for the employés of the privileged company than to board the vessels, capture their crews, and wreck the craft on the shores of the Bay.

But not thus could the Hudson Bay Company suppress competition from the interior. The French in the south were materially interfering with its trade, and the company found that to retain it its employés had to organize corps of traders and *voyageurs*, who would ascend the rivers and establish posts in the valleys of the Red River and Saskatchewan and the region of the Great Lakes. This was a matter that entailed no little difficulty and risk. To the "Hudson Bays" the interior was an unknown wilderness; and as yet they had not learned the craft of the Indian woodsman or the skill of the French *coureur de bois*. But they had more to contend with than the tyranny of nature and the perils of the way. The colony of New France by this time had grown to considerable proportions, and the French trader was to be met with all over the country. M. De Vaudreuil gives the population of New France in 1760 as 70,000, exclusive of *voyageurs* and those engaged in trade with the Indians. The French, moreover, held the two great waterways to the West—the St. Lawrence and the Mississippi. From these inlets their countrymen had spread far to the northwest; and in their traffic with the Indians of the Red River and Saskatchewan districts they had cut off much trade that previously had found its way to the Hudson Bay posts on the Albany, the

Nelson, the Churchill, and the Severn. Presently war with the English again broke out, and from across the Atlantic came the invading forces of Britain and contingents from her colonies on the coast. To some extent this withdrew the French traders to their posts on the meadows of the Mississippi and to those on the Ohio and the Alleghany. The time was therefore favorable to the Hudson Bay Company employés in again diverting the fur-trade to the old posts by the northern sea. More effectually to secure this trade, the company sent its servants to establish posts in the south, and by the year 1774 Cumberland House was founded on the Saskatchewan, and at a somewhat later day an extensive circle of forts, tributary to that at York Factory, was established and equipped.

Of the character and trade of these forts we get an intelligent idea from a graphic sketch of the Hudson Bay Company, in an English periodical published in 1870.[1] The writer is an old employé of the company:

"A typical fort of the Hudson Bay Company was not a very lively sort of affair at best. Though sometimes built on a commanding situation at the head of some beautiful river, and backed by wave after wave of dark pine forest, it was not unpicturesque in appearance. Fancy a parallelogram, enclosed by a picket twenty-five or thirty feet in height, composed of upright trunks of trees, placed in a trench, and fastened along the top by a rail, and you have the enclosure. At each corner was a strong bastion, built of squared logs, and pierced for guns that could sweep every side of the fort. Inside this picket was a gallery running right around the enclosure, just high enough for a man's head to be level with the top of the fence. At intervals, all along the side of the picket, were loopholes for musketry, and over the gateway was another bastion, from which shot could be poured on any party attempting to carry the gate. Altogether, though incapable of withstanding a ten-pounder for two hours, it was strong enough to resist almost any attack the Indians could bring against it. Inside this enclosure were the storehouses, the residences of the employés, wells, and sometimes a good garden. All night long a *voyageur* would, watch by

[1] "The Story of a Dead Monopoly:" *Cornhill Magazine*, August, 1870.

watch, pace around this gallery, crying out at intervals, with a quid of tobacco in his cheek, the hours and the state of the weather. This was a precaution in case of fire, and the hour-calling was to prevent him falling asleep for any length of time. Some of the less important and more distant outposts were only rough little log-cabins in the snow, without picket or other enclosure, where a 'postmaster' resided to superintend the affairs of the company.

"The mode of trading was peculiar. It was a system of barter, a 'made' or 'typical' beaver-skin being the standard of trade. This was, in fact, the currency of the country. Thus an Indian arriving at one of the company's establishments with a bundle of furs which he intends to sell, proceeds, in the first instance, to the trading-room: there the trader separates the furs into lots, and, after adding up the amount, delivers to the Indian little pieces of wood, indicating the number of 'made-beavers' to which his 'hunt' amounts. He is next taken to the store-room, where he finds himself surrounded by bales of blankets, slop-coats, guns, scalping-knives, tomahawks (all made in Birmingham), powder-horns, flints, axes, etc. Each article has a recognized value in 'made beavers'; a slop-coat, for example, may be worth five 'made beavers,' for which the Indian delivers up twelve of his pieces of wood; for a gun he gives twenty; for a knife two; and so on, until his stock of wooden cash is expended. After finishing he is presented with a trifle besides the payment for his furs, and makes room for someone else."

Of these trading-establishments of the Hudson Bay Company the writer adds: "There were in 1860 more than 150, in charge of twenty-five chief factors and twenty-eight chief traders, with 150 clerks and 1200 other servants. The trading-districts of the company were thirty-eight, divided into five departments, and extending over a country nearly as large as Europe, though thinly peopled by about 160,000 natives, Esquimaux, Indians, and half-breeds."

The Northwest Fur Company of Montreal was for nearly forty years an active and formidable rival of the Hudson Bay Company. It was a Canadian venture, a private joint-stock company, composed of French, Scottish, and, to some extent, half-breed traders, without charter, or, so far as we can make out, license from the Government. Its object was to pursue the peltry trade, and to traffic with the Indians. Next to the Hudson Bay Company, it was the most powerful trading-organization that ever entered the field of commerce in the Northwest. Its history is marked by chronic feuds with the employés of its great English rival, and by a sanguinary conflict with Lord Selkirk's settlement on Red River. In its encounter with the latter, twenty-two lives were lost, including the Hudson Bay governor. Toward the colony of the Scottish nobleman it pursued a relentless, cruel policy. In its hostility it was actuated by the same spirit of opposition that actuated the English company in resisting the entrance of a rival in its own field. This jealousy it became the purpose of the Hudson Bay Company to inflame. By every art it embittered the feeling between the Nor'westers and the colony; and afterward it readily lent its aid as an ally in the strife.

The feud with the Scotch immigrants of the Selkirk colony was only an incident, though a prominent one, in the history of the conflict between the two trading-organizations, locally known as the "Nor'westers" and the "Hudson Bays." The intrusion of the former into what was deemed the exclusive possessions of the latter was the occasion of a long and bitter strife. The Northwest Company, organized in 1783, was not long in building up a successful trade, for its operations were conducted with skill, vigor, and enterprise. From the period of the Conquest to that of the establishment of the Canadian company, many private traders had penetrated into the Northwest. The head of Lake Superior was their common rendezvous. Thence the usual route to the west was by Rainy River, the Lake of the Woods, and the Winnipeg. Reaching Red River they gradually extended their operations as far west as the Saskatchewan, and, ere long, to the forks of the Athabasca. There they intercepted the trade that was wont to seek the Hudson Bay posts on the Churchill. This rivalry at last woke the English company from its lethargy, and it determined to send traders inland to recover its monopoly. By this time, however, the Montreal company was not only in the field, it was strongly entrenched. Already it had possession of the trade of Red River, and had established a fort at the mouth of the Souris.

But the Canadian company was not only active, it was shrewd. The principle on which it was organized was cooperative; it gave its servants a share in the profits of the business. The effect of this was to strengthen the company and to make it a formidable rival. Every year saw its enterprising traders extend their operations farther west. This could not go on undisturbed. The Hudson Bay Company, now fully alarmed, bestirred itself to oppose it. Wherever the Nor'westers constructed a fort, the Hudson Bays established a rival one. Each claimed a right to the territory, the one by virtue of its charter, the other by right of discovery and first occupancy.

Now began a many years' conflict. The Hudson Bay Company was a newcomer in the territory; the French had been actively in possession for more than a century. As early as 1627, forty years before the Hudson Bays had obtained their charter, a body of French traders, known as the "One Hundred Associates," was trafficking on the plains of the Northwest. King Charles's deed to the Hudson Bay Company seems, indeed, to have been issued with a knowledge of this circumstance, for it cedes only those lands "*not* possessed by the subjects of any other Christian King or State." The French historian Charlevoix, who visited Canada in 1720, speaks scornfully of the pretensions of the English in these regions. The Nor'westers had another and a demonstrative ally in their employés, the Métis, or *Bois-brules*, who, of course, took the French view of the case. These "half-breeds," who to-day form a considerable and an unsettled portion of the population of the Northwest, were the progeny of the early French *voyageur* who had mated with the Indian. Later, the Scotch trader and company's employé was not loath to follow the example of his French countryman.

At the time of which we write, the Métis were almost entirely of French extraction, and were exclusively in the employ of the Northwest Company. At a later date, when the Hudson Bay Company began to trade in the south, an English, in contradistinction to a French half-breed race, in process of time sprang up. But as yet the half-breed was of French descent and owned allegiance to the Canadian company. To that company he naturally looked for employment; and he took to its service not only with alacrity but with ancestral pride. For his duties he was admirably fitted; for the half-breed possesses, in addition to the Frenchman's versatility and ready resource, the Indian's skill as a canoeist and his intuitive knowledge of the woods. The pride and stately dignity of the old French *noblesse*, and the magnificence of the Highland laird, who had now become an opulent fur-trader and possessor of large interests in the vast domain of the west, attracted the eye and won the heart of the simple child of the woods. This was true, indeed, not only of the half-breed, but of the full-blooded Indian. To the French both were drawn by characteristics of race which found no counterpart in the English. The French race was quick to merge into the Indian, and to pick up the habits, and not infrequently the vices, of the dusky children of the woods.

Such were the characteristics of the French Canadian and the half-breed who eagerly entered the employment of the Northwest Fur Company, and worked long and unweariedly in its interests. For a time no other race or class of men could have been more serviceable to the company. They were inured to hardships; they were at home in the woods; their relations with the Indians were of the happiest; and they were never homesick or out of humor with their surroundings. Furthermore, they were always loyal to the company.

French trading operations were always joined with the motive of discovery. It was the invariable policy of the French Government, through its representatives at Quebec, to encourage geographical research and advance the possessions of the Crown. As early at 1717 M. De la Noue, a young French lieutenant, was commissioned by M. De Vaudreuil, the Governor, to proceed to the west on a mission of trade and discovery. By this and the enterprises that immediately followed it, the whole vast interior, as far west as the Rocky Mountains, became known to the French; and in the region they speedily established their forts. In 1731 they erected Fort St. Pierre at the discharge of Rainy Lake, and in the following year founded Fort St. Charles on the Lake of the Woods and Fort Maurepas on the Winnipeg. In 1738 all the district of the Assiniboine was within the area of their operations, and Fort la Reine, on the St. Charles, and Fort Bourbon, on the Rivière des Biches, were established. Five years later the Vérendryes took possession of the Upper Mississippi and ascended the Saskatchewan in the interest of French trade. In 1766 the famous post of Michilimackinac, at the entrance of the *Lac des Illinois* (Michigan), was established. Other parts of the continent were also covered by the operations of the French traders and discoverers.

Hudson Bay had early been reached by way of the Saguenay and Lake St. John, by the Ottawa, and by Lakes Nipigon and Winnipeg. The Kaministiquia, at the head of Lake Superior, was the base of supplies for operations in the west, and the great rallying-place of the French trader and *voyageur*. In short, the whole country was probed and made known to the outer world by the enterprise of the French and the French Canadians. As a consequence any maps of the interior that were at all trustworthy were those of the French: the charts of the English, until long after the Conquest, were ludicrously inaccurate. Hence the opposition to the assumptions of the Hudson Bay Company, and the hostile rivalry which it engendered. After the Conquest, it is true, the French for a time abandoned their western possessions; but the old trading habit returned, stimulated by the sturdy Scotch and the organization of the Canadian Nor'-westers. The success of this company was remarkable. It had, however, its periods of trade depression and its years of disaster. A scourge of smallpox sometimes broke out among the Indians, and for the season destroyed its trade. Again, there were great floods in the west, and trade was impeded, if not wholly lost. Then came the era of strife with the Red River colony and collision with the Hudson Bays. In these engagements forts were fired and fur-depots destroyed. For a time hostilities were keen and continuous, and on both sides ruinous. Finally, the Hudson Bays and the Nor'westers coalesced; and from 1821 the amalgamated corporations traded under the old English title and charter of the Hudson Bay Company. This coalition gave great strength to the united company; it brought it an accession of capable traders and intelligent *voyageurs* and discoverers. In the service of the Northwest Company were men—Alexander Mackenzie and David Thompson among the number—whose names will be forever identified with discovery in the Northwest.

To the fur trade we chiefly owe the opening up of the vast

region embraced in the Dominion of Canada, from the slender thread of settlement on the banks of the St. Lawrence westward to the Pacific, and from the shores of Hudson Bay to the 49th parallel, which in 1846 became the international boundary. South of this line the principal voyages of exploration across the continent, at the beginning of the century, were the American expeditions in 1804–1806 of Lewis and Clark, up the Missouri and down the Columbia Rivers, and the later trading operations of John Jacob Astor, who established Astoria, the great western emporium of the fur trade. In this trade Astor laid the foundations of his colossal fortune. Closely following on these enterprises, and growing out of them, came the prolonged international controversy on the Oregon question, which from 1818 to 1846 formed a bone of contention between Great Britain and the United States. The treaty of 1846 established the Canadian boundary line and settled the question of the national ownership of the northern California coast.

Lewis and Clark accomplished for the United States what Sir Alexander Mackenzie had accomplished for Canada. They opened up an overland route to the Pacific, and divested the region of much of its terror to the heart of incoming civilization. Much of the territory opened up by these explorers French enterprise had already traversed. Indeed, to the French and the Scotch belong the honors of discovery over most of the continent. The whole country west of the Great Lakes was early made known by Frenchmen. In 1679 La Salle erected Fort Michilimackinac, at the entrance of Lake Michigan, and followed the Mississippi to the Gulf of Mexico. In the same year Du Luth reached the western extremity of Lake Superior and took possession of the sources of the Mississippi. About the same period Perrot and Le Sueur journeyed over the region and established forts by order of the French Governor. In 1742 Vérendrye reached the country of the Mandans, in what is now the territory of Dakota, and tracked the upper waters of the Missouri. Later he roamed over the vast plains of the Saskatchewan and probed the continent as far west as the Rocky Mountains.

In the track of the French traders a series of posts was established, extending from Sault Ste. Marie and the Kaministiquia to the distant Saskatchewan and the hyperborean Athabasca.

Later still was established the chain of trading-establishments of the Northwest Company, that linked the country from New Brunswick Post, at the source of Moose River, to the distant Fraser, the Thompson, the Peace, and the Mackenzie. Then came the cluster of Hudson Bay posts that figure so prominently in connection with the fur trade in the Northwest.

But in this enumeration we by no means exhaust the enterprise or tell the whole story of Franco-Canadian and Scottish-Canadian trade. In addition to Mackenzie's work on the west of the Rocky Mountains were the labors of James Finlay, another Scotchman, who ascended Peace River four years after Mackenzie, and explored the branch of that river to which he gave his name. In this region the name of another Scot is associated with the waters of the Fraser; while the other great river of British Columbia bears the name of still another Scotchman, David Thompson. All three were employés of the Northwest Company, of Montreal.

On the Walla-Walla and Columbia rivers the Northwest Company had in its service a whole colony of Scotchmen. The area of the company's trading operations was by no means confined to the district of Red River. The Nor'westers did a thriving trade on Columbia River, in Oregon, where they had an important and lucrative post. Their business on the coast was also extensive, reaching from California to New Archangel. On the Pacific slope, in 1817, the company had more than three hundred Canadians in its employ. From its ports three or four ships were annually despatched to London, by way of Cape Horn, freighted with furs. The ships on the return passage brought supplies for the establishments on the coast.

The Northwest Company had here no Hudson Bay rival; its chief competitor was John Jacob Astor. In 1810 this young German trader founded Fort Astoria, the great fur-mart on Columbia River, familiar to readers of Washington Irving's narrative of the western fur trade. Astor, it appears, was desirous to attach to his service some of the more prominent Scotchmen among the Nor'westers. He even made overtures to the company to join him in partnership. The advantage of an alliance, he pointed out, was his ability to ship furs in American vessels to India and China, which the Northwest Company was unable to do in consequence of the East India Company's monopoly of trade. The resident agents took the matter into consideration, but after an exchange of views with the wintering partners in the interior the proposition was declined, and it was decided to give Mr. Astor and his Pacific Fur Company a lively opposition in Oregon territory. This, of course, occurred long before international boundaries were determined; indeed, it happened within two years of the breaking out of the War of 1812.

But if Astor could not form an alliance with the Canadian company, he could seduce from its employment the men he sought to aid him in his enterprise. By dint of offers of partnership and rapid promotion he enticed twenty Canadians to enter his service. Placing these men at the head of two expeditions, Astor despatched one overland, and the other he sent round Cape Horn to the mouth of the Columbia. The breaking out of the war, and the active competition of the Northwest Company, made havoc of Astor's plans, and ere long broke up the arrangement between him and his Montreal Scotchmen. On the Pacific, Britannia's "wooden walls" were cruising about, and made trading operations too hazardous to be profitably engaged in. Fort Astoria, in the fortunes of war, and through the ceaseless rivalry of the Nor'westers, changed hands and became Fort George; but by the Treaty of Ghent, in December, 1814, the post was restored.

With the collapse of Astor's project, his Scotch partners returned to their former allegiance, and reëntered the service of the Northwest Company. Among these Scotchmen, and their countrymen who had remained in the service of the Canadian company, now gathered in the Oregon district, we find representatives of almost all the clans whose patronymics have the prefix of *Mac*.

In 1818, when Fort Astoria again changed its flag after its restitution to the Americans under the Treaty of Ghent, most of the Canadian traders returned to Fort William, to Red River, and to Montreal. Donald Mackenzie was the only one of the influential partners to remain. For several years he continued to trade on the Willamette and Snake rivers and in the country of the Nez Percés, having Fort Walla-Walla as his headquarters. But in 1822 he crossed the mountains to York Factory, and three years later he succeeded Robert Pelly in the governorship of the Red River colony. The departure of the Canadians from Oregon is thus graphically sketched by Bancroft: "It was a grand affair, this journey of the Northwest brigade from the mouth of the Columbia to Fort William and Montreal; it was at once a triumph and a dead-march. Ten canoes, five of bark and five of cedar, each carrying a crew of seven and two passengers, ninety in all, and all well armed, embarked at Fort George (Astoria). Of the party were McTavish, McDonald, John Stuart, David Stuart, Clarke, Mackenzie, Pillot, Wallace, McGillis, Franchère, and others, some of whom were destined for the upper stations. Short was the leave-taking for so large a company, for now there were not many left at the fort to say farewell. The *voyageurs* donned their broadest bonnets; arms were glittering, flags flying, the guns sounded their adieu, and, midst ringing cheers, in gayest mood the party rounded Tongue Point, and placed their breasts under the current. On April 17th they arrived at Rocky Mountain House on their way to Athabasca River. This post was more a provision-depot for the supplying of the Northwest Company's people in their passage of the mountains than a fur-hunting establishment. The glittering crystal eminences on which was perched the curved-horn mountain-goat, beyond the reach even of hungry wolves; the deep dense forests, snow-whited and sepulchral; the resting streams, laughing or raging according as their progress was impeded; the roystering torrent which no cold, dead, calm breath of nature could hush—these and like superlative beauties met the eye of the footsore travellers at every turn."

From the company's supply-house in the mountain-pass the Scotch traders pushed forward to the Athabasca, down whose waters the gay flotilla proceeded at a rapid pace. From the Athabasca they portaged across to Beaver River, descending which they entered Moore River and traversed Moore Lake. From this point the route lay across the plains to Fort Vermilion on the Saskatchewan, thence to Cumberland House and to English Lake. Crossing this they proceeded to Lakes Bourbon and Winnipeg, thence by the Winnipeg River to the Lake of the Woods, and over the portage to Fort William, where they arrived about the middle of July.

At Fort William the Nor'westers were greatly exercised over the discussion in the English Parliament of the affairs of the rival trading companies. Both companies had considerable influence in English politics. Each was eager to have its own version of the Selkirk affair laid before the House and the country. Neither hesitated to resort to sharp dealing to accomplish its purpose. Associated as was Lord Selkirk with the Hudson Bay Company, it does not seem that the latter very warmly espoused his interests. Its concern was more about its charter and its rights in the territory. He was no trader, but a lover of his kind. Stock in the Hudson Bays he purchased only to give influence to his name in the territory, to secure facilities in the transport of his people to Red River, and, as he hoped, protection when they got there. The whole matter of his colony's troubles was brought up in the House of Commons, and a blue-book was the result of the call for papers and correspondence. Little else, however, was done. From London the broken-spirited nobleman retired for rest to the Continent; but the most untroubled rest he could find was in the grave. This true patriot and baffled philanthropist died at Pau, France, on April 8, 1820.

With the death of Lord Selkirk the occasion for further dissension between the rival fur companies in some measure ceased. The English Government, though it did not see its way to effect anything by legislative enactments, endeavored to do something by mediation. With its aid, and the interposition of the Hon. Edward Ellice, one of the most influential of the resident English partners of the Northwest Company, a basis of agreement between the companies was arrived at. This agreement developed into a joint-stock partnership, which was entered into on March 26, 1821.

With the union of the companies, fur-stock again rose to a premium. Dividends that for years had fallen to 4 per cent., and even to nothing, now mounted to 10 and even to 20 per cent., with a handsome rest and an occasional large bonus. Posts that had fallen into decay were reëstablished, and trade was extended in all directions. Nor was amalgamation without its benefit on both human and brute life in the territories. The demoralization of the Indians, occasioned by the introduction of intoxicating liquors during the period of strife, ceased; while hunting "out of season," which was now strictly forbidden, had its effect upon the peltries and tended to conserve trade. But the country, in the years of even the poorest yield, was drained to an enormous extent of game. The fur yield of the Northwest Company for 1800 was as follows: 106,000 beaver, 2100 bear, 5500 fox, 4600 otter, 17,000 musquash, 320 marten, 1800 mink, 600 lynx, 600 wolverine, 1650 fisher, 100 raccoon, 3800 wolf, 700 elk, 1950 deer, and 500 buffalo! The gross returns of this one company for the year 1790 amounted to forty thousand pounds sterling ($200,000). Fifteen years later, when the Nor'-westers had absorbed the X.Y. Company, a rival Canadian institution, the gross value of its trade was one hundred twenty thousand pounds.

THE OPENING OF THE SUEZ CANAL

A.D. 1869

GARDINER GREENE HUBBARD

One great enterprise made memorable in history the otherwise ineffectual reign of Said Pacha, Viceroy of Egypt, who was the son of Mehemet Ali, sometimes called the "Peter the Great of Egypt." By the concession that made possible the construction of the Suez Canal this weak son of a powerful father made his name secure in the history of Egypt and of the world. This great work also conferred a still higher title to remembrance upon another name, that of Ferdinand de Lesseps (1805–1894), the French engineer, projector of the undertaking.

While he was French consul at Alexandria (1832) De Lesseps conceived the idea of connecting the Mediterranean and Red seas by a ship canal. Mehemet Ali, then Viceroy, one day said to him: "Remember, my young friend, that if in the course of your life you have anything important to do, you must rely only upon yourself." De Lesseps remembered the advice, although perhaps he did not need it. At all events, self-reliance sustained him through many crises when those in whom he trusted failed him. For some years, after 1849, he studied the works and plans of ancient and modern engineers for facilitating commerce between the East and the West through Egypt. Upon the accession of Said Pacha (1854), with whom De Lesseps was already acquainted, the engineer was invited to visit the Viceroy, whom he afterward accompanied on a journey across the desert. During this trip De Lesseps laid his plans before Said and obtained a concession for the canal. The terms of the concession, and the accomplishment of the great work for which it opened the way, are set forth in a clear and interesting account by Hubbard, whose special mastery of the subject is evident throughout.

THE concession obtained by De Lesseps from Said Pacha granted for ninety-nine years from the opening of the Suez Canal: "The exclusive power of organizing and directing a universal company for constructing through the Isthmus of Suez a water-canal between the two oceans, open forever as neutral ways to every commercial vessel proceeding from one sea to the other, without distinction, preference, or exclusion either of person or nationalities."

The concession required the approval of the Sultan of Turkey, as suzerain of Egypt, and that the annual profits, after the payment of 5 per cent. interest on the shares, should be divided as follows: To the Egyptian Government, 15 per cent.; to the stockholders of the company, 71 per cent.; to the original promoters, 10 per cent.; to the administration, 2 per cent.; and to the employés, 2 per cent.

Six additional concessions were obtained between 1856 and 1866. In February, 1855, De Lesseps went to Constantinople to obtain the approval of the Sultan, but failed through the opposition of Great Britain, by its representative, Sir Stratford de Redcliff. This opposition was continued without cessation until the completion of the canal.[1]

De Lesseps believed it was essential to the success of the great plan that the channel should be deep enough for the largest vessels to sail through without interruption from locks or gates, and that there was no insuperable obstacle to such a scheme. He was not an engineer; and therefore, realizing the necessity of a competent survey before proceeding further, he invited the ablest engineers of Europe to meet at Paris in October, 1855. They accepted this invitation, and after a full consultation appointed a subcommittee to examine the route. After several months of careful survey they reported that the plan was feasible, "and the solution of the problem of the junction of the two seas."

In 1857 De Lesseps presented to Lord Palmerston, then Prime Minister of England, the report of the engineers, for his approval. Lord Palmerston refused, saying: "All the engineers in Europe may say what they please; I know more than they do; my opinion will never change one jot; and I shall oppose the work to the very end." Thomas Stephenson, the engineer, supported Lord Palmerston, declaring that "the scheme was physically impracticable, except at an expense too great to

[1] "As if by the irony of history" the first ship that passed through the canal flew the English flag. Within twenty years Great Britain had come to contribute more than 80 per cent. of the traffic. In 1875 the British Government bought the shares of the original capital that belonged to the Khedive, Ismail Pacha. The acquisition thereby of a controlling interest in the canal was one of the conspicuous triumphs of Disraeli. In 1870 the number of vessels using the canal was 486; in 1899, 3607; receipts in 1870, about $1,031,865; in 1899, about $18,263,755.—ED.

warrant any expectation of returns." In Parliament the motion of John A. Roebuck, "that the power and influence of the country should not be employed in obliging the Sultan to withhold his consent," though supported by William E. Gladstone, was defeated by a vote of sixty-two in favor, two hundred twenty-eight in opposition. The press and the public were almost unanimous in condemnation of the project; the *Edinburgh Review* insisted that "the canal would neither shorten the passage to India nor materially facilitate the intercourse between the mother-country and its dependencies."

De Lesseps returned to Paris disappointed and disheartened; but the opposition of England had aroused the interest and enthusiasm of the French. The Emperor gave his public support to the company, Prince Jérôme Napoleon was appointed protector, and subscription-books were opened for the capital, fixed at $40,000,000, divided into 400,000 shares of $100 each. The French people subscribed for 207,100 shares; the Viceroy of Egypt, for 177,653 shares; others, for 15,247 shares.

Not a share of stock was taken in Great Britain. De Lesseps immediately began the surveys, procuring plans and arranging the numerous details of this vast undertaking. August 25, 1859, De Lesseps struck his spade into the earth, saying, "We strike the first blow that shall open the commerce of the East to the commerce and civilization of the West." At the same time the Viceroy of Egypt issued his circular, prohibiting the beginning of the work before the consent of the Sublime Porte had been obtained. This protest did not hinder De Lesseps, though he was greatly delayed in collecting materials and laborers. The work was begun at the most difficult places on the line of the canal, and on the harbors in the Mediterranean and Red seas.

In 1862 a small channel had been cut from the Mediterranean to Lake Timsah, about fifty miles, when England, not content with opposing this project through its representatives in Constantinople, through its press and its financiers, took more effective measures to stop the work.

The concession provided that four-fifths of the laborers should be natives, furnished by the Viceroy, and paid from one and a half to two piastres a day, with rations to the value of an additional piastre, equal, in the whole, to fifteen cents a day, or one-half more than the usual wages. The concession also authorized the company to construct the Sweet-Water Canal, and granted the company large tracts of land on the line of the Sweet-Water and Suez canals, with the right to have any goods or merchandise required for the use of the canal company entered without payment of any duty, and with the right to take tolls from all vessels passing through either of these canals. England contended that this labor was *corvee* or forced labor; that the laborers were not properly treated, and that Said Pacha had no right to alienate any land without the consent of the Sultan. De Lesseps replied that this was the only labor by which the great works of Egypt had been executed; that the *corvee* had been employed with the knowledge of England, and without protest, by English contractors and the Pacha in building railroads and in constructing the Mahmudieh Canal, where one thousand laborers are reported to have perished in one day; in digging irrigating canals, and in the cultivation of cotton plantations of Said Pacha; that England was influenced, not only by a desire to stop the work on the canal, but to obtain cotton, as a cotton famine prevailed from 1862 to 1865, during the Civil War in the United States. England proved to the Pacha that by transferring the twenty thousand laborers from the canal to his cotton-plantations, a large quantity of cotton could be raised and sold at an extravagant price. This argument was too strong to be resisted; and the laborers were withdrawn with the regret that "poor De Lesseps must go to the wall."

At that time the engineer reported that with the steady labor of thirty thousand *fellahs* the canal could have been completed in three years. The English press was satisfied; the *Times* declared "that as forced labor was to cease, the canal ceased," that "the canal was almost forgotten, its building looked on as De Lesseps's folly."

De Lesseps protested, and the French Government interfered. In 1863 Said Pacha died, and Ismail Pacha mounted the throne of Egypt. Gifted with high intelligence, and by nature a lover of progress, the new sovereign was wise enough to see that he could gain considerable advantages for his government, and at the same time assure the completion of the great canal by a prompt and considerable sacrifice, which would prevent serious complications in his relations with France. The concession had given to the company, in addition to the lands and the free entry of goods, certain municipal privileges, which seriously affected the revenues and threatened in time to create vicious entanglements in the relations between Egypt and the European Powers. Ismail seized this opportunity, and wisely agreed to submit to arbitration all questions between Egypt and the canal company, accepting, without hesitation, as arbiter, Napoleon III, Emperor of the French. This he did, well knowing that while the judgment against him would probably be heavy, it would be final, as the decision made by that arbiter would never be questioned by the company. An examination was made by a commission appointed by the Emperor, which decided that Ismail Pacha should pay the canal company for the withdrawal of *fellah* labor: An indemnity of 1,520,000 pounds ($7,600,000); for a cession of all rights of the company in the fresh-water canals, 400,000 pounds ($2,000,000); as compensation for tolls relinquished, 240,000 pounds ($1,200,000); as compensation for lands surrendered, 1,200,000 pounds ($6,000,000); total, 3,360,000 pounds ($16,800,000).

This was paid in 1864, and the work was resumed. Thus, a second time, the opposition of Great Britain resulted most advantageously to De Lesseps, furnishing the means for the continuation of the work, compelling the company to substitute machine for hand labor, and that which at first sight seemed to threaten destruction to the enterprise led to its success.

The Sultan's approval was still delayed, and not until March 19, 1866, was the *firman* issued granting "our sovereign authorization for the execution of the canal." While the arbitration was pending there was a practical cessation of work, from the withdrawal of *fellah* labor; but De Lesseps was not idle—he was planning for the substitution of machine for hand labor; seventy-eight dredgers of different kinds (some with iron spouts two hundred twenty feet long), engines, locomotives, cars, tugs, and other apparatus were constructed. The channel was dredged, the sand raised, thrown into the spout, and carried along its whole length by running water, raised by a rotary pump. Other dredgers were provided with buckets drawn from endless chains; others had short spouts, and some were ordinary dredgers tended by seagoing lighters and numberless tugs; where the dredger could not work, tramways, with dirt-cars and locomotives, were used. The first cost of the machinery was between ten million and twelve million dollars, and the cost of fuel when in full operation was two hundred thousand dollars a month. The machines were more economical and rapid than the *fellah* labor, excavating monthly when in full operation two million cubic metres of earth, a quantity sufficient to fill Broadway [New York city] from the Battery to Union Square, as high as the second stories of the houses. The digging of the canal presented no great engineering difficulties. The canal for part of the way was simply a trench cut through the desert, which is gritty, not sandy; for another part of the way through salt lakes too shallow for navigation; the rest through hills, whose rugged outlines break the dead level and uniform monotony of the desert; the highest elevation was near Suez—sixty feet.

The canal is 100 miles long: From Port Said through Lake Menzaleh to Kantara, 27 miles; from Kantara through Lake Ballah, 3 miles, to Ismailia, 21.47 miles; from Ismailia through Lake Timsah, 3 miles, to Bitter Lakes, 15 miles; through the Bitter Lakes, 21 miles; from Bitter Lakes to Suez, 15 miles; total, 99.47 miles.

It is supposed that formerly the waters of the Red and Mediterranean seas were connected; that the Isthmus has gradually risen, leaving several great depressions—salt-lakes, or great salt-marshes. In the deepest parts of these depressions the bottom was from ten to twenty feet below the sea-level, shelving to a few inches at the margin. A channel was dredged through these lakes, when they were filled with salt water, making great reservoirs preventing currents through the canal; for, though the waters of the two seas are at the same level in calm weather, when the wind blows the waves into Port Said and out from Suez there is a difference of several feet in the level. The current then flows through the canal into these lakes, but they are large enough to prevent currents through the canal.

Ismailia, the chief city of the Isthmus, is on Lake Timsah, half way across the Isthmus, where the railway from Cairo to Suez and the Sweet-Water Canal strikes the line of the Suez

Canal. The Great and Bitter lakes, forty leagues in circumference, required 440,000,000,000 gallons of water and six months to fill them.

The ancients opened a canal from the Nile to the Red Sea, but were unable to open one to the Mediterranean, for want of a harbor. A harbor was essential to the success of the scheme. De Lesseps was therefore compelled to construct "a harbor against nature," where there was no fresh water within thirty miles, neither port nor open roadstead, and only two or three feet of water, gradually deepening to twenty-five and thirty feet two miles from the shore. A sand-bank from three hundred to five hundred feet wide separated the sea from Lake Menzaleh—a vast salt-marsh. Over this bank the waves broke at every high sea. Land must be made, stone piers built to deep water, and, as there was no stone near, great blocks of artificial stone weighing twenty-two tons were made with cement brought from France and sand from the desert, and with these blocks piers two miles in length on the west and one mile on the east side were built out into the sea. The channel between these piers and in the harbor was dredged to a depth of twenty-seven feet, and the material used for making land. Here now stands Port Said, with a population of ten thousand, having one of the best harbors in the Mediterranean; its pier lighted with electric lights; its fresh water brought from the Nile at Cairo, one hundred sixty miles distant.

There was no fresh water nearer than the Nile, as rain rarely falls on the Isthmus. A large supply of drinking-water was required for the laborers and inhabitants of Port Said, Ismailia, and Suez and for the use of the vessels. To provide for this want, a canal eight feet deep and six feet wide was dug from the Nile at Cairo across the desert to a point near Ismailia, thence along the line of the Suez Canal to Suez, one hundred forty-nine miles, including the Ismailian branch. At Ismailia the water is pumped into reservoirs, and conducted in pipes to Port Said. It was finished to Ismailia, January, 1862, and to Suez, December, 1863. The canal between Cairo and Ismailia has since then been greatly enlarged by the Egyptian Government, and is a wide navigable canal with locks connecting the Nile at Cairo with the Red Sea. As all the rights in this canal were retroceded by De Lesseps to the Khedive, he was compelled to bear the cost of its construction, which was nominally $5,750,000, but in reality much greater, and probably $8,000,000.

In October, 1867, the first steamer went from Port Said to Ismailia. In the summer of 1869 the work grew near its completion. August 6th the Khedive struck the blow which united the waters of the Red Sea with those of the Mediterranean. In September De Lesseps sailed through in a small steamer and telegraphed:

"SUEZ, September 29, 1869.

"We left Port Said this morning, and, after an uninterrupted voyage by steamer, arrived here in fifteen hours."

The grand religious ceremonies of the inauguration took place at Port Said, November 16, 1869, beginning at about 2 P.M., in the presence of the Khedive, the Empress of the French, the Emperor of Austria, etc. During the night of the 16th, in order to be ready, the Khedive left Port Said in his yacht in advance of his royal guests, to receive them at the entrance of Lake Timsah.

The grand line of royal yachts left Port Said at 8 A.M., November 17th, the Aigle leading, with the Empress Eugénie and De Lesseps on board. That afternoon the fleet arrived in Lake Timsah, and were there received by a salute from Egyptian war-vessels which had come from Suez.

The evenings of November 17th and 18th were given up to festivities and excursions at Ismailia. At noon of the 19th the fleet left Lake Timsah, and at 5 P.M. anchored in the Bitter Lakes. During the night of the 19th the Khedive proceeded to Suez to await his guests in that harbor, and at 11.30 A.M. on the 20th the fleet came out of the canal into the head of the Red Sea. The inaugurating fleet was composed of sixty-nine vessels, bearing the flags of France, Austria, North Germany, Holland, England, Egypt, Russia, Italy, Norway, and Portugal, and representatives from all the courts of Europe and from every great newspaper in the world.

The expenditures on the Suez Canal at the time of opening, December 31, 1869, were: For construction, $58,271,000; for interest, including sinking-fund, $16,582,000; for negotiations and commissions, $2,208,600; for management, $2,836,505; for sundries, $3,266,650; total, $83,164,755.

This amount was raised from various sources: Subscriptions to 400,000 shares, at $100 per share, $40,000,000; loans of 1867 and 1868, $19,755,500; indemnity paid by Egypt, $16,-800,000; sundries, $6,609,255; total, $83,164,755.

The banks of the canal were faced with stone for a portion of the distance, and this work was steadily carried on until all the banks were lined. The width at the surface of the canal varies from 190 feet, where the banks are above the general level of the desert, to 328 feet, where they are low. The width at the bottom is 72 feet; the depth in 1871 was 23 feet. It has been deepened from time to time, and is from 25 to 28 feet deep. Fourteen steamers drawing 24½ feet passed through the canal in 1883. The actual time required for steaming through the canal is about nineteen hours; on account of delays, principally from vessels passing one another and because vessels are not permitted to sail by night, the average time from entering Port Said to leaving Suez is forty-eight hours. Vessels sailing in the same direction are not allowed to pass, and are required to stop at *gares* (or passing-stations) that vessels sailing in the other direction may pass. These *gares* are the sidings in this single-track road, three times the usual width of the canal, so that ships may pass on either side; with one exception they are on the east side of the canal.

The highest speed permitted is five miles and three-quarters an hour, but at this rate steamers are often obliged to use full head of steam, as the water, instead of flowing off all around the vessel, is heaped up in front of it. Wherever the channel is of uniform width, a vessel keeps its course without the use of the rudder, as the pressure is equal on both sides; but where the channel broadens on either side, the ship yields to the greater pressure, and heads directly for the opposite bank. Therefore, vessels frequently strike the banks or the bottom, and occasionally run into each other. Lighters and all needful appliances for assisting vessels are provided at short distances.

This canal, constructed not only without the aid of Great Britain, but in spite of her continued opposition, owes its success to her commerce, for four-fifths of its tolls come from British ships. No sooner was it opened than her steamers began using the canal, for a new and shorter route was opened to her empire in the East.

England desired to obtain some control in the canal, and the poverty of the Viceroy—the Khedive, since 1867—soon gave her the desired opportunity. The shares held by the Khedive, Ismail Pacha, entitled the owner to a certain control in the management, but the dividend on them was waived in 1869 for twenty-five years as the consideration for certain properties given by the Khedive to the company, subsequently purchased by him of the company on the demand of Great Britain.

The opening of the canal has produced a greater change in the commerce of the world than any other single event since the discovery of America. Formerly the commerce of the East was carried on mainly in sailing-vessels, under the English flag, around Cape of Good Hope and Cape Horn; now, in steamers through the canal. Sailing-vessels have great difficulty in sailing through the canal and the Red Sea, and so rarely use this route, while steam navigation by the canal is more economical than sailing-vessels via Cape of Good Hope; hence a large increase of steamers. The average time between London and India before the opening of the canal was ninety days, the passage fare seven hundred dollars; in 1875 it was less than thirty-six days, the passage fare three hundred forty dollars. Freights have been reduced in the same ratio with passenger fares.

The trade with the East is now by steam; and French, Russian, Austrian, and Italian vessels participate in it, and are doubling and tripling the number of their vessels, and will before long become powerful competitors with the British. The Mediterranean is no longer a closed sea, but from all its ports, and from beyond Gibraltar, all vessels bound east sail through the Suez Canal for India, China, and Australia.

The opening of the Suez Canal has not only transferred the commerce from sailing-vessels to steamers, but has also brought commerce to the maritime countries of the Mediterranean, France, Italy, and Austria. Before the Suez Canal was opened, ships very rarely sailed from these countries to the East. The commerce was all carried on under the flags of England and Holland. Now every ship to India and China passes their shores, and some steamers of the largest of the English lines start from Italy. French, Italian, and Austrian steamers were naturally drawn through the canal bearing the manufactures of their countries to the East, receiving in exchange the coffee and sugar of India, the teas and silks of China.

The East, too, has gained largely by the opening of the canal; for cheaper freights and competition have reduced the price of cotton goods, and they are now extensively used by the millions of India and China, while the labor of India and the products of that labor command higher prices. Thus action and reaction take place, and Europe and Asia are equally benefited. England foresaw the effect of the opening of the canal in developing the commerce of the Mediterranean and the competition of the Continent, and therefore was so persistent in her opposition to it. She did not anticipate the enormous development of her own commerce that would result from the facilities furnished by the canal.

Egypt, in her desire to aid the construction of the canal, agreed to furnish laborers at a stipulated price, to give liberally of her desert lands and the right to construct and use a fresh-water canal. England compelled her to withdraw the laborers and to regain the land.

For this labor and land and these rights she paid the canal company 3,360,000 pounds; the loss on the Elwady estate sold to the canal company and bought back by the Viceroy was 326,000 pounds; cost of the fresh-water canal was over 1,244,000 pounds; expenses of missions to Europe and cost of opening canal, 1,011,000 pounds; she sold her shares to Great Britain at cost, but was required to pay 5 per cent. per annum interest for twenty years on this cost, 4,000,000 pounds; total, 9,941,000 pounds ($49,705,000).

Fifty million dollars was exacted from Egypt as her contribution to the canal. Even this statement, according to the best authority, largely underestimates the cost. It does not include the loss to Egypt in impost duties, nor the vast sums paid out in interest on the sums paid in 1864, amounting, up to 1880, to not less than twenty million dollars, for which, as well as for the principal, she received only what she had previously given to the canal company. Egypt, alone of all nations, receives little, if any, benefit from the canal. The commerce of the East, which formerly paid tribute to her people as it crossed from Suez to Cairo and Alexandria, is now carried by foreign steamers without stopping, and pays tribute only to the Suez Canal. When England was at war with Egypt (1881–1885), the Suez Canal and the line of the Sweet-Water Canal afforded the surest way to invade and overcome Egypt. Arabia listened to the requests of De Lesseps, and forbore to destroy the canal or interrupt the flow of fresh water. Lord Wolseley disregarded these requests, closed the canal to all commerce, and made it the base of his line of operations.

THE COMPLETION OF THE PACIFIC RAILROAD

A.D. 1869

JOHN P. DAVIS[1]

When the United States had acquired California from Mexico, the desirability of a railroad across the continent became apparent at once. And this was emphasized two years later, when a stream of gold-seekers was moving slowly over the mountains and through the desert with ox-teams. After a few years the "Pony Express" was established, which carried the mails and a few passengers, and before the era of railways would have been considered an excellent means of rapid transit. While the railways were in process of construction, the route of that famous express grew steadily shorter, till the rails met as described in this chapter, when its day was over. The most urgent need of a railroad was seen when the Civil War broke out in 1861. Partly because of the great cost of transportation, but more from fear that the Pacific States would secede if called upon for troops, the Government omitted them in its requisitions for men. The fear was by no means groundless, since separation or union was the question at issue, and separation appeared so easy for those far-off commonwealths. As a fact, they had no thought of it, and California made liberal contributions of money for raising regiments at the East, so that her famous poet wrote:

"Honor's ringing gold shall chime
With valor's flashing steel."

The projection and execution, by four men in San Francisco, of a railroad eastward across the Sierras, for which nearly every pound of iron must be brought round Cape Horn, was one of the most daring achievements ever undertaken in the industrial world. Less than a century before, the bell at Philadelphia had rung out for freedom, and on that exciting spring day in 1869 there was a popular feeling as if a great bell Roland had proclaimed union throughout the land. The only large country in the world that borders on both the great oceans was then bound together with a band of iron — the first of many — realizing the dream of unity of interest and common brotherhood.

[1] From John P. Davis's *The Union Pacific Railway* (Chicago: Scott Foresman and Company), by permission.

WRITERS and public speakers of every class have wellnigh exhausted their resources of expression in detailing the attributes of the Pacific-railroad project, its promotion, accomplishment, and effects. Asa Whitney assured his readers in 1845, "You will see that it will change the whole world, allow us to traverse the globe in thirty days, civilize and christianize mankind, and place us in the centre of the world, compelling Europe on one side and Asia and Africa on the other to pass through us." Thomas H. Benton passionately pleaded that the great line "be adorned with its crowning honor, the colossal statue of the great Columbus, whose design it accomplishes, hewn from the granite mass of a peak of the Rocky Mountains, overlooking the road, the mountain itself the pedestal, and the statue a part of the mountain, pointing with outstretched arm to the western horizon, and saying to the flying passenger, 'There is the East! There is India!'" The congressional orator has not considered himself justified in addressing his fellow-members (or his constituents) on the subject of a Pacific railway without crowning his effort with a fulsome peroration on the greatness and grandeur of the project. Senator Butler (South Carolina) once complained: "It was said of the Nile that it was a god. I think that this Pacific-railroad project comes nearer being the subject of deification than anything else I have ever heard of in the Senate. Everyone is trying to show his zeal in worshipping this great road." Charles Sumner, greatest scholar of them all, when invited in 1853 to attend the celebration of Independence Day in Boston, apologized profusely in a letter to the mayor of the city for his inability to attend, and added: "The day itself comes full of quickening suggestions, which can need no prompting from me. And yet, with your permission, I would gladly endeavor to associate at this time one special aspiration with the general gladness. Allow me to propose the following toast: 'The railroad from the Atlantic to the Pacific—traversing a whole continent and binding together two oceans, this mighty thoroughfare, when completed, will mark an epoch of human progress second only to that of our Declaration of Independence. May the day soon come!'" The favorite rhetorical figure of the Pacific-railway orator was a comparison of his theme with the Seven Wonders of the ancient world, and a declaration, not admitting of contradiction, that they "dwindled into insignificance" in the comparison. Senator Rusk (Texas) in a letter to the Philadelphia Railroad Convention, in 1850, referred to the Pacific railway as the "Colossus of *Rhodes*," and another dignified Senator, with less originality, afterward referred to it in debate as the "Colossus of *Rail-Rhodes*."

Before the building of the Pacific railroad, most of the wide expanse of territory west of the Missouri was *terra incognita* to the mass of Americans. The interest of Thomas Jefferson in the new national purchase of Louisiana had inspired the "novel and arduous undertaking" of Lewis and Clark in 1804, 1805, and 1806, and the tales of bears, snakes, and buffalo, and descriptions of weird Indian customs compiled in their reports had excited the curiosity of many readers. The trappers and fur-traders of the Northwest had brought back from the wilderness, at long intervals, a mass of astonishing information of the fierce savages, strange animals, and peculiar vegetation of Oregon and the mountains. The widely circulated reports of Frémont's three explorations, and of the dangers and perils of the mountains and the desert West, had made the Pathfinder a hero and a presidential candidate. The *Pacific Railroad Surveys* from 1853 to 1855 added to the fund of popular information; and as each succeeding volume left the hands of the public printer, with its wealth of illustration and description, the naturally keen Anglo-Saxon appetite for adventure and acquisition was only whetted the sharper. The acquisition of California and Texas served only to heighten the ardor of the people to explore the "Great West." The discovery of the precious yellow dust in California hung up before the imagination of the "Argonauts of '49" a golden fleece that stimulated thousands of them to risk the dangers and privations of "prairie-schooner" voyages. And the later discovery of precious metals in Nevada and Colorado, in 1860 and 1861, swelled the ranks of the wealth-seekers. The Mormon rebellion, 1848, and the periodical outbreaks of the western Indians, followed by the Civil War and the impending loss to the Union of the Pacific coast territory, made the Pacific railroad, in the minds of most men, a national military necessity.

The inducements offered by the Act of 1862 were insufficient to attract to the Union Pacific individual capitalists desirous to display industrial heroism and save the nation, but doubling the amount of the prizes by the amendments of 1864 had the desired effect, and a beginning was made by the completion of eleven miles of the Union Pacific by September 25, 1865, and of forty miles by the end of that year. On October 5, 1866, the mileage had increased to two hundred forty-seven. By January 1, 1867, the road was finished and operated to a point three hundred five miles west from Omaha. In 1867 two hundred forty miles were built. The year 1868 produced four hundred twenty-five miles; and the first four months of 1869 added the one hundred twenty-five miles necessary to complete the road to its junction with the Central Pacific at Promontory Point. Work on the Central Pacific had been begun at Sacramento more than a year before it was begun on the Union Pacific at Omaha; and by the time the first eleven miles of the latter had been completed, the former had attained a length of fifty-six miles, increased by January 1, 1867, to ninety-four miles. In 1867 forty-six miles were built; in 1868 three hundred sixty-three miles were added; in 1869 the remaining one hundred eighty-six miles were covered, and Promontory Point was reached. The Union Pacific had built one thousand eighty-six miles from Omaha; the Central Pacific had built six hundred eighty-nine miles from Sacramento.

The natural obstacles presented by the mountains and desert land, the absence of timber on the prairies, of water in the mountains, and of both in the alkali desert, had made the work exceptionally difficult and expensive. The Central Pacific, though under the necessity of getting its iron, finished supplies, and machinery by sea, *via* Cape Horn or Panama, had the advantage of Chinese cooly labor and the unified management of its construction company; while the Union Pacific, having no railway connection until January, 1867, was subjected to the hardship of getting its supplies overland from the termini of the Iowa railways or by Missouri River boats, and had to depend on intractable Irish labor and the warring factions of the Crédit Mobilier. The Sierra Nevada furnished the Central Pacific all the timber needed for ties, trestlework, and snowsheds, but the Union Pacific had little or no timber along its line, except the unserviceable cottonwood of the Platte Valley, and many boats were kept busy for a hundred miles above and below Omaha on the

Missouri River in furnishing ties and heavy timbers. Both roads were being built through a new, uninhabited, and uncultivated region, where were no foundries, machine-shops, or any other conveniences of a settled country. The large engine used in the Union Pacific Railway shops was dragged across the country to Omaha from Des Moines. Twenty-five thousand men, about equally divided between two companies, are said to have been employed during the closing months of the great work. Several thousand Chinamen had been imported to California for the express purpose of building the Central Pacific. On the Union Pacific, European emigrant labor, principally Irish, was employed. At the close of the Civil War many of the soldiers, laborers, teamsters, and camp-followers drifted west to gather the aftermath of the war in the work of railway construction.

The work was essentially military, and one is not surprised to find among the superintendents and managers a liberal sprinkling of military titles. The surveying-parties were always accompanied by a detachment of soldiery as a protection against interference by Indians. The construction-trains were amply supplied with rifles and other arms, and it was boasted that a gang of track-layers could be transmuted at any moment into a battalion of infantry. And assaults on the trains by the Indians were not infrequent. "There was nothing we could ask them [the United States army] for that they did not give, even when regulations did not authorize it, and it took a long stretch of authority to satisfy all our demands. The commissary department was open to us. Their troops guarded us, and we reconnoitred, surveyed, located, and built inside their picket line. We marched to work to the tap of the drum, with our men armed. They stacked their arms on the dump and were ready at a moment's warning to fall in and fight for their territory. General Casement's track-train could arm a thousand men at a word; and from him, as a head, down to his chief spiker, it could be commanded by experienced officers of every rank, from a general to a captain. They had served five years at the front, and more than half of the men had shouldered a musket in many battles.

"An illustration of this came to me after our track had passed Plum Creek, two hundred miles west of the Missouri River. The Indians had captured a freight-train and were in possession of it and its crew. It so happened that I was coming down from the front with my car, which was a travelling arsenal. At Plum Creek station word came of this capture and stopped us. On my train were perhaps twenty men, some a portion of the crew, some who had been discharged and sought passage to the rear. Nearly all were strangers to me. The excitement of the capture and the reports coming by telegraph of the burning train brought all men to the platform; and when I called upon them to fall in to go forward and retake the train, every man on the train went into line, and by his position showed that he was a soldier. We ran down slowly until we came in sight of the train. I gave the order to deploy as skirmishers, and at the command they went forward as steadily and in as good order as we had seen the old soldiers climb the face of Kenesaw under fire." Such is the testimony of General Grenville M. Dodge, chief engineer of the Union Pacific during its construction.

The military coloring of the work of building the Union Pacific is well described in the following quotation from a newspaper of the day: "One can see all along the line of the now completed road the evidences of ingenious self-protection and defence which our men had learned during the war. The same curious huts and underground dwellings, which were a common sight along our army lines then, may now be seen burrowed into the sides of the hills or built up with ready adaptability in sheltered spots. The whole organization of the force engaged in the construction of the road is, in fact, semi-military. The men who go ahead, locating the road, are the advance-guard. Following them is the second line, cutting through the gorges, grading the road, and building bridges. Then comes the main line of the army, placing the sleepers, laying the track, spiking down the rails, perfecting the alignment, ballasting, and dressing up and completing the road for immediate use. This army of workers has its base, to continue the figure, at Omaha, Chicago, and still farther eastward, from whose markets are collected the materials for constructing the road. Along the line of the completed road are construction-trains continually pushing forward to 'the front' with supplies. The company's grounds and workshops at Omaha are the arsenal, where these purchases, amounting now to millions of dollars in value, are collected and held ready to be sent forward.

The advanced limit of the rail is occupied by a train of long box-cars, with hammocks swung under them, beds spread on top of them, bunks built within them, in which the sturdy, broad-shouldered pioneers of the great iron highway sleep at night and take their meals. Close behind this train come loads of ties and rails and spikes, etc., which are being thundered off upon the roadside to be ready for the track-layers. The road is graded a hundred miles in advance. The ties are laid roughly in place, then adjusted, gauged, and levelled. Then the track is laid.

"Track-laying on the Union Pacific is a science, and we, pundits of the Far East, stood upon that embankment, only about a thousand miles this side of sunset, and backed westward before that hurrying corps of sturdy operators with a mingled feeling of amusement, curiosity, and profound respect. On they came. A light car, drawn by a single horse, gallops up to the front with its load of rails. Two men seize the end of a rail and start forward, the rest of the gang taking hold by twos, until it is clear of the car. They come forward at a run. At the word of command the rail is dropped in its place, right side up with care, while the same process goes on at the other side of the car. Less than thirty seconds to a rail for each gang, and so four rails go down to the minute! Quick work, you say; but the fellows on the Union Pacific are tremendously in earnest. The moment the car is empty it is tipped over on the side of the track to let the next loaded car pass it, and then it is tipped back again, and it is a sight to see it go flying back for another load, propelled by a horse at full gallop at the end of sixty or eighty feet of rope, ridden by a young Jehu, who drives furiously. Close behind the first gang come the gaugers, spikers, and bolters, and a lively time they make of it. It is a grand 'anvil chorus' that those sturdy sledges are playing across the plains. It is in triple time, three strokes to the spike. There are ten spikes to a rail, four hundred rails to a mile, eighteen hundred miles to San Francisco. Twenty-one million times are those sledges to be swung, twenty-one million times to come down with their sharp punctuation, before the great work of modern America is complete!"

The only settlements between Omaha and Sacramento in 1862 were those of the Mormons in Utah, and Denver and a few mining-camps in Colorado and Nevada. Colorado was given over to the Kansas Pacific, and Salt Lake City was left for a branch line; Ogden, a Mormon town of a few hundred inhabitants, was the only station between the termini of the Union-Central Pacific. The necessities of the work of construction created new settlements and stations as it progressed, and as fast as the road was completed to each convenient point it was operated to it, while the work went on from the terminus-town as a headquarters or base of operations; thus, when the entire line was put in operation, July 15, 1869, such places as North Platte, Kearney, and Cheyenne had "got a start," while other towns, being made the termini of branch lines, secured the additional impulse due in general to junction towns. Some of the "headquarters towns," like Benton, enjoyed only a temporary, Jonah's-gourd existence, and nothing is now left to mark their former location. The life in them was rough and profligate in the extreme. An extract from the journal of a few days' sojourn in Benton in August, 1868, is instructive:

"Westward the grassy plain yields rapidly to a desert; at Medicine Bow we took final leave of the last trace of fertility, and traversed a region of alkali-flats and red ridges for fifty miles. In the worst part of this desert, just west of the last crossing of the Platte, we found Benton, the great terminus-town, six hundred ninety-eight miles from Omaha. Far as [we] could see around the town, not a green tree, shrub, or spear of grass was to be seen; the red hills, scorched and bare as if blasted by the lightnings of an angry god, bounded the white basin on the north and east, while to the south and west spread the gray desert till it was interrupted by another range of red and yellow hills. All seemed sacred to the genius of drouth and desolation. The whole basin looked as if it might originally have been filled with lye and sand, then dried to the consistence of hard soap, with glistening surface tormenting alike to eye and sense. Yet here had sprung up in two weeks, as if by the touch of Aladdin's lamp, a city of three thousand people; there were regular squares arranged into five wards, a city government of mayor and aldermen, a daily paper, and a volume of ordinances for the public health. It was the end of the freight and passenger, and beginning of the construction, division; twice every day heavy trains arrived and departed, and stages left for Utah, Montana, and Idaho; all the goods formerly hauled across the plains came here by rail and were reshipped, and for ten hours daily the streets were thronged with motley crowds of railroad men, Mexicans, and Indians, gamblers, 'cappers,' and saloon-keepers, merchants, miners, and mule-whackers. The streets were eight inches deep in white dust as I entered the city of canvas tents and pole-houses; the suburbs appeared as banks of dirty white lime, and a new arrival with black clothes looked like nothing so much as a roach struggling through a flour-barrel. It was sunset, and the lively notes of the violin and guitar were calling the citizens to evening diversions. Twenty-three saloons paid license to the evanescent corporation, and five dance-houses amused our elegant leisure.

"The regular routine of business, dances, drunks, and fist-fights met with a sudden interruption. Sitting in a tent door, I noticed an altercation across the street, and saw a man draw a pistol and fire, and another stagger and catch hold of a post for support. The first was about to shoot again when he was struck from behind and the pistol wrenched from his hand. The wounded man was taken into a tent near by and treated with the greatest kindness by the women, but died the next day. It was universally admitted that there had been no provocation for the shooting, and the general voice was, 'Hang him!' Next day there was a great rush and cry on the street, and looking out I saw them dragging the murderer along toward the tent where the dead man lay. The entire population were out at once, plainsmen, miners, and women mingled in a wild throng, all insisting on immediate hanging. Pale as a sheet and hardly able to stand, the murderer, in the grasp of two stalwart vigilantes, was dragged through the excited crowd, and into the tent where the dead man lay, and forced to witness the laying out and depositing in the coffin. What was the object of this movement nobody knew, but the delay was fatal to the hanging-project. Benton had lately been decided to be in the military reservation of Fort Steele, and that day the general commanding thought fit to send a provost guard into the city. They arrived just in time, rescued the prisoner and took him to the guardhouse, whence, a week later, he escaped.

"Transactions in real estate in all these towns were, of course, most uncertain; and everything that looked solid was a sham.

Red-brick fronts, brownstone fronts, and stuccoed walls were found to have been made to order in Chicago and shipped in (pine) sections. Ready-made houses were finally sent out in lots, boxed, marked, and numbered; half a dozen men could erect a block in a day, and two boys with screw-drivers put up a 'habitable dwelling' in three hours. A very good gray-stone stucco front, with plain sides, twenty by forty feet, could be had for three hundred dollars; and if your business happened to desert you, or the town moved on, you only had to take your store to pieces, ship it on a platform-car to the next city, and set up again.

"Ten months afterward I revisited the site. There was not a house or tent to be seen; a few rock-piles and half-destroyed chimneys barely sufficed to mark the ruins; the white dust had covered everything else, and desolation reigned supreme."

It had been expected that the Central Pacific, chartered by the State of California, would build east to the Nevada boundary, and that the Union Pacific, chartered by the National Government, would build westward from Omaha through the Territories to a meeting at the California boundary. But the object of the Pacific-railroad charter was to secure a railway from the Missouri to the Pacific, by whomsoever constructed, and its terms (section 10 of the Act of 1862) had provided that "in case said first-named [Union Pacific] company shall complete their line to the eastern boundary of California before it is completed across said State by the Central Pacific Railroad Company of California, said first-named company is hereby authorized to continue in constructing the same through California until said roads shall meet and connect, and the Central Pacific Railroad Company of California, after completing its road across said State, is authorized to continue the construction of said railroad and telegraph through the Territories of the United States to the Missouri River, including the branch lines specified, until said roads shall meet and connect."

This was changed in the Act of 1864 (section 16) to a provision that the Central Pacific might "extend their line of road eastward one hundred fifty miles on the established route, so as to meet and connect with the line of the Union Pacific road." Of which change Collis P. Huntington, of the Central Pacific, has said: "'One hundred fifty miles' should not have gone into the bill; but I said to Mr. Union Pacific, when I saw it, I would take that out as soon as I wanted it out. In 1866 I went to Washington. I got a large majority of them without the use of a dollar." Accordingly the Act of 1866 renewed the original provision of the Act of 1862, and provided (section 2) that "the Central Pacific Railroad Company of California, with the consent and approval of the Secretary of the Interior, are hereby authorized to locate, construct, and continue their road eastward in a continuous completed line, until they shall meet and connect with the Union Pacific Railroad."

The renewed provision resulted in the greatest race on record. The Central Pacific had to surmount the Sierra Nevada range at the beginning of its course, but the "Big Four," under the legal disguise of Charles Crocker and Company, were plucky, and the rise of seven thousand twelve feet above the sea-level in the one hundred five miles east of Sacramento to Summit was accomplished by the autumn of 1867. The Central Pacific did not wait for the completion of its fourteen tunnels, and especially its longest one of more than one thousand six hundred feet, at Summit, but hauled iron and supplies, and even locomotives, over the Sierra Nevada beyond the completed track, and went ahead with track-laying, to be connected later with the track through the tunnels. The Union Pacific had comparatively easy work from Omaha along the Platte Valley and up the slope to the summit of the Rocky Mountains, and boasted that its line would reach the eastern side of the Sierra Nevada before the Central Pacific had surmounted it. But the boast was not warranted.

In the autumn of 1867 the invading army of Mongolians emerged from the mountains on the west, while the rival army of Celts had reached the summit of the Black Hills and were beginning their descent into the Great Basin on the east. Every mile now meant a prize of $64,000 to $96,000 for the contending giants, with the commercial advantage of the control of the traffic of the Salt Lake Valley in addition. The construction of road went on at the rate of four to ten miles a day. Each of the two companies had more than ten thousand men at work.

For the purpose of facilitating the work, the amendatory Act of 1864 had permitted, on the certificate of the chief engineer and government commissioners that a portion of the work required to prepare the road for the superstructure was done, that a proportion of the bonds to be fully earned on the final completion of the work, not exceeding two-thirds of the value of the portion of the work done, and not exceeding two-thirds of the whole amount of bonds to be earned, should be delivered to each company; the full benefit of this inducement was sought by each of the contestants. The Union Pacific company had its parties of graders working two hundred miles in advance of its completed line in places as far west as Humboldt Wells, but financial difficulties prevented its following up this advantage. The Central Pacific Company, on the other hand, had its grading-parties one hundred miles ahead of its completed line and thirty miles east of Ogden.

When the two roads met at Promontory Point, it was found that the Central Pacific had graded eighty miles to the east that it never would cover, and the Union Pacific had wasted a million dollars on grading west of the meeting-place that it could not use. The Central Pacific had obtained from the Secretary of the Treasury an advance of two-thirds of the bond subsidy on its graded line to Echo Summit, about forty miles east of Ogden, before its completed line had reached Promontory Point; while the Union Pacific had actually laid its track to and westward from Ogden, and appeared thus to have gained the advantage of controlling the Salt Lake Valley traffic from Ogden as a base. The Union Pacific was pushing westward from Ogden with its completed line about a mile distant from and parallel with the surveyed and graded line of the Central Pacific, and the two companies were each claiming the right to build the line between Ogden and Promontory Point on their separate surveys. The completed lines were threatening to lap as the graded lines already lapped, when Congress interfered and tried to clear the muddle by statute. Before Congress could reach a conclusion, the companies compromised their differences, and Congress then approved the settlement by a joint resolution, April 10, 1869, "That the common terminus of the Union Pacific and the Central Pacific railroads shall be at or near Ogden; and the Union Pacific Railroad Company shall build, and the Central Pacific Railroad Company pay for and own, the railroad from the terminus aforesaid to Promontory Summit, at which point the rails shall meet and connect and form one continuous line." In the following year Congress, by further enactment, fixed "the common terminus and point of junction" at a particular point about five miles "northwest of the station at Ogden"; later the Union Pacific leased to the Central Pacific the five miles of track between the station at Ogden and the point fixed by Congress; thus Ogden became the actual point of junction of the two links of the completed Pacific railway.

It had at first been generally assumed that the transcontinental railway would pass through Salt Lake City and south of Great Salt Lake, and the Mormons had used their influence to obtain such a route; but before the final surveys were made, the north line was found by the Union Pacific to be more acceptable and was approved by the Government. Brigham Young thereupon called a meeting of the dignitaries of the Mormon Church, and an order was issued that no Mormon should make further grading-contracts with the Union Pacific. As the Mormon traffic was one of the prizes of the railway race, and the assistance of Mormon contractors was highly needful, the Union Pacific management awaited with some apprehension the action of the Central Pacific, but the latter also decided in favor of the route along the north shore, and Zion had to be content with the prospect of a future branch line. The Mormons then resumed their old relations with the eastern company, and many miles of well-graded roadbed bear witness of their participation in the enterprise.

The disputed question of the point of junction did not interfere with a due celebration of the meeting and joining of the two "ends of track" at Promontory Point on May 10, 1869. A space of about one hundred feet was left between the ends of the lines. Early in the day, Leland Stanford, Governor of California and president of the Central Pacific, arrived with his party from the west; in the forenoon Vice-President Durant and Directors Duff and Dillon, of the Union Pacific, with other men, including a delegation of Mormon "saints" from Salt Lake City, came in on a train from the east. The National Government was represented by a detachment of regulars from Fort Douglas, with the opportune accessories of ornamental officers and a military band. Curious Mexicans, Indians, and half-breeds, with the Chinese, negro, and Irish laborers, lent to the auspicious little gathering a suggestive air of cosmopolitanism. The ties were laid for the rails in the open space, and while the coolies from the west laid the rails at one end, the Irishmen from the east laid them at the other end, until they met and joined. The last spike remained to be driven. Telegraphic wires were so connected that each blow of the sledge could be reported instantly on the telegraphic instruments in most of the large cities from the Atlantic to the Pacific; corresponding blows were struck on the bell of the City Hall in San Francisco, and with the last blow of the sledge a cannon was fired at Fort Point. General Safford presented a spike of gold, silver, and iron as the offering of the Territory of Arizona; Tuttle, of Nevada, performed with a spike of silver a like office for his State. The tie of California laurel was put in place, and Doctor Harkness, of California, presented the last spike of gold in behalf of his State. A silver sledge had also been presented for the occasion. The driving of the spike by President Stanford and Vice-President Durant was greeted with lusty cheers; and the shouts of the six hundred persons present, to the accompaniment of the screams of the locomotive whistles and the blare of the military band, in the midst of the desert, found hearty and enthusiastic echoes in the great cities east and west.

After the last spike had been driven, the Central Pacific train was backed up, and the Union Pacific locomotive, with its train, passed slowly over the point of junction and back again; then the Central Pacific locomotive, with its train, went through the same ceremony.

The "driving of the last spike" was announced simultaneously by telegraph in all the large cities of the Union. Telegraphic inquiries at the Omaha office, from which the circuit was to be started, were answered: "To everybody. Keep quiet. When the last spike is driven at Promontory Point, we will say 'Done.' Don't break the circuit, but watch for the signals of the blows of the hammer." Soon followed the message from Promontory Point, "Almost ready. Hats off; prayer is being offered"; then, "We have got done praying. The spike is about to be presented," and—"All ready now. The spike will soon be driven. The signal will be three dots for the beginning of the blows." The magnet tapped—One—Two—Three—then paused—"Done!" Wires in every direction were "hot" with congratulatory telegrams. President Grant and Vice-President Colfax were the recipients of especially felicitous messages. In San Francisco it had been announced on the evening of May 8th from the stages of the theatres and other public places that the two roads had met and were to be wedded on the morrow. The city could not wait; the celebration began at once and continued practically through the 10th. The booming of cannon and the ringing of bells were united with the other species of noise-making in which jubilant humanity finds expression for its feeling on such an occasion. The buildings in the city and the shipping in the harbor were gay with flags and bunting. Business was suspended and the longest procession that San Francisco ever had seen attested the enthusiasm of the people. At night the city was brilliant with illuminations. Free railway trains filled Sacramento with an unwonted crowd, and the din of cannon, steam-whistles, and bells followed the final message. At the eastern terminus in Omaha, the firing of a hundred guns on Capitol Hill, more bells and steam-whistles, and a grand procession of fire-companies, civic societies, fraternities, citizens, and visiting delegations from surrounding places echoed the sentiments of the Californians. In Chicago a procession four miles in length, a lavish display of decorations in the city and on the vessels in the river, and an address by Vice-President Colfax in the evening were the evidences of the city's feeling. In New York, by order of the mayor, a salute of a hundred guns announced the culmination of the great undertaking. In Trinity Church the *Te Deum* was chanted and prayers were offered, and when the services were over the chimes rang out *Old Hundred*, the *Ascension Carol*, and national airs. The ringing of bells at Independence Hall and the fire-stations in Philadelphia produced an unusual concourse of citizens to celebrate the national event. In the other large cities of the country the expressions of public gratification were hardly less hearty and demonstrative.

THE BATTLE OF SEDAN

A.D. 1870

VON MOLTKE VON BISMARCK

One of the most noteworthy victories of modern times was that won at Sedan by the German army, under King William I of Prussia, over the French, commanded by Napoleon III and his generals, MacMahon and Wimpffen. This event led to the fall of the French Empire and the establishment of the Third Republic. It also marked the culmination of the Franco-Prussian War of 1870–1871. While the immediate ostensible cause of this war was the nomination by the Cortes of Prince Leopold, who was related to the Hohenzollerns, as successor to the Spanish throne, the underlying causes were of much greater import. After her triumph over Austria in 1866, Prussia rose to great prominence, and soon she appeared to be supplanting France as the leading State of Continental Europe. Napoleon III wished to add to his territory on the Rhine, but Prussia refused to cede the coveted lands. She also thwarted his attempt to purchase Luxemburg from Holland.

After these rebuffs the Emperor only awaited some pretext for war, although France had seldom been so poorly prepared. He eagerly seized upon the choice of Leopold for Spain, objecting on the ground of that Prince's relationship to the royal house of Prussia. Napoleon obtained from King William the withdrawal of Prussia's consent to Leopold's candidacy, but when the Emperor demanded also of the King a promise that never, in any circumstances, should Leopold accept the Spanish crown, William declined to make such an agreement. Napoleon regarded this refusal as a valid excuse for war. But Prussia was equally desirous of a conflict, and the statecraft of Bismarck took the form of subtle intrigue that made the rupture inevitable.

Napoleon meant to take a strong initiative and invade Germany; but after his declaration of war (July 19, 1870), he found the movements of the German armies too quick for him. The first important battle was fought at Weissenburg in Lower Alsace, August 4, 1870, and was won by the Germans. The French were turned back, and their enemies became the invaders. German victories followed in rapid succession—Woerth, Spicheren, Colombey-Nouilly, Vionville, Gravelotte were all won by August 18th—the French were driven from all sides toward Sedan, and there, on September 1st, the decisive battle of the war was fought. Moltke's account of this engagement, which, on the German side, he directed as chief of staff under King William, forms a part of his famous history of the Franco-Prussian War. The letter of Bismarck that follows

Moltke's narrative was written to Bismarck's wife, but never reached her. It was captured in the mail by French soldiers, and was published in a French newspaper. Bismarck, the "Creator of German Unity," was at this time chancellor of the North German Confederation, and was often present with the armies in the field.

COUNT HELMUTH VON MOLTKE

WHILE the Fifth French Corps were still fighting at Beaumont,[1] and before the rest of the army had crossed the Meuse, General MacMahon had given orders that it was to concentrate on Sedan.

He did not intend to offer battle there, but it was indispensable to give his troops a short rest and provide them with food and ammunition. He meant to retreat afterward via Mézières, whither General Vinoy was just then proceeding with the newly formed Thirteenth Corps. The First Corps, which had arrived at Carignan early in the afternoon, detached two of its divisions to Douzy in the evening to check any further advance of the Germans.

Though pursuit immediately after the battle was prevented by the intervening river, the retreat of the French soon assumed the character of a rout. The troops were worn out with their efforts by day and night, in continuous rain, and with but scanty supplies of food. The marching to and fro, to no visible purpose, had undermined their confidence in their leaders, and a series of defeats had shaken their self-reliance.

Marshal MacMahon must have known that the only chance of safety for his army, or even part of it, was to continue immediately the retrograde movement on September 1st. Of course the Crown Prince of Prussia,[2] who held the key to every passage over the Meuse, would have fallen on the flank of the retiring army, and would have pursued it to the frontier, a distance of little more than a mile. That the attempt was not risked is probably owing to the state of the worn-out troops. They were as yet incapable of a retreat in close order; they could only fight where they stood.

[1] Here, August 30, 1870, the Germans defeated a division of the French army under General MacMahon.—ED.

[2] The Crown Prince Frederick William in the Franco-Prussian War commanded the Third Army.—ED.

The Germans, on their side, still believed that the enemy would make for Mézières. The Army of the Meuse was instructed to attack them in their position and detain them there; the Third Army to press ahead on the right side of the river, leaving only one corps on the left bank.

The rear of the French was protected by the fortress of Sedan. The Meuse and the valleys of the Givonne and the Floing offered formidable obstructions, but this line of defence must be obstinately held. The Calvary of Illy [Calvaire d'Illy] was one of their most important points, strengthened as it was by the Bois de Garennes in its rear, whence a ridge extends to Bazeilles and offers protection in its numerous dips and shoulders. The road ran past Illy, should it become necessary to enter neutral territory. Bazeilles, on the other hand, which, as regards situation, formed a strong *point d'appui* for the line facing the Givonne, stands on a promontory, which, after the loss of the bridges across the Meuse, was open to attack on two sides.

In order to cooperate with the Army of the Meuse and hem in the French in their position, General von der Tann sent his first brigade over the pontoon bridges toward Bazeilles by four o'clock in the morning in a thick mist. The troops attacked the town, but found the streets barricaded, while they were fired on from every house. The company at the head pressed forward to the north gate, suffering great losses, but the others were driven out of the western part of Bazeilles, while engaged in street fighting, on the arrival of the Second Brigade of the French Twelfth Corps. However, they kept possession of the buildings at the southern end of the town and thence issued to repeated assaults. As fresh troops were constantly coming up on both sides, and the French even were reënforced by a brigade of the First and one of the Fifth Corps, the murderous combat lasted for many hours with wavering success; the fight for the Villa Beurmann, near the end of the high street and commanding its whole length, was especially fierce. The citizens took active part in the struggle, and they too had to be shot down.

The strong array of guns drawn up on the left ridge of the valley of the Meuse could not be brought to bear on the crowded streets of Bazeilles, now blazing in several places; but when, at eight o'clock, the Eighth Prussian Division had arrived at Remilly, General von der Tann ordered his last brigade into action. The walled park of Monvillers was stormed and an entrance was gained to Villa Beurmann. The artillery crossed the bridges about nine o'clock, and the Eighth Division was required to give its aid in a struggle begun by the Bavarians at La Moncelle, to the south of Bazeilles.

Prince George of Saxony had despatched an advanced guard of seven battalions from Douzy in that direction at five o'clock in the morning. They drove the French from La Moncelle, pressed ahead to Platinerie and the bridge there, and, in spite of a hot and steady fire, took possession of the houses on the other side of the Givonne, which they immediately occupied for defensive purposes. Communication with the Bavarians was now established, and the battery of the advanced guard was drawn up on the eastern slope; but the brave assailants could not be immediately reënforced by infantry.

Marshal MacMahon had been struck by a splinter from a shell at La Moncelle at 6 A.M., and he nominated General Ducrot as his successor in command, passing over the claims of two senior leaders. When General Ducrot received the news at seven o'clock, he issued orders for concentrating the army at Illy and for an immediate retreat upon Mézières. Of his own corps he despatched Lartigue's division to cover the passage at Daigny; Lacretelle and Bassoigne were ordered to assume the offensive against the Bavarians and Saxons, so as to gain time for the rest of the troops to retire. The divisions forming the second line immediately began to move toward the north.

The Minister of War had appointed General von Wimpffen, recently returned from Algiers, to the command of the Fifth Corps, *vice* General de Failly, and had also empowered him to assume the chief command in case the Marshal were disabled. General von Wimpffen knew the army of the Crown Prince to be in the neighborhood of Donchery, he regarded the retreat to Mézières as an impossibility, and was bent on the diametrically opposite course of forcing his way to Carignan, not doubting that he could rout the Bavarians and Saxons, and so effect a junction with Marshal Bazaine. When he heard of the orders just issued by General Ducrot, and, at the same time, observed that an assault upon the Germans in La Moncelle appeared to turn in his favor, he determined, in an evil hour, to exercise his authority. General Ducrot submitted without remonstrance; he was perhaps not averse to being relieved of so heavy a responsibility. The divisions of the second line that were about to march were ordered back; and the weak advance of the Bavarians and Saxons were soon pressed by the first line, who at once attacked them.

By seven in the morning one regiment of the Saxon advanced guard had marched to the taking of La Moncelle; the other had been busy with the threatening advance of Lartigue's division on the right. Here the firing soon became very hot. The regiment had marched without knapsacks, and neglected previously to take out their cartridges. Thus they soon ran short of ammunition, and the repeated and violent onslaught of the zouaves, directed principally against the unprotected right, had to be repelled with the bayonet. On the left a strong artillery had gradually been formed, and by half-past eight o'clock amounted to twelve batteries. But Lacretelle's division was now approaching on the Givonne lowlands, and dense swarms of *tirailleurs* forced the German batteries to retire about nine o'clock. The gunners withdrew to some distance, but then turned about and reopened fire on the French, and, after driving them back into the valley, returned to their original position.

The Fourth Bavarian Brigade had meanwhile reached La Moncelle, and the Forty-sixth Saxon Brigade was coming up, so the small progress made by Bassoigne's division was checked. The right wing of the Saxon contingent, which had been hard-pressed, now received much-needed support from the Twenty-fourth Division, and they at once assumed the offensive. The French were driven back upon Daigny, and lost five guns in the struggle. Then joining the Bavarians, who were pushing on through the valley to the northward, after a sharp fight, Daigny and the bridge and farmstead of La Rapaille were taken.

It was now about ten o'clock, and the guards had arrived at the Upper Givonne. They had set out before it was light, marching in two columns, when the sound of heavy firing reached them from Bazeilles and caused them to quicken their step. In order to render assistance by the shortest road, the left column would have crossed two deep ravines and the pathless wood of Chevallier; so they chose the longer route by Villers-Cernay, which the head of the right column had passed in ample time to take part in the contest between the Saxons and Lartigue's division, and to capture two French guns.

The divisions ordered back by General Ducrot had already resumed their position at the western slope, and the Fourteenth Battery of the guards now opened fire upon them from the east. At the same hour (ten o'clock) the Fourth Corps and the Seventh Division had arrived at Lamécourt, and the Eighth at Rémilly, both situated below Bazeilles; the advanced guard of the Eighth stood at the Rémilly railway station.

The first attempt of the French to break through to Carignan eastward had proved a failure, and their retreat to Mézières on the west had also been cut off, for the Fifth and Eleventh Corps of the Third Army, together with the Wurtemberg division, had received orders to move northward by that route. These troops had struck camp before daybreak, and at six o'clock had crossed the Meuse at Donchery, and by the three pontoon bridges farther down the river. The advanced patrols found the road to Mézières clear of the enemy, and the heavy shelling, heard from the direction of Bazeilles, made it appear probable that the French had accepted battle in their position at Sedan. The Crown Prince therefore ordered the two corps that had arrived at Brigne to march to the right on St. Menges; the Wurtembergers were to remain to keep watch over Mézières. General von Kirchbach then pointed out Fleigneux to his advanced guards as the next objective, to cut off the retreat of the French into Belgium, and maintain a connection with the right wing of the Army of the Meuse.

The narrow roadway between the hills and the river leading to St. Albert, about two thousand paces distant, was neither held nor watched by the French. It was not till the advanced guard reached St. Menges that they encountered a French detachment, which soon withdrew. The Germans then deployed in the direction of Illy, two companies on the right taking possession of Floing, where they kept up a gallant defence for two hours, without assistance, against repeated attacks.

The first Prussian batteries that arrived had to exert themselves to the utmost to hold out against the larger force of French artillery drawn up at Illy. At first they were protected only by cavalry and a few companies of infantry, and as this cavalry managed to issue from the defile of St. Albert it found itself the misleading object of attack, for the Marguerite cavalry division halted on the Illy plateau. General Galliffet, commander of the division, at nine o'clock formed his three regiments of Chasseurs d'Afrique and two squadrons of lancers into three divisions, and gave the order to charge. Two companies of the Eighty-seventh Regiment were the first in the line: they allowed the cavalry to approach within sixty paces, and then fired a volley that failed to stop them. The First Division rode on a little farther, then wheeled outward to both flanks and came upon the fire of the supports established in the copse. The Prussian batteries, too, sent a shower of shrapnel into their midst, when they finally retired to seek protection in the Bois de Garennes, while a trail of dead and wounded marked their way.

About half an hour later, that is, at ten o'clock, and at the same time when the assaults of the French in Bazeilles and at Daigny were being repelled, fourteen batteries of the Eleventh Corps were erected on and beside the hill range southeast of St. Menges; those of the Fifth Corps were soon added to this artillery park.

Thus, with the powerful infantry columns advancing upon Flegneux, the investing line drawn around Sedan was nearly completed. The Bavarian corps and the artillery reserves remaining on the left embankment of the Meuse were considered strong enough to repel any attempt of the French to break through in that direction. Five corps were standing on the right flank, ready for concentric attack.

The Bavarians and the Saxons, reënforced by the advanced guard of the Fourth Corps, issued from the burning town of Bazeilles and from Moncelle, and drove sections of the French Twelfth Corps, in spite of a stubborn resistance, from the east of Balan back to Fond de Givonne. Having thus taken possession of the spur of Illy, while awaiting a fresh attack of the French, the most necessary step now was to re-form the troops, which were in much confusion.

When this was done the Fifth Bavarian Brigade advanced on Balan. The troops found but feeble resistance in the village; but it was only after a hard fight that they were allowed to occupy the park of the castle, at the extreme end. Thence, soon after midday, the foremost battalion got close to the walls of the fortress and exchanged shots with the garrison. The French were now trying to take up a position at Fond de Givonne, and a steady fire was opened on both sides. At one o'clock the French had evidently received reënforcements, and when, after the artillery and mitrailleuses had done some preliminary work, they assumed the offensive, the Fifth Bavarian Brigade was driven back a little distance, but, assisted by the Sixth, regained its old position after an hour's hard fighting. Meanwhile the Saxon Corps had spread itself in the northern part of the valley toward Givonne. There the foremost companies of the guards were already established, as also in Haybés. The Prussian artillery forced the French batteries to change their position more than once, and several of them had already gone out of action. To gain an opening here, the French repeatedly tried to send ahead large bodies of *tirailleurs*, and ten guns were got into Givonne, after it had been occupied, but these were taken before they could unlimber. The Prussian shells also fell with some effect among the French troops massed in the Bois de Garennes, though fired from a long range.

After the *Franctireurs de Paris* had been driven out of Chapelle, the cavalry advanced through Givonne and up the valley, and at noon the hussars had succeeded in establishing a connection with the left wing of the Third Army.

The Forty-seventh Brigade of that body had left Fleigneux to ascend the upper valley of the Givonne, and the retreat of the French from Illy in a southern direction had already begun. The Eighty-seventh Regiment seized eight guns that were being worked, and captured thirty baggage-wagons with their teams and hundreds of cavalry horses wandering riderless. The cavalry of the advanced guard of the Fifth Corps captured General Brahaut and his staff, besides a great number of infantry and one hundred fifty pack-horses, together with forty ammunition- and transport-wagons.

At Floing there was also an attempt on the part of the French to break through; but the originally very insufficient infantry posts at that point had gradually been strengthened, and the

French were driven from the locality as quickly as they had entered. And now the fire from the twenty-six batteries of the Army of the Meuse was joined by that of the guards' batteries, which took up their position at the eastern slope of the Givonne Valley. The effect was overwhelming. The French batteries were destroyed and many ammunition-wagons were exploded. General von Wimpffen at first thought the advance of the Germans from the north a mere feint, but recognized his mistake when he himself proceeded to the spot toward noon. He therefore ordered the two divisions in the second line, which was behind the Givonne front of the First Corps, to return to the height above Illy and support General Douay.

On rejoining the Twelfth Corps he found it in full retreat on Sedan, and urgently requested General Douay to despatch assistance in the direction of Bazeilles. Maussion's brigade marched thither at once, followed by Dumont's, as their position in the front had been taken by Conseil Dumesnil's division.

All these marches and countermarches were executed in the space south of the Bois de Garennes under fire of the German artillery on two sides. The retreat of the cavalry heightened the confusion, and several battalions returned to the doubtful protection of the forest. General Douay, it is true, when reënforced by sections of the Fifth Corps, retook the Calvaire, but was forced to abandon it by two o'clock; the forest, at the back of the Calvaire, was then shelled by sixty guns of the guards.

Liébert's division alone had so far maintained its very strong position on the hills north of Casal. The assembling in sufficient strength of the German Fifth and Eleventh corps at Floing could be effected only very gradually. At one o'clock, however, part of them began to scale the hill immediately before them, while others went round to the south toward Gaulier and Casal, and more marched down from Fleigneux. These troops became so intermixed that no detailed orders could be given; a fierce contest was carried on for a long time, with varying fortunes. The French division, attacked on both flanks, and also shelled, at last gave way, and the reserves of the Seventh Corps having already been called to other parts of the battle-field, the French cavalry again devoted themselves to the rescue.

General Marguerite, with five regiments of light-horse and

two of lancers, charged out of the Bois de Garennes. He fell among the first, severely wounded, and General Galliffet took his place. The charge was over very treacherous ground, and, even before they could attack, the ranks were broken by the heavy flanking fire of the Prussian batteries. Still, with thinned numbers but unflagging determination, the squadrons charged on the Forty-third Infantry Brigade and its reënforcements hurrying along from Fleigneux. Part of the German infantry on the hillside were lying under cover, others were fully exposed in groups. Their foremost lines were broken through at several points, and a detachment of these brave troops forced their way past eight guns, through a hot fire, but the reserves beyond checked their further progress. A troop of cuirassiers, issuing from Gaulier, fell on the German rear, but encountering the Prussian hussars in the Meuse Valley galloped off northward. Other detachments forced their way through the infantry as far as the narrow way by St. Albert, where the battalions holding it gave them a warm reception; others again entered Floing only to succumb to the Fifth Jaegers, who fell on them front and rear. These attacks were repeated by the French again and again, and the murderous turmoil lasted for half an hour with steadily diminishing success for the French. The volleys of the infantry, fired at short range, strewed the whole field with dead and wounded. Many fell into the quarries or over the steep precipices, a few may have escaped by swimming the Meuse; and scarcely more than half of these brave troops were left to return to the protection of the fortress.

But this magnificent sacrifice of the splendid French cavalry could not change the fate of the day. The Prussian infantry had lost but few in cut-and-thrust encounters, and at once resumed the attack against Liébert's division. But in this onslaught they sustained heavy losses; for instance, the three battalions of the Sixth Regiment had to be commanded by lieutenants. Casal was stormed, and the French, after a spirited resistance, withdrew at about three o'clock to their last refuge, the Bois de Garennes.

When, between one and two o'clock, the fighting round Bazeilles at first took a favorable turn for his army, General von Wimpffen returned to his original plan of overthrowing the Bavarians, exhausted by a long struggle, and making his way to Carignan with the First, Fifth, and Twelfth corps; while the Seventh Corps was to cover their rear. But the orders issued to that effect never reached the generals in command, or arrived so late that circumstances forbade their being carried out.

In consequence of his previous orders, Bassoigne's division, with those of Gozo and Grandchamp had remained idle. Now, at about three in the afternoon, the two last named advanced from Fond de Givonne over the eastern ridge, and the Twenty-third Saxon Division, which was marching in the valley on the left bank of the Givonne, found itself suddenly attacked by the compact French battalions and batteries, but with the aid of the left wing of the guards and the artillery thundering from the eastern slope they soon repelled the French, and even followed them up, back to Fond de Givonne. The energy of the French appears to have been exhausted, for they allowed themselves to be taken prisoners by hundreds. As soon as the hills on the west of the Givonne had been secured, the German artillery established itself there, and by three o'clock twenty-one batteries stood in line between Bazeilles and Haybés.

The Bois de Garennes, where corps of all arms had found refuge and were wandering about, still remained to be taken. After a short cannonade the First Division of guards ascended the hills from Givonne, and were joined by the Saxon battalions, the left wing of the Third Army at the same time pressing forward from Illy. A wild turmoil ensued, some of the French offered violent resistance, others surrendered by thousands at a time, but not until five o'clock were the Germans masters of the fortress.

Meanwhile long columns of French could be seen pouring down on Sedan from all the neighboring hills. Irregular bands of troops were massed in and around the walls of the fortress, and shells from the German batteries on both sides of the Meuse were continually exploding among them. Columns of fire soon began to rise from the city, and the Bavarians, who had gone round to Torcy, were about to climb the palisades at the gate, when, at about half-past four, flags of truce were hoisted on the towers. The Emperor Napoleon had refused to join with General von Wimpffen in his attempt to break through the German lines; he had, on the contrary, desired him to parley with the enemy. On the order being renewed, the French suddenly ceased firing.

General Reille now made his appearance in the presence of King William, who had watched the action all day from the hill south of Frénois. He was the bearer of an autograph letter from the Emperor, whose presence in Sedan had till now been unknown. He placed his sword in the hands of the King, but as this was only an act of personal submission, the answer given to his letter demanded that an officer should be despatched thither, fully empowered to treat with General von Moltke as to the surrender of the French army. This sorrowful duty was imposed on General von Wimpffen, who was in no way responsible for the desperate straits into which the army had been brought.

The negotiations were held at Donchery during the night between September 1st and 2d. The Germans were forced to consider that they must not forego the advantage gained over so powerful an enemy as France. When it was remembered that the French had regarded the victory of German arms over other nationalities in the light of an insult, any act of untimely generosity might lead them to forget their own defeat. The only course to pursue was to insist upon the disarmament and detention of the entire army, but officers were to be free on parole.

General von Wimpffen declared it impossible to accept such hard conditions, the negotiations were broken off, and the French officers returned to Sedan at one o'clock. Before their departure they were given to understand that unless these terms were agreed to by nine o'clock next morning, the bombardment would be renewed. The capitulation was signed by General von Wimpffen on the morning of the 2d, further resistance being obviously impossible.

It is difficult to understand why the Germans celebrate September 2d when nothing at all remarkable happened but that which was the result of the previous day's work; the day the army really crowned itself with glory was September 1st. This splendid victory had cost the Germans 460 officers and 8500 men. The French losses were far greater: 17,000 were killed or wounded—the work principally of the strong force of German artillery—and 21,000 were taken prisoners in the course of the action, and 83,000 surrendered. Three thousand men had been disarmed on Belgian territory.

The trophies at Sedan consisted of 3 standards, 419 field-pieces, and 139 guns; 66,000 stands of arms; more than 1000 baggage- and other wagons, and 6000 horses fit for service.

COUNT OTTO VON BISMARCK

VENDRESSE, September 3 [1870].

MY DEAR HEART:

I left my present quarters before early dawn the day before yesterday, came back to-day, and have in the mean time witnessed the great battle of Sedan, in which we made about thirty thousand prisoners, and threw the remainder of the French army, which we have been pursuing since we were at Bar-le-Duc, into the fortress, where they had to surrender themselves, along with the Emperor, prisoners of war. Yesterday morning at five o'clock, after I had been negotiating until 1 A.M. with Moltke and the French generals about the capitulation to be concluded, I was awakened by General Reille, with whom I am acquainted, to tell me that Napoleon wished to speak with me.

Unwashed and unbreakfasted, I rode toward Sedan, found the Emperor in an open carriage, with three *aides-de-camp* and three in attendance on horseback, halted on the road before Sedan. I dismounted, saluted him just as politely as at the Tuileries, and asked for his commands. He wished to see the King; I told him, as the truth was, that his Majesty had his quarters fifteen miles away, at the spot where I am now writing. In answer to Napoleon's questions where he should go to, I offered him, as I was not acquainted with the country, my own quarters at Donchery, a small place in the neighborhood, close by Sedan. He accepted, and drove, accompanied by his six Frenchmen, by me and by Carl (who in the mean time had ridden after me), through the lonely morning toward our lines.

Before coming to the spot, he began to hesitate on account of the possible crowd, and asked me if he could alight in a lonely cottage by the wayside. I had it inspected by Carl, who brought word that it was mean and dirty. "*N'importe*," said Napoleon, and I ascended with him a rickety narrow staircase. In an apartment of ten feet square, with a deal table and two rush-bottomed chairs, we sat for an hour; the others were below—a powerful contrast with our last meeting in the Tuileries in 1867. Our conversation was a difficult thing, if I wished to avoid touching on topics which could not but affect painfully the man whom God's mighty hand had cast down.

I had sent Carl to fetch officers from the town and to beg Moltke to come. We then sent one of the former to reconnoitre, and discovered, twenty-one and a half miles distant, in Frénois, a *chateau* situated in a park. Thither I accompanied him with an escort of the Cuirassier Regiment of Life-Guards, which had meantime been brought up, and there we concluded with the French General-in-Chief, Wimpffen, the capitulation, by virtue of which from forty thousand to sixty thousand Frenchmen—I do not know, accurately, at present—with all they possess, became our prisoners. Yesterday and the day before cost France one hundred thousand men and an emperor. This morning the latter, with all his suite, horses and carriages, started for Wilhelmshohe, near Cassel.

It is an event of great weight in the world's history, a victory for which we shall humbly thank the Almighty, and which decides the war, even if we have to carry it on against France shorn of her Emperor.

I must conclude. With heartfelt joy I learned from your and Maria's letters that Herbert has arrived among you. Bill I spoke to yesterday, as already telegraphed, and embraced him from horseback in his Majesty's presence, while he stood motionless in the ranks. He is very healthy and happy. I saw Hans and Fritz Carl, both Buelows, in the Second Dragoon Guards, well and cheerful.

Good-by, my heart; love to the children. Your v. B.

COMPLETION OF ITALIAN UNITY

A.D. 1870

PIETRO ORSI

The unification of Italy, for which Italian patriots had longed and labored through many generations, was one of the most signal events of the nineteenth century. After the proclamation of the Kingdom of Italy, in 1861, Italian unity was acknowledged by England, France, Russia, and Prussia. In 1862 a new Italian Ministry was formed by Urbano Rattazzi, Cavour having been dead almost a year. It was the aim of Rattazzi, as it had been that of his two predecessors since Cavour, to continue the methods of that great statesman, who represented the highest civil glories of the Italian movement. The new Government had many difficulties to face. Naples, Tuscany, Modena, and Parma, which had been annexed to the Kingdom of Italy, aimed to recover their autonomy; Austria threatened invasion; the Pope used all his powers against the State that menaced his temporal throne; and Napoleon III, who had formerly assisted the Italian cause, was now mastered by adverse influences. At the same time the party of Garibaldi, impatient to finish the work they had done so much to advance, were eager to wrest Venice from Austria, and Rome from the Pope.

Disorganization everywhere hindered administrative progress. In the south, brigands, assisted by Francis II, the proscribed King of the Two Sicilies, committed alarming depredations, and a bold attempt was made to reinstate that Bourbon ruler. A futile scheme of Garibaldi's to move on Rome caused the Government much perplexity. Garibaldi was held prisoner for a few months, and in March, 1864, he went to London, where sympathy for his cause led him to hope for official support. That, however, was withheld. Meanwhile French troops occupied Rome, and their presence in the city was denounced by Italians throughout the Kingdom. Wishing to soothe the irritation, Napoleon III induced Minghetti, who had succeeded Rattazzi, to consent to a convention, September 15, 1864, whereby it was agreed that the French soldiers should be withdrawn from Rome, and that the Italian Government should respect the frontier of the Papal States and transfer its capital from Turin to Florence.

Such was the state of affairs at the time when Orsi, the Italian historian, begins his concise but comprehensive narrative of the final steps leading to the unification of all Italy under her own chosen sovereign.

THE Roman question still awaited solution. Napoleon III, in pursuance of the Convention of 1864, had, by degrees, withdrawn his troops from Rome: thus, by the end of 1866, the seventeen years of foreign occupation were at an end. The Pontifical Government now found itself face to face alone with its subjects. Thereupon, while some secret societies in Rome were seeking to foment an insurrection, the "party of action" determined to interfere, and with the greater readiness, since Urbano Rattazzi was again at the head of the Italian Ministry. Garibaldi traversed several provinces of the Kingdom to incite the citizens to war. By September, 1867, the preparations for the rising were well matured, but on the 23d of that month the Italian Government, which up till then had allowed them to go forward, was sufficiently influenced by the attitude of Napoleon III, now posing as the defender of the Pope, to have Garibaldi arrested and sent to Caprera, where his movements were watched by four vessels.

Notwithstanding the absence of Garibaldi, bands of volunteers were organized and marched into the Pontifical States. On the evening of October 22d, a futile attempt at revolt was made in Rome by Monti and Tognetti, two masons, who tried by means of a mine to blow up the Serristori barracks, while a hundred young men took possession of Porta San Paolo; but this movement had hardly broken out when it was quenched in blood. Hoping to find the city still in insurrection, the brothers Enrico and Giovanni Cairoli, with seventy followers, passed the frontier of the Papal States, to hasten to the aid of the insurgents; they descended the Tiber to a point within two miles of Rome, and there took up a position on the Monte Parioli, near a villa called Glori, in expectation of receiving news of the rising. They were surprised instead by a strong body of the papal police, and a hand-to-hand struggle rather than a battle ensued, wherein seventy in all fell dead or wounded. Enrico Cairoli died on the spot; Giovanni, after receiving serious wounds, was made prisoner, but obtained his liberty through the mediation of an English bishop, only to drag out, for little more than another year, an existence full of suffering caused by his wounds.

Thus, this valiant family, of which one had already fallen gloriously at Varese in the campaign of 1859, and another had died in Sicily of exhaustion during the toilsome march of "the Thousand," now yielded a fresh contingent to the band of Italian martyrs in the cause of freedom. A few days later the papal troops surrounded a factory in the Trastevere quarter of Rome, wherein several patriots were engaged in making cartridges. The besieged retorted on their assailants by fusillades and bombs, but were vanquished and in great part massacred. Among the dead was Giuditta Tavani-Arquati, who, in spite of her sex, had courageously assisted in the defence.

Napoleon III, indignant at the aspect events had assumed in Italy, prepared a fleet at Toulon to go to the aid of the Pontiff: such a step was all the more promptly taken, seeing that Garibaldi had effected his escape from Caprera. On the night of October 16th the veteran hero had put out alone in a small boat, managed to evade the surveillance of the watchful crews, and had reached Maddaloni, whence he made for Tuscany. Meantime Rattazzi, feeling himself incapable of coping with the existing state of affairs, resigned. During this ministerial crisis no one had the courage to take decisive steps, and thus the Garibaldian movement made progress. Garibaldi, having arrived at Florence, publicly incited the population to war, and then put himself at the head of the armed bands already assembled.

After passing the frontier, he encountered and defeated the papal troops at Monte Rotondo, on October 26th. But although a French division had debarked at Civita Vecchia, Garibaldi prevailed on his men to continue the struggle. On November 3d there was another engagement at Mentana, where at first the old hero succeeded in routing the papal troops, but in the rear came the French soldiers. The volunteers, armed with bad muskets, could not hold out long against the *chassepots* of the French, which, according to the opinion expressed in such *mal a propos* terms by General De Failly, the commander of the expedition, "worked wonders." Garibaldi, having retreated, disbanded his men and, recrossing the frontier, was once more sent back to Caprera by order of the Italian Government. Thus failed the Garibaldian expedition of 1867.

As if to emphasize the estrangement that these events produced between Italy and France, Rouher, President of the French Ministry, uttered the following words in the Chamber: "In the name of the French Government, we declare that Italy shall never take possession of Rome; never will France tolerate such violence done to her honor and to Catholicism. If Italy marches on Rome, she will again find France blocking the way."

However, the thoughts of all Italians were now fixed on Rome, and even in the December of that same year (1867) Giovanni Lanza, on assuming the office of speaker in the Chamber, announced that "all unanimously desire the accomplishment of national unity," and that "Rome, through the very nature of things and the exigencies of the times, must, sooner or later, be the capital of Italy." Afterward, when the growing animosity between France and Prussia had caused Napoleon III to desire a closer alliance with Italy and Austria, the Government of the former stipulated, as a condition of such an alliance, that Rome should be evacuated by the French troops which had returned there in 1867. Napoleon, still swayed by the clerical party, would not hear of this, so the plan fell through. After the first defeat sustained by the French in 1870, Napoleon asked help from Victor Emmanuel, without fixing any terms whatever. The King would gladly have gone to the assistance of his old ally of 1859, but public opinion in Italy was unfavorable to Napoleon III; besides, the Italians, although they had fought side by side with the French in 1859, had been allies of the Prussians in the Austro-Prussian War of 1866. Thus it was that on the night of August 6th–7th the council of ministers voted for neutrality.

On August 24th Prince Napoleon, the King's son-in-law, arrived in Florence to beg for the support of Italy, leaving the latter free to solve the Roman question as she would, but it was now too late.

When, after the disaster of Sedan, the Parisian population rose and proclaimed the Republic, the Italian Government felt itself absolved from the observance of the agreement made with the French Emperor in 1864; hence the question of intervention in the Papal States could now be debated. Victor Emmanuel wrote a letter to Pius IX in which he implored him, with filial affection, to consider the state of Italy and to renounce the temporal power; but the Pontiff replied that only violence would compel him to do the latter.

On September 19th the Italian troops, under General Raffaele Cadorna, arrived at the gates of Rome; on the 20th, after a short encounter at Porta Pia, they made a breach in the walls. Pius IX, who had wished merely to demonstrate the employment of armed force by the Government, then gave orders to his soldiers to withdraw. Thus was effected one of the most important facts in modern history—the abolition of that temporal power which, originally given by Pépin, had lasted for eleven centuries and had always hindered the unification of Italy.

On the occasion of the opening of the new Parliament in Florence, on December 5, 1870, Victor Emmanuel could with just pride exclaim: "With Rome as the capital of Italy, I have fulfilled my promise and crowned the enterprise that, twenty-three years ago, was initiated under the auspices of my magnanimous father. Both as a monarch and as a son, my heart thrills with a solemn joy as I salute all the representatives of our beloved country, gathered here together for the first time, and pronounce the words: 'Italy is free and united; it only depends on us to make her great and happy.' "

The Italian Parliament, before transferring its sessions to Rome, passed a law—known as the "Law of Guarantees"—by which the Pope was insured the enjoyment of all his prerogatives and honors as a sovereign, was awarded the palaces of the Vatican and the Lateran, as well as the villa of Castel Gandolfo—all exempt from any tax or duty—and was assigned an annual income of three million two hundred twenty-five thousand Italian *lire*. The Pontiff refused to recognize this law or to accept the allowance, and still persisted in maintaining his unavailing protest against the Italian Government.

On July 2, 1871, Victor Emmanuel entered Rome in state, and took up his abode in the palace of the Quirinal, uttering the famous words: "We are at Rome, and here we remain." The Chamber of Deputies monopolized for its sittings the Montecitorio palace, while the Senate took possession of the Madama palace—so called from Margaret of Austria, daughter of Charles V, who formerly lived there.

THE THIRD FRENCH REPUBLIC

A.D. 1870

JULES FAVRE

One might say, reasoning *a priori*, that of all the peoples of Europe those of France were best fitted to establish and maintain a republican form of government. Their lack of reverence for prescriptive rights and customs, their quick responsiveness, and their fearlessness in radical movements, whether social or economical, all point to republicanism as their natural government. Yet three trials were necessary before they arrived at that as a permanence. The Republic that was proclaimed in the presence of defeat and disaster, with a powerful foreign enemy at the gates, has endured four times as long as the combined periods of the other two, and is not likely to be overthrown in any future crisis. No longer can France be dazzled and led to bondage by a Napoleonic name, for the last of the Bonapartes perished in 1879—providentially, as some think—at the hands of the Zulus, where he had gone, in a quarrel not his own, to acquire a military reputation that should assist him in regaining his father's throne. When the Third Republic was established, there was nothing in it of the "red fool fury of the Seine," but the calm judgment and patriotic courage of statesmen equal to their country's need. It is a pleasure to read the simple account of the action written by one of their number, and to hope that what they founded in wisdom will endure through the centuries.

THE news of the capitulation of Sedan and the surrender of the Emperor spread throughout the city, causing universal indignation. In the evening immense crowds thronged the boulevards; the police strove in vain to disperse them by means that had been hitherto successful but now only excited popular rage. Cries were heard from the crowd demanding the fall of the Government. Many persons were armed. There was no more time for illusions; the insurrection had begun; the Government had virtually fallen; not a moment was to be lost in constituting a new one.

We visited M. Joseph Schneider at 9 A.M. to consult with him regarding the forming of a new government. We begged him to lose no time in convoking the Assembly; and I did not hide from him that I desired, in my own name and that of my friends, to propose the question of the deposing of the Emperor. In his endeavor to retain the Regent and the Prince Imperial, and thinking to avoid a revolt by gaining time, he brought forward objections — moderate, sad, but courteous — and disputed the hopelessness of the situation.

We persuaded him to convene the Assembly, which could easily be done, as nearly all our colleagues were in the Salle des Conférences, or in the antechambers of the Palace. We saw him again at half-past eleven; the conversation was long, but it resulted in nothing decisive.

In the interval we had arranged our plan. This was to bring about the assumption of supreme power by the Chamber. To this we added the deposing of Napoleon III, who had already practically acquiesced in it by his surrender at Sedan.

We were at this critical moment as free from personal interest as we had been on August 7th, when I had sought an audience with M. Schneider, the President. We had no other design than to consummate, without a revolution, an act of justice which had now become inevitable. On this occasion, if the Chamber had voted as we requested, the insurrection of the morrow would have had no cause to take place, and we should have been excluded from the new Government chosen by the majority.

I can affirm, without hesitation, that not one of us aspired to take part in it. M. Thiers, M. Ernest Picard, and I discussed names. We thought the Comte de Palikao should be retained on account of his knowledge of the military operations already begun. We included M. Schneider, President of the Corps Législatif. M. Picard and I endeavored to persuade M. Thiers to form the third member of the Commission. He opposed this suggestion, and was proposing the names of other colleagues, when we were informed that the President had taken his seat. It was one o'clock in the morning; the 4th of September had dawned.

In spite of the gravity of the news received, in spite of the agitation of the population of Paris, the Cabinet had not thought proper to meet. The Minister of War was found in bed, and, after saying that Sedan had capitulated and that the Emperor had been taken prisoner, he requested that the deliberations should be postponed until noon, that he might have an opportunity of consulting his colleagues. It would have been in vain for us to oppose this delay, which the Chamber hastened to accord; but we thought it our duty to give notice of the proposition for the dethronement. Paris required to know, on awakening, that its representatives had not lost courage. I quote from the *Officiel* the few words I spoke for the Opposition:

"If the Chamber is of opinion that, in the grave and painful situation described by the Minister of War, it is wise to postpone the deliberation till noon, I have no motive for opposing it; but, as we have to urge deliberation upon the part to be taken, in the absence of all authority, we request permission to place on this table a proposition which I shall do myself the honor to read, without at present adding any further remarks:

" 'We beg the Chamber to consider the following motion:

" '1st Article. Louis Napoleon Bonaparte and his dynasty are declared to have forfeited the power given to them by the Constitution.

" '2d Article. A government commission shall be named by the Corps Législatif, composed of (you will fix the number of members you think fit to choose from your majority), which will be invested with full authority of government, and whose express mission shall be to resist the invasion to the last, and to expel the enemy from our territory.

" '3d Article. General Trochu shall retain his office of Governor of the City of Paris.

" 'Signed. Jules Favre, Isaac Crémieux, Barthélemy St. Hilaire, Desseaux, Etienne Garnier-Pages, Larrieu, Gagneur, Steenakers, Magnin, Dorian, Ordinaire, Emmanuel Arago, Jules Simon, Eugène Pelletan, Wilson, Ernest Picard, Léon Gambetta, Comte de Kératry, Guyot-Montpeyroux, Tachard, Lecesne, Rampon, Giraud, Marion, Léopold, Javal, Jules Ferry, Paul Bethmont.'

"I will add nothing to this proposition, which I offer to your wise deliberations, and to-morrow, or rather to-day at noon, we shall have the honor of giving the urgent reasons that appear to oblige every patriot to adopt it."

The Chamber then separated, without offering any opposition

—for the following words of M. Pinard cannot be called such, and, for my part, I did not hear them:

"We can take provisional measures; we cannot declare the dethronement."

M. Thiers offered me a seat in his carriage. At the Place de la Concorde a dense crowd stopped us. The excitement was intense. We were asked whether the motion for dethronement had been voted upon. We replied that it would be voted upon at noon. We begged the populace to remain calm; wisdom and moderation were more than ever necessary; an exercise of these qualities would enable us to remain firm and so to fulfil our duty to the end. The people applauded M. Thiers, and we sought the repose that was so necessary to us.

September 4th, which dawned warm and bright like a fête-day, drew the population of Paris from their dwellings to enjoy the brilliant sunshine. All was calm during the early part of the day, and the appearance of the city was the same as usual. The approaches to the Corps Législatif, as well as the courtyard of the Hôtel de Ville, were filled with troops. In the Palace of Industry six hundred mounted gendarmes stood ready for an emergency. No announcement was made of the resolution the Cabinet had been obliged to take, and to this hour I do not know by what means it came to consider our proposition (continually ignored since August 9th) for the nomination of a commission invested with authority from the Government; the only addition it made was the dictatorship of M. de Palikao, under the form of a general lieutenancy. This tardy and ridiculous idea could not be received; it had no longer in its favor even the majority, which had at last opened its eyes and recognized, when too late, the duty it had refused to perform. The possession of the supreme power seemed to the Cabinet a necessity from which escape was impossible. Nevertheless it hesitated, through an honorable scruple, which several of its members had explained to us at different times before we laid down our proposition. It did not consider itself freed from its oath, and repudiated the idea of voting for the dethronement. It feared to imitate the Senate of the First Empire, lest it should be rejected in a similar manner. It therefore sought a formula that should allow the thing to be done without pronouncing the word. The deputies tried different forms, after which they entered into negotiations with us. They begged us to abandon that expression in our proposition which wounded their consciences. We wished for nothing more than to smooth all difficulties, provided only that the necessary steps were promptly taken. It appeared to us to be of the first importance to decide upon the course necessary to pursue, and to make known our intentions to the populace. Knowing well the excitement and indignation we might expect to arouse, we were ready to renounce the motion for dethronement if it could be made known that it had been virtually accepted.

After a lively discussion, we agreed upon this form, which seemed to conciliate all parties: "Considering the vacancy." This was the most attenuated expression of the idea that was indispensable to be made known. The paper was covered with signatures. We entered the Chamber, where probably the proposed form would have been accepted unanimously, when several members of the majority, regretting their consent, withdrew, with their colleagues, to the Salon de la Paix, where they had just been consulting. They then substituted for the words "Considering the vacancy" these: "Considering the circumstances"—which had no meaning. We could not admit them; it was agreed that each should make his own proposition; and President Schneider took the chair. It was a quarter past one.

In the ninth bureau, in which I was, the discussion at once turned upon M. Thiers's proposition, and that of the Left. Those among my honored colleagues who opposed dethronement repeated the laudable sentiments which I have already mentioned, though they appeared to me to arise from a mistaken view of their duties. This I endeavored to show, and the discussion, though lively, was being conducted with order, when a loud noise was heard in the courtyard outside the room in which we were deliberating. My friend M. de Pelletan, who had left the room to ascertain the cause, returned in a state of agitation, blaming the officers that had given the order for preparing arms and directing them against the crowd that surrounded the palace. Soon afterward we beheld the soldiers that were placed against the windows form in line to protect the entrances. Distant clamors reached us. A deputy entered hastily to inform us that the Chamber was invaded by the populace.

I refused at first to believe it, as I had observed no premonitory sign of such an event. We all quitted the room precipitately. The antechambers were filled with the mob, who appeared more embarrassed than enraged; nevertheless, some individuals, accosting me, demanded the fall of the Government. "We are aiming at that," I replied, "but you will not help us by interrupting us violently in our deliberations." I begged them earnestly to depart and to leave us to vote freely. I promised them that their desires should be accomplished. It was difficult to carry on a conversation in the midst of the tumult. I hastened to the sitting.

The *Journal Officiel* declares that "at half-past two the Chamber was invaded by the crowd stationed on the Place de la Concorde and in front of the Palais Bourbon; that, rushing through the anterooms and stairways, it was precipitated into the public galleries, raising the cry 'Dethronement!' joined with cries of '*Vive la France!*' '*Vive la Republique!*'"

The tribune was vacant for some minutes, when M. Gambetta appeared.

"Citizens," said he, "it is necessary that all the deputies present in the anterooms and leaving their bureaus (where they have been deliberating upon the question of the dethronement) should be at their posts to pronounce it.

"It is necessary also that you, citizens, should await the arrival of the representatives with dignity and tranquillity. We have sent for them; I beg you to keep a solemn silence until they return: it will not be long. There is no need to say that we shall not leave this place till we have obtained an affirmative result."

The applause following this address was soon followed by a tremendous noise. The doors of the hall gave way to the pressure of the crowd, which had penetrated tumultuously into the interior. M. de Piré wished to ascend the tribune; many of his colleagues attempted to restrain him. He yielded to them, but cried: "I had a duty to fulfil; I desired to protest against the present proceedings."

At this moment the Minister of War, who had several times appeared and disappeared, left the hall. The published account thus describes the end of the sitting:

"President Schneider said: 'Deliberation under such circumstances is impossible. I declare the sitting at an end.'

"A large number of National Guards, in uniform or without it, and bearing arms, entered the halls by the anterooms and also by the gates of the amphitheatre. A tumultuous crowd rushed in at the same moment, occupied all the benches, filled all the aisles, and descended into the semicircle, surrounding the secretaries' table as well as the reporters' desks, exclaiming, 'Dethronement! Dethronement!' '*Vive la Republique!*' President Schneider left the chair, walked slowly down the staircase on the left of the bureau, and quitted the hall. It was then a few minutes past three o'clock."

I was not present at the scenes just described. Shortly afterward I entered the hall and hastened to the tribune, to beg the crowd to retire. The tumult was at its height and I was powerless to quell it, when, turning toward that side by which, unknown to me, M. Schneider had left, I saw the dishevelled heads of two men, who were evidently in the highest state of excitement. One of them was ringing the bell loudly, and appeared to be preparing to propose some decree. The recollection of May 15th flashed upon my mind. I recalled that Barbès had made the mob vote foolish measures. I did not hesitate; and, feeling the full import of the step I was about to take, I succeeded in making a few words audible in the midst of this tempest. As there was a demand on all sides that I should proclaim the Republic, I said: "Such a proclamation must not be made here, but at the Hotel de Ville. Follow me; I will go thither at your head." This course, which had suddenly occurred to me, had the advantage of freeing the Chamber, of preventing a sanguinary conflict within its walls, and of preventing an attack that would have rendered a violent faction master of the movement. It is true we exposed ourselves thereby to the peril of a march through the disturbed city. I was utterly ignorant of the state of affairs in the streets; but there was no time to hesitate. My proposal was received with acclamation, and I left the tribune in the midst of the cries of "To the Hotel de Ville!" At the door that leads into the gallery of Pas-perdus I was surrounded by several of my colleagues, among whom were M. Emile de Kératry and M. Jules Ferry. They came to my side, and we set off.

When we reached the Quay, I soon perceived that the crowd marching behind me had nothing to fear. The steps in front of the Palais Bourbon were covered with citizens and National Guards, who hailed us enthusiastically. A similar gathering awaited us on the steps of the Church of the Madeleine. The Pont de la Concorde and the Place de la Concorde resounded with shouts of sympathy. We proceeded slowly, exchanging tokens of sympathy with persons of all ages who crowded toward us. It was with difficulty that the National Guards could clear the way before us.

At the end of the bridge arose a formidable cry: "To the Tuileries!" We made an energetic signal for the crowd to pass along the quays, and it obeyed. We had just passed the Solferino Gate, when among the throng I saw General Trochu coming toward us, followed by his lieutenant-major. Our line halted instantly. I made my way through the crowd, and holding out my hand to the General explained in a few words the events of the day. "There is no longer any government," I added; "my friends and I are on the way to constitute one at the Hotel de Ville; we beg you to return to your part of the town, and there to await our communications." The General offered no objection, and galloped off toward the Louvre.

The clock indicated five minutes to four when we arrived at the Place de la Grêve. There the crowd was dense. A long stream of people had made their way along the left bank of the river, and were prepared to cross the Pont d'Arcole to join us. We were carried, rather than pressed, into the large hall of the Hotel de Ville. It was full to overflowing; nevertheless they made way for us to the benches at the farther end. I spoke a few words, which were received with the cry of "*Vive la Republique!*" This was in reality the overmastering desire of the excited populace, and it included the fall of the Empire and resistance to the foe. On these two points all were agreed—"the Republic" was the formula representing the country and liberty.

While I was speaking, my colleagues, MM. Picard, Gambetta, Simon, Pelletan, and Emmanuel Arago, had arrived; M. Crémieux soon followed; a large number of deputies accompanied them. It was necessary to deliberate, and to that end we had to escape from the frightful tumult in the large hall. We found an entrance into a small committee-room, lighted by a wide window; it was soon filled by the crowd, but we secured a table and chairs. We immediately agreed to form a government, with the cooperation of the Paris deputies and those who had been elected; it was the only means to cut short the discussions between the leaders of different parties. Violent speeches were addressed to M. Gambetta, who had energetically opposed the name of M. Felix Pyat; but, for the same reason, it was impossible not to admit that of M. de Rochefort.

We were just installed. A message had been sent to General Trochu, who had had some difficulty in reaching us. He had laid aside his uniform, but he came to place himself at our disposal. His language was clear and firm.

"I beg of you," said he, "permission to place a preliminary question before you: Will you protect the three institutions—Religion, the Family, and Property—in promising me that nothing shall be done in opposition to their interests?"

We assured him of this.

"Upon that condition," said he, "I am with you, providing you make me head of the Government of National Defence. It is indispensable for me to occupy this post. As Minister of War or as Governor of Paris I should not control the army; and if we wish to defend Paris, the army must be in our hands. I am not a statesman; I am a soldier; I know the sentiments of my comrades; if they do not see me at your head, they will leave you, and your task cannot be fulfilled. It is not ambition that dictates to me this course; it is the conviction that unless it is followed nothing can be done. If we are to reach success, we can accomplish it only by concentrating all power in the hands of one man. As military commander, my authority must be without limit. I shall not in any way interfere with you in the exercise of civil power; but its action must be in cooperation with that of the defence, which is our supreme duty. Nothing that concerns this double movement can be ignored by me; it is a question of responsibility and of safety."

The frankness of this unexpected declaration did not displease one among us. We were not blind to the responsibility and the danger of the burden which our country's disasters had imposed upon us. It was impossible that we should hesitate to share it with an illustrious, courageous, and popular general, and even to leave the heaviest share of the load to be borne by him, who, in the terrible situation to which we were reduced, had evidently the largest stake at issue. We accepted his conditions, and he departed to take possession of the War Office.

The Government constituted at the Hôtel de Ville was composed of nine deputies from the Seine, of M. Picard and M. Jules Simon, named also for Paris, and of General Trochu, accepted by us in the terms I have already given.

That same evening the Government nominated its Ministry, which was composed of the following members: M. Picard, Minister of Finance; M. Gambetta, Minister of the Interior; M. Crémieux, Minister of Justice; Général Leflô, Minister of War; Admiral Fourichon, Minister of the Marine; M. Simon, Minister of Public Instruction; M. Favre, Minister of Foreign Affairs; M. Dorian, Minister of Public Works; M. Magnin, Minister of Agriculture and Commerce. Five members of the Government—MM. Trochu, Garnier-Pagès, Pelletan, Emmanuel Arago, and De Rochefort—received no portfolio.

These measures were adopted without debate, except in the case of the Ministry of the Interior, upon which a vote had to be taken. M. Gambetta had a majority of two votes over M. Picard. At the same time the Government announced its accession by three short proclamations addressed to the nation:

"Frenchmen: The nation has taken precedence of the Chamber, which hesitated. In order to save the country from danger, it has demanded a republic.

"It has placed its representatives not in power, but in peril.

"The Republic saved the country from invasion in 1792. Another republic is proclaimed. The revolution is effected in the name of public safety.

"Citizens, watch over the city, which is confided to you; to-morrow you, aided by the army, will be the avengers of the country."

The following was addressed to Paris:

"Citizens of Paris, the Republic is proclaimed. A Government has been appointed by a unanimous vote. It is composed of the following citizens [giving the names as above]. General Trochu is invested with full military power for the

National Defence. He is appointed head of the Government. The Government urges all to be calm. The people will not forget that they are in the face of the enemy. The Government is above all a Government of National Defence."

Finally the Government appealed to the National Guard:

"Those men upon whom your patriotism has just imposed the formidable duty of defending the country, thank you from their hearts for your courageous devotion. To your resolution is due the civic victory that has restored liberty to France. Thanks to you, this victory has not cost a drop of blood. The personal power exists no longer. The entire nation again takes up its liberty and its arms. It has arisen ready to die for the defence of our territory. You have restored its life, which despotism had suffocated. You will maintain with firmness the execution of the laws, and, rivalling our noble army, together you will show the way to victory."

M. Etienne Arago was appointed Mayor of Paris. M. Emile de Kératry became Prefect of Police.

After prescribing those measures that seemed necessary to the maintenance of public tranquillity, we left M. Jules Ferry and M. Etienne Arago at the Hôtel de Ville.

Paris never had been more peaceful; and although at that late hour many shops were still open and many passengers in the streets, although at every step were armed men, neither disputes nor violent words were to be heard. No one thought of the possibility of resistance to the great movement that had been just accomplished. And how could it have been suspected? There had been neither conspiracy nor combat. The Empire had not been overthrown by a sudden blow. Its fall was only the natural and inevitable consequence of a series of faults, equivalent to crimes, which irrevocably condemned it. It had accomplished its own ruin; and if Paris had not risen against the Empire, the monarchy would none the less have disappeared. In several towns the Republic was proclaimed on the morning of September 4th. This time France was not influenced by the capital. France preceded Paris, and resolved of itself to provide for its honor and safety. Thus there was nowhere the shadow of conflict. All those numerous champions of the dynasty, who were so much spoken of, all those docile functionaries, disappeared as by an act of magic, without one of them dreaming of risking himself by an act of fidelity or devotion to the fallen monarch. This was not from lack of courage, still less from calculated defection; it was the instinctive acknowledgment of a superior force which it would have been madness to oppose; this force was no other than that of the human conscience, awakened at length by misfortune, and manifesting itself in the unanimous reprobation of the man and of the system that had ruined France.

THE SIEGE OF PARIS AND THE END OF THE FRANCO-PRUSSIAN WAR[1]

A.D. 1871

CHARLES F. HORNE

Events in the Franco-Prussian War followed one another with amazing rapidity, and the entire struggle, gigantic as it was and momentous in results, included little more than six months of military operations. This war, unparalleled in modern times for its brevity, compared with the scope of its action and the reach of its consequences, is equally remarkable for its one-sidedness. In every great battle and in every siege the French were defeated.

After the surrender of Napoleon III at Sedan (September 2, 1870), the tide of Prussian success swept quickly on to final triumph. From the proclamation of the Republic, two days after the capitulation of the Emperor, to the preliminary settlement of peace—followed by the definitive Peace of Frankfort, May 10, 1871—Charles F. Horne gives a concise but comprehensive view of the Third Republic in its unavailing struggle against the might of Prussia.

THE republic that was proclaimed in Paris, September 4, 1870, amid the gloom and terror caused by Napoleon's surrender, is the present Government of France. At first it had neither constitution nor president. Indeed, it had no legal authorities whatsoever.

The feeble Assembly that had helped Napoleon III to govern felt itself out of place amid the tumult that followed upon his downfall. One of its few members who really represented the people was Jules Favre. At his demand, and under the menace of a gathering mob, the Assembly declared France a republic. Then most of its members hastened to disappear into the oblivion whence they had come.

The Parisians were left to form a government of their own. Favre and a few other leaders declared themselves temporarily the "Government for the National Defence," and began arranging for the election in October of a regular Assembly, to be truly representative of the nation. This election was prevented by the

[1] From Charles F. Horne's *Story of France* (New York: F. R. Niglutsch), by permission.

advance of the German armies; and the self-constituted "Government for the National Defence" continued to rule France until the war was over.

In energy and resource its members proved themselves not inferior to the Jacobins of 1792. Their lack of legal authority to enforce any command made their work infinitely difficult; and their patience, honesty, and devotion to France deserve all our praise. Chief among them were Jules Favre, a lawyer of ability and proven patriotism, and Léon Gambetta, a fervid, hot-headed young orator hardly thirty-two. They offered the renowned statesman and former prime minister, Louis Adolphe Thiers, a place among them, but he declined the dangerous honor.

The first effort of the Republicans was to restore peace. They asserted that Prussia had no cause for quarrel with them, and that the senseless dispute had vanished with the Empire that had originated it. They were willing to compensate Prussia for the expense she had been under, and would pay her a heavy indemnity, but, as Favre put it: "Not a foot of our territory! Not a stone of our fortresses!" If the war were forced upon them, they would fight to the utmost.

Bismarck, at that time Chancellor of the North German Confederation, was by no means willing to recognize this new Government. He would have much preferred dealing with the Empire, whose chief was in his hands. When Favre was sent to negotiate with Bismarck, the Chancellor treated him with neglect and harshness. A great outcry had already risen in victorious Prussia for the restoration of her ancient borders, the return of the provinces of Alsace and Lorraine, which had been wrested from her in the time of Louis XIV, two centuries before. Bismarck made this demand the first condition of peace. All France upheld Favre in his indignant refusal.

So the war continued, under conditions directly reversed from its beginning. Defeated France sought only peace. It was triumphant Prussia that now demanded concessions and surrender of territory. There were two ways by which the country might be saved: by finding allies among the other nations, or through the uprising of the whole united people to destroy the Germans. Both methods were attempted. M. Thiers, upon his own authority and that of the Provisional Government, made the round of the capitals of Europe in quest of alliances upon any terms. But none of the Powers cared to treat with an ambassador of such doubtful legality or to involve themselves in a cause that seemed already lost.

Meanwhile the utmost efforts were put forth to rouse the French people of the provinces. These had enthusiastically accepted the new Republic. Indeed, many of the provincial cities had themselves proclaimed its existence, without waiting for news from the capital. Yet now they held back doubtfully. They were jealous of the pretensions of the Government at Paris. They dreaded the excesses of the Paris mob.

The position of military affairs was briefly this. Several French fortresses along the eastern frontier still held out, notably Strasburg; but these were compelled to surrender one by one. The only considerable French army of regular troops that remained was under Marshal Bazaine, shut up in Metz. It consisted of nearly two hundred thousand men; and about three hundred thousand Germans surrounded it, while a second German army, almost equal to the first, marched toward Paris.

General Trochu was made military commander of the capital, and it was hastily prepared to resist either an assault or a siege. Around the city stretched a gigantic wall which King Louis Philippe had planned and Napoleon III had built. It was now nearly completed, thirty feet in height, and was protected at every angle by huge forts and heavy guns. The defences were strengthened as much as possible, and provisions were gathered from all quarters. Fugitives from the surrounding villages flocked into the city, swelling its total population to nearly two and a half millions of excited and determined people.

From these nearly four hundred thousand men were enrolled as soldiers, but of course the great majority were untrained and unreliable, noisily patriotic, but little better than a mob clamoring through the streets. General Trochu had only eighty thousand regular troops on whom he felt he could rely.

The Prussians first appeared before the desperate city on September 18th. They made no attempt at an assault, but, extending their lines around the walls and forts, settled down to the most stupendous siege of modern times. They were less numerous than the French troops, but they were a thoroughly disciplined army and were everywhere successful in the little preliminary skirmishes by which they established themselves.

At first the Parisians found their greatest trial was being shut out from all news of the outside world. They organized a balloon service, and pressed carrier-pigeons into use. Early in October the fiery Gambetta escaped from the city in one of these balloons, and establishing himself at Tours soon perfected an efficient organization extending over all the country. His glowing speeches thrilled his countrymen to action, and outside of Paris he became the dictator of France.

There was no longer any question of apathy among the provinces. If Paris would really fight, they would not be behind her in heroism. France responded as one man to Gambetta's appeals. At one time he had probably a million and a half of volunteers under arms. But alas, armed men are not armies! These raw recruits, undrilled, lacking proper weapons, half starved, and, as time went on, half naked, proved no match for the German troops. There were armies of the North, armies of the South, and armies of the West, attacking the invaders furiously all over France. But the brave peasants sacrificed their lives in vain. They met only repeated defeats. Not one genuine French victory brightens the record of this disastrous and one-sided war.

Most notable perhaps of these feeble yet glorious armies was one gathered on the Loire and placed under the command of General de Paladines. A plan was formed for him to advance toward Paris from the south, while the Parisians were to make a sortie to meet him; and at the same time Marshal Bazaine was to break out of Metz, and threaten the Prussian rear.

Bazaine, however, instead of liberating his enormous army, surrendered it bodily (October 29th). About one hundred seventy-five thousand troops, most of whom, at Gravelotte, had proved themselves worthy of better things, were yielded, without further effort, to a foe not greatly outnumbering them. The case is without a parallel in history! After the war Bazaine was tried as a traitor. He pleaded that his provisions were exhausted, that a battle would have meant only useless sacrifice of life, and above all that he was a servant of the Emperor, that no legal government had superseded Napoleon, and hence he knew not what or whom to fight for. "There was still France," was the noble answer of the Duc d'Aumale; and the court judges condemned Bazaine to death. His sentence was reduced to imprisonment, and he afterward escaped.

His surrender of Metz prostrated the last hopes of Frenchmen. It brought a long succession of evil consequences in its train. During the siege of Paris one of the most serious difficulties of the Provisional Government was the controlling of the lower classes of the populace. The majority of these were "Red Republicans" or anarchists; and their leaders, hoping to seize upon power for themselves, took advantage of every fresh disaster to rouse the ignorant multitude to tumult.

The news of Bazaine's surrender stirred the Red Republicans to indiscriminate fury. A mob assailed the Government for the National Defence, and threatened its leaders with instant death. Favre and the others sat calmly in their seats awaiting the inevitable. Someone showed General Trochu a way of escape, but he declined it, saying, "Friend, a soldier dies at his post of duty." Warning of the perilous situation of the Government finally reached the regular troops; and they hastened to their chief's defence and suppressed the tumult. Its consequences they could not suppress. Negotiations for peace with Prussia had been once more under way; but at news of the rioting in Paris, Bismarck broke them off, on the old plea that here was still another government, and he knew not with which to deal. Doubtless he felt that if the jarring factions meant to destroy each other, he could make better terms with the exhausted remnant.

Another evil which sprang from the disaster at Metz was that the huge German army was left free there, and these troops hastened to reënforce their brethren before Paris, who were in urgent need of help. The French army of the Loire under General de Paladines had performed its part in the general plan, by attacking the invaders from the south. At the same time the Parisians sallied out upon them repeatedly, in force. There was severe fighting all through November.

The arrival of the second German army upon the scene made the struggle hopeless, yet it was persistently maintained. A body of fifty thousand troops under General Ducrot fought their way out from Paris as far as Champigny, on the farther shore of the river Marne. They had three days of sickening carnage, during which more Frenchmen fell than the armies of Napoleon III had lost at Woerth or Gravelotte. The besiegers also lost heavily. But the army of the Loire was defeated and scattered; so Ducrot and his men fell back upon Paris to await the end.

The defences of the metropolis were strong—impregnable, her newspapers had once boasted; and the most difficult problem of the sorely harassed Government became the feeding of the vast multitude within the walls. These soon stooped to mule-meat, next to fancy foods from their zoological gardens, antelope steak and elephant trunk, and then to dogs and cats, and even vermin. The suffering became intense. "Poor little babies," says one who was among them, "died like flies." The German engineers pushed their lines of intrenchments ever nearer to the doomed city. Shells began to fall upon its houses; and a regular bombardment opened, which could result only in the capital's complete destruction.

Desperate sallies were made again and again all through January, but never with more than momentary success. At last the Government for the National Defence gave up in despair. There seemed no longer any hope for Paris or for France. Favre was again commissioned to confer with Bismarck, and to secure the best terms he could for the surrender of the city. The siege came to an end January 29, 1871.

One of the arrangements of the capitulation was that there should be a truce long enough to permit the election of a free French Assembly, which could with some show of legal authority negotiate a final peace, whose terms would thus become binding upon all France. The truce did not, however, include the last and only remaining one of those pathetic "armies of the provinces" which the genius of Gambetta had raised. This force, under General Bourbaki and the Italian hero Garibaldi, was struggling against the Germans in eastern France, trying to get around their armies and invade Prussia itself.

The effort failed. The weather was intensely cold, and Bourbaki's half-naked troops suffered all the tortures of freezing and starvation. They were half surrounded, their leader shot himself, and finally the perishing remnant of the men was compelled to retreat into Switzerland. There, as they had invaded a neutral country, they were disarmed—probably much to their own relief—and the active operations of the war came to an end (February 1, 1871).

Meanwhile the Assembly for which the capitulation of Paris had provided was elected. It met in February, chose Thiers as its President, and deputed him to settle terms of peace with Bismarck. Favre assisted him. It was a terrible trial to both of these patriots thus to aid in tearing apart their beloved country, and Thiers, a man of more than seventy years, broke down frequently in the course of the long negotiations.

Considering how complete had been Prussia's victory, the final terms seem not over-severe, though of course bitterly humiliating to the proud Frenchmen. Alsace, which had been French for two hundred years, whose people spoke French and were devoted to the country, was given up to Prussia. So was about one-fifth of Lorraine; and an enormous money payment, nearly a billion dollars, was to be made to the victors as quickly as possible. Until the money was delivered, the French fortresses were to be held by German troops.

The treaty was laid before the Assembly and finally accepted, March 2, 1871. On the same day thirty thousand German troops were paraded through the streets of Paris, as a visible sign of her surrender and captivity. Then they withdrew, and the war was at an end.

THE UNIFICATION OF GERMANY

A.D. 1871

EMIL REICH

Before the end of 1870, while the Franco-Prussian War was in progress, the North German Confederation made federative treaties with the Southern States of Germany, and thus the foundations of Germanic unity were laid, and in the following year the present Empire was established. This fulfilment of a long-cherished dream of German patriots was one of the two chief results of the war with France, the other being the establishment of the Third Republic on the ruins of the Second Empire.

After the surrender of Napoleon III at Sedan (September 2, 1870) and the proclamation of a republic by the French, the German armies marched on Paris and laid siege to the city. Soon a large French army that had been shut up in Metz surrendered; and when on January 28, 1871, Paris itself capitulated, the German triumph was complete. Already it had been suggested in Germany that the possession of presidential rights in the new confederation by King William I of Prussia should "be coupled with the imperial title." Later the suggestion took the form of Parliamentary and diplomatic request, presented to King William in an official address at Versailles, December 18, 1870; and there, in the palace, January 18, 1871, he was proclaimed German Emperor.

William formally assumed the imperial dignity in the presence of all the German princes or their representatives, and of many military officers. The ceremony was conducted by the Crown Prince Frederick William, and a proclamation to the German people was read by Prince Bismarck, first Chancellor of the new Empire. On March 17th the Emperor returned to Berlin, and in April a constitution for the German Empire was adopted and published.

In the following pages Emil Reich, who has devoted particular attention to the development of modern Europe, treats the making of the German Empire not after the manner of the ordinary chronicler, but in the profound spirit of the philosophic student. His survey of the historical antecedents of this unification of national life is especially illuminating.

THE unity of Germany forms in many ways one of the most instructive chapters of history. For it is in Germany perhaps more than in most countries that the old perennial and terrible fight of man against nature has been fought out, and finally led to results perhaps all-important. Like all the other nations of Europe the Germans, too, have always tried to make the limits of their country conterminous with the limits of their language. Europe has at no time been given to the Roman ideal, and just as a united states of Europe is impossible in the near or in the far future, so it was impracticable in the last two thousand years. Europe consists at present of more than forty highly organized polities, each of which clings to its personality in language, law, custom, and every other feature of national life with uncompromising tenacity. Each of these States has at all times tried to combine and unite its members and to separate itself from its neighbors. The centripetal forces in Europe have always been in the minority, and even the greatest emperors and conquerors have found that their dreams of uniting Europe under one rule were short-lived and sterile.

This work of union, this attempt to bring together in one highly differentiated state the members of one and the same nation, this old historical endeavor of the European peoples, has been realized in some countries earlier than in others.

Of the diverse elements of what was called the Holy Roman Empire of the Germanic nation in previous centuries, it is very difficult to form a definite idea. The number of sovereigns, from a small lord to the Emperor, who all had sovereign rights over their respective subjects, is amazing. The Emperor had no fixed nor considerable revenue; he had no standing and efficient army; and being at the same time the ruler of Austria and Hungary he had no vital interest in the welfare of his Provinces outside his Danubian monarchy. In fact, the interest of the Hapsburg emperors was rather the other way. The more Germany was split up into innumerable little sovereignties, the more it was unable to offer very great resistance to the Hapsburgs. The great international Treaty of 1648, the so-called Peace of Westphalia, had really increased the almost anarchic state of Germany, and by its terms Sweden and France stood as guarantors or perpetuators of this condition. It is almost impossible to realize the confusion, the chaos, the incredible disorder, that reigned in Germany in consequence of this political dismemberment. Each sovereign had coins of his own, had customs-lines of his own, had little armies of his own, separate individual codes of law of his own; the religion of the sovereign decided as a rule the religion of his subjects, and a very considerable portion of Germany was "under the crozier," belonging as it did to powerful ecclesiastical potentates such as the Archbishops of Cologne, of Mainz, of Trèves, and the Bishops of Bamberg and Wurtzburg. Litigation in the courts of these small sovereigns, and appeals to the central court of the Emperor, were, as a rule, exposed to the most exasperating delays and to ruinous expense.

The German poet Schiller, in his tragedy *Kabale und Liebe* ("Intrigue and Love"), has given us a terrible picture of the cruelty and oppression practised by these petty tyrants. Commerce flourished very little, and the German towns had long fallen from that commercial importance which they had reached in the fourteenth and fifteenth centuries. The people were indifferent to their lot, and did not even rise when the Landgrave of Hesse sold them like chattels to the English to fight the Americans in the war of 1775–1783.

The position of the women, especially in the seventeenth century, was most degrading. The German woman, at no time credited with any superior intellectual energy, was in the seventeenth century an altogether obscure and insignificant partner of her husband. It is true that in the first half of the eighteenth century the *status* of German women was considerably raised, and we hear of many an energetic, highly intellectual, and cultivated woman in that century.

The Germans, while politically paralyzed and unable to shake off the torpor that had fallen upon them since the end of the Thirty Years' War in 1648, had yet one great ideal in common. While Germany was practically a mere geographical expression, *Deutschthum* ("Germandom") as they call it themselves, soon began to exert itself. To put it in plain words, the unity of the Germans was, in contrast with that of the English and the French, at first not a political unity, but an intellectual one. They were politically as diverse as if they had been total foreigners to one another. But intellectually, in the second half of the eighteenth century, they had begun to learn the immense value of their language in scientific and literary works, and so to feel a consciousness of German nationality which, although still lacking political union, yet prepared the way for it. In this sense the history of German literature is even more important to the historian than is the history of French or English literature. The works in which for the first time the unparalleled resources of the German language were made use of were the greatest possible incentive to a feeling of nationality in Germany.

Even up to the middle of the eighteenth century all the most valuable works published in Germany were still written in Latin or in French. When, however, in the second half of that century, Lessing, Herder, Goethe, Wieland, Schiller, and other German writers manifested the power of the German idiom, its adaptability to prose and poetry alike, its capacity for the highest philosophical researches as well as for the lowest comedy, its force in narrative, didactic and descriptive style alike—when all this became clear to the enthusiastic readers of these authors, the Germans felt that a new era had begun in their history. As in the sixteenth century the spiritual effect of the Reformation had brought home to the Germans their spiritual unity, so in the second half of the eighteenth century and in the first half of the nineteenth the constantly increasing number of classical works written in German impressed upon the Germans the fact that they were fast becoming united intellectually.

The military disasters that fell upon the Germans in 1805–1807 could not but impart to every German a feeling that a nation cannot rest with a unity that is only intellectual and spiritual. More than that was needed. Political unity was required, and it now became not only a dream, but a practical interest, for all Germans to consolidate their political edifice in order to reap the full benefit of their spiritual and intellectual unity. At that time the question really was, not whether the political unity of Germany should be attempted—for on that point all German-speaking nations were at one—but which German power should realize the unity? The house of Hapsburg played, even in 1815, a considerable *role* in the so-called German Confederation; and until 1850 the King of Prussia, the only rival of the Hapsburgs, could not secure any ascendency or hegemony in that Confederation; and thus it was that many expected the unity of Germany to come from Austria. The problem, therefore, which the Germans had to solve in the second half of the nineteenth century was, whether their political unity should come from South Germany or Austria, whence had come their spiritual and intellectual unity, or whether it should come from North Germany or Prussia, which had hitherto done little or nothing for the intellectual regeneration of the nation except the establishment of a few universities, and which in 1806 and 1807 had proved itself to be utterly helpless, disorganized, and decadent. Those who hoped to see the unity of Germany realized by Austria were singularly mistaken about the nature of that power. The Hapsburgs, for reasons that are not quite clear, have never been able to unite any of the nations that have come under their rule in a real union. Austria (or rather the Hapsburgs) has at all times been unsuccessful in its attempts at bringing about that political and national unity which in the latter half of the nineteenth century many a patriotic German hoped to see introduced into his own country.

In order to understand this important point very clearly, we must hark back for a moment to the times of a struggle that took place long before the period here treated, but the influence of which is clearly evident at the present day. We mean the famous Silesian wars, which, with the interruption of a few years (1748–1756) raged from 1740 to 1763. In 1741 Frederick the Great succeeded, by one victory, in wresting from Austria the large and fertile Province of Silesia. Prussia, which obtained the heterogeneous elements of three portions of Poland in 1772, 1793, and 1795, was yet rich in her German Provinces, especially after the Congress of Vienna in 1815, when she obtained large provinces on the Rhine; and her national unity was infinitely superior to that of Austria. She occupied a very considerable part of Germany proper, had German people as subjects, and a unity of language and also largely of religion; all that she lacked was some one great statesman who might realize the old hope. On the other hand, Austria's ethnography was a bar to any statesmen who should have tried to realize the unity of Germany. Prussia, indeed, wanted great men; Austria could not have done much even with the greatest man at the helm. Moreover, Austria had neither a powerfully organized and united army, nor a regular and well-stocked exchequer. Prussia, through the reforms introduced by non-Prussian statesmen—such as Stein, Hardenberg, Scharnhorst, and Altenstein—from 1807, had created a system of national education both in law- and high-schools, by works both scientific and literary; and in her army as well as in her national revenue she had made herself highly efficient.

The old question whether Athens made Themistocles or Themistocles made Athens is to the mind of many a historian an insoluble problem. However, we find that in any case of a really great man in history the possibilities of his career had long been prepared by the state or the nation to which he belonged. It cannot be denied that the influence of Bismarck after he came to power and to the enjoyment of the complete confidence of King William of Prussia was a decisive factor in the history of that country and of Germany. Yet it is equally certain that without the previous reforms made by such men as Luther, Melanchthon, and Brenz, and the still greater literary and artistic lights of Germany, Bismarck's genius alone could not have effected anything.

From the Revolution in 1848 to the end of the 'fifties Prussia was still held to be subordinate to Austria in point of influence in Germany; and an attack on Austria was not considered in any way as promising sure success for the Prussian army. At the same time the Prussian army, since the great defeat of Jena in 1806, had been reformed and improved and made a fighting-instrument second to none in Europe, and, as subsequent events have proved, superior to most.

When Austria in 1859 had been defeated by France, and had been deprived of most of her territory in Italy; when at the same time the uncompromising position of the Hungarians toward Austria rendered her interior security more than problematic—a new view of the relation of the Danubian monarchy to Prussia was taken by Prussian statesmen. Of those men, Bismarck was even at that time the most important. He came from a small family in North Germany, and had to recommend him neither wealth nor remarkable personal connections. His strongest recommendation was his extraordinary political genius. All his measures were based on information regarding the persons and circumstances he was called upon to deal with, such as very few statesmen have ever used. In addition to a perfect knowledge of Prussia, and of the influential men and women of recent history, Bismarck had a rare insight into the general political state of Europe. He was master of the French language, and had also a surprising command of English; and when he was ambassador in Russia he acquired a working knowledge of Russian. Of the courts and the political situation of the Powers in Europe he had acquired from personal study and from a judicious course of reading such ample and accurate knowledge that as a rule he was better informed about the tendencies and character of political events than most men dealing with them directly or indirectly. Accordingly, he was seldom mistaken in the strategy of his actions, though at all periods of his life the wisdom of his methods was challenged, doubted, attacked, and even ridiculed by men in important and commanding positions.

Bismarck had firmly seized the necessity of bringing about the unity of Germany under Prussian ascendency by the most careful conduct of Prussia's foreign policy. He knew that the consummation of the great work could not be effected by introduction or academical spread of mere ideas. He knew it was preëminently a matter of diplomacy and war. He clearly indicated, in letters and speeches, that while some nations may bring about their national unity through treaties, or the slow work of mutual assimilation, the Germans, he rightly held, could not possibly realize their secular hope without establishing themselves as a great military power. This is the sense of his famous utterance that history is made by blood and iron. Nobody admired Cavour, the unifier of Italy, more than did Bismarck; likewise nobody acknowledged the surpassing merit of Francis Déak in bringing about the unity of Hungary in a peaceful way more than did Bismarck; but nobody saw more clearly that the problems with which Déak or Cavour had to contend, although identical in object with that of Bismarck, yet had a character so different that for their realization other means were required. As diplomatic reverses at home or abroad could never discourage him, even so the greatest triumphs in the field or in diplomatic negotiations were never able to beguile him into excessive actions. We must admire both his courage and his moderation.

His adversaries were numerous. It is well known that the Empress Frederick III, the daughter of Queen Victoria, was the persistent and implacable enemy of Bismarck; the historian Mommsen was likewise continually hostile to him; and it is certain that the great man lived in a world of incessant intrigues directed against his person and against his work. His greatest successes did not persuade the Empress Frederick that she was in error, and all his enemies and opponents were conspiring to shake the nerve of the Titan.

In addition to physical resources of the rarest strength, Bismarck, like most great men, had also an unusual amount of good luck. Like Richelieu and Mazarin, Bismarck could, under all circumstances, count on the unswerving attachment and friendship of his sovereign. Against this powerful friendship and steadfast confidence of the monarch all the shafts of envy and jealousy were hurled in vain. Not that the Emperor always shared the opinions or the desires of Bismarck; in fact, he was, in 1864, in 1866, and in 1870, very reluctant to accept the policy of his great minister. But in the end he consented to it.

The victories of the Prussians in 1866, the ascendency of Prussians in Germany since the day of Sadowa, were events the importance of which was clear to every statesman and diplomatist in Europe. Thiers, Edgar Quinet, and other politicians and public men of France pointed out clearly that Bismarck could not possibly rest on the laurels of his Austrian campaign; that he was necessarily striving to complete the unity of Germany, which in 1867 was yet far from complete. Bismarck in 1866 had united the Northern States of Germany into the North German Confederacy; but the Southern States—Bavaria, Wurtemberg, and Baden—were not yet combined with Prussia. It has been said that if his military success over Bavaria in 1866 had been as complete as his success over Austria, Bismarck might very well have forced Bavaria and other Southern States of Germany to join the North-German Confederation. In that way the Franco-Prussian War might have been avoided, and the unity of Germany secured in a peaceful manner, without the terrible loss in men and money entailed by that gigantic war.

It cannot be denied that in these arguments there are some elements of truth; and Bavaria might have been persuaded to join the North German Confederacy without the terrible war against France. On the other hand, Bismarck's considerations were of a deeper and, on the whole, of a juster nature. He felt that the South German States could not be permanently held as members of a united Germany unless a great and successful war should put an end to any attempt at separation.

Moreover, those Southern States—in 1867 as well as in 1740 or in 1645—were always coquetting with France, and had, by secular tradition and habit, a policy of friendship, nay, of alliance with the French. These old historical traditions and tendencies, Bismarck rightly felt, could not be efficiently combated by anything short of a successful war against France, in which the Bavarians too would be obliged to undergo the sufferings and accept the sacrifices necessary to the completion of the great plan. Bismarck, therefore, made no definite attempt at persuading the Southern States from 1866 to 1870 to join the North German Confederation.

The war between Prussia and France at once manifested the inner unity of the German nations; for the Southern States at once joined Prussia and the Northern States; and under the leadership of Moltke, of the Crown Prince Frederick, and of Prince Frederick Charles, the German armies invaded France, and in nearly every single battle worsted the French, even when, as at Gravelotte, the Germans had not a superiority of numbers.

At the first blush it appears inexplicable that the German generals, none of whom had seen or experienced a great war—except the war of 1866, which lasted only a few weeks—should prove so immeasurably superior to the French generals, every one of whom had gone through numerous campaigns previous to 1870. In fact, it must be said that in 1870 theory proved superior to practice; and the German officers, mere theorists, so to speak, undid all the plans, practice, and routine of the French generals. The explanation of this remarkable puzzle may be found in the fact that the experience of the French generals was great indeed, but it had been acquired, not in Europe and against European armies so much as in Mexico, in Algeria, in China; that is, against nations of a civilization and science inferior to those of Europe. The Germans were prepared for that war, and for more than two generations had studied its possibilities in minutest detail.

After the terrible disasters of Sedan and Metz came the siege of Paris. The French, maddened by their unprecedented reverses, accepted for a time the guidance of Gambetta, a man of energy and insight, but one who lacked the ruthless powers of an efficient dictator. He was able to create new armies, to offer to the Germans a resistance on the Loire and in the north of France which in many ways was more efficient than that offered to the Germans by the old regular army of France. The Germans, after October, 1870, were unable to repeat those wholesale captures of armies which characterized the first stage of their war with France; yet Gambetta was not quite equal to the different situation created in France through the German victories.

We now know, from German military writers, that the Germans could not have continued the war for another three months, after January, 1871. The winter was terribly cold; Bismarck, as he tells us himself in his memoirs, spent sleepless nights in apprehensions of international interference; the financial resources of Germany began to be exhausted, and a popular and implacable war, in the manner of the Spanish resistance to Napoleon, would have forced the Germans to retreat, and may have possibly deprived them of Lorraine, if not also of Alsace.

However, in France, as usual, there were strong parties filled with personal ambition, who, in the collapse of the old *regime*, welcomed an opportunity for raising themselves to power. Of these parties Adolphe Thiers was the head. He wanted peace, and peace by any means, for he knew that peace meant his own coming to power. He had been unsuccessful in his long and wearisome travels to the various courts of Europe asking for help and intervention. Bismarck—and that was his greatest diplomatic feat—had so completely isolated France that neither England nor Russia seriously thought of intervening. After the occupation of Paris, France was obliged to accept, in 1871, the terms of peace dictated by Bismarck at Frankfort-on-the-Main, by the terms of which France lost Alsace altogether, and of Lorraine the portion inhabited by German-speaking people; and, moreover, she was obliged to pay an indemnity of $1,000,000,000. The real cost of the war to France was $5,000,000,000, and but for the immense wealth of the country the war would have ruined it financially, as it did politically.

The Germans at Versailles—that is, in the very palace of Louis XIV, who in the seventeenth century had so deeply humiliated the Prussian Elector and the Germans generally—constituted themselves into the German Empire. King William of

Prussia accepted the new dignity of the imperial crown rather reluctantly; and there were great difficulties about the title, which was finally settled as King William, German Emperor. Thus the great purpose of Bismarck, to bring about the unity of Germany by a successful war with France, rather than by negotiations and treaties with and between German sovereigns themselves, was completely realized; and Germany, which hitherto had been a lax and inefficient conglomeration of small and great sovereignties, was now launched on a career of political and commercial prosperity, and speedily became a world-power.

THE RISING OF THE COMMUNE

A.D. 1871

GABRIEL HANOTAUX[1]

Immediately following the Franco-Prussian War occurred a crisis in France that precipitated a new reign of terror. This was the uprising of the Commune in Paris against the authority of the Assembly—the legislative body of the Third Republic. After the conclusion of a preliminary peace agreement between Prussia and France (March 2, 1871), Paris was abandoned by nearly all the ruling and influential men. Those who remained in the city—Jules Favre, Ernest Picard, and Jules Ferry—were unpopular and left the direction of affairs to Generals Vinoy and Paladines. Paris was filled with unrest and apprehension. It was rumored that the Republic was threatened with a *coup d'état*, and Paris with the entrance of the Germans. The walls of the city were placarded with calls to resistance. The actual entry of German troops (March 1st), in accordance with the preliminaries of peace, was declared by Thiers to be one of the principal causes of the insurrection.

The revolutionaries embraced several parties—Blanquists, followers of Louis Blanqui, traditional insurrectionists; the later Jacobins, violent partisans of a strong republican government; socialists of various schools; and the International or workingmen's party. These were the chief elements that formed the politico-social body known as the Commune of Paris, which had its precursor in the revolutionary committee of 1789–1794, also called the Commune. The city was full of idle persons, among whom were many of the more than two hundred fifty thousand soldiers just released from active service; a great influx came from the provinces; fragments of the army of Garibaldi in the late war gathered; and below all others was "a nameless collection" of the criminal population. Arms were plentifully supplied for the rising, and the streets were barricaded. How far the National Guard could be trusted by the Assembly no man could tell. It mainly went over to the Commune.

Such was the condition of Paris after the withdrawal of the German troops from the city (March 3d). At this point begins the narrative of Hanotaux, the noted French statesman and historian, who has made valuable additions to our knowledge of these exciting events.

[1] From John Charles Tarver's translation of Gabriel Hanotaux's *Contemporary France* (New York: G. P. Putnam's Sons), by permission.

AFTER the foreign troops left Paris, fifteen days passed away in alternations of fear and hope. The question of the government was raised at Bordeaux, the question of disarmament at Paris. A conclusion was necessary. Both sides made their preparations.

On March 8th Duval, the future general of the Commune, established an insurrectional section at the Barrier d'Italie, and organized for resistance. The Central Committee approached the International. Meanwhile M. Jules Ferry, Mayor of Paris, was still writing to the Government on March 5th: "The city is calm; the danger is over. At the bottom of the situation here, great weariness, need of resuming the normal life: but no lasting order in Paris without government or assembly. The Assembly returning to Paris can alone reëstablish order, consequently work which Paris so much needs; without that, nothing possible. Come back quickly."

Then came the news relative to the law of debts and the question of rents, to the transferrence of the Assembly to Versailles; it was affirmed that a *coup d'etat* was in preparation. M. Thiers, head of the Provisional Government, installed himself, March 15th, at the Ministry of Foreign Affairs. The moment had come to act. It was necessary to proceed to disarmament. Paris could not be left thus, beside herself, rifle in hand.

The knot was at Belleville and Montmartre. A council of ministers was called on the 17th at the Ministry of Foreign Affairs. The subject of deliberation was the opportuneness of a stroke on the part of authority which was defined in this formula: "Recover the guns."[1] M. Thiers says: "The general opinion was in favor of recovering the guns." He says again: "An opinion in favor of immediate action was universally pronounced." He says again: "Many persons, concerning themselves with the financial question, said that we must after all think of paying the Prussians. The business men went about everywhere repeating: 'You will never do anything in the way of financial operations unless you finish with this pack of rascals, and take the guns away from them. That must be done with, and then you can treat of business.' " And he concludes: "The idea that it

[1] Many cannon had been removed to these places by the National Guard and the Commune.—ED.

was necessary to remove the guns was dominant, and it was difficult to resist it. In the situation of men's minds, with the noises and rumors that circulated in Paris, inaction was a demonstration of feebleness and impotence."

The stroke was decided on; it consisted in bringing into the interior of Paris the guns that were guarded on the heights of Montmartre. There were at most twenty thousand troops of the Assembly to execute the plan.

It was arranged that action should begin at two o'clock in the morning. M. Thiers was at the Louvre, anxious, with General Vinoy, who answered for success. The operation seemed at first to be succeeding. General Lecomte occupied the plateau. The whole hill was surrounded. But a large number of teams would have been necessary to operate such a colossal removal before daybreak. The teams were not there; the army had no longer any horses. Several days were necessary to take away all the guns. Then it was seen that the operation was badly planned. However, seventy guns were carried off, and the remainder were guarded by troops, waiting with grounded arms.

Little by little the news that the guns were being taken away spread in Montmartre. The alarm-bell was rung. Some shots were fired and roused the quarter. The eminence and surrounding regions were astir. There was a shout of "*Coup d'etat!*" The National Guards assembled. The crowd of women and children pushed around the soldiers who were guarding the guns. "Hurrah for the Line!" they cry on all sides. "You are our brothers; we do not wish to fight you." They penetrate into the ranks of the soldiers, offer them drink, disarm them. They hold up the stocks of their rifles, disbanding themselves. General Lecomte was surrounded and taken prisoner, along with his staff.

M. Thiers returned to the Ministry of Foreign Affairs. At the Hôtel de Ville, where the Mayor of Paris, M. Jules Ferry, remained permanently on duty, they waited for news. At first it was good; then it was worse; at half-past ten the disaster was defined; the head police-office telegraphed: "Very bad news from Montmartre. Troops refused to act. The heights, the guns, and the prisoners retaken by the insurgents, who do not appear to be coming down. The Central Committee should be at the park in the Rue Basfroi!"

At the Ministry of Foreign Affairs the Government sat in permanence in the great gallery that looks upon the garden and over the quay. Men bringing news come in and go out. The generals deliberate in a corner.

The old Marquis de Vogué was among the chance comers. He pulled out of his pocket his deputy's scarf of 1848, and he went from one to the other, bent, his voice broken, saying: "I know how it is done. You put that round your body, and you get yourself killed on a barricade."

General Leflô, Minister of War, who had gone as far as the Place de la Bastille to get information, returned between twelve and one o'clock.

It was decided to order the general call to arms to be beaten, to assemble the battalions of the National Guard, which, it was thought, could be relied on. Only six hundred men presented themselves.

M. Thiers, in a state of great emotion, wished to learn from General Vinoy what was the exact military situation.

Already by midday or one o'clock he was beginning to declare that it would be necessary to resolve to abandon Paris. In his impatience he went as far as the Pont de la Concorde to meet the troops, who were retreating in good order with General Faron at their head. Toward three o'clock he returned to the Quai d'Orsay.

The news in Paris was worse and worse. The barracks were taken or evacuated. However, the Hôtel de Ville, relying on the troops of the Lobau barracks and occupied by Jules Ferry, who refused to abandon it at any price, still held out.

M. Thiers had hardly returned to the palace of the Quai d'Orsay when drums and clarions were heard, and from the windows three battalions were seen passing; they were the National Guards of the Gros-Caillou, who were going to join the movement. In the palace there was only half a battalion of light infantry. In spite of the wavering of Jules Favre, Jules Simon, and Ernest Picard, "whom it was difficult to convince of the necessity for this retreat," the Government knew the chief of the executive power could not remain thus exposed. For the rest M. Thiers cut the question short. He decided that he should leave Paris, and betake himself to Versailles. It was half-past three or four o'clock. "Foreseeing that," says General Vinoy, "I had doubled my escort. I had had my carriage prepared, and all was ready. I said to M. Thiers: 'Put on your overcoat; the gate of the Bois de Boulogne is guarded; your escape through it is assured.' I had sent a squadron there. But before starting he gave me the order to evacuate Paris." M. Thiers, in fact, calling up, as he has himself said, recollections of February 24, 1848, and of Marshal Windischgraetz, who after leaving Vienna reëntered victoriously some time afterward, was strengthened in his opinion by the state of disorganization and demoralization in which he felt the army to be.

He was insistent with General Vinoy to learn what troops there were that could be counted on. The General told him there was not one sure except the Daudel brigade. M. Thiers repeated again and again: "Send me the Daudel brigade to Versailles." There was no written order.

After the departure of M. Thiers, General Leflô, Minister of War, insisted on the necessity of complete evacuation. He affirmed that it would be impossible to hold out anywhere, even at the Trocadéro or at Passy. He signed the order and accepted all the responsibility.

Now, the Daudel brigade occupied the forts, including Mont Valérien. Chance willed it that the two battalions of light infantry, which it was proposed to withdraw from Paris, were on duty at this fort; this for a whole day was the entire garrison.

In the night between the Sunday and Monday General Vinoy, toward one in the morning, wrote a letter to M. Thiers, which Mme. Thiers read to him without his getting up, and in which he begged for authority to have Mont Valérien reoccupied. M. Thiers ended by consenting. Otherwise this fort, like those of Issy, Vanves, and Vincennes, would have been in the hands of the Commune. Mont Valérien was reoccupied on March 20th in the morning; the Fédérates presented themselves there hours afterward and in vain summoned the commander to surrender.

Meanwhile in Paris the Central Committee, taken at first by surprise, ordered the beat to arms. Montmartre, Belleville, the Buttes Chaumont, were in full insurrection. The Panthéon, Vaugirard, the Gobelins, rose to the voice of Duval. The battalions of the middle-class quarters did not respond to the call. At Montmartre a tragic scene settled the implacable character of the outbreak. General Lecomte, who had been arrested in the morning, was kept under surveillance in the house No. 6 of the Rue des Roziers. Clément Thomas, a former General of the National Guard, who had very imprudently mixed with the crowd in civil attire, was arrested and shut up with him. After some hours of frightful anguish Clément Thomas was seized and shot at close quarters just as he was going down the staircase; General Lecomte was shot in his turn in the garden, and, it is said, by his own soldiers.

In the evening M. Jules Favre hurled at a deputation, consisting of MM. Sicard, Vautrain, Vacherot, Bonvalet, Méline, Tolain, Millière, and others, who tried to intervene in the name of the mayors, the formidable words, "There is no discussion, no treating with murderers."

The Central Committee, up to that time wavering, gave orders that Paris should be invaded and occupied. At the Hôtel de Ville M. Jules Ferry still held out. He received repeated orders to evacuate. At 9.55 P.M. he left the Hôtel de Ville, the last man to do so, carrying away his papers, and taking the servants with him. He crossed the centre of Paris, already in the hands of the insurgents, escorted by the troops of General Derroja, who forced their way with fixed bayonets.

So then a new siege of Paris was to begin; the insurrection now became general, occupying the city and the forts on the south and west; M. Thiers and the National Assembly at Versailles; both parties under the eye of the German army, which, in conformity with the terms of the preliminaries, kept all the forts on the north and east.

Events hurried on with rigorous logic. Revolutionary measures multiplied. At the outset the Commune made some show of government; it maintained order in Paris up to a certain point and with some method in its deliberations. Something resembling that "gain of reason" attributed to it by Bismarck can be discovered in it. But it soon fell into clumsy imitation of the first revolution. The decree of hostages copied the list of suspects; the guillotine was suppressed, and then solemnly burned in front of the statue of Voltaire, but it was replaced by the rifle.

In default of practical reforms, the crowd was allowed free

feeding for its antireligious violence; suppression of the public worship fund, separation of the Church from the State, arrest of the Archbishop of Paris, Monseigneur Darboy, of several members of the clergy, and Protestant congregations. Liberty of the press was effectively suppressed. Chaudey, deputy to the mayor of the First Ward, and a member of the International, was arrested at the office of the *Siecle*, of which he was editor.

Divisions, hatred, rose to fever-point among all these desperate men. Disorder, indiscipline, were everywhere. There was no longer any common understanding even for action, for self-defence. Rigault, a fellow with an insolent carriage, was like a madman unchained at the Prefecture of Police. In the end he was removed from his post; but, imitating Fouquier-Tinville, he got himself appointed Attorney-General to the Commune. Violence was only just arrested in front of the Bank of France, thanks to the energy of M. de Ploeuc, the relative moderation of the aged Beslay, and the coolness of Jourde, delegate of finance. For the rest, the Bank of France was in some sort paying its ransom by advancing (with the authority of the Government at Versailles) the money necessary for the pay of "thirty sous."

Paris at length had opened her eyes. On April 18th, at the supplementary elections, in which eleven quarters were to take part, out of 280,000 electors on the register, only 53,000 took part in the votings; 205,000 abstained—that is to say, 80 per cent. of the registered electors. Half the vacant seats were unfilled. Clément and Courbet belong to this day. Henceforth there was nothing but the most manifest tyranny in the great city.

On May 14th Fort Vanves was occupied. The circle drew closer. Delescluze, though dying, was everywhere; he tried to rouse the battalions, whose effectives were diminishing. On May 16th, at nightfall, the Vendôme column was flung from its pedestal and shattered. The minority of twenty-two members separated from the majority. Soon it joined them again; on May 17th, at the Hôtel de Ville, sixty-six members present still remained at the roll-call.

The forts being taken, the walls were on the point of yielding. It was necessary to think of the classic strife of insurrection, barricade-fighting. But the military men of the Commune—Cluseret, Rossel—infatuated with their ideas of the great war, had made no preparations. Men felt themselves taken by surprise. What was to be done? Then the idea of destruction, of annihilation of the town in the last hours of the catastrophe, began to haunt those fated brains. Delescluze and his colleagues of the Nineteenth Ward placarded: "After our barricades, our houses; after our houses, our ruins." Vallès wrote, "If M. Thiers is a chemist, he will understand us."

An intense horror spread over the town, no longer knowing the nature of the awakening at hand. The population, which had let things take their course, was now reduced to shutting itself up in the houses. The National Guards ran hither and thither in the empty streets, with the stocks of their rifles forcing suspected houses or shops to open. Some timid efforts were distinguishable on the part of the National Guards to prepare resistance from the inside. M. Thiers received numerous suggestions, proposals of all kinds. One day a promise was made to deliver one of the gates of Paris to him. He spent the night with General Douay in the Bois de Boulogne, waiting for the signal that never came. Meanwhile he was informed that he would find a counter-movement all ready as soon as the troops crossed the lines of defence. Tricolor sleeve-badges were prepared. The great mass of the population waited in a state of terrible anxiety for the entrance of the regular troops.

The Commune felt that it was surrounded by enemies. It decided to draw up lists of suspects. Amouroux recalled that a law of hostages was in existence, and cried out, "Let us strike the priests!" Rigault, on the 19th, inaugurated the sittings of a jury on accusation. On all sides shooting began at the moment when the terrible contact was on the point of taking place.

The works of approach now permitted the bombardment of the gates of La Muette, Auteuil, Saint-Cloud, Point-du-Jour. The Fédérate troops, worn out by their ceaseless efforts, refused to serve. The breach was made; the wall, untenable under the projectiles, was abandoned. The assault was fixed for the 23d.

On the 21st, toward three o'clock in the afternoon, a man appeared upon the ramparts near the Saint-Cloud gate and waved a white handkerchief. In spite of the projectiles, he insisted, he shouted. Captain Garnier, of the Engineers, on service in the trenches, drew near. The man declared that the gate and the wall were without defenders, and the troops could penetrate into the town without striking a blow. He gave his name. It was Ducatel, a foreman in the municipal service.

He was believed and followed; the gate was crossed: the troops of Versailles entered Paris. M. Thiers looked on at this unexpected movement from the top of the battery at Montretout. At one moment the soldiers were seen coming out again, and a cry rose around him, "We are repulsed." But confidence was soon restored. By the aid of glasses "two long black serpents were distinguished gliding toward the gate of the Point-du-Jour, through which they entered." The officers in command, on being informed, stopped the fire directed upon the ramparts. The troops slipped inside from one place and another along the wall, without at first penetrating into the town.

From this moment there was war in the streets, but a war without method, without guidance, without a chief, a war without discipline, the struggle of despair. Each quarter, each group, fought for itself. The positions that had been prepared for the internal defence were guarded or abandoned, as chance willed.

In the night between the Sunday and the Monday seventy thousand men under arms from Versailles had slipped in some way along the fortifications forming a vast semicircle from La Muette to the Champ-de-Mars, by the Auteuil viaduct. General Douay had advanced by Auteuil and Passy to the Trocadéro. There was some fear that the ground was mined. But Ducatel, walking some paces in advance of the General, declared that there was nothing to fear.

On Monday, May 22d, in the morning, a proclamation of Delescluze was posted up announcing the entrance of the men of Versailles. It was a call to arms: "Room for the people, for the bare-armed fighting men! The hour of the revolutionary war has struck!"

During this day the Versailles troops occupied Paris as far as the Palais de l'Industrie, the left bank along the quay, the Ministry of Foreign Affairs, the Champ de Mars, the Ecole Militaire, and soon Vaugirard, the Invalides, the Palais Bourbon, the Montparnasse station; on the right bank the whole region included between the Saint-Lazare station and the Place Clichy. One would say that the end was now possible in a single blow. M. Thiers telegraphed to the prefects on May 21st, 6.30 P.M.: "The Saint-Cloud gate has just fallen under the fire of our guns. General Douay has hastened to the spot, and is at this moment entering Paris with his troops. The corps of Gernerals Ladmirault and Clinchant are moving forward to follow him."

If the Versailles troops had hurried the movement, perhaps they would have profited by the confusion of the Fédérates and rapidly taken the whole town. But it was desirable to avoid a check at any cost; the explosion of mines was feared; the advance was surrounded with precautions; it was made with prudence and often with sapping, suspected houses being searched.

In the night between Monday and Tuesday the insurgents took fresh courage. A burning sun illumined the city. The alarm-bell sounded: the call to arms was beaten. The Fédérates descended from the suburbs. All came and, conscious of great numbers, lent mutual courage. The barricades were occupied; fresh ones were thrown up; it is said that there were five hundred in Paris. The central quarters formed, as it were, a formidable block, having as its front the defences formed by the Place de la Concorde, the Rue Royale, the Boulevard Malesherbes, the Place Clichy, on the right bank; the barricades of the Rue du Bac, of the Rue Vavin, the Rue de Rennes, the Rue de la Croix-Rouge, the Rue du Panthéon on the left bank; and as a redout Montmartre, the Buttes-Chaumont, Père la Chaise, the Gobelins, the Butte-aux-Cailles. It was a fortress inside a fortress. The real battle was about to open. The psychological condition was no longer the same. On both sides a hideous rage blinded all these men to the sense of humanity.

On Tuesday, the 23d, at four o'clock in the morning, the troops that had bivouacked in the street resumed the attack. Montmartre was the objective. A smart fight was expected. The height was carried about two o'clock, almost without a blow. It is said that this formidable operation was rendered easier by the agency of money. Dombrowski, beaten at La Muette, fell back. He was mortally wounded; and he died uttering words that showed his preoccupation—"And they say that I betrayed them!" His body was carried to the Hôtel de Ville, and laid in Mlle. Haussmann's bed, and on the following day the Fédérates accompanied it with a kind of funeral procession to Père la Chaise.

The fighting was terrible in the Faubourg St. Honoré, in the Boulevard Malesherbes, at the Madeleine, in the Rue Royale, on the Terrace of the Tuileries. Brunel was in command there; he, too, had come from prison.

However, this position was turned by the capture of Montmartre. Brunel, in obedience to the orders given by Delescluze, began the conflagration by setting fire to the houses in the Rue Royale, which were close to the barricades.

The Tuileries and the Louvre were surrounded. Bergeret held a council of war in the great hall of the Tuileries. He had the rooms soaked with petroleum, caused barrels of powder to be brought up, and gave the order for burning the palace.

On the left bank, the troops that were marching upon the Panthéon were stopped at the Croix-Rouge, at the Rue de Rennes, at the Bellechasse barracks. They moved on, however, as far as the quay by the Rue de Légion-d'Honneur. But before retreating the Fédérates set fire to the Rue de Lille, the Palais du Conseil d'Etat, and the Cour des Comptes, to the Palais de la Légion-d'Honneur, where "General" Eudes, before decamping, did not forget to deliver his stroke.

After two hours' fighting, the Fédérates who had defended the barricade in the Rue Vavin fell back, but first they blew up the magazine of the Luxembourg. The whole of the left bank was shaken as if by an earthquake. At the town hall of the Eleventh Ward, where Delescluze was dying, he was speaking in low tones, and his appearance was so heart-breaking that in the midst of such a day he still appealed to the emotions of those present. In accordance with his orders, the defence of the Bastille and the Faubourg Saint-Antoine was prepared.

When night came, Brunel abandoned the Rue Royale. At three o'clock in the morning Bergeret blew up the Tuileries. Notre-Dame and the Hôtel-Dieu were saved only by the courage of the staff of the hospital, led by M. Brouardel. Everything was burning; explosions were everywhere. It was a night of terror. The Porte Saint-Martin, the church of Saint-Eustache, the Rue Royale, the Rue de Rivoli, the Tuileries, the Palais-Royale, the Hôtel de Ville, the left bank from the Légion d'Honneur to the Palais de Justice and the Police Office were immense red braziers, and above all rose lofty blazing columns. From outside, all the forts were firing upon Paris. Inside Paris, Montmartre, now in the hands of the Versailles troops, was firing upon Père la Chaise; the Point-du-Jour upon the Butte-aux-Cailles, which returned the fire. The gunners were cannonading one another across the town and above the town. Shells fell in every direction. All central quarters were a battlefield. It was a chaos; bodies and souls in collision over a crumbling world.

The night was dark, the sky black; a violent wind arose; it came from the south, and spread the flames, the smoke, the horror of the immense conflagration in a squall of fire toward the west, toward the enemy, toward Versailles, and toward those slopes of Saint-Cloud from the heights of which the members of the Government, the members of the Assembly, came to look on at a catastrophe in which the city was on the point of sinking.

M. Thiers had returned to Paris on Monday, the 22d, at three o'clock in the morning, by the Point-du-Jour gate. M. Jules Ferry, Mayor of Paris, had accompanied the first battalion of infantry, which, following the left bank, had occupied the Ministry of Foreign Affairs, just quitted by M. Pascal Grousset. Here was the seat of government; here Marshal MacMahon established his headquarters. M. Thiers, however, maintained constant relations with the National Assembly, which continued to sit at Versailles.

Prisoners were already coming in. But the Commune was not yet defeated. In the city all the furies were unchained. In the course of a deadly struggle, in which all minds appeared to lose their balance, the blood frenzy became universal. The most hideous rumors spread abroad; the soldiers were being murdered, were being poisoned; the firemen were putting petroleum in their engines. Then it was affirmed that the Commune, in a last convulsion of its rage, had assassinated the hostages.

In fact, on Wednesday, the 24th, in one quarter, police agents, prisoners, were shot in cold blood at Sainte-Pélagie by order of the pretended revolutionary tribunal presided over by Raoul Rigault. At La Roquette, in the night between the 24th and 25th, on the written order of Ferré, transmitted by Genton, a magistrate of the Commune, a squad commanded by a Fédérate captain, Vérig, massacred Georges Darboy, Archbishop of Paris, Abbé Deguerry, Fathers Clerc, Ducoudray, and Allard, and M.

Bonjean. Death was everywhere. On both sides henceforth the word of command was to be, "No quarter." On the same day, at ten o'clock in the morning, fifteen members of the Commune met at the Hôtel de Ville and determined to burn it down. The fire was started in the roof, and soon the ancient municipal building was in flames.

On the 25th, Thursday, the new line of defence was at the bridge of Austerlitz, resting on Mazas. Another siege began and a second assault had to be made. The troops were exhausted. But the last combatants were resolved to perish. Women and children were on the barricades and delivered fire. A strange frenzy excited these brave but feeble beings, and they continued to struggle after the men had left the barricades. At Mazas the civil prisoners revolted. At the Avenue d'Italie the Dominicans of Arcueil and their servants were killed by National Guards of the 101st Fédérate battalion, commanded by Serizier.

Meanwhile the bridge of Austerlitz was carried. The Butte-aux-Cailles, where Wroblewski resisted with energy, was occupied. The whole left bank was taken as far as the Orléans station. Fighting was still going on at the Chateau-d'Eau and the Bastille. The Place de la Bastille was turned by way of the Vincennes railway. All the survivors of the struggle, the desperates, met at the town hall of the Eleventh Ward, on the Boulevard Voltaire, around Delescluze, who was still obeyed; Vermorel on horseback, wearing the red scarf, was visiting the barricades, encouraging the men, seeking and bringing in reënforcements. At midday twenty-two members of the Commune and the Central Committee met, and Arnold informed them of the proposal of Mr. Washburne, Minister of the United States, suggesting the mediation of the Germans. Delescluze lent himself to this negotiation; he wished to make for the Vincennes gate, but he was repulsed by the Fédérates, who accused him of desertion. He came back, returned to the town hall, and wrote a letter of farewell to his sister.

Toward seven o'clock in the evening Delescluze set out, accompanied by Jourde and about fifty Fédérates, marching in the direction of the Place du Chateau-d'Eau. Delescluze was dressed correctly—silk hat, light overcoat, black frock-coat and trousers, red scarf round the waist, as he used to wear it; he was distinguished by his neat civilian costume from his company with their tattered uniforms. He had no arms, and supported himself on a walking-stick. He met Lisbonne, wounded, who was being carried in a litter, then Vermoral, wounded to death, held up by Chièze and Ayrial. Delescluze spoke to him and left him. The sun was setting behind the square. Delescluze, without looking to see whether he was being followed, went on at the same pace, the only living being on the pavement of the Boulevard Voltaire. He had only a breath left, his steps dragged. Arriving at the barricade he turned to the left and climbed the paving-stones. His face was seen to appear with its short white beard, then his tall figure. Suddenly he disappeared. He had just fallen, stricken to death.

In the night, while the centre of Paris was one immense furnace, the conflagration reached the quarters that were still being defended. Fire at the Chateau-d'Eau, fire at the Boulevard Voltaire, fire at the Grenier d'Abondance. The Seine, whose waters were already dyed with blood, rolled through Paris like a bed of fire; straws from the granary, papers from all the different records, made a rain of sparks; the air was scorching.

From Thursday, the 25th, there was a multiplication of executions. At the Saint-Sulpice Seminary an ambulance full of Fédérates, under the direction of Doctor Faneau, were slaughtered; it is said that some combatants had taken refuge here and had fired on the troops. Everywhere upon the barricades National Guards taken with arms in their hands were shot. The houses were entered and searched; everything that was suspicious, everything that seemed suspicious, was in danger. The soldiers, black with smoke, were the blind instruments of public vengeance —sometimes also of private grudges. They no longer knew what they were doing. Their chiefs did not always take account of the formal orders that had been given by Marshal MacMahon forbidding useless violence. Often, too, the officers tried in vain to restrain the fury of the exasperated troops. A National Guard's jacket, trousers with red stripes, blackened hands, a shoulder appearing to be bruised by the rifle-stock, a pair of clumsy boots on the feet, a suspicious mien, age, figure, a word, a gesture, sufficed.

Courts-martial were opened at the Chatelet, at the Collège

de France, at the Ecole Militaire, in several town halls. The prisoners, collected in crowds at all the points where resistance had been offered, and, one may say, over the whole city, were sent before these improvised tribunals, which proceeded to a summary classification. Whether in the streets, or even before these tribunals, how many premature executions were there? How many decisions equivalent to these executions?

On Friday, the 26th, the fighting was concentrated first at Belleville and the Place du Trône. At Belleville, at the town hall of the Eleventh Ward, the remnant of the Central Committee had resumed the direction of affairs along with Varlin. The command was intrusted to Hippolyte Parent. Ferré was carrying out to the very end the horrible mission he had imposed upon himself. After a hideous procession in the streets, which was but one long agony of death, forty-eight hostages—priests, policemen, Jesuit fathers—were massacred in the Rue Haxo. Toward evening, Jecker, the banker, was shot at Père la Chaise.

On the other side, at the Panthéon, Millière, who took sides only at the last moment, Millière, who had long intervened, Millière, upon whom fatality and perhaps an implacable hatred were weighing, Millière was shot on the steps of the Panthéon.

The Bastille yielded at two o'clock. La Villette was still holding out. Indescribable sufferings overwhelmed the exhausted combatants. The fighting was now centred in the extreme quarters, not far from the advanced guards of the German army, who looked on at this spectacle, impassive, contenting themselves with herding back the fugitives.

Fighting was still in progress on Saturday, the 27th. The weather was awful; the sky livid, first a fog, then torrents of rain. There was fighting at La Villette, fighting at Charonne, fighting at Belleville. The centre of resistance was still the town hall of the Eleventh Ward, the Buttes Chaumont, and the Rue Haxo. Ranvier brought the last combatants up to the barricades. Ferré was leading a troop of prisoners of the line, whom he still purposed to shoot; they were delivered by the crowd. He went back to La Roquette to fetch fresh victims, but the three hundred men imprisoned there showed fight. Those alone perished who tried to escape, and soon Ferré fled as fast as his horse could gallop at the sound of "Here are the Versailles men."

On Saturday evening two centres of resistance remained in the Eleventh and Twentieth wards. Five or six members of the Commune—Trinquet, Ferré, Varlin, Ranvier—still held out at Belleville. Some hundreds of the Fédérates threw themselves into Père la Chaise, to fight and die behind the tombs.

On Sunday, at four o'clock in the morning, Père la Chaise was carried after a short struggle. The two wings of the Versailles army, which had enveloped Paris, met at the Rue Haxo, where they captured thirty pieces of artillery from the Fédérates. The town hall of the Eleventh Ward was taken after a desperate resistance. The last groups of the Fédérates led by Varlin, Ferré, Gambon, wandered from the Twentieth Ward to the Rue Fontaine-au-Roi in the Eleventh. Louis Piat hoisted the white flag and surrendered with about sixty combatants. The last barricade was in the Rue Ramponneau. One single Fédérate was defending it; he escaped; the last shots were fired. By one o'clock all was over. The tricolor floated over the whole city. On the 29th the Fort of Vincennes, defended by three hundred seventy-five infantrymen, of whom twenty-four were officers, surrendered after vainly trying to negotiate with the Germans. In the evening nine officers were put to death in the ditches.

On Sunday at midday Marshal MacMahon caused to be posted a proclamation addressed to the inhabitants of Paris, saying: "The army of France has come to save you. Paris is delivered. Our soldiers carried at four o'clock the last positions held by the insurgents. To-day the conflict is over, order is reëstablished, work and safety will again come into being."

THE GENEVA ARBITRATION

A.D. 1872

THEODORE DWIGHT WOOLSEY

The most important example of international arbitration in modern times was that by which were settled the claims growing out of the depredations on American commerce by the Confederate cruisers during the Civil War. Some of these cruisers, in violation of the laws of neutrality, had been built or fitted out in British ports, and this gave the United States a claim against Great Britain for damages. In 1868 and 1869 Reverdy Johnson, United States Minister at the Court of St. James, negotiated two treaties for the settlement of the so-called "Alabama Claims," both of which were rejected by the United States Senate. But on May 8, 1871, a treaty was signed at Washington, negotiated by a high commission composed of Hamilton Fish, Robert C. Schenck, Samuel Nelson, Ebenezer Rockwood Hoar, and George H. Williams—on the part of the United States; and Earl De Grey and Ripon, Sir Stafford Northcote, Sir Edward Thornton, and Sir John A. Macdonald—on the part of England. The ratifications were exchanged in London in the following month. This treaty provided for a tribunal of arbitration, to sit at Geneva, Switzerland, which should consist of five members, to be appointed as follows: one by the President of the United States, one by her Britannic Majesty Victoria, one by the King of Italy, one by the President of the Swiss Confederation, and one by the Emperor of Brazil. The arbitrators thus appointed were Charles Francis Adams, Sir Alexander Cockburn, Count Frederic Sclopis, Jacob Staempfli, and Baron d'Itajubá. J. C. Bancroft Davis was appointed to act as agent of the United States in presenting the claims, and Lord Tenterden as agent of Great Britain. Counsel was employed, those for the United States being William M. Evarts, Caleb Cushing, and Morrison R. Waite. The first meeting of the tribunal was held on December 15, 1871, and the award was made at the final meeting, September 14, 1872. This was signed by all the members except the British representative, Sir Alexander Cockburn, who did not agree. The British Government had put in a counter-claim for an increased award on the treaty concerning the Canadian fisheries, on the ground that the privileges conceded by it to American fishermen were more valuable than its concessions to Canadians. The tribunal, while awarding damages to the amount of fifteen and a half million dollars for the destruction wrought by the Confederate cruisers, allowed an offset of five million dollars on account of the fisheries. The method by which the British Government paid the balance was not by shipping the gold, but by buying in Europe ten and a half million dollars of United States bonds, and delivering them to the American representatives.

THE claims generically known as the "Alabama Claims," after vain attempts to have them settled, were at length submitted to a tribunal of arbitration. On the part of the United States untenable ground was taken in regard to the Queen's proclamation at the beginning of the Civil War. On the part of Great Britain there was a feeling that municipal law was the measure of international duties, and a seeming willingness that the United States should fall to pieces, which gave rise here to indignation and disgust. The war came to a close with the Union preserved; cotton was exported, intercourse and industry returned to their old channels. Meanwhile that healthy opinion in regard to the breadth of international obligation, which such men of state as Cobden and such jurists as Phillimore had professed, found other open advocates. Even members of the Cabinet expressed regret at the escape of the vessels that violated the laws of neutrality. It was felt that in another turn of things the United States would observe their neutrality law with one eye shut. Expeditions on the land must follow the same rule as those on the sea. Who could tell what unneutral want of due diligence, what boldness in relying on the carelessness of officials in the United States, what Fenian raids, what chronic hostile feeling, the conduct of England might provoke?

One evidence of a wiser state of feeling in Great Britain was the appointment of a neutrality-laws commission in 1867, which after twenty-four meetings reported in 1868. This body, consisting of some of the most eminent publicists of the kingdom, as Phillimore, Twiss, and Vernon Harcourt (Historicus), as well as of eminent judges, and of lawyers, such as Roundell Palmer, with one warm friend of the United States, William E. Forster, represented, of course, various shades of opinion, and sought for light from various persons. The report recommended, among other things, that any person, within her Majesty's dominions, who shall fit out, arm, despatch or cause to be despatched, or shall build or equip any ship "with intent or knowledge that the same shall or will be employed in the service of any foreign Power in any war being waged" against any belligerent Power not at war with Great Britain, or shall commence or attempt to do, or shall aid in doing, any of these acts, every person so offending shall be deemed guilty of a misdemeanor. Extensive powers also are given to the Secretary of State, or other person beyond the seas having chief authority, to issue a warrant for the arrest, search, and detention of such ships, until they can be condemned or released by process of law. The owners or agents can apply for their release, and the nearest court of admiralty is to act upon the application, with the usual admiralty appeal to the Privy Council. But from this resolution were excepted foreign commissioned ships, and also those foreign noncommissioned ships coming into the country under stress, upon which "no fitting out or equipment of a warlike character shall have taken place in the country."

Two other special recommendations made by the commission deserve notice. One was that prizes, "not entitled to recognition as commissioned ships of war," when captured by vessels violating the neutrality of Great Britain, shall, if brought within British jurisdiction, on due proof in the Admiralty Court, at the suit of the original owner or his agent, be restored. This was not to hold, however, when the ship was brought into the realm without due notice of the unlawful fitting out of the capturing vessel. The other was that no vessel of a belligerent, built, equipped, fitted out, armed, or despatched contrary to the act shall in time of war be admitted into any British port.

Vernon Harcourt dissented from this report as it represented the *building* of vessels. A law constituting this, under the conditions supposed, a misdemeanor would, he thought, be difficult of execution; would impose a new responsibility by its nonexecution; would be odious within the country, and, if not executed, give just ground of complaint to foreigners; and would put the trade of the country at an uncalled-for disadvantage.

Other persons who were consulted by the commission, expressed very strict notions of the duties of neutrals. Sir Robert Phillimore would be expected to do this in regard to munitions of war obtained by a belligerent within a neutral territory, since in his commentaries he had advanced the same opinion. He says that "in the *memoire justificatif* (*i.e.*, the memorial written by Gibbon, the historian) it will be seen that England *then* considered that the permission accorded by the French Government for the export of munitions of war from French ports to the revolted colonies was one justifying cause of the war which England had declared against France." And although a neutral may be impartial in allowing both belligerents to supply themselves with the means of mutual destruction within the neutral territory, yet the theoretically equal permission to both belligerents may be practically illusory and false. He adds that to such a degree "may the advantage of this permission preponderate in favor of one belligerent over the other" "that it may be a necessary measure of defence on the part of one belligerent to make war upon the country which supplies his adversary with the means of prolonging the contest."

Another eminent legal gentleman, Mr. Rotheny of Doctors' Commons, goes still farther in his view of what neutrals owe to their position of neutrality. He raised the question whether it would not be expedient to prohibit altogether the building of ships-of-war by private shipbuilders, without the express permission of the Government. He would have not only the building of ships made illegal without such sanction, but the export also of munitions of war to the belligerents, "and possibly also, and within certain conditions, the precarious and demoralizing trade of blockade-running." He would allow the diplomatic agent of a friendly State, equally with the Government, to initiate in the Court of Admiralty proceedings under the neutrality laws; and, lest this should be objected to as a great power given to an agent of a foreign State, he remarks that "the same power is given to a common seaman whose wages exceed fifty pounds; to any person who has rendered service, in the nature of salvage, to a ship; and to any person who has sustained loss or injury by a collision with a ship." Still further, in the case of a vessel-of-war escaping from a British port, whether fully equipped for war or not, and thereupon beginning depredations on the commerce of a friendly State, he proposed, if she should receive a commission, to regard this as a proof that the State that had commissioned her connived at her violation of neutrality, had knowingly violated a neutral sovereign's rights, and in the transaction had made Great Britain a base of operations against its enemy. There would then be a perfect right to demand satisfaction for the outrage; to demand that the vessel should be restored to British jurisdiction, to refuse it admission into British waters, and to lay hands on it if it voluntarily came thither. "The fact of the violation of neutral rights by its escape would be a warrant for its condemnation; the ship would have been *ipso facto* forfeited to the neutral State, and would remain so forfeited into whosesoever hands it passed. To hold that its character would be purged by the completion of the voyage or by its being taken into the service of the belligerent was founded on entire misapprehension," he thinks—"it was the belligerent who had committed the offence, and it did not rest with him to condone it." This opinion favored a stricter neutrality than most persons even in this country were willing to advocate, especially in the matter of furnishing munitions to belligerents.

The report of the neutrality commission was not acted upon in Parliament until the year 1870. Then a law founded on it was passed, August 9th, at the time when Prussian armies were on their victorious march into France. It was a great improvement on the old law; but in exempting any commissioned ship of any foreign State or body invested with belligerent power from forfeiture for violating its provisions, it might prove a source of new difficulties hereafter.

A few months after this the proposal was made by the British Government to that of the United States to appoint a joint high commission for the purpose of settling the questions that had arisen respecting the fisheries on the coasts of British America, as well as all those that affected the relations of the United States toward her Majesty's possessions in that part of the world. The United States modified this proposition so as to include the claims generically known as the "Alabama Claims." The enlarged plan of work for the High Commission was accepted, and out of this grew the Treaty of Washington.

It was hoped that the two Powers might come to some understanding, within the Commission itself, about the claims just spoken of, without resorting to further measures; but this was found to be impossible, and so resort was had to an arbitration, which was to be guided in its judgments by three important rules laying down the duties of neutral States, and by other principles of international law not inconsistent with them. The offer of arbitration came from the British Commissioners, the three rules from the American.

In international arbitration it may happen not infrequently that one of the parties will refuse to obey the sentence, on the ground that the arbitrator, or the tribunal of arbitration, has given a decision on questions that were not submitted.

The British Commissioners who negotiated the treaty represented to their Government that they understood that the consequential damages or indirect claims were not to be put forward by the United States. But, when the case appeared, they were put forward; and the appalling amount of possible damages greatly excited the British public. Sir Stafford Northcote publicly used the following words: "We, the Commissioners, were directly responsible for having represented to the Government that we understood a promise to be given that these claims were not to be put forward, and were not to be submitted to arbitration." The American Commissioners, one and all, denied knowledge of any such understanding.[1] A little before this was known in England, the Marquis of Ripon corrected what his fellow-Commissioner had asserted — "the claims were mentioned," said he, "in a manner which in substance is described in that protocol on your lordship's table," and Sir Stafford Northcote authorized a friend to make the explanation, in the

[1] See pamphlet published by the United States Government, entitled "The American Commissioners and the Statement of Sir Stafford Northcote" (Washington, 1872). The commissioners in general content themselves with denying that any promises not to urge the indirect claims were ever made. Mr. Hoar adds that he "always thought and expected that those claims, though incapable from their nature of computation and from their magnitude incapable of compensation, were to be submitted to the tribunal of arbitration, and urged this as a reason why a gross sum should be awarded, which should be an ample and liberal compensation for our losses by captures and burnings, without any petty details." This, as we understand it, means that when, in the progress of negotiations, the Commissioners on the two sides had agreed that there should be an arbitration, it was expected that this species of claims, although incomputable and incapable of compensation, should be urged as a makeweight; and it frees Mr. Bancroft Davis from the charge that has been made of putting the indirect claims into the case on the sole responsibility of the State Department.

House of Lords, that in what he had publicly declared as to claims for indirect losses he referred to the statement voluntarily and formally made by the American Commissioners at the opening of the Conference of the 8th of March, which he, for one, understood to amount to an engagement, that the claims in question should not be put forward in the event of a treaty being agreed upon.

The question arose whether this understanding or interpretation was authorized by the protocol itself, and to this we must answer in the negative. The American Commissioners did not mean that these claims would be waived "in the event of a treaty being agreed upon," but in the event of a gross sum being agreed to by the British Commissioners, so that further proceedings—before arbitrators, for instance—should be rendered unnecessary. They said in effect: "We have two kinds of claims; give us a gross sum off-hand to satisfy one species of them, and we will consider it an end of the whole matter." This surely did not mean that if the British Commissioners should not accede to their proposition, and should carry the case up to another court, they would still continue the offer.

After dividing the claims into two classes, the direct and the indirect, and remarking that the pecuniary amount of the direct losses could be easily ascertained, they added "that in the hope of an amicable settlement no estimate was made of the indirect losses—without prejudice, however, to the right of indemnification on their account, in the event of no such settlement being made." The question shifted to this: What did they mean by amicable settlement? The words occur elsewhere in the correspondence between the governments and in the preface to the treaty, where they denote a settlement, not by force, but in the way of friendly agreement. In the protocol, however, they are restricted to settlement within the board of Commissioners. For as yet nothing appears to show that they thought of arbitration, and they feel full power for whatever arbitrators could do in the way of an immediate agreement. They therefore propose the payment of a gross sum in satisfaction of all claims—meaning, or course, as yet direct claims—and interest thereon.

The others denied that Great Britain had failed to discharge her duty in regard to the cruisers, and declared that she had showed her readiness to adopt the principle of arbitration. Now for the first time they make the offer of arbitration, to which the American Commissioners declined to give their consent, "unless the principles which should govern the arbitrator in the consideration of the facts could first be agreed upon." This was accepted at length by the other party; the three rules were adopted, and the great difficulty was overcome.

The protocol then left it free to make demand of indemnification for indirect losses. But when we come to the treaty, it seems almost certain that its terms are inconsistent with the supposition that these losses were to be brought into account. We lay no stress whatever on the vague words in the First Article, "difficulties growing out of" and "claims growing out of acts committed by" certain vessels, for the very question was, Cannot claims grow remotely as well as directly out of acts? But the Tenth Article seems decisive. If Great Britain had been found to have failed to fulfil any duty as a neutral, and the arbitrators had not awarded a gross sum, a board of assessors was to be appointed who should decide what amounts were to be paid to the United States "on account of the liability arising from such failure [of duties] as to each vessel, according to the extent of such liability as decided by the arbitrators." When these words were made a part of the treaty, no reasonable man who assented to them could have thought of the indirect losses. For in that case the assessors would have been called upon to decide what effect the Alabama, what the Florida, etc., had had upon the transfer of American ships to the British flag, upon enhanced payments of insurance, upon the prolongation of the war, and upon the increase of the cost of the war—a problem which no mortal man could solve, and of which no sane man would seek a solution.

In the confidential memorandum submitted to our Commissioners by the State Department, the claims are mentioned as: (1) Claims of the United States consisting of claims for outlay in the pursuit of rebel cruisers, and also of increased premium and enhanced freights growing out of the risk caused by the operations of rebel cruisers fitted out in English ports; and (2) as claims of individuals who had lost vessels or goods owing to the same cruisers. No other losses were mentioned. Moreover, when the case was prepared, the five first chapters were sent to several persons for examination and remark; but, as we learn from the report of the agent of the United States before the Tribunal at Geneva, Mr. Bancroft Davis, the sixth chapter, in which alone the mention of the indirect claims occurred, "was not sent out for criticism, as the others had been." As far as any pledge to the British Commissioners was concerned, the author of the case had certainly a right to bring these claims forward; and so very short a chapter could not demand criticism apart from its subject; but the fact that no criticism was called for on so important a subject seems to show that at the eleventh hour it had been resolved to call in the auxiliary forces of indirect losses, and to make a grand attack on the enemy's flank.

The British Government denied that in the case, as submitted by them, anything but direct losses was thought of, and they were ready to stay further proceedings unless a supplementary convention with the United States could explain or limit the treaty to their satisfaction. As early as April 15th, when the British counter-case had been presented to each of the arbitrators, the English agent made known to them the feelings of his Government in regard to the claims in the American case. Our Government, on the other hand, asserted that the tribunal at Geneva ought to decide whether claims for indirect losses properly came before them for consideration. Both were right. A tribunal must determine what is the extent of its powers. Great Britain had a right to withdraw its case from the tribunal on the ground that the opposing party brought forward what never had been submitted. Of course, in such disagreements there is risk of exasperation and even of war. But it was better that the British Government should take their measures at the beginning than that they should refuse at the end, after long sitting and arguments, to comply with the judgment. The result of the final adjudication depended mainly upon the three rules contained in the Treaty of Washington—how they should be interpreted—and upon the facts of the treatment of insurgent cruisers by British authorities. Other principles of international law, of course, entered into the decision, and as to these the arbitrators were unfettered. They had a right to follow Roman law, or

English law, or their own views of equity, or any other rule that seemed to them good. The three rules were these:

"A neutral government is bound: First, to prevent the fitting out, arming, or equipping, within its jurisdiction, of any vessel which it has reasonable ground to believe is intended to cruise or to carry on war against a Power with which it is at peace; and also to use like diligence to prevent the departure from its jurisdiction of any vessel intended to cruise or carry on war as above, such vessel having been specially adapted, in whole or in part, within such jurisdiction, to warlike use.

"Secondly, not to permit or suffer either belligerent to make use of its ports or waters as the base of naval operations against the other, or for the purpose of the renewal or augmentation of military supplies or arms or the recruitment of men.

"Thirdly, to exercise due diligence in its own ports and waters and as to all persons within its jurisdiction to prevent any violation of the foregoing obligations and duties."

These rules are expressed with at least the ordinary clearness of diplomatic papers, yet they gave ground for debate as to their real meaning.

The Tribunal of Arbitration, passing from a declaration of their principles to a decision upon the facts of the case, found that Great Britain failed by omission to fulfil her duties, as laid down in one or more of the three rules, in regard to the Alabama, the Florida, and the Shenandoah, but was responsible for the acts of the latter only from the time of her leaving Melbourne, February 18, 1865. The tenders of the two former vessels were subjected to the decision given in relation to the principal ships. Four of the arbitrators, for the reasons given in the award, and Sir A. Cockburn for reasons separately assigned by him, found Great Britain to have incurred liability under the first and third rules, as far as the Alabama was concerned; four of them decided that there was a failure to fulfil all the rules in the case of the Florida, and three to fulfil the second and third rules in the case of the Shenandoah. They found that there was no such failure in regard to the other vessels presented to them, although, in the case of the Retribution, two out of five were inclined to give a decision casting blame on Great Britain. Several vessels were excluded from consideration for want of evidence.

After finding that, in regard to the vessels above named, there had been a failure to fulfil some of the "duties set forth in the three rules, or recognized by the principles of international law not inconsistent with them," the arbitrators might have proceeded at once to award a sum in gross, to be paid to the United States; but they wisely chose to give the reasons that weighed with them in their determination of the amount of the indemnity. This they did in the way of passing judgment upon certain of the claims of the United States; and first they decided that "there is no ground for awarding any sum by way of indemnity for the costs of the pursuit of the cruisers specified in the award." The reason alleged for this was that these costs were not properly distinguishable from the general expenses of the war. Next, they expressed themselves to be unanimously of opinion that there was no ground of award on the head of "the prospective injuries," which as depending in their nature on future and uncertain contingencies, could not properly be made subject to compensation. Sir Alexander Cockburn, in his dissenting opinion, was far from objecting to claims of whalers for loss of prospective catch; only he would cut down greatly those that were actually presented; he would award a reasonable percentage on the value of the vessels and outfits.

Next they say that, in order to arrive at an equitable compensation for damages sustained, it was necessary to set aside all double claims for the same losses, all claim for gross freight, so far as it exceeded the net freight; and it was just to allow interest at a reasonable rate. Having expressed these opinions, which commended themselves at once, they awarded, by a vote of four to one, fifteen and a half millions of dollars in gold to be paid in satisfaction of all claims made by the United States, and they declared that "each and every one of said claims, whether the same may or may not have been presented to the notice or laid before the tribunal, shall henceforth be considered and treated as settled and barred." These words were in substance those of the treaty, which also requires payment of the gross sum awarded within twelve months of the award.

It was an important question how far the United States were bound to respect the decisions of the tribunal in regard to the various classes of claims that were brought before them. The tribunal declared on the 19th of June that the losses in the transfer of the American commercial marine, the enhanced payments of insurance, and the prolongation of the war, and the addition of a large sum to the cost of the war, do not, according to the principles of international law, furnish good foundation for an award of compensation or computation of damages between nations. In their award the claim for pursuit of the cruisers was rejected. There remained, then, only the first out of the five classes of claims mentioned in the cases, that for direct losses growing out of the destruction of vessels and their cargoes by insurgent cruisers; and from this the item of prospective earnings or profits was excluded, while the item of wages and that of interest also are allowed. Also freight was taken to mean net, not gross freight.

The arbitrators gave their award on the ground that a vessel violating laws of neutrality could not wipe out its guilt by a subsequent commission, and that, if found in the waters of the offended nation, it may have the privilege of exterritoriality denied to it. The new foreign enlistment act, good in other respects, appeared to fail at this point. Nothing in the act, it was said, subjected any commissioned vessel to forfeiture, or gave to a British court any jurisdiction that it did not have before. And a foreign State was defined to include "any person or persons exercising, or assuming to exercise, the powers of government in, or over, any foreign country, colony, province, or part of any province, or people." It was true that captures effected by a vessel breaking the neutrality laws of England were pronounced illegal; and a vessel so captured, and afterward brought within the British dominions by the captor, or his agent, or his government, or by any other person, with knowledge that the capture was made under such circumstances, might be restored by act of court to the original owner; and this, as we understood the law, would be the case although the court of the guilty vessel's nation might have decreed it to be a lawful prize. But this would go no further than to teach the captor, and those to whom a title was passed, to avoid British waters in such cases. The fact still remained that in future years, if an order in council and the royal prerogative are not adequate to prevent the admission of such vessels into British ports, the same complaints would arise which the United States made, and which helped their cause so materially before the arbitration. Vernon Harcourt endeavored to provide a partial prevention of this source of evil. He was a member of the commission on the foreign enlistment act, and he dissented from their report so far as to be unwilling to extend the penalties of the law and the preventive authority of the executive to the building of ships, apart from the question of their arming and despatch from the realm. He made one valuable suggestion against "the recognition of belligerent commissions to vessels on the high seas, by which such vessels became at once raised to the position of lawful belligerent cruisers, though they sailed from no port, and, in fact, derived no support from the natural and legitimate naval resources of those in whose behalf they wage war." "It seemed to me," he continued, "that for all reasons it was wise to discourage such a practice. As there was no rule of international law that forbade such delivering of commissions on the high seas, we could not, of course, refuse to recognize the title of such a cruiser to all the legitimate rights of war, in places beyond our jurisdiction. But we were masters of our own hospitality within the realm. Though, therefore, we could not dispute the validity of such a commission on the high seas or the legality of captures made by such a vessel, we might refuse to admit into our ports any vessel that had not received its commission in a port of its country." Such a rule, if made six years before it was proposed, would have driven the Alabama, the Florida, and the Susquehanna from all British ports, and very materially diminished the grievances of the United States against Great Britain.

The example of this arbitration at Geneva, renewing a policy of nations that had long since fallen into comparative neglect, the hope of gaining, by peaceful ways, what could only be gained by war at a vast loss; the conviction that most wars have been unnecessary, if only some amicable settlement and impartial judge could have been found—these considerations, which are worth many times fifteen and a half million of dollars, will, as many hope, help the spread of peace over the world. At all events, the world will ever honor the two great and proud nations for the course they took.

CHRONOLOGY OF UNIVERSAL HISTORY

EMBRACING THE PERIOD COVERED IN THIS VOLUME

A.D. 1861–1872

DANIEL EDWIN WHEELER

CHRONOLOGY OF UNIVERSAL HISTORY

EMBRACING THE PERIOD COVERED IN THIS VOLUME

A.D. 1861–1872

DANIEL EDWIN WHEELER

Events treated at length are here indicated in large type; the numerals following give volume and page.

Separate chronologies of the various nations, and of the careers of famous persons, will be found in the INDEX VOLUME, with references showing where the several events are fully treated.

A.D.

1861. Secession of the Cotton States from the American Union and formation of the Confederacy; inauguration of President Lincoln; bombardment of Fort Sumter; President Lincoln calls out the militia; secession of Virginia. See "SECESSION OF THE SOUTHERN STATES," xviii, 1.

Victories of the Unionists in West Virginia; Richmond made the capital of the Confederacy.

"THE BATTLE OF BULL RUN." See xviii, 26.

Missouri saved to the Union; Commissioners Mason and Slidell arrested on the British ship Trent.

Austria reorganized as a constitutional kingdom under the Emperor Francis Joseph.

Victor Emmanuel proclaimed King of Italy.

France, England, and Spain send fleets to Mexico to enforce financial claims.

1862. Victories of the Unionists in Tennessee; Grant captures Fort Donelson.

"THE MONITOR AND THE MERRIMAC." See xviii, 38.

Grant wins the Battle of Shiloh; slavery abolished in the District of Columbia.

"THE CAPTURE OF NEW ORLEANS." See xviii, 46.

"McClellan's Peninsula Campaign." See xviii, 53.

Second Confederate victory at Bull Run; Lee's invasion of the North; Battle of Antietam.

"Emancipation in the United States." See xviii, 70.

Renewed Federal advance on Richmond, and defeat at Fredericksburg.

France despatches troops to Mexico.

Garibaldi attacks Rome in the interests of Italy; is defeated by Italian troops at Aspromonte.

1863. Battle of Chancellorsville; Lee again repulses the Federal advance, and again invades the North, the "high-water mark" of the Confederacy. See "The Battle of Gettysburg," xviii, 77.

"The Fall of Vicksburg." See xviii, 110.

Draft Riots in New York city; Battle of Chattanooga establishes Federal supremacy in Tennessee.

France defeats the Mexicans, and the Austrian Archduke Maximilian is created Emperor of Mexico.

Rebellion in Poland; the German Confederation quarrels with Denmark and seizes the Danish duchies.

1864. Grant is made General-in-Chief of all the Federal armies and begins his celebrated "hammering" campaign against Richmond.

"Destruction of the Alabama." See xviii, 124.

Farragut captures Mobile; Sherman captures Atlanta.

"Sherman's March to the Sea." See xviii, 135.

Unsuccessful struggle of Denmark against Austria and Prussia.

France agrees to withdraw her troops from Rome.

Organization of the International Association of Workingmen. See "Career of the International," xviii, 141.

Final subjugation of the Tai-ping Rebellion in China.

1865. Inauguration of President Lincoln for a second term; capture of Richmond by the Union troops. See "The Surrender of Lee," xviii, 153.

President Lincoln assassinated. Andrew Johnson succeeds to the Presidency; he issues a proclamation of amnesty. The Thirteenth Amendment proclaimed as part of the United States Constitution.

Florence made the capital of Italy.

1866. President Johnson disputes with the United States Congress over the "reconstruction" of the South.

"The Laying of the Atlantic Cable." See xviii, 175.

Prussia quarrels with the other States of the German Confederation; war declared; Prussian troops easily defeat the forces of the lesser German States and attack Austria. Italy joins the war against Austria; Italians defeated at Custozza; Prussians victorious in the great Battle of Sadowa; Austria sues for peace; Italian fleet destroyed at Lissa. See "The Austro-Prussian War," xviii, 163.

Reconstruction of the German Confederation under Prussia; Italy secures Venetia.

Grand congress of the International Association of Workingmen at Geneva.

Brief War of Peru and Chile against Spain.

1867. The United States Congress establishes military government in the Southern States.

"THE PURCHASE OF ALASKA." See xviii, 206.

French troops withdraw from Mexico at the demand of the United States; capture and execution of Maximilian. See "THE FALL OF MAXIMILIAN," xviii, 186.

"CANADIAN CONFEDERATION." See xviii, 196.

Final establishment of constitutional government in Austria, recognition of the Hungarians, and reorganization of the empire as the double State of Austria-Hungary.

Garibaldi again attacks Rome, and French troops return to protect it; defeat of Garibaldi at Mentana.

Napoleon III seeks to extend French territory in the Rhineland and is checked by Bismarck.

French advances in Annam; British war in Abyssinia; the Mikado of Japan abolishes the authority of the Shogun.

"THE DISCOVERY OF DIAMONDS IN AFRICA." See xviii, 225.

1868. Impeachment of President Johnson before the United States Senate.

"REVOLUTION IN SPAIN." See xviii, 243.

The Fourteenth Amendment proclaimed as part of the United States Constitution.

1869. Ulysses S. Grant inaugurated as President of the United States.

"THE COMPLETION OF THE PACIFIC RAILROAD." See xviii, 287.

The Hudson Bay Fur Company surrenders its charter to the British Government. See "THE ABOLITION OF THE FUR COMPANIES," xviii, 258.

The Spaniards vote for a monarchy and look for a king.

"THE OPENING OF THE SUEZ CANAL." See xviii, 275.

1870. The Fifteenth Amendment proclaimed as part of the United States Constitution; the end of the "reconstruction" acts.

Dispute between France and Prussia over the Spanish kingship; France declares war. The lesser German States join Prussia. Defeat of the French at Woerth, at Gravelotte and other places.

"THE BATTLE OF SEDAN." See xviii, 302.

"THE THIRD FRENCH REPUBLIC." See xviii, 321.

Paris besieged by the Germans; Gambetta organizes the armies of the French provinces; surrender of Metz; bombardment of Paris begun.

The Papal Council proclaims the dogma of "infallibility"; the French forces withdraw from Rome; Italian troops seize it after armed resistance. See "COMPLETION OF ITALIAN UNITY," xviii, 316.

1871. Great fire in Chicago.

King William of Prussia proclaimed Emperor of Germany at Versailles. See "THE UNIFICATION OF GERMANY," xviii, 340.

Final defeat of the French armies of the provinces.

"THE SIEGE OF PARIS AND THE END OF THE FRANCO-PRUSSIAN WAR." See xviii, 333.

Election of a National Assembly in France, and election of M. Thiers as Chief Executive; removal of the Government to Versailles.

"THE RISING OF THE COMMUNE." See xviii, 351.

Partial burning of Paris and reëstablishment of the Versailles government under M. Thiers.

Rome made the capital of United Italy; opening of the Mont Cenis tunnel.

African explorations of Stanley in search of Livingstone.

Slavery abolished in Brazil.

1872. The judges selected to pass upon the Alabama question make an award in favor of the United States. Great Britain accepts the decision, and international arbitration is thus established. See "THE GENEVA ARBITRATION," xviii, 367.

Great fire in Boston.

Trouble between the German Government and the Roman Catholic Church.

Carlist insurrection in Spain.

END OF VOLUME XVIII